Copyright ©

All rig

No part of this publication may be reproduced, distributed, or transmitted in any form or by any means, including photocopying, recording, or other electronic or mechanical methods, without the prior written permission of the author, except in the case of brief quotations embodied in critical reviews and certain other non-commercial uses permitted by copyright law.

First edition: November 2025

ISBN: 9798275893496

Imprint: Independently published

Disclaimer

In some sections of this book, names have been changed or omitted to protect the identity of individuals.

Think of Something Publishing and Keith Budden as an individual accept no responsibility for any information contained within this book and disclaims and excludes any liability in respect of the contents or for action taken based on this information.

A Lifetime of Moments

Dedicated to Paige Turner

If you've opened this book, you might be expecting a neat little autobiography.
The sort where the author is born, grows up sensibly, achieves a few respectable milestones, and finishes with something wise and tidy about life.

This... is not that book.

This is the story of a man who somehow turned medical dramas into comedy sketches, business trips into soap operas, and friendships into lifelong romances-without-the-label. It's full of moments I never planned, challenges I never asked for, and people I absolutely couldn't have lived without.

It's also full of coincidences so outrageous you'd swear I'd made them up.
(I didn't. I promise. Even I'm not that creative.)

Inside these pages you'll meet the people who shaped me, saved me, challenged me, kissed me, shouted at me, held me up, and occasionally stripped naked in hotel bathrooms to demonstrate regional Scandinavian logic. You'll see how humour became my armour, love became my compass, and how laughter sometimes turned out to be the only sensible response to absolute chaos.

So settle in. Turn the page.

Because once you start, you'll realise what I eventually did:

A life isn't one big story.
It's a lifetime of moments.

And these are mine.

Before we go any further, one small thing.

This is not a "look how brave I am" memoir.
It's a "look how ridiculous life can be… and how wonderful it still is" one.

Some of what you'll read will make you laugh.
Some of it might make you wince.
A few moments may catch you unexpectedly in the throat.

If you're reading this because life has been a bit much lately, you're very welcome here.
If you're here for humour, heart, honesty, and the occasional raised eyebrow, you're in exactly the right place.

There's no test at the end.
No lesson you're required to learn.

Just stories, told as they happened, by someone who has been knocked sideways more than once and discovered that standing back up is often overrated, sometimes sitting down with a cup of tea works just as well.

Right then.

Let's begin properly.

Foreword

f you're holding this book in your hands, or scrolling, or listening to it in that soothing audiobook voice I've done my best to imagine, then let me start with a simple, heartfelt thank you.

This book wasn't supposed to exist.

Not because I didn't want to write it, but because for most of my life I never expected to live long enough to write it. Between Marfan syndrome, cancer, neuropathy, pacemakers, political misadventures, the occasional fire brigade rescue, and whatever cosmic force seems determined to keep my life interesting, I've had more plot twists than a Netflix series with commitment issues.

And yet... here we are.

People often tell me my life is "inspirational."

I've heard it from friends, relatives, medical staff, and the occasional stranger who's just watched me wrestle a rollator into a car boot.

But honestly? I've never felt like I've lived an extraordinary life. I think I've always been too close to the wood to see the trees.

When you're living moment to moment, medical crises, family chaos, love, loss, laughter, and the odd naked streaker at Ascot, it all feels fairly normal. Or at least... normal for me.

Only when I sat down to write did I realise how many threads had woven themselves together along the way.
That's really what this book is: a tapestry of moments.
Pull any one thread and the whole thing changes.
Follow them long enough, and you might even spot the pattern.

This isn't a traditional autobiography.
No neat timeline. No straight line from A to B. My life has been more "A to Q via L, with a brief stop at F because someone fell out of a tree."
What you will find here is honesty.
And humour.

And the occasional chapter that makes you laugh and say, "Oh, Keith... honestly."

I wrote this book because stories matter. Moments matter. Memories matter. And because if I don't write some of them down now, they'll escape.

I hope as you read, it feels less like a book and more like sitting with me over a cup of tea (or a Belgian bun), hearing the stories the way they were meant to be told, with a smile, a sigh, and the occasional raised eyebrow.

Thank you for being here.
Keith

PS: *Warning - Reading this book may cause laughter, unexpected emotion, and a sudden desire to hug people, eat cake, or phone someone you love. If symptoms persist, please continue reading and consider sharing copies generously.*

PPS: *You **can't** rewind to the beginning.*
*But you **can** start from where you are now and change the ending.*

Life is like a game of poker

Some days you wake up feeling like the world has finally tilted in your favour. The sun's on your face, your back doesn't creak quite as much as usual, and life deals you something that looks suspiciously like a royal flush.

Other days?
Well... other days you're handed a two-seven off-suit, the kettle packs up, the toast lands butter-side down, and you wonder whether getting out of bed was a tactical misstep.

But that, in a nutshell, is life: a poker game where the cards are constantly changing, and the dealer has a wicked sense of humour.

We don't get to choose the hand we're dealt. Never have, Never will.

What we *do* get to choose is how we play it.

I've had days when everything aligned so perfectly it felt choreographed: the right people in the right place at the right time, paths opening, opportunities appearing, the sense that the universe was giving me a rare wink and whispering, "Go on then, this one's yours."

Those days are magic. We treasure them.

But I've also had days when the chips were down, the cards were dreadful, and the best I could hope for was keeping a straight face while the world tried to knock me sideways. Health scares, disappointments, setbacks, the kind of moments that make you wonder if you're even sitting at the right table.

And still... I played.

Because that's the only real secret: **you've got to stay in the game.**

Poker teaches you that bluffing works occasionally, luck works sometimes, but grit works *every time.*

Confidence isn't pretending you've got pocket aces; it's knowing that even if you haven't, you can still play with intent, courage, and a little bit of cheek.

Sometimes you hold firm.
Sometimes you fold.
Sometimes you shove all your chips in the middle and hope you've read the room right.

The only bad move?
Not playing at all.

Over the years I've realised resilience doesn't come from the hand, it comes from the player. You don't need perfection to move forward; you just need enough courage to take the next step, whatever it looks like.

And when life deals you a truly terrible hand?
That's when your character shows.
That's when the real lessons arrive, about yourself, about others, about what genuinely matters.
Those are the moments that grow you, shape you, sharpen you.
So, whether today brings you a royal flush or a pile of cards better suited for recycling, remember this:
You're still in the game.
Play it.
Smile at the bad hands, celebrate the good ones, and keep your seat at the table.

Live for today, don't get tangled in yesterday, and don't borrow trouble from tomorrow.

Because tomorrow?

That's a fresh shuffle, a clean deal, and a whole new hand waiting to be played.

Threads theory - or how the universe became my personal PA

You'll find a later chapter in this book called *God, The Universe, and Everything In Between*, where I go properly into my faith and how it has shaped my life.

But this chapter needs to sit earlier.

Because if you read the rest of this book without this one, you'll get the stories, the characters, the chaos… but you might miss the quiet thread that runs through almost everything that's happened to me.

I call it my **Threads Theory**.

It's simple. Not in the *two-minute YouTube explainer* way, but in the *this quietly explains half my life* way.

Whether you believe in God in the traditional sense, or your god is nature, or you believe in absolutely nothing except gravity and a decent supermarket loyalty card… let's just call it **The Universe**.

It saves me having to write "God-or-trees-or-nothing-at-all" every time, and frankly I don't have the energy for that level of Ctrl+C, Ctrl+V these days. (Mac users, mentally swap Ctrl for Cmd. You're included. Calm down.)

So, here's the theory.
If you meet someone once, that's just life.

If you meet someone twice, that might still be coincidence.

But if someone appears in your life **three times or more**, in different settings, at different stages, wearing different hats… then The Universe is no longer being subtle.

At that point it's basically waving a giant neon sign above their head saying:
"Pay attention. This one matters."
And that person becomes a **thread**.

Some threads become romantic partners.
Some become business partners.
Some become the people you ring when the sky falls in.
And some are simply... there.

Steady. Reliable. Quietly woven into your story long before you realise how much you need them.

Every person who appears more than once in this book - Vik, Ruth, Enma, Michelle, Rolf, Roy, Roger - they're all threads. Each arrived with a purpose, and almost never the purpose I expected.

But one thread crystallised this theory for me.

Vik.

No full name, partly to respect her privacy, mostly because if I ever upset her I want plausible deniability. She knows exactly who she is.

The First Crossing

I met Vik at an affiliate networking event in London.

What struck me first were her eyes, not romantically, but in that rare *I'm actually listening to you, not rehearsing my reply* way.

We talked. Properly talked.
Nothing dramatic. No lightning bolts.
But I left thinking:
Good soul, that one.

The Second Crossing

Six months later, another event.

Same smile. Same eyes.
Same seamless continuation of a conversation we'd paused half a year earlier, as if no time had passed at all.

Two crossings.
Still could be coincidence.
Still could be The Universe doodling in the margins.

The Third Crossing
(The Universe Stops Being Subtle)

I boarded the train at Liss.
Sat down.
Relaxed into the journey.

At Liphook, the doors opened... and who should step on, through *my* door, into *my* carriage, and very nearly into *my* lap?

Yes. Vik.

We both did that startled double-take dance, the one where your brain needs a second to catch up, and then talked all the way to Waterloo.

That was crossing number three.
Level unlocked.
The Universe chuckling quietly in the background.

When Life Started Choreographing

A few months later, Vik changed jobs.

At exactly the same time, I'd just moved into photobook software.

Her new employer needed, wait for it, photobook software.

Neither of us knew about the other's shift.
The Universe, however, did its smug little shuffle.

Coincidence? Maybe.
But it was starting to look less like coincidence and more like The Universe running a spreadsheet with our names colour-coded.

And Then Came 2014

This part is covered properly later in the book, but here's what matters here:

I was in hospital.
A real health crisis.

Real fear.
Real darkness.

On day two of being properly conscious again, an email arrived from Vik. She was in Australia, enjoying the trip of a lifetime.

"How are you?" she asked.
I replied with the standard British dishonesty:
"I'm fine."
(I wasn't. Not even close.)

The next morning, another email arrived.
Just four words:
"How are you, *really*?"

She had no way of knowing where I was.
No social media posts.
No public updates.
Nothing.

But she knew.
Somehow, she knew.

The Universe whispered.
Vik listened.

And in the weeks that followed, she became the person I could tell everything to, the fear, the pain, the darkness I couldn't bring myself to put on Michelle, or Roy, or Roger.

She wrote every single day.

No judgement.
No drama.
No fixing.
Just steady, consistent, unshakeable presence.

It wasn't romantic.
It wasn't dramatic.
It wasn't anything Hollywood would buy the rights to.

It was simply a thread doing exactly what threads do.

Holding you together when you're not entirely sure you can do it yourself.

I'm convinced I wouldn't have made it through that time without her.

She already knows that.
But I'll say it here too, permanently:

Thank you, Vik. From the bottom of my heart. Because without you, that heart may not still be beating.

Don't Call Me Brave

People often say to me, "Keith, you're so brave."

Brave.

It's a word I've never quite known where to put. **It doesn't feel like it belongs to me.**

Yes, I've lived through a fair few storms, more than I'd have ordered, if life had come with a returns policy. Illness. Disability. The heartbreak of losing my partner far too soon. Watching my daughter fight her way out of a destructive relationship. Watching her children, my grandchildren, go into foster care. The business ups and downs. The hospital corridors that know my footsteps a little too well.

But still, I stumble over that label: Brave.

To me, bravery looks like a firefighter running into a burning building when everyone else is running out. It looks like a soldier signing up, knowing full well what the risks are, and choosing to do it anyway.

That is courage.
That is choice.

Me? I didn't choose most of what's happened to me. The cards landed where they landed. **All I really chose was to keep playing.**

I didn't decide to lose the people I loved. I didn't put my name down for the medical rollercoaster. I didn't ask for grief, or pain, or fear. But I did decide, sometimes through gritted teeth, not to stop.

Not because I'm heroic.
Not because I'm fearless.
But because... honestly, what else was I going to do?

I've cried behind closed doors.
I've had days where getting out of bed felt like climbing Everest in slippers.
I've asked myself "why me?" more times than I could count.

I've smiled in public when my heart felt like it was held together with string and hope.
I've cracked jokes because sometimes humour is the only shield you've got left.

That isn't bravery.
That's survival.

That's putting one foot in front of the other and choosing, quietly, stubbornly, not to stop walking.

So, when someone calls me brave, I say thank you, because I know it comes from kindness. But inside, I always want to gently correct them.

I don't think I'm brave.
I think I'm human.

And if there's one thing I've truly learned, it's this:
You don't need bravery to keep going.
You just need someone, or something, you care about enough to try.
A reason. A purpose. A spark.

That's not heroism.

That's what ordinary people do every day, often without even realising it.

That's humanity.

Born in a storm (literally) - and apparently because my parents were bored

I arrived on the 14th of October 1964, the third son of George and Olive Budden - though not, as I later learned, the final act of a carefully planned trilogy.

Oh no. I was meant to be the **third of three**, not the **last of five**. My Mum had fallen pregnant with two girls before me, but both pregnancies heartbreakingly ended early. It seems my mum and dad were destined for sons. Daughters simply weren't part of the Budden script.

I made my grand entrance at St Mary's Hospital in Portsmouth, in the middle of a thunderstorm. Proper cinematic stuff. Lightning. Thunder. Crashing skies. I'm slightly surprised I wasn't christened *Thor*, *Zeus*, or the very on-brand *Keith, God of Static Electricity*.

Mum later told me I wasn't just born in a thunderstorm; I was conceived in one too. Apparently, my entire existence is down to the weather throwing a tantrum.

There was a nine-year gap between me and Roger, and a sixteen-year gulf between me and Roy. When I eventually became old enough to wonder why my brothers were practically old enough to claim a pension by the time I arrived, I asked Mum what had happened.

With that mischievous glint she reserved for stories she absolutely *shouldn't* enjoy telling a child, she said: "Well, love... you weren't planned. There was a thunderstorm, the electricity went off, no TV, no radio, nothing to do... so, well... there you are."

Thank you, Mum. Nothing says "cherished" quite like being the human equivalent of *"What else shall we do this evening?"*

I was born early, a few weeks premature, and in the 1960s that was serious business. The staff gently asked my mum whether she wanted me christened immediately because, to put it bluntly, they weren't entirely convinced I'd live long enough for them to ask again.

When they asked what name they should put on the christening record, Mum said:
"Oh, Keith will do."

I'm glad she stuck with her choice, because Dad's plan was to name me after both of my grandfathers: **Edwin Arthur**. Lovely men, both of them, but let's be honest: "Edwin Arthur Budden" sounds less like me and more like someone who owns a monocle collection and speaks fluent Latin.

So, Keith it was.

And here I am.

A product of thunderstorms, power cuts, and my parents running out of evening entertainment.

A perfectly on-brand start to a rather unpredictable life.

Nan, Vale Cottages and the spiders of doom

By the time I arrived on Planet Earth, both my parents were already what we'd politely call "the upper end of the parenting age bracket." This meant that of my four grandparents, only one was still alive: my dad's mother, Nelly, my Nan.

And what a woman she was.

I'm pretty sure her personality could have powered a small village. She was tough, superstitious, stubborn, loving, and just a tiny bit terrifying, basically the entire Romany starter pack of personality traits, all wrapped up in one formidable lady.

Dad worshipped her. In fairness, she adored him too, he was her only surviving child, but even so, the loyalty levels were... intense. Mum used to joke that she'd married my father only to become the "other woman." Occasionally this led to what the BBC would call "robust discussions." (Those of us who grew up in the seventies would translate that as "walls vibrating and Dad suddenly becoming very interested in washing the car.")

Dad worked as a Signal & Telegraph Technician for British Rail, which explains both his love of routine and my own lifelong obsession with trains. His evenings followed a schedule so precise NASA could have used it:

5:30pm: Home.
5:31pm: Wash and shave.
5:35pm: Dinner with Mum, Roger, and me.
6:15pm: Out the door, off to collect Nan.
6:30pm – closing time: The pub circuit of Petersfield.
Closing time + 5 minutes: Drop Nan home.
Closing time + 15 minutes: Dad returns, smelling faintly of Gales HSB and cigarette smoke, and collapses into bed.

Weekends were the extended edition of this routine.

On Saturdays, he'd pick Nan up at lunchtime, bring her home for a hearty lunch, and together they'd settle down to watch *World of Sport*. Nan loved the horse racing, but her true passion was the wrestling at 4pm, Big Daddy, Giant Haystacks, all the greats. Her commentary consisted mainly of sharp intakes of breath and the occasional "Well, he deserved that."

Honestly, you could set Big Ben by that woman.

Which brings me neatly to **Kent Walton**, the legendary *World of Sport* wrestling commentator. When I worked for the Department of Health and Social Security, he was one of my clients. Elderly by then, still working, and, as I discovered, still claiming to be ten years younger to ITV.

Every year I'd process his National Insurance refund, and every year he'd grin and say, "Let's keep this between us, shall we?" I admired him enormously. Anyone who clings to a job they love that fiercely deserves a medal. Or at least an extraordinarily strong cup of tea.

But back to Nan.

Saturdays always ended the same: Dad and I would drive to the fish and chip shop, pick up Roger from Bassetts the Ironmongers, head home for tea, and then Dad would chauffeur his mother back to the pub for the evening's entertainment.

Nan lived in 3 Vale Cottages, Sheet, a house so old that historians could probably carbon-date the wallpaper. The ceilings were low enough that once I shot up in my teens, I had to walk through the house like a question mark, bent in the middle. Heating was supplied by a single open fire. The toilet was outside and so cold in winter you'd practically need crampons.

The spiders, however, thrived.

These weren't normal spiders. These were creatures that, to this day, I'm convinced were big enough to apply for planning permission.

One eight-legged resident once looked at me as if *I* was the intruder.

I never went upstairs. Ever. The tiny door beneath the staircase might as well have had a sign reading *Abandon Hope All Ye Who Enter Here*. Whatever was up there, bedrooms, storage, ghosts, was left entirely to the imagination.

When I was preschool age, we visited often because Nan had something we didn't: a television. A tiny black-and-white screen no bigger than a dinner plate, encased in a wooden cabinet roughly the size of a wardrobe. We'd sit and watch *Watch with Mother*, which I loved, though I suspect Mum mostly enjoyed the free babysitting.

I adored my Nan. Completely. Even when she was fiery, even when she scolded Dad, even when she insisted on telling fortunes using methods I'm fairly sure weren't approved by the Church of England.

She passed away when I was in my mid-teens.

I still think of her sometimes, especially when I'm scrolling on my phone, a device that can stream live horse racing, hold a video call with someone in Australia, and order dinner in under two minutes.

Nan would have loved it. She would have used it exclusively for gambling, bossing people around, and tracking Dad.

In other words: perfectly.

Aunt Nell and the secret biscuit syndicate

Although I only had one official Nan, I grew up with a sort of honorary one as well: Aunt Nell.

Now, I have absolutely no idea how Mum and Aunt Nell first met, though given Mum's lifelong knitting obsession, I strongly suspect it involved wool, tea, and someone saying, "Would you mind just casting on these 112 stitches for me?"

Mum could knit with her eyes closed.

But Aunt Nell?
Aunt Nell could knit with her eyes *closed* and still outperform most sighted people.

Which was particularly impressive, considering she was about 90% blind.

We visited her flat often, especially during school holidays, and there was something wonderfully calm about the place. She'd ask Mum to find a specific Braille knitting pattern (which always impressed me, because to small Keith those raised dots might as well have been alien hieroglyphs).

If she was working on a multicoloured jumper, she'd ask Mum to lay out the wool in order, each colour neatly clipped with a clothes peg so she could switch shades with the efficiency of a seasoned stage magician.

Her world may have been smaller than most, but it was beautifully complete: her knitting, her radio, the hum of afternoon plays, and long, gentle chats with Mum.

Her kitchen, however, was straight out of *Tomorrow's World*.

She had a gadget that clipped onto a cup and beeped when the tea was nearly at the top, basically the 1970s version of a proximity sensor. She could fill a cup, pop it onto a saucer, and glide across the room without spilling a drop. I couldn't manage that *with* 20/20 vision.

Only in later years, when her balance wobbled a bit, did she reluctantly swap to mugs.

She was bright, funny, endlessly curious, and absolutely brilliant company. And she always, without fail, offered me tea and a couple of digestive biscuits.

Now, Mum had a strict rule: **"Only two biscuits."**

Aunt Nell had a slightly different interpretation of this:

Two biscuits for when Mum was watching...

...and an extra one if she wasn't.

Every time she slipped me that illicit third digestive, she'd lean in, tap my hand, and whisper conspiratorially, *"Don't tell your mother."*

I never did.

And Mum, being Mum, probably knew anyway.

Aunt Nell wasn't related to us by blood. But she was, in every way that mattered, family. The warm kind, the gentle kind, the kind who teaches you that love doesn't require shared DNA... just shared tea, shared stories, and the occasional shared biscuit-based crime.

Tea cosies, taxi runs and the art of getting on with it

If I ever needed proof that work ethic can be inherited, I only have to look at Mum and Dad. Between the two of them, they could have powered the National Grid with sheer graft alone.

Mum, for as long as I can remember (and probably long before that), was *always* working on something. Packing envelopes, helping at Murphy's egg outlet, cleaning schools, caretaking schools... and, quite often, surviving schools. She did it all. And then she'd come home and immediately start doing all the household jobs.

And *then* she'd start her real passion: knitting.

And when I say passion, I don't mean "nice hobby."
I mean "full-blown industrial operation."

By the late 70s our living room looked less like a family home and more like the research wing of the Wool Marketing Board.

Mum had knitting machines in the same way other people have teaspoons: one in every corner and more appearing whenever nobody was looking.

When I was about twelve, she taught me to knit. Back then it wasn't exactly the height of playground masculinity, this was the era of football stickers, Action Man, and pretending not to own a teddy bear, but I absolutely loved it. It felt peaceful. Logical. Almost rebellious in a quiet sort of way.

Mum did crochet and embroidery too, but knitting? That was her superpower. She knew her work was good. People knew it was good, and as a result half of Petersfield seemed to be walking around wearing something Mum had conjured out of wool, caffeine, and determination.

She also found not one but two niche markets long before "find your niche" became a business seminar cliché.

Niche #1: Tea cosies.
Not just any tea cosies, *architectural* tea cosies.

Her speciality was thatched-cottage teapot hats. Some looked like brick buildings, some like timber-framed pubs, and every single one looked like the sort of place Miss Marple would pop into for a quiet cuppa before the next murder. They sold faster than she could knit them.

Niche #2: Soft toys.
These she knitted on her machines: guardsmen, footballers, farmers, policemen, sailors... and Santa Claus by the battalion.

November and December in our house looked like Santa's workshop had exploded and the emergency response team was made of knitting needles. School fairs loved them. Local shops loved them. Dad sold them by the armful to people he knew down the pub with Nan.

If Etsy had existed in 1981, Mum would have retired a millionaire.

Now Dad, his work ethic came from a different angle.

His day job was with British Railways as a Signal and Telegraph Engineer, something that later played no small part in my own railway obsession. But when he wasn't doing *that*, he was in the garden.

Not just our garden.
Oh no.
Ours, the neighbours,' people three streets over...

He collected gardens the way Mum collected knitting machines.

And when winter arrived and gardening calmed down, he drove taxis instead. If he had an airport run to Gatwick or Heathrow and the back seat wasn't full, he'd take me along. I loved everything about those drives: the hush of pre-dawn starts, the smell of diesel, the rhythm of tyres slicing through wet tarmac, the murmur of passengers making small talk they'd instantly forget.

Now, I didn't inherit Mum's knitting genius or Dad's enthusiasm for soil.

But their work ethic?

Oh absolutely.

That stuck.

The graft.
The discipline.
The "if there's work to do, do it properly" mentality.

The habit of scanning the world for opportunities, woolly or otherwise.

And that, dear reader, is as good a legacy as anyone could wish for.

The great newspaper coup of '78

It was with one of my good friends, Ian, that I first dipped my toes, well, more like plunged head-first, into the world of business.

Like most kids of our era, hitting thirteen meant one thing: a newspaper round. Ours were with John Menzies, delivering the Portsmouth Evening News, a fine publication that still exists today (now simply called *The News*, presumably because the full name took too long to shout across the shop).

Ian had a bike, which meant he got the nice, spread-out housing estates on the edge of Petersfield. I, lacking both balance and any hope of carrying a bag the size of a small anvil on two wheels, was assigned the town centre: shops, flats, stairwells, and enough front doors to make a postman cry.

We'd head straight to Menzies after school, collect our bundles, and set off like two underpaid carrier pigeons with poor pay and no union representation.

I don't remember exactly what we earned per paper, probably about two pence. Saturdays were the big money: three pence per paper because they contained the football results supplement. "Supplement" is doing a lot of heavy lifting; it was essentially a small phone book glued inside the sports pages.

Just down the High Street was The News' tiny editorial office. It served Petersfield's sister paper, the *Petersfield Post*, and it smelled gloriously of ink, paper, and mild despair, like all good newspaper offices should.

And then... came the economics lesson.

Ian and I had just been introduced to the magical concept of *profit margins*. The difference between what something costs and what you can get away with charging for it. To our thirteen-year-old brains, this was less "an accounting principle" and more "the cheat code to life."

John Menzies bought the papers at one price and sold them at another. We were the ones doing the arduous work, the delivering, the dodging of dogs, the climbing of three flights of stairs when lifts mysteriously "didn't work again."

So why, we reasoned, couldn't *we* buy direct?

Cut out the middleman. Classic business strategy.

Especially when you are The Middleman's Employees of the Month. (Well… employees.)

So, one afternoon, armed with the confidence of two boys whose voices were one hormonal tremor away from breaking, we walked into The News office.

Ian, coward, made me do the talking.

A manager in a wood-panelled office listened politely as I explained that we wanted to buy the papers wholesale and deliver them ourselves. And to our utter shock, he said:

"Yes, that's fine. That's how small newsagents do it."

No laughter. No ejection. No "Come back when you're old enough to shave."

He even told us we could return unsold copies for credit.

Then he gave us the price: **four pence below the cover price.**

We practically floated out of the building. It was flawless. Perfect. Bulletproof.

We were basically Rupert Murdoch, but with shorter trousers.

We recruited Ian's sister, Elvina, to become Head of Customer Services (which is to say, she'd answer the phone if anyone called after school). Our flyers proudly proclaimed:

"Call Elvina after 4pm if you'd like to change your delivery."

We didn't have bank accounts, so everything was cash-in-hand. Proper old-school trading. Very Dragons' Den, but with more acne.

We did the maths:

- Customers saved six pence.
- We earned six pence per paper instead of two.
- We even added a delivery charge (because, as our economics teacher said, "people don't value what they don't pay for").

Honestly, it was capitalism with training wheels.

For a week, we slipped flyers inside every newspaper we delivered… discreetly, or so we thought.

By day four, disaster.

One of our customers, no doubt a loyal friend of Big Business, handed our flyer straight to the manager at Menzies.

That afternoon, when we arrived to collect our rounds, he summoned us into his office with the tone of a man preparing to roast children over a spit.

He slapped the flyer down like Exhibit A at a trial.

"So?" he said. "What have you got to say for yourselves?"

There was no point pretending. We were caught.

"You're both fired," he said. "Now get out."

I paused.

"What about tonight's rounds?"

"GO!"

So, we went.

Heads high.
Futures bright.

Because what he didn't know was this:

The next morning, our first business venture officially opened.

The day I tried to hide a sink disaster with a dishcloth

One of my earliest childhood memories - and given how many times I've been knocked unconscious since, it's a wonder I remember anything at all - took place in our kitchen.

We had one of those deep white Belfast sinks, the kind that always looked spotless no matter how many potatoes, muddy carrots, or small children were dunked in it over the years.

On this particular day, four-year-old me was standing on a chair beside it, doing what every four-year-old does best: being dangerously curious.

On the draining board sat a cast-metal kettle stand. Now, when I say "heavy," I mean the sort of thing a blacksmith would use as a paperweight. It was absolutely *not* designed for small hands, or, frankly, for my hands now.

But I decided to pick it up anyway because... well, because I was four. That was the full extent of my risk assessment.

Predictably, it slipped. Not gracefully, either.

It bounced off the edge of the sink with a clang so loud it probably woke the neighbours, took a neat bite *out* of the enamel, and landed in the base of the sink with a final, damning thud.

Mum rushed in.

She looked at me. Looked at the kettle stand. Looked at the chunk missing from her pristine sink. Then back at me.

The full sequence, like a crime-scene investigator putting the pieces together.

"You silly boy," she said, in that tone all mothers have mastered, calm, disappointed, and mildly terrifying. "You know that's too heavy for you. What if it had been hot? You could have burned yourself! And *look* what you've done to the sink. Just wait until your Daddy gets home, he's going to be very cross with you."

Now, I knew I was in trouble.

But I also knew I was *resourceful*.

So, I pointed at the chip and, with the optimism only a small child can muster, asked:

"Could you not just... put the dishcloth over it? Then maybe Daddy wouldn't notice?"

Reader, diplomacy was not my strong point.

My mother was not, in any universe, a violent woman. But even the Saint of Petersfield would have lost patience with that suggestion.

She brought her hand down sharply on the back of one thigh, then the other. It stung, and the tears came instantly.

"Owww! That hurt, Mummy!" I sobbed.

"Good," she said, matter of fact. "It was meant to."

This was definitely not going as I'd hoped.

"Get down off that chair and go to your room," she said. "And I don't want to hear another squeak out of you before your Daddy gets home."

"Sorry, Mummy," I sniffed, and trudged upstairs with the heavy tread of a man off to face a firing squad.

I perched on my bed with one of my comics but couldn't concentrate. I just sat there waiting for The Return of the Father, the sequel no child ever wants.

Eventually I heard the familiar growl of the car outside.

I ran down, wrapped myself round his leg like a koala on a eucalyptus tree. He took one look at my blotchy face.

"Have you been crying, son?"

I nodded.

"Why? What's happened?"

"Mummy smacked me," I sniffed, expecting sympathy.

Instead, he raised his hand and delivered a matching swat to the back of my thigh.

"Owww! Daddy! You didn't even let me tell you what happened!"

"I don't need to hear what happened," he said calmly. "If your mother lost her temper, you must have done something really bad. Now come on, you're going to apologise properly, or you'll have something real to cry about."

And that was that.

Due process? Not in our house.

He marched me into the kitchen.

"Keith wants to say something to you," he announced.

I looked at Mum, still red-eyed. "I'm really, really sorry, Mummy."

"Do you mean it?" she asked.

I nodded like a small, terrified woodpecker.

"Do you promise never to touch things in the kitchen without asking first?"

"Yes, Mummy."

Her expression softened. "Good. Then we're all square. Now go wash your hands for tea."

And just like that, it was over.
No drama. No lectures. No follow-up.

Dad found a replacement sink a few weeks later, life returned to normal and, as with so many family mishaps, it was never mentioned again.

But did I forget it?

Not a chance.

Some lessons stay with you… especially the ones delivered to the back of your legs.

The family web: please take notes

If you've made it this far, dear reader, you probably deserve a medal, preferably one with a diagram of my family tree on the back, because you're about to need it.

Yes, it's time to explain the Budden family structure.

Think of it like assembling flat-pack furniture without the instructions: everything fits together in the end, but there *will* be moments when you stare into the middle distance and question your life choices.

Let's begin.

Mum, Dad, and a Café Called Monty
As you already know, my parents were Olive and George.

They met in 1947, though technically Mum had already lived in Liss for years, thanks to being evacuated from Walthamstow during the war. She lived with a couple called Frank and Dollie - my "Auntie Dollie."

Not actually an aunt. In fact, the only thing "aunt-like" about her was that she tolerated small children and made sure Mum didn't starve.

Mum was working with Auntie Dollie in the Monty Café when Dad wandered in one day during his lunch break, still serving as a soldier. He claimed it was "the food" that brought him back daily.

Spoiler: it wasn't the food.

Dad had recently returned from the war, Macedonia, to be precise, after spending months helping move military vehicles across Europe. By the time he settled in Sheet with his mum, my Nan, he was a trained lorry driver with impeccable manners and what Mum later called "a smile a girl could fall for."

He flirted, but never quite plucked up the courage to ask her out.

Then fate (and a no-show boyfriend) stepped in.

One Saturday night, he passed the Savoy Cinema, Petersfield's social hotspot, and spotted Mum looking forlorn outside.

"The chap who was meant to meet me hasn't turned up," she told him.

"Well," Dad said, summoning every ounce of courage in Hampshire, "you could always come in with me instead."

And she did.

One movie, one walk home, and the rest is history.

They married in Sheet Church. Roy arrived in October 1948, Roger in March 1955, and then, after a nine-year gap, me, in 1964.

Yes, I was the plot twist.

Dad's Side of the Family
Dad had six siblings, none of whom survived into adulthood.

By the time I was born, only he and his mother, my Nan Nelly, remained.

Nan, as you know, was… how shall I put this… a character.

Romany traits, strong opinions, a healthy collection of superstitions, and the sense of humour of someone who had absolutely no time for nonsense.

Mum's Side of the Family
Mum had two brothers: Ben and Jim.

Jim, I met much later in life, but Uncle Ben was a permanent fixture, married to my Auntie Mollie, with cousins Matthew and Andrew completing their branch of the tree.

Here's where things get… interesting.

Mollie had two sisters: Hazel and Julie.

Julie moved to Gosport.

Hazel… married my brother Roy.

Yes.

That makes Hazel my sister-in-law *and* my auntie-by-marriage.

Please take a moment. Have a biscuit if needed.

Every family has "a story."
This is one of ours.

The Roy & Hazel Saga (Or: Why the Red Cross Man Came to Visit)

Hazel had facial disfigurement from birth complications and was tiny in stature, but sharp as a tack and possessed a laugh loud enough to startle livestock.

Roy didn't realise she was technically his aunt (not by blood, but still).

My parents were horrified. Hazel's family probably were too. The whole thing escalated into a level of drama that made *EastEnders* look underplayed.

And then Roy and Hazel eloped.

The shock nearly finished Mum.

A Red Cross man came to the house (back when they helped locate runaway adults as well as missing persons). They tracked the couple to Birmingham. Both were safe, both working... but not ready for contact.

Years passed.

Then came Taro Fair - centuries old, beloved, chaotic.

I had just won a goldfish, proudly parading it like I'd just solved world peace, when Roy and Hazel appeared pushing a pram.

It was awkward, emotional, halting...
but it was the beginning of healing.

From that day on, we slowly knitted ourselves back into one family.

Their son, Grant, made me an uncle at age six, something my friends delighted in teasing me about. ("Are you collecting your pension yet, Keith?")

Roger

Roger had cerebral palsy from birth and epilepsy that wasn't properly controlled until his twenties.

He never married, but he lived his life with humour, kindness, and stubborn resilience, very much the Budden trademark.

He died in December 2024, a loss I still feel sharply.

And Then There's Me

You will read the rest of my health adventures later - there are plenty - but familywise, here are the women who shaped my life:

- **Elizabeth**, my childhood sweetheart
- **Ali**, my university, and early-twenties partner
- **Ruth**, whose story intertwines through fate and serendipity.
- **Sandra**, a gentle, important chapter
- **Enma**, my fiancée, who would have been my wife had she lived a few months longer.

Enma brought with her two children, Richard and Michelle.

Michelle later blessed me with five grandchildren, Shona, Bethany, Hugh, Lucy, and Davy, and they, in turn, have given me three great-grandchildren: Jane, Debbie, and Abie.

I didn't mind "Grandad."

But "Great-Grandad" made me feel like I should start dispensing Werther's Originals from a tartan tin.

So we settled on **Gramps**.
Much more my style.

The Family, in All Its Beautiful Chaos

And so there you have it: the Budden family.

Complicated? Yes.
Occasionally dramatic? Certainly.

But full of love, loyalty, and more laughter than a BBC sitcom.

We might not have been rich in worldly goods, but we were wealthy in the only currency that mattered:

Care.
Connection.
And the kind of family stories that would make even the scriptwriters of *Coronation Street* **say,**

"Bit far-fetched, isn't it?"

Wait... we have to go back?

I hadn't been to nursery school, so the idea of starting infants' school felt impossibly exciting, like I was finally being invited into the secret world of "the big kids.
The ones who got to carry satchels, smell faintly of crayons, and talk knowingly about something called "assembly."

The big day arrived.

Mum dressed me with the loving precision usually reserved for sending a child to a royal garden party. Crisp white shirt. Red jumper. Grey shorts so long they almost qualified as formal trousers. Shoes shining with enough polish to illuminate an airstrip. And a satchel that was clearly designed for a much larger child, or possibly a medium-sized pony, hanging proudly off my shoulder.

Hand in hand, Mum marched me through the school gates. "I'll pick you up this afternoon," she said, smiling like someone who absolutely knew what was coming and chose not to warn me.

I don't remember much about that first day's *lessons,* because who cares about phonics when there's a sandpit the size of the Sahara? I spent most of the morning there, building sandcastles using the exact technique Roger had taught me on our trips to Littlehampton and the Witterings. (He'd have been proud. I was producing three-turret masterpieces with impressive structural integrity.)

At some point a teacher handed me my very first reading book: **Red Book 1**.

Just the sight of it made me feel like a scholar. A proper reader. Practically a professor.

The rest of the day passed in the blissful ignorance that only a four-year-old can achieve. Then the bell rang. I sprinted into the playground with the momentum of a small, excited cannonball. There was Mum, waiting. Arms open. Smile ready. I dashed toward her, satchel flapping wildly against the backs of my legs like an angry leather pigeon.

We walked home, and I spent the entire journey, and the next hour in the kitchen, giving her a blow-by-blow account of my day. The sand. The book. The bucket. The other children. The sheer *joy* of it all.

She listened beautifully, the way only mums can, half cooking tea, half nodding at the right moments, entirely encouraging.

When she put my plate down, she said,
"I'm so glad you enjoyed your first day at school."
"Oh yes, Mummy," I beamed. "It was fun."

And that's when she dropped the bombshell.
"So, you won't mind going back *tomorrow* then?"

I froze.

"Wait... what? You mean I have to go *again*?"

"Yes, darling," she said, doing a heroic job of not laughing. "You get holidays at Christmas, Easter, and in the summer... But other than that, you'll go every day, Monday to Friday, until you're sixteen."

Reader, I stared at her like she had just told me Father Christmas had resigned.

"Oh," I said eventually, in the small, betrayed voice of a child who has just discovered the fine print of life.

Inside, though, my tiny brain was in full crisis mode.

Every day? Until I'm SIXTEEN?

Nobody had mentioned this in the brochure.
That was the precise moment I realised school wasn't a jolly little outing.

It was... a commitment.

Still, I went back the next day, and, unbelievably, the day after that, proving even four-year-olds can adapt when bribed with sandpits and storybooks.

The day the bull came to assembly

Current residents of Liss might struggle to picture it, but when I was little, the spot where Tesco and its parade of shops now stand was... fields.

Just fields.

No car park.
No flats.
No meal deals.

Just grass, the occasional muddy puddle, and, most importantly, livestock belonging to Mr Mitchell, the local butcher.

Yes, you read that right. The butcher kept the animals behind the shop.

I spent years thinking they were simply family pets who rotated out when they got bored. It never occurred to me why Mum discouraged me from "naming the cows," or why Bessie, Daisy, and Buttercup all mysteriously vanished every few weeks.

Back then, Liss was thriving enough to support *two* butchers, Mitchells in the village and Berrimans in Liss Forest. Both gone now, although the excellent Butcher & Larder has restored honour to the village and, speaking as someone who has tested their sausages thoroughly, I can confirm they're superb.

But I digress.

Let me take you to **The Day It Happened**.

It was a perfectly ordinary school day. Red brick buildings. Packed lunch in a Tupperware box older than the British Constitution. Everything utterly normal.

Then we saw him.

A bull.

Not the gentle, slightly bewildered steers we were used to, but a *proper* bull, with a nose ring and the attitude of someone who had just read his own name on tomorrow's Specials Board.

At some point that morning, his handler decided it was time to move him into the slaughterhouse.

The bull disagreed.

For reasons known only to him, possibly spiritual awakening, possibly sheer bloody-mindedness, he ripped free, ploughed straight through the fence, and charged directly into the school playground.

We knew something was wrong when we heard pounding footsteps, frantic shouting, and a teacher yelling:

"Keep the children in your classrooms! A bull has escaped, it's in the playground! But don't panic!"

This was, objectively, the worst possible thing to say.

Naturally, we panicked by running straight to the windows like meerkats on Red Bull.

And there he was.

Huge.
Snorting.
Pawing at the ground.

Breath billowing in the autumn air like a steam train that had skipped anger management classes.

One of the butcher's men tried to grab the rope attached to the bull's nose ring.

The bull took one look at him, lowered his head, and charged.

I've never seen an adult run so fast.

He practically levitated onto the boundary wall. The children in my class applauded.

What followed was several adrenaline-soaked minutes of man-versus-bull theatre: the men lunging bravely forward, the bull lunging even more bravely back, while two hundred small children narrated the action like excitable sports commentators.

Eventually, three men managed to corner him, grab the rope, and wrestle him towards the gap in the fence.

The bull made his displeasure extremely clear, but resistance was futile: three determined butchers beat one very annoyed bovine.

And just like that, the crisis was over.

A huge cheer went up - pupils, teachers, probably even the school caretaker who had just watched his newly painted fence explode into kindling.

A Strange Legacy
Even now, every Sunday when I cook my sirloin steak, I sometimes wonder whether that moment, watching the furious dignity of a bull refusing to go quietly, embedded itself somewhere deep in my subconscious.

There's probably a philosophical lesson in there about courage, survival, or the futility of resisting an inevitable fate.

But honestly?

I just remember thinking:

"Well... that was much better than maths."

The view from Bude

With Mum and Roger being regular fixtures at the Methodist Church in Petersfield, it was only a matter of time before Mum gently steered me away from the Cub Scouts and toward the Boys' Brigade. Not a shove, just that classic Mum manoeuvre, the kind where she *"suggests"* something, but you somehow already know the decision has been made.

They met once a week in the church hall. Mum introduced me to the group leader, who gave me that chipper, slightly rehearsed line:
"Why not come along for a couple of weeks and see if you like it?"

Translation: *You're one of ours now, son.*

And as it turned out, I did enjoy it. There weren't many lads from Liss, but I got to know boys from Petersfield and the surrounding villages. Fresh faces, new mischief, new badges to earn (and yes, that mattered).

Uniform was a big deal, dark shoes, dark trousers, blue shirt, blue jumper, and a cap that bore a suspicious resemblance to an RAF hat. Even at ten years old I felt ever-so-slightly important wearing it, like I might be called upon to taxi a Lancaster Bomber at a moment's notice.

Part of Boys' Brigade life meant attending at least one church service a month. Since Mum and Roger were in the pews every week anyway, that wasn't exactly a hardship. I tagged along, polished shoes and all.

But the real highlight, the thing we all waited for, was the summer camp.

Ours was just outside Bude, in Cornwall. I must've been around ten the first year I went, buzzing with excitement and nerves in equal measure. I'd never been away from home before, so this was big. *Proper* big.

We piled into a couple of hired minibuses. I waved goodbye to Mum from the church car park with a brave face while my bottom lip did its own, less convincing thing.

When we arrived, the tents were already pitched: four boys to a tent, plus separate tents for the leaders and their wives (who I always suspected were the ones actually keeping everything running).

That first afternoon was pure bliss: rounders on a big green field, barbecue food (a novelty to me, we weren't a barbecue household), and that fizzy excitement of being somewhere new and away from adults... or so we thought.

Of course, I'd smuggled my teddy into the bottom of my rucksack. Did I dare take him out? Not until the other boys were asleep. A lad can only withstand so much teasing.

Lights out came sooner than expected. The leaders did their rounds, switching off lanterns, and suddenly the tent was dark, chilly, and very, very not home. I lay there missing my bed, my Mum... and most of all, Chum, our cat.

Chum's usual sleeping spot was on top of my wardrobe, until he'd roll over in the night and plummet down the gap between wardrobe and wall with all the grace of a sack of bricks. Then, after a suitable period of reflection (or sulking), he'd re-emerge and leap right back up again. I wondered if Chum missed me. I hoped so. I certainly missed him.

Next thing I knew, Reveille blared outside the tent. So much for sleeping in.

Breakfast got the blood going, and the days flew past in a blur of games, sea breezes, and sunburn. Nights flew considerably less, turns out canvas isn't known for its heat-retention properties, but overall, camp was brilliant.

One moment stands out above all the others: standing at the top of the cliffs, looking out at the vastness of the ocean. No Isle of Wight in the distance to reassure you, just water stretching all the way to America.

I checked the atlas back at camp.

It really was just sea, all the way across the Atlantic.

I remember thinking: *One day I'll go there.* I'll stand on a cliff on the other side, look back toward Bude, and wonder if there's some kid doing exactly the same thing in reverse.

Ah, the magic of being ten and being convinced you've invented philosophy.

Sadly, I never got to go back. Over the winter, our group leader got a new job and moved away. None of the other leaders wanted to take over, and just like that, the group folded.

I suppose I could've joined the Scouts instead. Plenty of my friends did. But for whatever reason, it never happened.

And so, my Boys' Brigade chapter ended, short, sweet, and full of memories... plus one very well-travelled teddy, who survived the trip entirely unscathed and, most importantly, undetected.

Tractors, Tea, and the Thrill of the Engine

I've always had a soft spot for anything that moves, trains, planes, ships, buses, trams, even the odd lawnmower if it makes the right sort of noise. But nothing, *nothing*, gripped mini-me quite like the mighty farm tractor.

I've no idea where the obsession came from. We weren't farmers. We didn't *know* any farmers. We didn't even live near a farm big enough to cause a traffic jam. But show me a tractor and I was instantly hypnotised.

The noise. The size. The slow but determined *"I've got a field to plough, and I'll get there in my own time, thank you very much"* attitude.

Loved it.

Whenever we were out in the car, I'd beg Dad to slow down if one appeared in a field. There I'd be, nose pressed to the window, admiring some farmer carving perfectly straight lines into the soil, straighter than anything I ever produced in my school exercise books, despite the red margin line essentially begging me to behave.

I never announced that I wanted to *be* a tractor driver, but I talked about them so much my parents considered enrolling me in the Young Farmers just to give themselves some peace.

Then came the day to end all tractor-related days.

We were heading out of Petersfield, past Froxfield and towards Ropley, when something glorious caught my eye: a John Deere dealership. Rows of shining green-and-yellow machines, practically glowing under the autumn sun.

"Dad, STOP!" I pleaded.

To his eternal credit, he did.

The gates were locked, but I could still see them… a metallic army of agricultural perfection. I stood there gripping the bars like a very tiny prisoner serving a life sentence for loving diesel fumes too much.

At the time, I thought nothing could ever beat that.

But I was wrong.

Because I hadn't yet discovered the Massey Ferguson and Ford tractor showroom in Rowlands Castle.

We'd often pass through on the way home from Portsmouth. Mum and Dad would nip into The Castle Inn for a drink while I sat outside with colouring pens, a notepad, and a glass of Coke (or a bitter lemon when I wanted to feel sophisticated.) By the time we left, it was usually dark, and I was half-asleep in the back seat, so the dealership went unseen.

Until one evening... when my destiny changed.

We'd left Portsmouth early. As we drove past the dealership, the lights were blazing across rows of gleaming tractors, showroom open, machines on display, my eyes widening like saucers.

"STOP!" I yelled.

Dad braked hard, probably thinking we'd hit a pedestrian, a dog, or possibly the moon.

"What?!" he shouted.

"Look! TRACTORS!"

And bless him, he swerved straight into the nearest layby before Mum could protest.

We crossed the road and stepped inside. Mum must have silently accepted that her evening was no longer hers. The salesman, clearly a saint in overalls, let me climb into not one but *three* tractors in the showroom.

Then he took us into the yard.

He pointed at a huge machine, already impressive under the floodlights.

"Hop in," he said.

I think my soul left my body.

He checked it was out of gear, pressed the clutch, and then said the most beautiful sentence ever spoken to a small boy:

"Go on, son, start her up."

There was no chance I was going to say no.

I turned the key.

Chug... chug... chug... FROOOM.

The engine burst into life. The flap on the exhaust pipe fluttered like a flag in the wind. A puff of blue-grey smoke curled upwards. I pressed the accelerator gently, and the whole tractor growled.

It was pure, unfiltered magic.
Better than Christmas.
Better than birthdays.
Possibly even better than fish and chips (but don't tell Mum).

After that, every time we passed through Rowlands Castle, d daylight, moonlight, or technically "midnight and well past your bedtime", I insisted we stop and admire the tractors. Dad indulged me every time, a small act of kindness I've always remembered.

Even now, when I get stuck behind a tractor on a country lane, everyone else huffs and complains.

Not me.

I smile.

Because those rumbling engines, those giant tyres, those slow, determined chugs...

They take me straight back to a yard in Rowlands Castle, a kindly salesman, a roaring diesel engine, and the evening I felt like king of the farming world.

I want to be happy

I was 10 years old when I was asked what I wanted to be when I grew up and I said,
"I want to be happy."

I made it my life's mission.

Everyone else in the classroom gave sensible answers.
Fireman. Nurse. Pilot. Footballer.

One boy even said he wanted to work in IT, which, looking back, meant he was either a genius or terrifyingly lacking in imagination.

But me?

I sat there in my bowl haircut and Gola trainers and said the one thing every adult secretly wishes they'd had the courage to say:

I want to be happy.

The teacher smiled in that thin, controlled way teachers smile when they're not sure whether to be impressed or concerned.

"Well," she said, "that's very... nice, Keith. But what job do you want?"

"I don't know," I told her. "Just something that makes me smile."

She wrote *HAPPY* in the box on the form as if she was placing an order she knew the catalogue didn't stock.

But here's the thing:

I meant it then.
And I still mean it now.

Happiness has guided more of my decisions than common sense ever has.
Common sense would've kept me out of half the ridiculous situations I've walked into.

Happiness, on the other hand, has walked me *straight into them,* patted me on the back, and said, "Go on, it'll make a good story later."

And it usually did.

I'm not talking about the Disney kind of happiness, the musical-number, birds-tying-your-shoelaces variety.

I mean the real stuff.

The quiet contentment of knowing you're exactly where you're meant to be, even if where you're meant to be happens to be:

- sitting half-naked in a cardiac lab,
- dancing like a Dad on Red Bull to S Club 7,
- or standing in the pouring rain at a remembrance parade with a lump in your throat and pride in your chest.

Happiness hasn't always been easy to find.

Some years it felt like trying to tune into the radio with a bent coat hanger. Illness, loss, grief, disappointment, they all try to turn down the volume.

But every single time, something, or someone, has turned it back up again.

My brothers, with their unshakable loyalty.
My daughter and grandchildren, even in the hardest chapters.
Friends who became family when life felt too heavy to carry alone.

And yes, even the strangers:
The nurse who held my hand tighter than I technically needed.
The Danish woman who marched me through an airport like lost luggage.
The GP who once told me, "You're still here because you're too bloody stubborn to leave."

They were right.
I am stubborn.

Stubborn about living.
Stubborn about laughing.
Stubborn about getting back up when life would honestly be easier if I stayed on the floor a bit longer.

But that's what a 10-year-old signed up for.

Because happiness isn't a destination.
It's not a job title.
It's not something you stumble upon at the end of a long journey, like a service station selling cheap coffee and questionable sausage rolls.

It's a decision -
made daily,
sometimes hourly,
sometimes with gritted teeth and a muttered,
"Oh for God's sake, Keith, keep going."

If you're reading this, I hope you find your own version of happiness.
Not the one on inspirational posters with sunsets and people doing yoga on cliffs.
The real kind.
The messy kind.
The "smile at a stupid joke," "dance to a song you shouldn't like," "hold someone when they need it," "get back up again" kind.

The kind a 10-year-old could recognise instantly.

Because after a lifetime of moments -
some joyous,
some heartbreaking,
some downright absurd -
I've learned one thing:

Happiness is rarely found when life is easy.
But it's almost always found when life is honest.

And if little Keith, sat in that classroom with his Lego haircut, could see me now, he'd probably say:

"Well done, mate.
You played the long game."

The summer we all grew up (some faster than others)

We were a tight little tribe along our road, me, Mark, Jane, Ian, Ian's sister Elvina, and Martyn with his sister Tammy. All born within a couple of years of each other, which made us the perfect recipe for mischief: enough similarity to bond, enough difference to argue, and enough unspent childhood energy to power a small town.

Whenever Mum and Dad took a rare weekend away, I went to stay with Martyn and Tammy while Roger stayed with one of his friends. Roy had already flown the nest by then. It worked both ways too - if Martyn's parents, Mike, and Elaine, went away, Martyn and Tammy came to ours. We were like a low-budget timeshare scheme, but with more grass stains and fewer legal contracts.

I loved staying at Martyn's. His parents were younger than mine, which automatically made them cooler. Their weekends were full of walks in the woods, football matches on the green that lasted until someone lost the ball in the brambles, or rounders games played until the sun dipped below the rooftops. If the weather was good, Mike would pile us all into the car and take us to the beach.

My dad was a loyal Hayling Island man (pebbles, queues, and wind), but Mike always took us to the Witterings, - proper sand, the kind you could build empires out of. To this day, Wittering sand remains the gold standard by which I judge all other beaches.

I was about seven when all this started. Martyn had a bunk bed. He slept on the top; I slept on the bottom. Even then, my relationship with heights was best described as "respectful avoidance."

Evenings followed a set pattern: Elaine would run a bath for me, Martyn, and Tammy. All three of us together, splashing happily. Completely innocent. We knew Tammy didn't have a "winky," as we called it, but that was just an interesting biological footnote.

Elaine would lift Tammy out first, wrap her in a towel and send her off to get into her pyjamas. Then she'd come back for the two of us. It felt cosy. Safe. Ordinary.

And then, as these things do, everything changed.

Tammy started... well... developing.

We noticed.

In the subtle, understated way boys of nine or ten notice things without fully understanding what they are noticing.

One night, after Tammy had been lifted out of the bath and padded off to her room, Martyn announced, in a voice that could probably have been heard three streets away:

"She's getting BOOBIES!"

That was the end of communal bath time.

Elaine took about three seconds to make the executive parental decision that Tammy would, from that moment on, be bathing alone. Looking back, it was definitely the right call.

We were a gang of outdoor children. Tea was eaten at warp speed, then we vanished until it was too dark to see the ball, the bike, or each other. In winter or when it rained, we'd rotate between houses, playing board games or, in our more technologically advanced years, Binatone TV tennis. Two sticks, a dot, and a line in the middle pretending to be a net.

Cutting-edge!
Today's teenagers would faint with boredom.

But of all the memories from that gang, one remains a milestone.

It was Elvina who delivered it.

We were playing kiss chase on a warm evening. The kind where the air is thick with summer dust and laughter echoes across the gardens. We'd been tearing around the play area when Elvina darted behind her dad's shed. I followed, purely in the spirit of the game, of course.

I was in jeans and a T-shirt; she was still in her school blouse and dark blue skirt. She'd rolled the waistband to make it shorter, a teenage rite of passage, showing most of her thighs. Maybe it was that. Maybe it was the hint of perfume she'd started wearing. Maybe it was the faint outline of her bra, something mysterious and entirely new to me.

Or maybe it was the mischievous smile she gave me when I caught up with her.

Whatever it was... the air shifted.

We kissed.

Then we kissed again.

A nervous, shy, heart-thumping kiss. The kind that changes something in you, even if you can't explain what.

Her blouse rustled against my arm. Then, gently, she guided my hand onto her breast. My heart took off like a startled bird.

It didn't go any further, and honestly, it didn't need to.

It was sweet. Innocent. Unforgettable.

A small but seismic step in the long, bewildering, wonderful process of growing up.

The sort of moment that stays tucked into the scrapbook of your mind forever.

The year I accidentally grew up

Moving up to senior school felt less like an educational transition and more like being thrown into a much bigger, louder version of life. At nearly eleven, I was leaving behind the comfort of junior school and joining what Mum ominously referred to as "the real world."

There were only two options: Petersfield Comprehensive (now TPS), or Mill Chase in Bordon. Mum and Dad didn't need a family meeting to reach a decision, Bordon had a "reputation." Mum described it delicately as having a "rough edge." Translation: I was going to Petersfield Comp.

That summer, Mum marched me through Commercial Road in Portsmouth more times than was strictly humane. We got everything: new shoes, a proper white shirt (goodbye polo shirts), grey polyester trousers that could probably withstand nuclear fallout, and a navy blazer large enough to house a family of four. When I pointed out that the sleeves came somewhere near my fingertips, Mum chirped, "You'll grow into it!" A lie told by mothers since the dawn of time.

On the first day of term, I discovered every other mother had told the same lie. Thirty of us looked like child actors in an adult costume drama.

Mum sewed on my cloth school badge by hand, painstakingly, night after night while watching Crossroads. She also sewed name labels into everything I owned, including my underpants, just in case I suddenly forgot who I was.

The first day wasn't too bad, only the first years were in. But Monday arrived, and with it, the older pupils. Fifth formers who looked about 35, some sporting moustaches so advanced they could probably rent property. Suddenly I understood why Mum kept asking whether I thought I'd "adapt."

The school was filled with familiar faces, Mark, Jane, Ian, plus new arrivals from East Meon, Clanfield, Liphook and Greatham. We were sorted into forms of thirty, boys and girls together, and assigned form teachers who looked either incredibly kind or vaguely homicidal. Sometimes both.

Homework arrived like a tax bill, sudden, confusing, and non-negotiable. We lugged textbooks home every night. To protect them, Mum covered mine in brown paper or wallpaper offcuts. Anyone who damaged a book received a stern letter and a replacement bill, so I treated mine like museum artefacts.

PE was a problem.

I was medically exempt, though I didn't know why at the time. I assumed it was to prevent me developing epilepsy like Roger. Looking back, I suspect Mum already knew something wasn't quite right with me physically. For the first year, though, I still had to attend lessons, which meant two hours standing in the rain watching other boys chase a muddy ball around a field.

Eventually, the school relented and said I could spend Wednesday afternoons in the library instead. It felt like parole into paradise. Books, warmth, quiet, heaven.

Certain teachers have stayed with me:

- **Peter Walker (English)** - who still plays chess with Roy today, fifty years on.
- **Mr Dyson (Biology)** - gentle but firm.
- **Mr Smith (Technical Studies)** - could fix anything except our behaviour.
- **Mr Handley (Woodwork)** - whose lessons proved that I should never, ever be left alone with sharp objects.
- **Mr Prater (Art)** – owner of a beautiful vintage Rover and, I suspect, a deep belief that none of us possessed artistic talent.
- **Mr Stoodley (Geography)** - terrifying. Legend has it he could silence a classroom simply by entering the building. Years later... rumours surfaced. Another story, another time.

I loved **Home Economics** (cookery). Shepherd's pie, rock cakes, sausage plait, I made them all and carried them home proudly. My family always declared them delicious. Whether that was truth or self-preservation, I'll never know. But it sparked a love of cooking that's stayed with me ever since.

Drama was another favourite. I only ever acted in one school play, - a murder mystery. I was a vicar with a straw hat and umbrella, which already felt like typecasting.

My big line was:
"My flock in this village are not as innocent as they seem. Amongst them there is a wrong 'un or two, make no mistake."

Just reading it now, I realise... I was basically auditioning for *The Traitors* half a century too early.

We rehearsed flawlessly six times. Then came the final performance, the one with all the parents. I delivered my line perfectly, reached for my umbrella... and it wouldn't move. The tip had lodged itself in a knot hole in the stage.

The audience thought it was slapstick genius.
I tugged.
Nothing.

A teacher had to sprint on stage mid-scene to rescue me. Umbrella freed; the hall erupted in applause. I wanted the ground to swallow me whole. I vowed never to perform again. (I lied, but that's for later).

A few other memories remain sharp.

The cricket incident.
I was watching, not playing. One second the ball was hurtling toward the batsman, the next everything went black. I woke up on a lab table with Mr Davey and half my classmates hovering over me.

"You took a cricket ball to the forehead," he said cheerfully.

Today I'd have been airlifted to Southampton General. Back then, the treatment was:
   1. Cup of tea.
   2. Maybe a lie down.
   3. Back to lessons.

And then there was **my first real lesson in sex education**, delivered not by the school but by my classmates.

It was 1977.

Four of us, me, Stu, Elizabeth, and Tina, were at Elizabeth's house. Her mum was out shopping.

We'd run out of board games, when Elizabeth suddenly announced:

"I know, let's do *you show me yours and I'll show you mine*."

There was a pause.
Then: "Well... alright."

"Boys first," she said.

So, Stu and I undressed, awkwardly, fully, while the girls inspected us with the clinical detachment of trainee pathologists. Stu already had pubes. I did not. I made a mental note to start growing some immediately.

Then it was the girls' turn. Elizabeth went first, brown dress off, then green tights, then bra, then pants. I'd never seen a girl my age naked before. The world shifted slightly on its axis. Tina followed, shyly, but determined not to be outdone.

For a couple of minutes, no more, we simply stood there, four awkward teenagers. Staring. Fascinated. Confused. Thrilled. Terrified.

Then Elizabeth said,

"Quick, get dressed, Mum'll be home soon!"
We scrambled into our clothes at record speed.

Her mum came home carrying shopping bags.

"Who wants tea?"

"Yes please!" we all chimed, halos gleaming.

"What have you been doing?"

"Oh, just playing games," Elizabeth said smoothly.

And that, dear reader, was that. An utterly innocent, utterly unforgettable, utterly 1970s rite of passage.

Lessons from the Chicken Shed

My first proper job, the first time I was paid by someone who didn't share my surname, arrived when I was about fourteen.

Mum, being Mum, had already worked half the village by that point and was then selling eggs for a local farmer called Murphy at a stall in the Folly Market.

Murphy was a man of few words, most of them delivered through a permanent haze of cigarette smoke. Picture an Irishman with a gravelly voice, a van the size of a shoebox, and a cigarette that seemed to be attached to his lip by industrial adhesive, and you've got him.

One Saturday, Mum quietly suggested he give me a try-out on the farm.

And that's how, on a cold November morning, I ended up waiting beside her at the Folly Market, ready to climb into Murphy's tiny white Suzuki Super Carry, a vehicle that looked like it would struggle to carry a *super* bag of shopping, let alone trays of eggs and an adolescent boy.

"Hop in," he said, nodding at me.

We wheezed out of Petersfield as the cab filled with cigarette smoke thick enough to cure bacon. Halfway up Stoner Hill, the little engine sounded like it was reconsidering its life choices.

Eventually, though, we rattled into the gravel drive of the farm.

"Right lad," Murphy said as we climbed out. "We'll get you started in the packing room. If you don't break the place, maybe I'll teach you the other jobs later."

Friendly motivational style, that man.

He led me to one of the long wooden sheds.

"Mind," he said, "it's a bit smelly."

A bit?

When he opened the door, the smell hit me like a physical slap, ammonia, feathers, heat, and what I can only describe as Eau de Chicken Armpit. I did my best not to gag. I didn't want my first day to also be my last.

Inside were row upon row of wire cages stacked six or more high, each holding several hens. Today, people would be staging protests and chaining themselves to the gates. Back then, it was just how eggs were made.

Murphy took me to a side room with a conveyor belt carrying eggs past a sorting table. Two girls were working there: Melanie, a friendly twenty-something with a laugh that could shake dust off rafters, and Tracy, a slim blonde around my age who immediately made me wish I'd brushed my hair.,

"This is Keith," Murphy announced. "Show him the ropes."

Melanie handed me a green overall three sizes too big and a box of latex gloves. "Try a few pairs," she said. "Tea or coffee?"

"Coffee," I replied, trying to sound worldly, despite the fact that at home I only drank it when Mum made a cup strong enough to dissolve spoons.

The job itself was straightforward: wipe the muck off eggs, sort them, tray them, box them, and send them on their way. The work never stopped, a constant river of eggs that didn't care if you were bored, tired, or daydreaming about the girl opposite.

Week after week, which became my Saturday routine. Mum to the market. Murphy to the farm. Me to the conveyor belt.

Occasionally, if one of the girls needed a lift home, I'd be banished to the back of the Suzuki. Imagine a tin can with no seats and no windows, bouncing around like a loose onion whenever Murphy took a bend. "All right in the back, nipper?" he'd yell.
"Yes!" I'd shout back.
"Just checking the suspension!" he'd say, roaring with laughter.
Suspension, my backside.

After a while, Murphy decided I was ready for "proper" farm work. Feeding the hens.

The feeders were long metal contraptions that slid along rails in front of each cage. You pushed them manually, tipping grain into troughs as you went. In theory, simple. In practice, it was like wrestling a runaway shopping trolley with murderous intent.

The biggest risk was decapitating an over-excited hen. It didn't happen often, but when it did... well, let's just say the rest of the hens were not shy about expressing their feelings. Removing the unfortunate bird while being pecked by fifty of its closest friends was not my favourite task.

The sheds were normally deafening, but when the feeder started moving, everything went silent, thousands of hens waiting for breakfast. Heads stretched out; eyes fixed. The avian equivalent of the Boxing Day sales.

One summer, Murphy decided I was ready for outdoor duties. He sent me outside with a bucket of wood preservative to paint a shed. For once, I had fresh air, my Walkman, and no risk of poultry-based violence.

It was going beautifully, until I turned around and discovered an entire herd of cows blocking the exit.

They stood there chewing slowly, staring at me as if assessing whether I might be edible.

I tried "Shoo!"
Nothing.

I hit the bucket with my brush.
Nothing.

I made myself as big as possible.
They remained unimpressed.

Eventually Murphy wandered over, tapped them lightly with a broom handle, and they scattered like oversized toddlers. "They won't hurt you," he said cheerfully, as I quietly retrieved my heart from my boots.

Years later, at university, I found myself debating battery farming with a passionate vegan named Yvette. She found the whole concept horrifying.

I found it... complicated.

Cruel? Yes.
Normalised? Absolutely.
Simple? Never.

Those hens were born in cages, lived in cages, and died in cages.

I wasn't defending it, just acknowledging reality.

And looking back, that was probably one of the first genuine business lessons I ever learned about work, business and life:

You don't get to choose the world you start in.
You only get to choose what you do with it.

The man who gave me light

For as long as I'd known anything about my mum's family, I knew she had two brothers: Uncle Ben, who lived nearby and was woven into our daily lives... and Uncle Jim, who lived somewhere in the foggy outskirts of family mythology. Mum mentioned him occasionally, usually in the same tone she used for rationing or the Coronation, but I'd never met him, and for years he was little more than a name attached to a Christmas card.

Apparently, he'd been at Roy and Hazel's wedding, but I was only four at the time and entirely absorbed in the two vital questions of childhood:

1. When is cake happening?
2. If there's a photographer, what are the chances of me pulling a funny face in the background?

So, he lived in my memory the way characters in Dickens novels do, real, but only because someone else said so.

That changed when I was fifteen.

Mum announced, with the same solemn excitement she usually reserved for royal events, that Uncle Jim had got back in touch and was coming to visit. Dad, Roy, and Roger were all at work, so I was the welcoming committee, a fifteen-year-old with a 110 camera and approximately the photographic skill of a drunk pigeon.

By then I was well and truly obsessed with photography. Mum and Dad had bought me a little 110 camera for my birthday, and I adored it. I photographed trees, clouds, dogs, hedges, my own feet, anything that stood still long enough. Truprint and Bonusprint must have loved me; I kept them in business through blurry horizons, underexposed sunsets and at least ten photos where my own finger was the star of the show.

What I *really* wanted, though, what every photography book in the library told me I should want, was a 35mm SLR. A *proper* camera. One with knobs and dials and a lens that actually turned rather than just *suggesting* it might. There was a photography shop in Petersfield, tucked beside the goldfish pond in Dragon Court. While Mum did the weekly shop in Gateways, I'd press my nose to the window like an orphan in a Victorian novel staring at a roast goose.

The price tags, unfortunately, had more digits than I had savings. Mum told me I'd have to save every penny from my Saturday job with Murphy. I worked it out: even if I saved everything, even tea money, it would take me over a year. I briefly considered selling a kidney but assumed it would violate some obscure school rule.

So, when Uncle Jim arrived that summer, and Mum mentioned my hobby in passing, I wasn't expecting anything. But his eyes lit up.

He was a keen photographer too. Within minutes, he'd handed me a couple of his books, guides on shutter speed, composition, *seeing the ligh.*" I devoured them. It was the first time anyone had taken my interest seriously enough to talk to me like I wasn't just a kid with a toy from the Argos catalogue.

And then came the moment I'll never forget.

One afternoon, without ceremony, he said, "Well, I've upgraded my kit... so you might as well have this, Keith." And he handed me a Praktica SLR. with TWO lenses. A wide-angle and a telephoto.

My brain shut down.
My hands went numb.
I think I squeaked.

You know those TV moments where the heavens open and a choir goes "AHHHH"? That was me. Internally. Externally I just stood there, stunned into silence, clutching the most beautiful piece of machinery I had ever held.

It instantly became my most prized possession. I still have it, lovingly stored away. I haven't used it in years but selling it would feel like selling a piece of my own history.

When I moved up to the sixth form at TPS, Photography CSE was on offer. I signed up quicker than I've ever said yes to anything in my life.

The darkroom soon became my second home. There's nothing

quite like watching an image materialise in a developer tray, that slow, magical bloom under the red light. It felt like alchemy. Or coaxing ghosts into existence. That was the moment photography didn't just become a hobby; it rooted itself deep in my bones.

But my time with Uncle Jim was heartbreakingly short.

One evening, Mum, Dad, Roger, and I went to the torchlit tattoo at HMS Vernon in Portsmouth, long before it turned into the shopping-palooza now known as Gunwharf Quays. I'd taken my camera, of course, and spent the whole night trying to master low-light shots, convinced I'd just created the next *National Geographic* cover.

When we got home, laughing, chatting, smelling of fireworks and fried onions, Mum bent down to pick up the post. There was an envelope waiting for her.

I will never forget her face as she opened it.
The hallway went still.
Then her voice, trembling:

"Jim's been taken to hospital with chest pains… and… he passed away this afternoon."

It made no sense. We had been watching fireworks. He had been dying. Two worlds running side by side, divided by a single, terrible line.

I stood frozen on the doormat, unable to speak. Unable to breathe.

I barely had time to know him. But what a gift those months were.
And what a legacy he left me.

Because every time I frame a shot…
every time I pick up a camera…
every time the world lines up in that perfect fraction of a second…

Uncle Jim is there.
In the viewfinder.
In the light.
In everything I learned because of him.

The year we went to war (sort of)

If you grew up in Liss in the 1970s, you'll remember the annual carnival, part community celebration, part organised chaos, and now sadly extinct thanks to modern health-and-safety rules and insurance companies who clearly never experienced the joy of a badly-secured papier-mâché dinosaur on the back of a Bedford lorry.

Back then, though, the Liss carnival was glorious.

It wasn't the Petersfield carnival, which was the big one: all pomp and pageantry, winding through town from Cranford Road down to the Heath, where the funfair waited like a neon promise. No, Liss's version was smaller, scruffier, and infinitely more charming, organised every year by the Scouts and buoyed along by sheer enthusiasm and whatever ideas people could cobble together with duct tape and optimism.

Somehow, in amongst the homemade floats and crepe-paper creations, the Scout organisers occasionally managed to attract serious talent. One year, the Red Devils parachute team dropped in, literally. I still have their signed card somewhere in a memorabilia box, probably sandwiched between a half-melted Crackerjack badge and a school report politely suggesting I "apply myself more consistently."

The procession began at the West Liss recreation ground next to the Scout Hut, meandered through the village, and finished at Newman Collard playing fields. Waiting there would be stalls, tombolas, arena events, a helicopter from RAF Odiham, and the local garages proudly showing off their latest models.

And me?

I made it my personal mission to collect every single glossy car brochure on the field. I was a boy who believed nothing in life was more exciting than a new Ford Granada with headrests.

Then came the year everything changed.
The year we, three boys with more imagination than skill, decided to enter the carnival ourselves.

It must have been 1978 or 1979. We were obsessed with World War II, fuelled by Commando comics and Airfix kits that never looked remotely like the picture on the box. My Dad's British Racing Green Ford Cortina was, in our minds, practically a military vehicle already.

It just needed... embellishments.

So, we got to work.

Cardboard panels for the side windows.
A turret built from scrap wood and a curtain pole.
A very questionable machine gun painted black.
And a bit of wire to act as an aerial, because every good tank, and every bad replica, needs an aerial.

The only thing we hadn't figured out was how to actually *attach* the turret to the car.

Enter Dad.

Bless him, he took one look at our creation, one look at the Cortina, and, instead of forbidding us from coming within twenty yards of his paintwork, calmly fitted the roof rack, tied the turret on securely, and then, as if by magic, produced an entire roll of camouflage netting.

We draped it over the car like we were preparing for a covert operation in the jungles of Hampshire.

Our mums made us "army uniforms" (loosely inspired by actual uniforms but mostly inspired by what happened to be in the sewing box). Dad wore his old army beret and pinned on his medals. For one glorious afternoon, we were a military unit. A slightly lopsided one, admittedly.

We didn't win a prize.
Honestly, we weren't even close.
But it didn't matter.

We were in the carnival.
We were part of the village.
And for a few shining hours, we weren't just kids from the street, we were *The Tank Crew*.

Even now, all these years later, I still walk the same driveway at

Newman Collard Park that the procession used to follow. About two-thirds down, there's a cracked manhole cover, a battle scar from the year a traction engine rolled over it. The manhole cover lost, of course. There's only ever going to be one winner when Victorian steam engineering meets 1970s municipal cast iron.

But like the carnival itself, that scar is a small, stubborn memory of a time when life was simpler, community was everything, and a Ford Cortina could, with enough cardboard and enthusiasm, become a tank.

Steel, signals and the magic of movement

Looking back, it was probably inevitable I'd end up obsessed with railways. When your dad works for British Rail as a Signal and Telegraph Technician, trains become as much a part of childhood as Sunday roasts, itchy polyester shirts, and pretending you've definitely done your homework.

Dad occasionally took me with him on Saturday jobs, but only if he was working at a station. Even then, I wasn't allowed anywhere near the danger zone. I stood on the platform doing what any sensible small boy would do: absorbing every detail as if I were overseeing a major infrastructure project.

I adored the whole spectacle. The cranes lifting track panels. The crews replacing ballast. New sets of points going in with the precision of surgery performed by men in donkey jackets.

When a ballast train rumbled through, usually Sealion or Seacow wagons behind a Class 33, or better still a Class 73, it felt like the earth itself shook.

Nowadays everything seems to be hauled by a Class 66 "shed." Efficient? Yes. Characterful? Only if you think a fridge freezer has character. Back then, locomotives had faces, voices, moods. You could tell one from another the way some people can tell labradors from spaniels.

One machine fascinated me above all others: the tamper.

After the ballast was laid, this incredible contraption crawled down the track, lifting, adjusting, and smoothing until every sleeper sat just so. I could watch a tamper for hours. Dad, however, had mixed feelings. He admired their engineering, right up until one ripped straight through a cable he'd spent two days laying. That tended to cool the romance somewhat.

Dad could also get us into signal boxes. Petersfield became a second home, but the real thrill was Guildford's signalling centre. Compared to Petersfield's levers and clunks, Guildford was… futuristic. Banks of lights. Switches. Electronic diagrams. The sort of place a boy imagines if you tell him he's about to see "mission control."

I wasn't allowed to take photos, so I meticulously sketched the entire track layout into a notebook. It looked like a child's drawing of the London Underground after three Weetabix, but I loved it.

Alton signal box was another highlight. Just before it closed, the signalman gifted me a lever nameplate from an old frame. I still use it as a doorstop today, a small, solid reminder of when signals were pulled by muscle, not software updates.

Dad also took me to depot open days: Eastleigh, Old Oak Common, Swindon, Crewe, if it had oil, grease, and a "No Entry" sign, we went. Thanks to Dad's BR pass, he travelled free, and I went on a heavily discounted "privilege fare." There's nothing quite like wandering around a massive shed full of enormous engines while your dad points out something technical you nod at as if you understand.

We loved preserved railways too. The Watercress Line at Ropley and the Bluebell Railway were firm favourites. Steam engines felt alive, breathing, panting, occasionally leaking with the dignity of an elderly gentleman who refuses help with the stairs.

Years later, as Chairman of East Hampshire District Council, I got to travel behind the Flying Scotsman from Alresford to Alton. That, however, is a story for a later chapter, and a good one.

But the crown jewel of childhood rail memories?

An unofficial cab ride in a 4-VEP electric multiple unit.

Dad's mate was the driver. We climbed in through the driver's side door at Liss, squeezed into the little cab, and set off toward Waterloo. At Haslemere, Guildford or Woking, I'd duck into the vestibule in case someone official spotted an extra passenger. But when the line was clear, I watched the driver work the train like a concert pianist.

No screens.
No digital prompts.
Just knowledge, rhythm, and a lifetime of experience.

Those early days hardwired something into me. Trains weren't just vehicles, they were systems. People. Timing. Ccoordination.

A world running on trust and unseen skill.

And that's why even today, whether through model railways, train simulators, or chairing the Hills to Harbour and Wey Valley rail partnerships, the railway is still part of the rhythm of my life.

Dad once said,
"Good signalling isn't about trains. It's about people knowing where everyone is."

He wasn't wrong.

Turns out, that applies to life too.

Clearer air: further views

For all the times I've said I didn't learn many "life lessons" from my dad, there was one conversation, one quiet, unremarkable Sunday afternoon when I was about sixteen, that shaped the entire trajectory of my life.

I was sitting at the dining room table, surrounded by what looked like the early drafts of an Ofsted report gone wrong. Scraps of paper everywhere, half-baked plans, doodles, and the occasional attempt at serious thought. It was the era of CSEs and O Levels (yes, dear reader, gather round - I *am* that vintage). I'd done my mocks, had a rough idea of my predicted grades, and now faced the terrifying question of every teenager:

What next?

Dad wandered in, hands in pockets, wearing the expression of a man who had walked into a room and instantly regretted it.

"What are you doing, son?"

I sighed, the sigh of a sixteen-year-old who believes the fate of civilisation rests entirely on his shoulders.

"Well, Dad… you know I've got my final year next year."

"Ah-ha," he said, in that carefully neutral tone parents use when they sense something is about to become long and complicated.

"I'm trying to work out what to do. If I get the grades they think I will, do I stay on for sixth form? Do I go to college instead? Do I take the job Murphy offered me? It's not great money, but at least it's something. Or maybe I take a year out and help Roy with building for a bit, then go back to studying later. A kind of gap year."

Dad listened. Properly listened. Which already made this conversation unusual.

"Well, Keith," he said eventually, "it has to be *your* decision. You know your Mum and I will support you whichever way you go."

"That's great, Dad," I said, "but it doesn't help me actually **make** the decision. And it's a big one. I need to get it right."

He nodded… then paused.

"Can I borrow your pen and a sheet of paper?"

I slid them across. He drew a triangle. Then a horizontal line across it about two-thirds of the way up.

"Imagine this is a pyramid," he said. "The pyramid of life."

I nodded, unsure whether this was heading toward wisdom, metaphor, or an unexpected lesson in ancient engineering.

"This line here," he said, tapping the ledge he'd drawn, "this is where we are. Me, your mum, Roger, Roy, you. This is what hard work has earned us. A house. A car. Food on the table. We're doing alright."

He paused.

"But look at the rest of the pyramid above us."

He pointed to the peak.

"We're here. But you… you can go much higher. You're bright. You think. You work things out. You've got a chance to climb well above this line. You can give yourself, and your future family, a better view than we've ever had."

Then he delivered the sentence that hit me with such force it etched itself permanently into my bones:

"The higher you climb, the clearer the air, and the further you can see."

I felt it then, and I still feel it now. I've quoted it in talks, workshops, mentoring sessions, even in council meetings when I wanted people to understand why ambition matters.

I hugged him, or as close to a hug as Dad would tolerate, which was somewhere between "mild shoulder contact" and "accidental collision."

He turned to leave the room. Then, at the doorway, he stopped.

"And one more thing," he said. "Always hold out a hand to help other people as you're climbing up. Because you never know whose hand you'll need to grab when you're falling down again."

Two sentences.
Two mantras.
Two foundations for everything I went on to do.

Dad, if there *is* a heaven, and if, by some miracle, you have broadband up there, I hope you're looking down and smiling.

Your words didn't just guide me.
They built me.

And I've learned this along the way:

A rising tide really does lift all boats.
When we lift others up, we lift ourselves too!

Lessons beyond the classroom

By the time it came to choosing where I'd spend the sixth form, Mum and Dad had already marched me around half of Hampshire in search of the ideal institution.

We visited Alton College, Southdowns College, and Horndean College, each with its own atmosphere. Southdowns in particular felt wonderfully modern and *properly college"* the sort of place where people drank black coffee and debated politics, rather than hiding behind a stack of textbooks hoping no one noticed they hadn't opened one.

Had I known university was in my future, Southdowns probably would have been the perfect stepping stone. But hindsight, as they say, has 20/20 vision, mine, at the time, was operating at about 3/10.

In the end, staying put at The Petersfield School made the most sense.

I knew the teachers, I knew the layout, and crucially, I could get there under my own steam… which, admittedly, varied depending on the weather and what had been on television the night before.

Alongside my beloved CSE Photography course came the more "serious" A-level choices. At that time, I nursed vague ambitions of becoming a Physics teacher, an idea based largely on the fact that I liked Physics and was reasonably certain I could operate a whiteboard without injuring myself. So, Maths and Physics were easy choices.

That left one more subject.

Part of me wanted to take Art. Photography had awakened something creative in me, and Art felt like a natural extension of that. But in the spirit of being sensible (and with a gentle nudge from teachers keen for me to "stay focused"), I narrowed the choice to Biology or Chemistry. I'd never taken Chemistry to O-Level, and with Roy's work as a mental health nurse and my own involvement with the Red Cross, Biology felt like the more natural fit.
The lessons themselves were fascinating. The teachers were passionate, knowledgeable and supportive.

The problem wasn't them.
It was me.

What no one really explained, or perhaps what they explained repeatedly while I nodded enthusiastically and absorbed none of it, was that the biggest difference between school and sixth form wasn't the freedom.

It was what you were supposed to *do* with that freedom.

"Study time" sounded wonderfully grown-up. To my teenage brain, it translated as freedom to play table tennis at the youth club, keep up with developments in the Falklands War, drink tea in the common room, and practise composing dramatic photographs of raindrops on windowsills.

Technically, the photography counted as learning. Technically.

Then came the university visits, Surrey, Sussex, Southampton, and the polytechnics at Portsmouth and Kingston. I enjoyed them all, and by some miracle (or administrative oversight), I ended up with conditional offers from Surrey, Sussex, and Southampton.
My heart was set on Southampton.

Mum, unsurprisingly, preferred Surrey. It was commutable by train, which meant I could live at home. In hindsight, I suspect that was the real selling point, presented under the respectable banner of "saving money."

Fortunately, this didn't turn into a family debate, because... well... results day happened.

Let's just say that all those "study" sessions spent perfecting my backhand at table tennis and taking long-exposure photos of passing buses had finally declared themselves.

The offers evaporated.

It wasn't the end of the world, just one of life's early reminders that plans don't always unfold neatly, no matter how carefully you write them in your notebook.

And for what it's worth, it didn't close any doors. It just nudged me gently toward others I'd never noticed were open.

Sloggis, Sparky and the Speed-Freak Organist

I've written already about my love of books, but running alongside it, often louder, and occasionally in a key that could wake the dead, was music.

My first musical obsession was a crackly old record called *Sparky's Magic Piano*. Half story, half recital, all magic. A cheeky boy receives the gift of perfect technique from a talking piano... right up until the magic wears off and practice must take over.

Even at six I learned something valuable: talent is the spark, graft is the petrol, and if you rely on magic alone, you're buggered.

One of my favourite TV characters was Basil Brush, and I was over the moon when Mum bought me not only a Basil Brush glove puppet, but the Basil Brush record (yes, there really was one, it's on Youtube if you're interested).

It had lyrics like these:

Mr Frog went knocking on Mrs Mouse's door, hum, hum
He'd been there many times before, hum, hum
Mr Frog went knocking on Mrs Mouse's door
She said "I know what you're here for", hum, hum, hum, hum, hum, hum.

I still sing it to my great-grandchildren today, it always brings a wide smile to their face and they join in with the *hum, hums*.

Of course it was only later in life I realised the lyrics contained a double entendre.

Childhood innocence is a wonderful thing.

Like nearly every child of my era, my musical career began on the wooden recorder at primary school - an instrument whose entire purpose, I am convinced, was to teach teachers patience and to prepare parents for the sound of feral cats being strangled.

The lightning bolt arrived a couple of years later at junior school, when a classmate, one Timothy Peake (not the astronaut, but another Tim Peake entirely) played during assembly. He went on to become a proper concert pianist, played during assembly.

I was transfixed. If music could do *that*, I wanted in.

Mum arranged piano lessons with Philip Reder, a kind man with the patience of a saint and the posture of someone who had spent his entire life warning children not to slouch. Once I graduated from the "hesitant scales" phase, he invited me to a little Saturday group at his flat on Weston Road.

There were three or four of us, including Tim, all squashed into his living room like a miniature orchestra of earnest children. One unforgettable morning, we all piled into his wheezy Hillman Imp and drove to BBC Radio Solent to perform live on *Albert's Gang*. Mum and my brother Roger recorded it at home on cassette as if I'd just debuted at the Royal Albert Hall.

Around this time, we acquired an upright piano, at least fourth-hand, possibly fifth, and definitely tuned by someone who believed "close enough" was good enough. The neighbours were saints.

Then came the turning point.

One Saturday, wandering through Woolworths, I spotted a small single-keyboard home organ. Eight whole sounds! Chunky brown plastic straight from the golden age of 'must-have' electrical tat.

I was hooked.

To my astonishment, it appeared that Christmas.

Dad, not to be outdone by Woolworths, later discovered that the Army & Navy store in Guildford sold *proper* home organs: two keyboards and pedals.

Pedals!

Like a church organist!

He and I trudged up Guildford's hill (which gets steeper every time I remember it), tried several models, and settled on a sensible mid-range organ on the "never-never."

Space was tight, so the piano went off to a ballet school, at least it found a graceful retirement.

The organ stayed. The house shook.

Unfortunately, I was still playing the organ like a pianist, barely using the pedals, and treating the left-hand manual as optional. Then a small shop opened on Heath Road, run by Mike, his wife Barbara, and their daughter Izzy.

Mike listened to me play for thirty seconds and smiled the smile of a man who had just diagnosed something terminal in the left hand.

"You learned piano first, didn't you?"

Guilty.

"You're barely using your pedals. And your left hand - well..." He paused in a way that suggested my left hand might need counselling.

"Don't look glum," he said. "I can teach you."

And he did, twice-weekly lessons that became the heartbeat of my teens.

I spent so much time in that shop that I essentially became part of the furniture. And that is how teenage me came to learn far too much about Sloggi knickers.

One Friday evening, we were due to go to a John Mann concert in Haslemere. Dad dropped me off behind the shop. I went upstairs to the flat, and Barbara called down the hall: "Izzy, hurry up, Keith's here!"

Izzy emerged wearing an oversized blue T-shirt, bare feet, bare legs, and a complete lack of teenage self-consciousness.

"Where are my new knickers?" she said.

She rummaged in a shopping bag, produced a neat blue-and-white box (I had no idea women's underwear came in boxes, civilisation is full of surprises), and disappeared back into her room.

Two minutes later, she re-emerged, lifted the hem of her T-shirt just high enough to *model* the Sloggis, gave a little twirl, announced "They fit really well, don't they?" and vanished again.

Teenage me attempted nonchalance and instead achieved a facial expression best described as *giraffe swallowing a pineapple*.

Moments later she came out fully dressed in a long blue dress, looking beautiful, and off we went to hear a master at work.

John Mann was extraordinary. If Mike and I were League Two, John was Premier League on a Champions League night. After the concert, I queued for a signed programme and bought an LP purely on the strength of the cover photo. I floated home.

A few weeks later, Mike switched the shop to Eminent organs, John Mann's brand, and invited John to play an in-store launch. John ended up performing for more than three hours. Then he came upstairs for dinner. I peppered him with questions until Mike, fully aware I could continue until sunrise, changed the subject.

Talk drifted to the Haslemere concert.

"We should put something on in Petersfield," Mike said.

John looked at me.

"Find a date. Keith, fancy doing thirty minutes as the warm-up?"

My heart tried to escape through my ribcage. "Yes. A thousand times yes."

I needed practice.

Dad arranged for me to "warm up" the room at the Liss Royal British Legion before their resident organist, Bob, assisted by drummer Frank when he wasn't at bowls.

Most Saturdays I'd play for thirty to sixty minutes to an audience of forty or fifty mildly bemused regulars. It was priceless training: learning to cope with mistakes, find a rhythm, and keep going even when half the crowd was more interested in the bingo.

Concert night arrived. The stage lights hid most of the 200-strong audience, which was a blessing. I sat, breathed, played, a couple of slips only I noticed, and then soaked in a warm wave of applause. Then John Mann reminded everyone what real mastery sounded like.

A few weeks later, a BBC envelope arrived inviting me to a national talent-show audition in London. I went, played, left thinking "good, not great," and later received a rejection letter so gently phrased it could have been from a therapist delivering bad news.

Somewhere along the way, I also discovered the mysterious creature known as the *pipe organ*.

Roger, with the reckless confidence only brothers possess, told Reverend Doug Banyard at Buriton Church:
"My brother Keith can play."

A pipe organ, I learned, is nothing like an electronic organ. The keys require force, the pedals require precision, and the registrations must be chosen before you start.

Once you begin to play, there is no stopping to fiddle.

It's commitment in organ form.

Reverend Banyard opened the church specially so I could practise. He wandered around calling encouragements like a man training a Labrador.

Sunday arrived. I played quietly as the congregation entered.

During the hymns I relied entirely on Reverend Banyard's expression reflected in the little mirror above the keyboard.

He was smiling.

Mostly.

After the service he approached.

"How did it go?" I asked.

"Well," he said carefully, "the tunes were familiar, and there wasn't a note out of place... but the congregation isn't used to singing their hymns quite that fast."

They never asked me back.

Probably fearing that "Jerusalem" would become a military march.

Do I still play? Occasionally. I have a full-size keyboard now, there simply isn't room for a real organ at home unless I sacrifice the kitchen, and while I do love music, I also love toast.

The love of music never left: classical, military bands, theatre organ, and the occasional modern gem.

And if you forced me to pick just one desert-island record?

Peter Skellern - *Skellern*.

Track?

Cheek to Cheek.

Every time.

Nineteen steps and a thousand stories

Moving into sixth form didn't just change my timetable, it changed my Saturdays too.

My brother Roy had been head barman at the Folly Wine Bar for a couple of years, and when he offered me a Saturday job there, I jumped at it. At that stage, I wasn't allowed anywhere near the actual bar. My job was simple on paper: restock everything before opening time.

Easy, I thought.

It wasn't.

The Folly soon became something of a family business: Roy behind the bar, his wife Hazel working as housekeeper, and me, the Saturday lad, keeping the shelves full. It sounded straightforward... until you encountered **the staircase**.

Nineteen stone steps.
Nineteen.
A number seared permanently into my quads.

If the bottles and wine we needed weren't available in the main storeroom behind the bar, that meant descending those nineteen steps to the outside store, loading boxes onto a trolley, then carrying each one back up by hand. Some weeks it was four or five boxes; during December, it could be twenty.

Looking back, I'm amazed I didn't drop dead on the spot, especially once I learned, years later after my Marfan's diagnosis, that this was absolutely the kind of exertion I should *never* have been doing. But at the time it was just *what the job required*.

If nothing else, it kept me fitter than any gym ever has.

When I finally turned eighteen and was allowed behind the bar, the job transformed overnight. I loved it, the banter, the regulars, the characters, the sense of being part of the heartbeat of the place.

And oh, the characters.

The most unforgettable was **Keith "Gibbo" Gibson**, a man with a laugh that could rattle windows. Gibbo had a remarkable ability to vanish without notice and then return days later as if he'd only stepped outside to adjust his shoelaces.

One Thursday lunchtime he declared, "I fancy some sardines for lunch. I'll nip out and get a tin."

"Alright," I said. "See you in a bit."

A "bit" turned into nine days.

He wandered back in the following week, tied on his apron, and announced with complete sincerity: "Sorry I'm late. They were out of sardines, so I had to get pilchards instead."

He later admitted he *had* gone out for sardines and immediately bumped into two friends heading to Wales for a camping trip. Naturally, he joined them.

Another regular was Trevor, a charismatic local who went on to run his own bistro in Liss. And then, of course, there was the most famous customer of them all: **Erika Roe**, the legendary Twickenham streaker. She was warm, funny, and, as I quickly learned, an excellent tipper.

The Folly itself had bags of charm: exposed beams, quirky corners, a lively atmosphere, and staff like Gibbo and me who probably shouldn't have been left unsupervised.

One afternoon we tied a small plastic spider, the sort you get in Christmas crackers, to a long length of cotton, fixed it to a beam, and waited. When an unsuspecting lady sat beneath it, deep in conversation, we'd gently lower the spider onto her shoulder.

The shriek was always immediate.
The laughter was always universal.
The complaints were surprisingly non-existent.

Harmless mischief. Pure Folly spirit.

One Christmas, Roy and some of the staff staged a pantomime in the bar. We'd been granted a late licence, and the final night ran well past midnight. After ushering out the last of the merrymakers, I headed upstairs to do a final check and heard noises from the kitchen.

Curiosity got the better of me.

I opened the door.

There, sprawled across the stainless-steel prep table, skirt around her waist, tights, and panties halfway down her legs, was one of the waitresses. Behind her, trousers, and pants around his ankles, moving with unmistakable enthusiasm, was the chef.

I closed the door. Quietly.
I put on my coat.
And left them to it.

Some things, I decided, did not need reporting to management.

And that, really, was life at the Folly: chaotic, funny, full of character, never predictable, and utterly formative.

It wasn't just a Saturday job.

It was an education in people, pressure, humour, and the strange, wonderful things human beings get up to once you put a bar in front of them.

Three lads, a van, and an expired tax disc

Before mobile phones.
Before Spotify playlists.
Before anyone had even dreamt of Bluetooth speakers...

There were mobile discos.

And in the late 1970s and early 80s, they were *glorious*.

It began, as many bad ideas do, with Roy, a van, and a beer.

Roy sat me and my cousin Matthew down one evening and said, "Right lads, I've got a proposition."
(This sentence has never preceded anything sensible in the history of mankind.)

One of his mates was giving up his mobile disco business and wanted to sell the whole lot, lights, turntables, amplifiers, mixers, speakers, and crates upon crates of vinyl, all for a price so low it probably broke at least three consumer laws.

We thought about it for roughly eight seconds.

"Yeah, why not? Sounds fun."

And that was it.
We were in business.

Within weeks, we were out most weekends. By November and December, we were doing six nights a week, Christmas parties, social clubs, sports bars, pubs, you name it. If a room had a plug socket and people willing to dance, we were there.

We needed a name. After far too much discussion and possibly too many beers, we settled on:

The Gentle Green Giant Disco.

And yes... the logo bore an uncanny resemblance to the Incredible Hulk. In the modern world, Disney's lawyers would have us in court so fast our stylus would still be spinning. But back then, nobody cared. Or at least, nobody who mattered.

The gigs were brilliant.

Hauling the equipment in and out of the venues was less brilliant.

This was the era of filament light bulbs, huge, chunky things that became as hot as the surface of the sun. After three hours of flashing, spinning, and strobing, you couldn't touch them until they cooled. Move them while they were still warm and the filament snapped, and there went a few quid straight in the bin.

But once everything was set up, the lights pulsing, smoke machine puffing (when it worked), vinyl crackling under the needle, we'd watch a dance floor come alive.

There's nothing quite like seeing a room full of people belting out *Come On Eileen* at the top of their lungs while you're standing behind the decks, feeling like gods of the night.

We built a solid reputation locally. Regular bookings at the SEB Club in Heath Road and the Social Club in Station Road, soon spreading to other towns.

Which is where the **Great Tax Disc Incident** occurred.

Remember road tax discs?

Small circle of paper.
Stuck in the windscreen.
Needed to be in date.

Well... Roy's approach to renewing the disc could best be described as *aspirational*.

One night, we had a booking in Chichester. No sat-nav in those days, just an address scribbled on a scrap of paper. After driving in circles for ages, Roy had a moment of what he called "inspiration."

"I know!" he said. "I'll go into the police station and ask them."

And before Matthew or I could protest, he swung the van into the police station car park and parked right outside the main entrance. As in... right in front of the big glass doors.

He hopped out.

Matthew and I just stared at each other.

"Should I check it?" Matthew asked, pointing to the tax disc.

He turned it.
Expired.
By three months.

We were sitting in an illegal van, outside a police station, officers walking past us, the van proudly displaying its incriminating paperwork like a delinquent child waving a stolen sweet.

Eventually, Roy returned, beaming.

"Found it! Third on the left, all the way down."

We were laughing so hard we could barely breathe.

"What?" Roy demanded.

"You've just parked outside the police station with an expired tax disc!" Matthew managed between wheezes.

Roy glanced at it, shrugged, and said, "Oh yeah. Must sort that."

And off we drove, miraculously un-arrested.

Looking back now, I'm not sure whether it was luck, youthful confidence, or sheer stupidity.

Probably a bit of all three.

But that was the era.

Chaotic.
Fun.
Slightly reckless.
Absolutely unforgettable.

From table tennis to Tottenham

When my A-level results arrived, let's just say they didn't provoke any urgent calls from Oxford. Or Cambridge. Or, frankly, the local library.

Looking back, I probably should have spent fewer hours perfecting my table-tennis serve at the youth club with Paul and more hours learning, oh I don't know... physics. But hindsight is a wonderful thing and utterly useless at exam time.

So, there I was, working more or less full time at the Folly Wine Bar in Petersfield. It wasn't a "career," but it wasn't half bad either: Roy was head barman, Hazel worked as housekeeper, the regulars were colourful, and Chris Healey, the boss, was one of life's genuinely good men. Even now we still keep in touch.

Life felt steady. Comfortable. Predictable.

And then one Thursday, everything detonated in the best conceivable way.

I got a call behind the bar.

"Keith," Mum said, sounding suspiciously breathless, "Middlesex Polytechnic just phoned. They want to speak to you. They might have a place on their Natural Physics course."

I scribbled down the number on the back of a bar tab and rang them the moment I had five seconds of quiet.

Sure enough, they had a space. If I wanted it, I needed to come for interview the following Wednesday. Decision required immediately. Course starting in early October.

Everything in my life shifted half an inch to the left.

This was it. A door. A chance. A nudge from The Universe, or Mum, depending on who you asked.

Mum insisted on coming to London with me. She needed to "check the area," which was code for *make sure you're not moving to somewhere where the locals actively hunt students.*

The address they gave, Tottenham, didn't exactly soothe her nerves.

My London knowledge at that point was limited to:

1. the National Theatre
2. the Model Railway exhibition (naturally)
3. Big Ben

That was it.

We travelled up: Waterloo → Bank → Central Line → Liverpool Street → overground to White Hart Lane. Walked the short road to the campus.

Tottenham, Mum realised mid-stride, was not actually a swirling cauldron of crime and burning rubble. That seemed to calm her slightly.

The interview went well.

On the train home, I already knew the answer.
"I'm going," I said.

Mum nodded, half-proud, half-worried.

She always was.

To sweeten things further, I qualified for a maintenance grant, those magical unicorns from a bygone age, and I was guaranteed a room in halls. The course itself was based at the Bounds Green campus: hop on the W3 bus to Wood Green, one Tube stop, short walk, done.

The next ten days were a blur of packing, shopping, mild panic, and the slow realisation that I was actually leaving home.

I remember that Sunday vividly. Early lunch. Suitcase packed. Mum came outside to give me a hug goodbye. She held me for a little too long, then whispered:
"Be good. And if you can't be good... be careful."
Then she slipped something into my jacket pocket.
Only later did I discover the packet of condoms.

Classic Mum.

Dad drove me to halls. Carried my bags. Gave me a hug (the brief, masculine kind). Then he pressed £100 into my hand, neatly folded £10 notes, and headed home.

And suddenly I was standing alone in my new room.

My new life.

The room itself was... character-building. Green-painted walls, Marley-tiled floor, single bed, desk, tiny en-suite loo (no shower, that was communal). I shared the bathroom with exactly one person. Unfortunately, that person was our hall warden, the resident tutor.

Peaceful, yes.

Also: knocks on the wall if the music reached anything above "mildly enthusiastic."

I wandered upstairs to the communal kitchen. As I unpacked my shopping, I heard a voice behind me.

"Hello."
Soft Welsh lilt.
I turned to see a slim lad with brown hair and an easy grin.
"I'm Stuart. Everyone calls me Stu."

We chatted. He invited me to beers that evening in Andy's room, "he's across the hall from you." I agreed, relieved. My social life so far consisted entirely of checking my 12-inch black-and-white TV got all three channels.

At 7pm I realised I should probably bring drinks. I went to the student union bar and bought four cans of Double Diamond, marvelling at the prices.

At 8pm, I knocked on Andy's door.

He looked about thirty. I nearly asked if he was the lecturer.

"No, I'm Andy," he laughed. "I'm twenty-four. Army. Doing teacher training."

His room was a fog of cigarette smoke and conversation.

Inside were others: Brian and Glyn, two girls named Kathy and

Cathy, Cathy being a slim, tanned girl who immediately caught my attention, and a handful of others I'd come to know well.

Around 11pm, another knock.
In walked a stocky Yorkshireman with curly blonde hair.

"Hi," he said. "I'm Jan."

What I didn't know, what I **couldn't** have known, was that I'd just met my closest male friend for life. My honorary brother. The man who would one day stand at his wedding and describe our bond as "the closest two men can be without sharing blood or a bed."

He was right.
And I felt exactly the same.

Over the next week, the hall filled. Faces, names, stories: Peter, Nadesh, Andrew, Ali, Tracey, Janet, Barbara, the two Kathys, and of course, Cathy. We became a patchwork family of sorts.

Years later, Middlesex Polytechnic would become Middlesex University. A few of us reunited a decade on. But only Jan remained a constant in my life, until the day the world lost him far too soon.

But that first week?
That was everything.

The first time I'd stood completely on my own two feet.
A world away from Petersfield and the youth club and the table tennis table.

A new chapter.
A new hand dealt.

And for the first time, I was ready to play it.

The night the wizard lost his cape

It wasn't quite love at first sight; more love at second staircase.

Ali and I fell for one another within a couple of weeks of arriving at university. She lived on the first floor, right next to the communal kitchen; I was on the ground floor beneath her. There were two staircases between our rooms, and although the nearer one made far more sense, I mysteriously kept finding myself taking the long route... just in case she happened to be walking by.

Before long, she was doing the same, a head popping round my door if she heard me inside.

Looking back, it was wonderfully innocent. Young love without strategy or grand declarations. Just instinct, curiosity, and the quiet thrill of seeing that someone was pleased you'd turned up.

We spent more and more time together: drinks in the union bar, terrible instant coffee in one kitchen or the other, films in Wood Green, long conversations about everything and nothing.

Sometimes we went out in groups, sometimes we peeled away and found space for just the two of us.

Money was tight for me. Mum and Dad slipped me the odd tenner, or bailed me out if I was truly desperate, but mostly I lived on my grant. Ali came from a vastly different world, her father a barrister, her mother a solicitor, their family home a sprawling neo-Georgian mansion in Wiltshire. I counted twelve bedrooms.

"You could sleep in a different one each month," I told her, "And it'd be a whole year before you looped back to the start."

Her parents were relaxed when I stayed over, no fuss about separate rooms. Mine were less laissez-faire. At my house, Ali got the bed, and I was banished to the sofa. Mum would have set up motion sensors on the stairs if she'd had the technology.

By mid-term we'd reached what can only be described as the "enthusiastically affectionate" stage, intimate but still innocent, physical but still careful.

And then came the night everything changed.

The campus Halloween Ball had been delayed thanks to a union sit-in (this being the 1980s, such things were practically seasonal), and when it finally happened, we made a day of preparing.

In the fancy-dress shop in Wood Green, Ali found a green felt pixie costume, complete with bright green tights. I opted for a wizard outfit with a cape and wand that made me look less "powerful sorcerer" and more "children's TV presenter with delusions."

Back in her room, we got ready together. She slipped the pixie outfit over a T-shirt; I fastened my cape and attempted drama. She did her make-up... then mine.

By the time we stepped into the kitchen to meet our friends, we looked, if not exactly terrifying, then at least committed.

The party was brilliant. "The Monster Mash" blaring, drinks flowing, friends laughing, costumes shedding sequins at an industrial rate.

By 1 a.m. the music ended, and we trudged back across campus, a trail of felt, glitter and fake cobwebs marking our path.

Back in the hall kitchen, Ali perched on my lap as our friends peeled away one by one. By 2 a.m., it was just us.

We kissed, still half in costume. Something tore, my cape. Then something else, almost certainly still my cape. By the time we reached the corridor, we looked like two moths who'd lost a fight with a wardrobe.

Outside her door, she was down to her T-shirt. I was down to my boxers and a small, pathetic shred of cape hanging on for dear life. We stumbled into her room laughing.

And by the time we reached her bed... even those last scraps had surrendered.

What followed was funny, awkward, natural, and absolutely right, two young people trying their best, laughing at the clumsiness of inexperience, and discovering something intimate and tender in the middle of it all.

Whether it was her first time, I never asked.

It was mine.

Afterwards we lay together quietly, Ali's head resting on my chest, her breathing soft and steady, moonlight falling across her cheek. I kissed the top of her head.

"Thank you," I whispered.

I'd thought I knew what love was, the fluttering feeling, the anticipation, the endless planning of how often to "accidentally" appear near her staircase.

But that night, for the first time, I felt something deeper.

Not just loving someone.

Being in love with someone.

The night we played for more than points

I've mentioned before how Andy's room became the unofficial headquarters of our little university tribe. I'm still not entirely sure why. Maybe because it was closest to the main entrance, or because if anyone forgot their swipe card, all it took was a tap on his window and he'd let you in. Whatever the reason, we gathered there most evenings, talking, laughing, sharing cheap drinks and cheaper gossip, and occasionally playing card games that started innocent and didn't always stay that way.

One night, the group was its usual chaotic mix: Andy and his girlfriend Sue, who was visiting; Sarah; Ali; Cathy; Stu; and me. We'd been playing cribbage, helped along by a few ciders and that particular kind of student curiosity that tends to surface around midnight. At some point, someone, and I genuinely couldn't tell you who, said, "Why don't we play strip run?"

Andy looked at Sue, the way a man does when silently checking whether he's about to make a terrible mistake. Sue simply smiled. "Sure. You'll have to teach me the rules."

Strip run was simple. Fast-paced cards. Play your hand; if you ran out first, you were safe. Everyone else counted their remaining cards. Whoever had the most removed an item of clothing. Ties meant double trouble. It was ridiculous. Daft. And absolutely the sort of thing a group of late-teenage students would condsider a brilliant idea at eleven at night.

I won't bore you with the blow-by-blow, but fate wasn't particularly kind to me. Before long, I was down to just my boxer shorts. To my left, Ali had lost her top and sat there calmly in a cream lace bra, still in her jeans and far less flustered than I was. Around the room, various items had come off: Andy's socks, Sue's cardigan, Cathy's jumper, and Sarah, characteristically, a single stocking, removed with theatrical finesse.

Another round, another loss for Sarah. She reached into her trousers again, produced the matching stocking, and, with a flourish that would have impressed a stage magician, handed its toe-end to Pete to pull free. The room erupted.

Then Cathy lost. Off came the jeans, revealing a flash of purple thong that drew a mixture of cheers and mock scandalised looks.

And then it was Ali's turn. She stood, unbuttoned her jeans, stepped out of them, and looked down at her green cotton knickers and cream bra. "What a colour combination," she said, laughing. "I clearly wasn't expecting an audience tonight."

At this point, I was beginning to hope the universe had had its fun with me. It hadn't. Another hand. Another defeat. Sue plucked a tea towel off the radiator and passed it to me. "For modesty," she grinned.

So, tea towel in place, I let my boxers drop. There was cheering. There was laughter. Ali gave my backside a playful slap as I sat down. "Be seated, big boy," she teased.

That was the final straw for the evening; dignity, or what passed for it, had reached its limit. We ended the game and scrambled back into our clothes, still breathless with laughter.

As things settled, I noticed Sarah sitting on the edge of the bed, stockings in hand. Instead of folding them away, she unfastened her trousers and took them off. Beneath them she wore a black lace suspender belt and matching briefs, elegant, understated, and so far removed from anything I'd ever seen in real life that it caught me completely off guard.

My mum's undergarments had been industrial affairs: practical, reinforced, built for function rather than fantasy. This was something else entirely. Sarah caught me watching, smiled, and winked. "Enjoying the view?"

I stammered something incoherent, went a spectacular shade of beetroot, and suddenly found the pack of cards urgently in need of reordering.

It was a fleeting moment, daring, silly, innocent in its own youthful way. One of those snapshots of early adulthood that lodges itself firmly in the memory.

A time when friendships were intense, boundaries were elastic, and the world still felt like a place brimming with discovery.

Eight out of ten

Student life came with its own special menu of risks: hangovers, half-memories, questionable decisions, and the occasional lesson you didn't find in any lecture hall. I was sensible enough to minimise the hangovers with a pint of water before bed, a habit that probably saved me more than once, but sadly, water doesn't do much for the half-memories.

By second year, our group had moved into a large, slightly beleaguered Victorian semi in Wood Green. Two old houses knocked into one, it had all the charm you'd expect: peeling paint, creaking floorboards, and a stubborn band of rising damp that turned the hallway carpet into something resembling a wet sponge. We eventually admitted defeat, pulled it up, and embraced bare boards.

That hallway also turned out to be the ideal environment for slugs. Big ones. Bold ones. Enough to form an unofficial "Slug Grand Prix" on rainy evenings. The races ended abruptly when someone discovered that salt didn't speed them up, it melted them. That was, understandably, the end of the sporting season.

Bedrooms were a mixed bag. Most of us had narrow single beds, the kind that forced you to sleep with military precision. Andy had a double because his fiancée visited most weekends. Elaine's and Yvette's rooms had doubles too, for their own reasons. I didn't realise at the time that Yvette was gay; not that it mattered, it simply made sense in hindsight.

One Sunday morning remains etched in memory.

I woke to sunlight cutting between the slats of the blind, feeling pleasantly foggy after what I remembered as quite a lively evening. Yvette had friends over, the drinks had flowed, and laughter had filled the house. After that, my memory dissolved into something resembling wet tissue paper.

Still half-asleep, I became aware that I was lying right on the edge of my bed, odd, since it was pushed up against the wall. I tried to roll over.

I couldn't.

Something was behind me.

I propped myself up on my elbows, turned... and froze.

There was someone else in the bed.

Tracy.

Now, Tracy was perfectly pleasant, sharp-witted, loud-laughing, and full of personality... but she wasn't someone I'd ever fancied. Not even a little bit. And yet there she was, fast asleep, sharing approximately one and a half feet of mattress with me.

A cautious glance under the duvet revealed the full picture. I wasn't wearing anything. Her smooth back and buttocks confirmed she wasn't either.

The floor completed the crime scene: a breadcrumb trail of clothing leading from the door to the bed.

I eased myself out, located my boxers, and retreated to the en-suite to gather my thoughts, or at least the surviving fragments of them.

By the time I came back, she was stirring.

I put the kettle on. In moments of crisis, tea or coffee is always the correct answer.

She wrapped the duvet around herself and blinked blearily.

"Morning," I said. "Coffee?"

"Yes, please," she said, rubbing her eyes.

We surveyed the room. Then each other.

"Does this mean what I think it means?" she asked.

"I think so," I said.

"Oh, shit," we both said together, and then burst out laughing.

There was no awkwardness. No drama. Just two slightly sheepish students acknowledging an unexpected detour in the evening's events.

Before leaving, she paused at the door, pulled the duvet a little tighter around her, and gave me a mischievous grin.

"Oh, by the way," she said, "eight out of ten."

"Don't forget to bring my duvet back later" I said.

Then she was gone.

It became our unspoken secret. Years later, when I told Jan, he howled with laughter.

"I've been there too with Tracy, mate, got the T-shirt!"

We both laughed until our sides hurt.

Just another colourful square in the patchwork quilt of student life, the kind of moment you don't plan, don't repeat, but never quite forget.

Songs of praise
(featuring me... sort of)

The campus where our halls of residence were based was called **All Saints**, so it seemed only fitting, or perhaps tempting fate, that the BBC chose it as the venue for a live broadcast of *Songs of Praise* on All Saints' Sunday.

Now, this may have been an unusually bold decision on their part. All Saints had a Students' Union with a reputation... let's call it *enthusiastically militant*.

One memorable example: we once held a vote on whether to stage a sit-in protesting apartheid in South Africa. I emphasise *vote* because, while we were still inside the hall casting our ballots, the Union stewards were already outside chaining the doors shut. It's fair to say the sit-in passed comfortably, although democracy may have been sitting in the cheap seats that day.

But back to *Songs of Praise*.

We were told to assemble in the main sports hall by 2:30 p.m. for a full rehearsal. The BBC planned to record it just in case something went wrong during the live broadcast that evening.

Rows and rows of us filed in: students, staff, and a few rows at the front reserved for the Polytechnic choir, who all looked suspiciously polished for a Sunday afternoon.

The rehearsal began. As we gamely warbled our way through the hymns, members of the production team wandered between the rows handing out red and green cards. Nobody knew what they were for, but human nature being what it is, everyone assumed that green must be the "good" one.

Once the rehearsal was finished, the producer checked the recording, announced everything had gone smoothly, except for one hymn, which apparently needed another attempt. We were then released us for tea in the refectory. We were told to be back by 6 p.m. sharp for the live show.

When we returned, the great red-and-green mystery was solved.

The production crew directed those with green cards into one section and those with red cards, me included, were guided into another.

The producer took to the stage once more.

"When you hear the *Songs of Praise* theme," he explained, "you'll stand. When the theme ends, you are live on BBC One. Those of you with green cards are positioned under the microphones, so the audience at home will hear you clearly.

He paused.

Those with red cards... well... we won't be hearing *you* tonight. But do keep singing, the cameras will still be on you."

Ah. The delicate art of televised worship.
And, apparently, damage limitation.

The broadcast went without incident. Back in Hampshire, my parents watched proudly, sitting a little closer to the screen than usual. This was the pre-digital age, of course, no video recorder, no iPlayer, so I never actually saw the programme myself.

Mum said she couldn't spot me.
Dad and Roger insisted they had.

I didn't have the heart to explain the full truth: even if they *had* seen me, they definitely hadn't heard me.

Then again, Mum probably wouldn't have been fooled.

When I was about seventeen, I was in my room one evening, lying on my bed with my headphones on, singing along, enthusiastically, to a song I loved. I was lost in my own world until the door burst open and Mum rushed in, genuinely alarmed.

She thought I was in pain.

Apparently, my singing voice wasn't just off-key, it was a distress signal.

The night of the naked conga

There were many games played in halls, in our digs, in rooms where the décor could only be described as *charity shop chic*.

But one game sits above all the others, spoken of with the kind of reverence usually reserved for sporting triumphs or questionable miracle sightings.

This was *strip run*.

It happened in the summer term of our first year, when the future felt alarmingly uncertain, and the present felt too precious to waste. By then, we weren't just flatmates or classmates; we were a tribe. We'd survived breakups, hangovers, exam anxiety, and at least three kettles that had died heroic but overworked deaths. We knew one another's quirks and chaos so well that the "rules" of strip run had naturally... evolved.

Clothing was still forfeited, of course, this was strip run, not Scrabble, but now it came with an unwritten etiquette. No one ever pushed a boundary. We had a stop word everyone respected. And, crucially, the game didn't end when one person got naked. Sometimes two or three of us were starkers before the deck was finished. But it was never lewd, never pressured, always wrapped in trust, friendship, and an astonishing amount of laughter... helped along by cider and the peculiar invincibility that only early adulthood provides.

On that particular night, almost the entire gang was crammed into Andy's room: Andy and his visiting girlfriend Sue, Ali and me (she more or less lived on my lap by this point), Pete and Cathy, Jan and Tracy, Stu, Elaine, Sarah, and even Yvette, who rarely indulged our late-night nonsense.

The room was a sea of empty cans, card decks, and the accumulated clutter of students who had collectively given up on tidiness in favour of camaraderie. The first few rounds unfolded in the usual way: a mix of cheers, groans, and items of clothing being launched into the air like soft fabric fireworks.

Andy was soon down to his boxers. Sue had lost her jeans but maintained an air of elegant dignity, ankles crossed, knees drawn up. Cathy was already stripped to her T-shirt and white cotton knickers. Ali, sitting cross-legged on my lap, had lost her jeans but still had her green tights and cream top. Somehow, *somehow,* I had only lost my socks. I made the mistake of feeling smug. Which, as life has repeatedly taught me, is never wise.

Elaine, bless her, had chosen to wear a onesie, a tactical error of the highest order. One lost hand later, the zip came down and she was instantly reduced to her underwear, greeted with raucous applause and sympathetic laughter.

Tracy followed soon after, removing her trousers with an embarrassed grin that suggested she'd already accepted her fate.

Then someone, it may have been Pete, could have been Stu, raised a can, and declared:
"As it's our last game together here in halls, let's go all in! Everyone naked before the end. If you're already naked, you drink. Stop word still stands!"

And that was it. The room erupted in agreement. Sensible decisions, like study timetables and portion control, was officially off duty.

Stu was the predictable first casualty, his tea towel clutched heroically until it, too, gave up. Ali and I lost a hand together; I tugged her top over her head, and she pulled mine off in return. Cathy followed, slipping out of her T-shirt to delighted cheers. By now, modesty had left the building entirely.

Layer by layer, the room became a battlefield of abandoned clothing until only Tracy remained in her blue satin French knickers. Unfazed, she slipped them off without hesitation and flung them into the air like a victory pennant. We cheered as if we'd just witnessed a last-minute Cup Final winner.

And then, because youth, friendship, and cider are a volatile combination, someone shouted:
"Let's do a farewell conga! NAKED!"
And off we went.

A conga line of bare, giggling, cider-fuelled students snaking through the corridors, up staircases, down hallways, singing and laughing, tea towels waved like liberation flags before being abandoned in favour of momentum.

We reached the bottom of the final staircase and stopped dead.

There, blocking our path, stood our hall warden.
In pyjamas.
Arms folded.
Expression: somewhere between *thunderstorm* and *Old Testament judgement*.

"I'm guessing you're all in Andy's room as usual," she said calmly.

We nodded in unison. Naked. Silent.

"I'm giving you five minutes to get back in there and get dressed," she continued. "In five minutes, I will knock. If *anyone* is not fully dressed when I come in, you'll all be in the Head Tutor's office first thing tomorrow. Understood?"

We nodded again, suddenly eight years old, chastened, and acutely aware of the breeze.

Limbs diving into piles of clothing. Jeans, bras, jumpers, shirts, socks, some definitely belonging to the wrong people. Somehow, and I remain convinced divine intervention played a role, particularly as we had all taken part in Songs of Praise, we made it.

There was a knock.
The door opened.
The warden surveyed us.

Fully dressed. Mostly straight-faced. Barely breathing.

She nodded once.
"Off to bed. Quietly."
We obeyed without a word.

And that, dear reader, was the legendary night of the naked conga. A tale retold across countless pints, always ending the same way:
"Thank God the warden had a sense of humour."

Empty boxes, full lessons

My first real job in IT arrived, somewhat ironically, while I was home from university for the summer.

I was back behind the bar at the Folly, pulling pints and collecting empties, when a chance conversation nudged my life in an entirely new direction. One of our regulars, John Scott, overheard me chatting about computers, leaned over the bar and said:

"Fancy earning a bit more than tips? Come work for me."

His business, SCI (UK) Ltd, operated out of the old library building in central Petersfield. It sounded far more exciting than polishing glasses, so I didn't need asking twice.

On paper, the job was simple. SCI sold computer peripherals, mostly dot-matrix printers, and I was to keep the office systems running. They had two Apricot PCs, quirky but loveable little machines, and in the marketing department sat the first Apple Mac I had ever seen. It looked like a spaceship had deposited it on someone's desk.

I wasn't allowed within three feet of it. Only the head of marketing was trusted with that machine. It might as well have been kept under museum glass.

Most of my time was spent with the customer service team, automating repetitive tasks and writing bits of software to make their lives easier. This was pre-Word, pre-Excel, pre-anything-that-made-life-simple. If you needed a tool, you built it yourself. For a student who loved problem-solving, it was bliss.

The team was young, the atmosphere relaxed, and although the hours were long, 60 hours a week for £60, it was still double what I'd earned at the Folly. At university, that felt like serious money.

Then one morning everything changed.

I arrived at 8:30 a.m. to find the entire team standing outside on the pavement. The door was locked. No John. No keys. No explanation.

We waited.
Nine o'clock came and went.
By 9:15, it was clear this wasn't a simple delay.
This was before mobile phones. Before texts. Before "just dropping a message." If someone vanished, they were simply… gone.

Peter and I both knew where John lived, so we volunteered to drive over. On the way, we passed the warehouse, a barn opposite his house, and noticed the warehouse staff standing outside as well.

One of them said he'd knocked at John's front door but had no reply.

Peter and I split up to check the windows. He took the right side of the house. I took the left.

The first room I looked into was eerily empty. Just a rug on the floor. No furniture. No clutter. Nothing.

The kitchen was worse. Cupboards open. Almost bare. A single stray cereal box, abandoned like a prop from a crime drama.

We regrouped at the front.

"Looks like they've done a bunk," Peter said, calmly.

There was nothing else to do. We drove straight to the police station.

Peter went inside while I waited in the car. When he came back, he looked grim.

The police would meet us at the office.

By the time we returned, some colleagues had drifted home, but a handful of us lingered on the pavement, stunned, anxious, and quietly processing what we already knew. Eventually, a police officer arrived, followed by a man who introduced himself as the landlord's agent. He had keys.

As soon as the door opened, the alarm screamed into life. Peter silenced it, he knew the code, and we stepped inside.
The main office looked… normal.

John's office did not.

His safe hung open, completely empty. Desk drawers pulled out. Papers scattered. It looked like someone who had left fast, and deliberately.

Then Paula, his secretary, noticed an envelope on her desk. John's handwriting. Her name.

The officer opened it and read:
"Dear Paula, I am sorry for the inconvenience this will cause, but you must understand I had no choice. There is no money left in the business. You should speak to Mr Jones at Lloyds Bank in the Square, as the bank will probably want to put the company into liquidation."

Silence.

Paula rang Mr Jones immediately.

Twenty minutes later, he walked in, listened, and said calmly, "I suggest you all gather your things and head home. I can't make promises, but the bank recently lent the company money secured against the warehouse stock. You'll likely be paid for the work you've already done.."

Peter offered to accompany him to the warehouse. The rest of us drifted away, dazed, unemployed, and unsure what any of it meant.

A few hours later the phone rang. It was Peter.

"You're not going to believe this."

At the warehouse, they'd forced the door with a crowbar. Mr Jones asked the forklift driver to lower a pallet of printers. As it came down, the driver frowned, it felt far too light.

They opened the top layer. Those were real. Brand-new printers. Perfectly boxed.

Underneath?
Empty boxes.
Just polystyrene.

Another pallet: the same.
Another.
And another.

Over ninety percent of the warehouse stock, the collateral for the bank loan, the heart of the business, was a façade.

John had vanished.
The printers had vanished.
The money had vanished.

The police sealed the site. Mr Jones confirmed the bank accounts were empty. There would be no final pay packet. No compensation. Not a single penny.

It was the most dramatic introduction to the world of IT anyone could imagine.

But it taught me something priceless very early in life:

Sometimes the entire house of cards collapses, even when *you* have done everything right.

And when chaos hits, people don't look for the loudest voice.

They look for the person who stays calm, thinks clearly, and starts picking up the pieces.

I didn't know it then, but that lesson would shape more of my career than any textbook ever could.

At least now, I was in the game.

The bathroom burglars of Waterlooville

After Roy left his job at the Folly Wine Bar, he became a general handyman for John Day, millionaire owner of the Folly Market in Petersfield. John also owned a sprawling house just outside town, Causeway House, complete with its own stable block and a small army of staff who kept the place running.

During one of my university holidays, Roy was doing some work at a house in Waterlooville and asked if I'd lend a hand. The job sounded simple enough: strip the bathroom, remove the tiles, repaint the walls and ceiling, install the new suite, retile, and tidy up. We had three weeks while the family were away. What could possibly go wrong?

We'd barely started when there came a knock at the back door.

Roy went to answer it while I hovered halfway down the stairs, curious.

A small boy stood there.

"Hello. Can Johnny come out to play?"

"Johnny's not here," Roy said. "He's on holiday with his mummy and daddy."

"Oh," the boy replied. "What are you doing?"

"We're taking out the bath and wash basin."

The boy frowned. "Are you allowed to do that?"

This was precisely the wrong type of question to ask Roy, who never missed an opportunity for mischief.

"No," he said, solemnly. "We break into houses when people are away, steal their bathroom fittings, and sell them."

The boy's eyes widened. "That's very naughty!" he gasped, then sprinted away across the lawn.

Roy returned inside, struggling to contain his laughter.

"I heard all of that," I said.

Thirty minutes later, there was a much louder knock at the *front* door. This time it was Johnny's father... accompanied by a policeman..

"This man says you told his son you were stealing property from this house," said the officer. "Is that correct?"

Roy went pale. In record time, he produced the paperwork, the house keys, and an explanation of the "joke". The policeman chuckled, but did suggest, quite firmly, that perhaps Roy might like to recalibrate his sense of humour when small children were involved.

We apologised profusely and returned to the bathroom, suitably chastened.

Our next problem arrived moments later.

I was chiselling tiles from the bathroom wall when a tremendous crash came from the adjoining toilet. We ran in to find half the tiles from *that* wall now smashed on the floor. My enthusiastic hammering had shaken everything loose.

We ended up retiling the toilet ourselves, wiping out most of the profit.

Lesson learned: enthusiasm + plasterboard = bankruptcy.

It wasn't our only mishap.

On another job in Wickham, Roy dropped me off to tackle some joinery while he went elsewhere. Carrying long pieces of timber through the lounge, I misjudged the distance and clipped a China horse on the mantelpiece. It shattered cleanly in two.

The lady of the house appeared instantly.
"You careless oaf!" she snapped. "You just wait until your brother gets back!"

Two hours later, Roy returned.
"Your half-wit of a brother decapitated my horse!"

Without missing a beat, Roy sighed and said, "Really? That's a surprise, he's usually very good with animals."

I very nearly swallowed my own tongue trying not to laugh.

Roy promised the horse would be replaced out of my wages.

Miraculously, I tracked down the exact same China horse and bought her a replacement. Disaster narrowly avoided.

At Causeway House, John's live-in housekeeper provided lunch for the workers each day. At first it was generous fare: cottage pie, stews, fish and chips on Fridays. Then the "budget cuts" arrived.

One day lunch consisted solely of tinned peeled tomatoes on toast.

We protested, but John insisted he was "sharing the same hardships."

Something didn't sit right.

After lunch, I followed him into his office. Through the half-open door, I saw him sitting behind his desk... eating ham on toast.

"So," I said, leaning in, "you're suffering with us, are you?"

He looked up quickly. "Oh, this isn't for me. It's for Rory," he said, gesturing to his golden retriever.

I raised an eyebrow.
"Better give it to him then," I said. "Wouldn't want it getting cold."

He hesitated, then reluctantly placed the plate on the floor.

The next day, full cooked lunches were back on the menu.

Perhaps I had the makings of a negotiator after all.

Our biggest job for John was constructing a new steel-framed indoor riding arena. Roy oversaw the build; I got the less glamorous but far more dangerous roles, including driving a diesel forklift without a licence, and lifting a welder and his acetylene tank twenty feet in the air inside a cage we'd knocked together from pallets.

If Health and Safety had appeared, we'd have been jailed before lunchtime.

The welder was enormous but efficient. He finished quickly, leaving us to paint the steel beams with red oxide primer.

Roy climbed the ladders. I steadied them.

At one point we had two ladders side by side. Roy tried to step across... slipped... grabbed the far ladder... and dropped the heavy tin of paint.

The next thing I knew, I was waking up in the back of an ambulance on the way to QA Hospital.

The paint tin had fallen twenty-five feet and clipped the side of my head. I was lucky, just concussion and a monumental headache.

Roy looked stricken. "Best tell Mum you don't remember anything," he muttered.

I spent the night in hospital. A week later, I was back at university, bruised, humbled, and quietly convinced that my brief career in building had probably reached its natural conclusion.

From thermal printers to the Inter-City 125

After my early brush with the unpredictability of small-business life, it was gently (and repeatedly) suggested, mostly by my parents, that I needed something more stable. Something proper. Something with payslips and pensions and no risk of the boss vanishing with a warehouse full of empty printer boxes.

And that's how I found myself applying for a position in the Contributions section at the Department of Health and Social Security in Guildford, now the Department of Work and Pensions. The DHSS promised structure, routine, job security, and most importantly from Mum's perspective, it was only a half-hour train ride from home. I got the job. And so began my seven-year career in the Civil Service.

The Guildford office didn't really have computers. It had *a* computer, singular. A lonely terminal locked away in the typing room like some sacred relic from a lost civilisation. If you needed to look up someone's National Insurance record, you filled out a form by hand and delivered it to the typists before 4 p.m. The next morning, like magic, a printout would appear on your desk.

Unless you'd made a mistake in the name or NI number. In which case, you'd come in to find the dreaded "RECORD NOT FOUND," which was Civil Service speak for *You fool. Try again.*

About a month in, I was sent on a week-long training course at the Reading office. It was the first time I'd stayed away from home since university, and instead of halls or a hotel, I was billeted in a classic post-war semi in Tilehurst, run as a no-frills B&B for travelling salesmen and civil servants.

Dinner was at 6 p.m. sharp. Not 6:05. Not "just finishing this chapter." Six. One evening I got held up and arrived back at 6:45. The landlady met me at the door, arms folded.

"Your dinner," she said, "is in the bin."

A warm welcome back.

Back in Guildford, I started looking more closely at the monthly statistics reports our section produced. They were entirely manual: counting, tallying, mental arithmetic, and optimism. It struck me that surely, *surely*, there had to be a better way.

So, I went home, fired up my Sinclair QL, and wrote a simple program to generate the reports automatically.

The results were good. *Incredibly* good. I handed them to my manager, who was so impressed she marched straight into the management meeting waving them like the Magna Carta. That was my first moment of real recognition in the Civil Service: the system was rigid, yes, but it wasn't immune to improvement.

There was, however, one small flaw. My thermal printer. Leave one of my beautiful reports on a sunny windowsill, and by lunchtime it had faded like the Cheshire Cat, all spreadsheets, no grin. We had to warn people not to let direct sunlight anywhere near my statistics. "Progress," I told them, "But fragile progress."

A year in, a new opportunity surfaced. HQ in Newcastle was launching a trial for a modern National Insurance card, a plastic, credit-card-sized replacement for the old paper strip everyone kept in their wallets until it disintegrated into lint and regret. It sounded exciting: real computers, real innovation, and a chance to escape the monotony of forms and fountain pens.

My assistant manager remembered my interview, my enthusiasm for computing, and, thankfully, the monthly stats triumph. "You should apply," he said. I took that as a polite version of *For the love of God, go where your talents are.*

I applied and was invited to an interview in Newcastle. I'd never been further north than London, so this felt like a proper adventure. The Department paid for the train and hotel and gave me a ten-pound-a-night food allowance, practically a banquet by student standards.

I can still remember the journey:

Waterloo.
The Underground to King's Cross.
And then the main event, boarding a High-Speed Train.

To a train buff like me, it was bliss.

I'd watched Inter-City 125s streak past for years. This was the first time I'd actually *ridden* one.

And I was being paid to do it.

The journey flew by, and soon I was stepping off at Newcastle Central, suitcase in hand, heading toward the DHSS centre via the Tyne and Wear Metro, miles from home and buzzing with possibility.

I didn't know it then, but this was one of those quiet forks in the road.

The moment where I stopped being just a cog in the machine...

...and started becoming someone ready to help *change* it.

When opportunity whispers

Sometimes opportunity doesn't knock; sometimes it whispers quietly from the back pages of the local paper.

That's exactly how my next big career move arrived.

One evening, flicking through the *Bordon Herald*, an advert jumped out at me. A company called Digital Dynamics, based in Farnborough, was looking for computer programmers. The salary? £9,600 a year. Compared to the £6,800 I was earning at the DHSS, it felt like discovering a Wonka-style golden ticket, only with fewer Oompa Loompas and considerably more COBOL.

I didn't hesitate. I sent in my application, crossed everything crossable, and before long, I was invited for an interview.

The interview took place at their Farnborough office. I was met by the office manager, Dave, who introduced me to Barry, the Managing Director. Barry was immaculately dressed, formal in manner, short in stature, and crowned with a full mane of striking white hair that made him instantly memorable. He had the air of a man who expected clarity, precision, and thinking before speaking, qualities I immediately respected.

What was scheduled as a 45-minute chat turned into nearly three hours. We talked about everything: technology, problem-solving, ambitions, frustrations, their plans for growth, my ideas for how I could contribute. By the end, it felt less like an interview and more like two people sketching out the future on invisible whiteboards.

So, when a letter arrived a few days later offering me the job, I wasn't exactly shocked. But I was thrilled.

I accepted on the spot. Just like that, my Civil Service chapter came to a close, and I stepped properly into the world of private enterprise.

The Farnborough team was small back then: just Dave, Julian, Neil, and me. The bulk of the company was based in Harrogate, but down south, we were a tight little unit. There was an energy about the place, that *we're building something* spark, and I felt part of it from day one.

Then came an unexpected perk that made the leap feel even more real.

The company car.

Until then, I'd only driven second-hand bangers, each at least a decade old, held together by rust, luck, and the whispered hope that *please start* might somehow count as mechanical expertise.

Digital Dynamics handed me the keys to a beige Vauxhall Cavalier.

It wasn't new, it had belonged to someone who'd recently left, but at just 18 months old, it was the most modern car I'd ever sat in, let alone driven. I was absolutely chuffed.

Over the years, the Cavalier gave way to a crisp white **Peugeot 405**, then a bright red **Ford Orion**, and eventually a **British Racing Green Renault Laguna**. Each one marked a new stage of my working life.

And if you're wondering whether those cars had adventures of their own... don't worry. There's a whole chapter later in the book.

Digital Dynamics didn't just give me a salary bump and a shinier motor.

It gave me confidence.

Freedom.

A sense that I was back on the front foot, doing something I loved, surrounded by people who genuinely valued what I brought to the table.

Looking back, it was exactly what I needed.

A welcome break, yes.

But more than that -
a proper new beginning.

Always check your spools

We didn't have many rules in our Farnborough office, but one stood above all others:
whoever was last out at night had to run the backups.

There were two systems to look after, the IBM PC, which behaved itself, and the Data General mainframe, which absolutely did not.

The IBM backup was blissfully simple. It used a chunky cartridge drive. You grabbed the correct day's cartridge from the fireproof data safe (Monday to Friday plus a weekend special), slid it in, pressed a button, and waited for the reassuring whirr. Foolproof. Practically civilised.

The Data General, on the other hand, belonged on the bridge of the USS Enterprise.

It used a reel-to-reel tape drive: two great spools of magnetic tape, blinking lights, and mechanical clunks that suggested something terribly important was happening, even when it wasn't. It was the sort of machine that inspired both awe and quiet dread.

Loading it wasn't difficult, exactly, just very precise.

Left spool. Thread the tape through the heads. Up to the right spool. Anchor it. Wind for tension. Close the lid with a satisfying authoritative *thunk*. Press start.

Then, if the gods were smiling, the drive would form a vacuum and the reels would spin into life.

If the gods were not smiling, one of two things happened:

1. **The tape snapped** - often because it had survived more backup cycles than was medically advisable.
2. **The vacuum refused to form** - usually because the lid wasn't fully closed, or dust had settled on the sensor.

Julian, one of our senior developers, had shown me the fix for the second issue:
A sharp puff of breath onto the sensor.
Very scientific. Very Digital Dynamics.

As the junior developer, I was rarely first in or last out, so I'd only performed the dance a handful of times. I'd observed Dave and Julian do it often, but watching someone make toast doesn't mean you won't burn your first loaf.

Then, one evening, fate delivered my moment.

Everyone else left at five, Dave, Julian, Neil, gone like a fire drill had been sounded. I stayed behind to finish something, then wandered into the server room at around six.

PC cartridge backup? Easy. Done in minutes.

Then came the Data General.

I loaded the reel, threaded the tape, clipped it to the right-hand spool, wound it clockwise to tension, shut the lid, pressed start...

The air pump hissed - then *pop!*
The lid sprang open.
Not ideal.

I tried again.
Pump, hiss... *pop!*

Right. Sensor, then.

I lifted the lid, located the sensor, and, recalling Julian's sage advice, gave it a heroic puff of breath.

Closed the lid. Tried again.

Pump, hiss... *pop!*

At this point I had exhausted both my technical knowledge **and** my dignity.

It had to be a hardware fault.

Pinned above the drive were instructions and a reassuring notice about **24/7 engineering support**, complete with a phone number and our customer code. So I rang it.

After explaining my problem, the engineer on the other end said cheerfully, "Sounds like a fault! We'll have someone out to you within the hour."

I thanked him, retrieved the day's newspaper from the bin, and settled into my chair like a man expecting a tow truck.

Forty-five minutes later, there was a knock at the office door.

A friendly, middle-aged man with a ginger beard stepped inside. "Got a tape drive playing silly beggars?" he asked.

I led him to the server room, feeling equal parts relieved and deeply embarrassed.

He opened the lid, looked at my handiwork for perhaps **three seconds**, and chuckled.

"You haven't done this many times, have you?"

"No," I admitted. "First time unsupervised."

Still grinning, he unclipped the tape from the right-hand spool, turned the spool 180 degrees, reattached the tape, and wound it several turns **anticlockwise**.

Then he shut the lid, pressed the button...
Pump.
Silence.
Perfect vacuum.

The reels spun into life, smooth and confident, like a well-rehearsed ballet.

"You mean I wound it the wrong way?" I asked.

He laughed kindly. "Don't worry, lad, we've all been there. Got the T-shirt and the mug."

He filled out his service report, paused with pen hovering, then said, "Now... what shall we put? Ah yes, *'Contamination on lid rubber seal. Thoroughly cleaned.'* That sounds suitably technical."

He handed me the form.

"All sorted."

"Thank you," I said, "And sorry for wasting your evening."

"Not wasting anything," he replied. "Just remember, always check your spools before you call the cavalry."

A small humiliation at the time, but one that stayed with me.

Because sometimes the most important lessons in your career aren't about technology at all.

They're about slowing down.

Checking your assumptions.

And making absolutely sure the spool is turning the right way before you ask for help.

But all toast is brown

One of the unexpected perks of my Digital Dynamics years, later rebadged as Welcom, was the regular pilgrimage north to our headquarters in Harrogate, North Yorkshire.

As a project manager, and later a business development executive, I made the journey roughly every two weeks, until the M1 felt less like a motorway and more like a familiar old friend with questionable driving habits.

The route became muscle memory: M3, M25, M1 to Leeds, then the A61 through gentle hills and big skies. I knew every service station, every fondly remembered Little Chef, and every one of the radio black spots where Steve Wright in the Afternoon would abruptly vanish into static. After a while, I could have driven it with my eyes shut, though I wisely resisted the urge to test that theory.

One trick I mastered was timing the return journey so I hit Leicester Forest East services before nightfall. Two reasons:

1. It had a proper choice of food (a rare luxury on motorways in those days), and
2. From there to Farnborough, every mile was lit. After a long business trip, that steady ribbon of light felt like a small, merciful kindness.

In Harrogate, I always stayed at The Grants Hotel, a charming, family-run place within easy strolling distance of the town centre. I must have stayed there hundreds of times. Most visits blurred together into a pleasant haze of check-ins, cooked breakfasts, and office days. But one morning is etched permanently into my memory.

I was sitting in the restaurant awaiting my order, a luxury I still miss in the age of lukewarm buffet sausages, when a new trainee waitress approached, notepad trembling slightly in her hand.

"Are you ready to order, sir?"

"Yes, please. Full English. No egg, no black pudding. Extra bacon instead."

She nodded solemnly.

"And toast?" she asked.

"Yes please, strawberry jam."

She wrote it all down and stepped away. At that moment, the senior waitress, who was training her, called gently after her: "You didn't ask whether he wants white or brown toast."

The trainee stopped dead. Turned slowly. And said, with the absolute sincerity of someone stating an indisputable law of nature:

"But... all toast is brown."

I very nearly inhaled my coffee. If there were BAFTAs for earnest confusion, she'd have swept the board.

No visit to Harrogate was complete without a pilgrimage to Betty's Tea Rooms. If you've been, you'll understand. If you haven't, rectify that immediately, civilisation more or less begins with their tea and cakes.

Evening meals were often spent at Pinocchio's, a little Italian place whose garlic mushrooms should have been protected by UNESCO. Sadly, it eventually closed. Losing a favourite restaurant is like someone quietly redrawing the map of your life.

Two other Harrogate haunts live vividly in memory, though one has drifted into legend. The first was a Mexican restaurant where I once took a colleague called Bernard, a man proudly sporting what can only be described as a solar panel for a sex machine. "I love spicy food," he announced confidently. His sweating scalp told a very different story. I tried not to laugh. I failed.

The second was The Montpelier, still going strong, I believe.

Wednesday nights belonged to a local institution known affectionately as *Gyrating Jeff*. He was vertically challenged and danced energetically in the front window, coaxing passers by inside with moves that defied both physics and modesty. The place was rammed every week. His disco nights were pure Harrogate folklore. I spent many an evening there, pint in hand, chatting, laughing, and occasionally, against all natural instinct, dancing.

In the years since leaving Welcom, I've returned to Harrogate from time to time. Each visit feels like opening a time capsule.

Betty's still glows with quiet elegance.

The Montpelier still hums.

Pinocchio's is gone but never forgotten.

And the memories, those long drives, those familiar haunts, those tiny human moments like the waitress grappling with the existential nature of toast, remain some of the warmest of my working life.

For a while, Harrogate wasn't just a place I travelled to for work.

It was somewhere I lived, a fortnight at a time.

The night the Orion died

Most of my trips to Harrogate were pleasantly uneventful: long stretches of motorway, decent music on the stereo, and a company car that (usually) behaved itself. But one journey stands out, not for what went right, but for everything that went spectacularly wrong.

Bernard and I packed our bags into the boot of my red Ford Orion, my pride and joy at the time. We had our usual arrangement: I'd drive north, he'd handle the return. Simple. We've done it countless times. Nothing unusual. Nothing dramatic.

The M3 was fine.
The M25 was fine.
Most of the M1 was fine.

And then, about twenty miles south of Leeds, winter descended in that special northern way: suddenly, thick darkness swallowed the world beyond the headlights. That's when things took a turn.
First, the heater fan died without warning. Annoying, but survivable. "That'll be one for the garage," I muttered. The engine still purred, so we carried on.

A few minutes later, as I moved out to overtake a slower car, something distinctly odd happened. The Orion surged forward exactly as it should, lovely and smooth, but the rev counter dropped. Not climbed. Dropped.

"Bernard, take a look at this," I said.

He leaned over just in time to watch the needle fall again as I accelerated.

"That's not right," he said, in a tone that suggested he was wondering if we should draft our wills.

Neither of us fancied pulling onto the hard shoulder in the freezing pitch black, so we made a pact: get to Leeds. If the car died there, at least we'd be off the motorway. Miraculously, we made it.

And then, just as we left the city and joined the quiet stretch of the A61 to Harrogate, the dashboard lights gave up and died. All of them. I now had:

- No heating,
- A rev counter that behaved like it was auditioning for Most Unreliable Supporting Actor, and
- No idea how fast I was actually going.

Perfect conditions for night driving.

Those last eleven miles into Harrogate felt like a hundred. Too slow, and we risked the car finally giving up. Too fast, and a speeding ticket, or a ditch, beckoned. We were two men in a rapidly cooling Ford Orion, hurtling into darkness with all the confidence of a pair of blindfolded squirrels.

But somehow, by luck, prayer, or sheer Ford stubbornness, we rolled into the car park of Grant's Hotel. I switched off the ignition, exhaled deeply, and thought I'd better check whether it would restart.

Click. Click.

Then silence.

Dead as a doornail.

"Well," I said, half laughing, half groaning, "thank heavens we didn't stop on the motorway."

The next morning, we grabbed a taxi to the office. The receptionist gave me the number for the local Ford dealer. They came to collect the car, and just before lunch, they rang.

The mechanic's tone was calm, professional, and edged with disbelief.

"We've found the problem," he said. "A loose piece of bodywork has been vibrating while you were driving. Nothing unusual. But it's been rubbing against your main wiring loom... and it's cut straight through it."

There was a pause. A significant one.

"It's an expensive fix," he continued. "Honestly, sir... we'd recommend writing the car off."

A few days earlier, I'd thought the red Orion was the best company car I'd ever had. Now it was destined for the scrapyard.

Still, if you're going to have a catastrophic vehicle failure, the car park of a warm hotel in Harrogate beats the hard shoulder of the M1 in the freezing dark any day.

The night I set off my own alarm

One of the unavoidable downsides of visiting client sites while living in a second-floor flat was the sheer logistics of equipment. If I'd taken a PC, a monitor, or any other bit of kit with me, it was far easier to drop it back at the office on the way home than lug it upstairs like a pack mule.

Normally the process was simple:
Unlock door → deactivate alarm → dump equipment → reactivate alarm → go home.

A sequence so familiar I could (almost) have done it blindfolded.

Which, as it turned out, was exactly the problem.

It was a wet, miserable night just after 11 p.m. when I pulled up outside the office, rain hammering down in sheets. I decided I'd save myself a trip: grab the PC and keyboard in one go, dash to the door, drop them inside, and disarm the alarm before it threw a tantrum.

Spotting a bin bag in the boot, I thought: *Perfect - keyboard and mouse can go in there to keep them dry.*

Thus armed, I elbowed the boot shut and hurried to the door, juggling everything like a one-man circus act.

As soon as the door opened, the alarm began its ominous **beep... beep... beep...**

Thirty seconds to deactivate.

Plenty of time, I thought confidently, flicking the light switch.

Pop!

Two seconds of illumination, then total darkness.

Excellent.

I now had maybe twenty-five seconds left, standing in a hallway blacker than a cave, holding a PC, a bin bag, and my dignity by the thinnest margin.

A faint glow from the streetlight outside gave me just enough vision to avoid tripping over imaginary obstacles. No sign of the hallway chair that was *always* by the door. I gave up looking and lowered the PC gently onto the floor, and that's when the thirty seconds expired.

The alarm exploded into life.
WEE-WAH, WEE-WAH, WEE-WAH!

Dear God.
The noise was deafening. And, of course, that meant one thing: it had already alerted the police.

Perfect.

I stabbed the code into the panel like it owed me money.

Blessed silence.

Well, sort of, my ears were still ringing like church bells.

The screen confirmed it: **Police notified.**

The station was only half a mile away, so I figured they'd turn up in minutes. I retrieved the monitor, still in darkness, still no police. Then, as a gesture of sanity, decided to replace the bulb. At 6ft 3in, I didn't need a chair. A quick twist, click, and the hallway was bright again.

"Why was the chair under the stairs?" I muttered. "We never put it under the bloody stairs…"
I stopped myself, Basil Fawlty mode fully activated.

Still no police.

Midnight came and went. I debated leaving, but Sod's Law guaranteed they'd appear the second I locked up. So, I made a coffee. If they arrived mid-sip, I could always pour it down the sink.

One hour later, headlights finally appeared. Two officers stepped out. One circled the back; the other walked inside.

"Evening, sir," he said. "We're responding to an automatic alarm call. Did it alert you too?"

"No officer," I replied. "It was me. Lightbulb blew; I didn't reach the panel in time."

He eyed the newly lit hallway.

"It's working now," he observed.

"I know it's working now," I said, resisting the urge to flail like Basil. "In the time I've been waiting for you, I replaced it."

His colleague returned.
"No sign of a break-in," he announced.

I sighed. "I've just explained, it was me. I set it off."

"And you are?" he asked.

"Keith Budden."

"And are you allowed to be here?"

For a dangerous split second, the devil on my shoulder whispered:
No, officer, I broke in, the alarm went off, and I thought, well, it's raining, so I'll just make a coffee and wait for you.

Fortunately, common sense throttled that impulse.

"Yes," I said politely, "I work here."

I produced my licence, the office keys, and demonstrated that I knew both activation codes.
Satisfied at last, the officer nodded.

"Well, all seems in order. Goodnight, sir."

And just like that, they were gone.

I finished my coffee, rearmed the alarm, locked up, and finally stumbled through my own front door at 1:30 a.m.

"Dave and Julian are never going to believe this," I muttered.

They didn't. Until I told them.

Never eat before the Archbishop

One of the client accounts I was given to manage was the Roman Catholic **Archdiocese of Liverpool,** not your typical IT gig, and all the more memorable because of it.

I'll never forget my first visit. Driving along the M62 into Liverpool, I was struck by the contrasts: pockets of clear hardship sitting right alongside bright, vibrant communities. I checked into my hotel within sight of Anfield and made a mental note: *this is a city with stories.*

The next morning, I headed to the Liverpool Metropolitan Cathedral. Walking inside, I was instantly taken by its bold modernism, a circular sanctuary crowned with a lantern tower that poured coloured light like stained-glass rain. Locals call it **Paddy's Wigwam**, or **The Pope's Launchpad**. Both feel entirely fair.

I asked where I could find my contact, Father Swallow.

"Downstairs in the refectory," someone said.

I descended into the basement and was met by a hugely different atmosphere: the hush of the cathedral replaced by the warm bustle of students, clergy, and staff.

Father Swallow was exactly as his name suggested, genial, round-faced, cheerful. After a coffee, he walked me across the road to the administrative offices, where we spent the morning reviewing their systems and discussing improvements. By lunchtime, I was ready to collapse face-first into a plate of food.

The staff refectory was peaceful, long tables laid neatly. At each setting: cutlery, a plate, and a fresh bread roll with a small knob of butter.

I picked up the roll, sliced it open, spread the butter, and took a bite.

Lovely.

Then I noticed something odd.
No one else had touched theirs.
Not a single roll shifted.
Every knife remained exactly where it had been placed.

And that's when the Archbishop walked in.

Everyone stood. And the Archbishop began to say grace.

There I was, halfway through my roll, mid-chew, the only person eating during grace. Probably not a mortal sin, more of a lightweight, entry-level sin, but I could have melted into the floor all the same.

Lesson learned:
Never eat before the Archbishop.

A few months later, the Archdiocese gave me a *different* sort of religious experience, one involving much less holiness and much more humiliation.

It was winter. I'd been installing software updates all day, finally wrapping up around 6:30 p.m. The building was empty except for Father Swallow, who popped his head in on the way out.

"Do you need much longer?"

"About an hour."

"Alright. I won't set the alarm. Just lock up properly: close the wooden inner door into the porch, make sure it latches, then shut the glass door onto the pavement."

Simple.

An hour later, updates complete, I packed up, turned off the lights, and made my way to reception. I closed the wooden inner door, click, and turned to leave through the glass door.
It didn't move.
I pulled again.
Nothing.

Someone had locked it **from the outside**.

I was trapped in the porch, a narrow glass-fronted chamber barely eight feet deep, like an exhibit in the museum of "Men Who Should Have Left Sooner."

Passersby glanced at me with the sort of casual curiosity normally reserved for mannequins.

Thankfully, I had mobile signal.

"Hi Keith," said Father Swallow, cheerfully. "Everything alright?"

"Not exactly. I'm locked in the porch."

Pause.

"Oh dear... When I left, I bumped into the caretaker. We were chatting. He must have locked up behind us. Completely forgot you were still there."

He lived **forty minutes** away.

So, I waited. And watched people walk past. And tried not to look like a lost Labrador pressed against a window.

True to his word, forty minutes later he arrived, flustered and apologetic.

"Well," he said as he let me out, "I might as well set the alarm now."

"Excellent idea," I said. "And next time, I'll make sure I'm *on the correct side* of the glass door before you do."

Never follow fog lights

Sometimes the most important lessons in life arrive quietly. No fireworks, no fanfare, just a moment of clarity in the middle of an otherwise ordinary day. And so it is, dear reader, with this chapter.

I'd spent the day working at the Archdiocese in Liverpool, and although I needed to leave by 4:30 p.m. to make it to Harrogate in time for the Welcom Christmas Party at the Majestic Hotel, darkness had already settled in. December is good at that.

The M62 was familiar territory by then. Damp roads glistened under the moonlight after a day of rain. The plan was simple: M62 to Leeds, then north into Harrogate. I'd done the journey at least a dozen times.

Traffic thickened around Manchester, as it usually did, but once past that stretch I settled in. Radio on, heater humming, headlights carving a path ahead.

Then we began the climb into the Pennines.

It started with mist, gentle at first, then thicker, then so dense it swallowed the world. Fog lights flicked on ahead of me, red glows suspended in the void, and I followed suit.

Soon the traffic slowed to a crawl. Then stopped.

A wall of brake lights in front. An army of headlights behind.

I tuned into a Manchester radio station for updates. After a few minutes came the inevitable announcement: an accident in the fog. Eastbound M62 closed. Traffic to be diverted at the next junction.

This was long before the days of sat-nav. If you wanted a new route, you created one. So, I reached behind the passenger seat, grabbed my trusty AA Road Atlas, and unfolded it across my lap. With traffic at a standstill, I traced a rough plan eastward. Not ideal. But workable.
When the diversion finally came, I peeled off the motorway, headlights pushing through the fog as I threaded my way along unfamiliar A-roads. I aimed for Bradford, then around Leeds Bradford Airport, then up toward Harrogate, a route I'd done

once before, years earlier, in daylight, and without the near-zero visibility.

It felt like hours. The fog was relentless. The world reduced to two red dots ahead, the lorry's rear fog lights.

And although I knew I shouldn't, I found myself following them instinctively. Wherever they went, I went. The human brain loves something to latch onto in the darkness, even when it shouldn't.

Then, mercifully, the fog thinned for just a second.

I glanced left.

A sheer drop. A steep, unforgiving slope disappearing into blackness. Only a single post and a barbed-wire fence separating the road from a fall that didn't bear thinking about.

And in that instant, the truth hit me:
If that lorry had gone over, I would have followed it.

When the truck moved forward again, I didn't. I let it drift into the fog and kept my distance. The car behind me sounded an impatient toot, but I ignored it.

For the rest of the journey, I drove by a simple rule, one my father taught me when I first learned to drive at night:
"Never go faster than you can safely see in front of you."

Good advice for driving.

Excellent advice for life.

The great radio fayre that never was

I think we'd all *like* to claim we've never fallen for an April Fool's prank, even something as daft as the BBC's famous spaghetti-tree broadcast, but the truth is, I, along with several hundred others, was completely taken in by County Sound radio. Hook, line, and sinker.

Back then, I was a loyal County Sound listener. It kept me company on my daily commute from Liss to Farnborough and back again. I'd even won a runner-up prize on one of their phone-in competitions. Fame of the finest local-radio variety.

They had a regular sound effect, a cockerel crowing, that played several times every morning. One day, the presenter announced a competition to name the bird.

My suggestion was "Giblets."

Not everyone's taste, but it made the presenters laugh, and it earned me a mention on air. My claim to regional radio glory.

Years earlier, during my days at the DHSS in Guildford, County Sound had even interviewed me when I was a shop steward, talking about the impact of our strike action. So yes, I had a soft spot for them. A sense of local loyalty. A sense that we understood each other.

That was my first mistake.

April Fools' Day that year fell on a Sunday.

All morning, County Sound kept hyping a big event, a huge fayre at Stoke Park in Guildford. They played "live reports" from the showground: music, crowds, laughter, the works. It sounded brilliant.

I had no plans, and Liss to Guildford isn't far. I knew Stoke Park well.

So, I thought, *why not?*

A spontaneous day out. A bit of fun.

What greeted me instead was... nothing.

No banners.
No music.
No rides.
No stalls.

Just an empty park and a car park inexplicably full of hopeful, optimistic listeners.

I parked on a nearby side road and walked onto the grass, only to find around a hundred equally baffled people wandering around like extras from a low-budget zombie film.

"Are you here for the fair?"
"Yes."
"Where is it?"
"No idea."
"County Sound said it was here..."
"I know."

Eventually, we all realised the same thing: something didn't add up.

That moment of clarity arrived the second I got back to my car, turned the key, and the radio crackled into life:
"To all our listeners who've headed to Stoke Park this morning, we'd just like to remind you of the date... it is Sunday, April the 1st."

The penny dropped.
What a fool.
And what a well-executed prank.

I burst out laughing. What else can you do? I drove to Worplesdon Road, bought cod and chips, and ate them on a bench in the spring sunshine before heading home, still chuckling at my own gullibility.

A fine reminder, as the old saying goes:
If something sounds too good to be true... it probably is.

Escorted to Waterloo (no handcuffs required)

Of all the accounts I managed during my years at Welcom, one of my firm favourites was the Metropolitan Police Trading Service, headed by their General Manager, John.

So, when an invitation to John's retirement lunch landed on my doormat, I didn't hesitate. It was to be held in one of the committee rooms at New Scotland Yard. I wouldn't have missed it for the world. John was sharp, fair, and carried that old-school sense of honour you rarely see today. And I'm pleased to say the respect was mutual.

At that time, New Scotland Yard was still at 10 Broadway, just off Victoria Street, not yet the smart glass tower on Victoria Embankment. And for context later, the cab road running straight through Waterloo Station was still open back then.

I caught the train from Petersfield to Waterloo, changed at Clapham Junction, and reached Victoria just before noon. From there it was a brisk ten-minute walk. I paused outside the entrance to admire the famous rotating sign, the same one that appears on the news whenever someone reports "live from New Scotland Yard."

Looking back, I wish I'd taken a selfie, but this was the era when phone cameras produced images that made you look like you'd been drawn in charcoal by a blindfolded toddler.

Inside, the policewoman on reception checked me off the guest list and asked me to wait.

I wandered the foyer for a moment, stopping at the Eternal Flame, the elegant memorial that honours Metropolitan Police officers who lost their lives in service. The flicker of the flame reflected in the still pool of water beneath. A moment of calm before the celebrations.

"Mr Budden?" a voice said behind me.
I turned to see a young officer.
"That's me," I said.
"Please follow me, sir."

We navigated a maze of corridors until the muffled sound of conversation grew louder. When he opened the door to the committee room, I was greeted by a sea of suits, crisp uniforms, and easy laughter.

"Keith!" John called out from across the room. "Glad you made it, let me get you a drink."

I assumed wine. Possibly orange juice.
Instead, he handed me a whisky, a generous one. A *very* generous one.
"You're not driving, are you?" he said with a grin. "And I remembered, neat, no water, no ice."

I had no recollection of ever discussing whisky preferences with him, but John had a talent for remembering the minute details that made people feel valued.

The lunch that followed was brilliant: tasty food, enjoyable conversation, and, it must be said, a positively heroic amount of alcohol. Whisky, wine, beer, liqueurs, if it came in a bottle, it came our way. The afternoon drifted along on warm laughter and the clink of glasses.

Then John stood to give his retirement speech. Funny, touching, and full of gratitude.
And then, unexpectedly, he turned to me.

"Keith," he said, "is a brilliant IT man. If you've got an IT need, speak to him. He's sold me hundreds of thousands of pounds' worth of kit over the years... but he's never sold me a single thing I didn't need."

It remains one of the finest compliments anyone has ever paid me.

I raised my glass, nodded my thanks, and tried not to look too emotional.

As the evening wound down, people began drifting away with handshakes and hugs. John came over.

"Hope you enjoyed today," he said.
"I did," I replied. "And I hope retirement treats you very well, you've earned it."

"Which station are you heading to?"

"Victoria's closest," I said, "but Waterloo's more direct for me."

"No problem," he said. "I'll have a couple of the lads run you there."

A few minutes later two uniformed officers appeared, polite and businesslike. They escorted me outside into the cool London air. I must admit, by this point I was well and truly sozzled. They bundled me into the back of a police patrol car and off we went.

Rather than dropping me outside Waterloo like normal mortals, the driver swung confidently through the old cab road *into the middle of the station itself.*

"Thanks, lads," I said, trying to sound sober. I don't think I succeeded.

"No problem, sir," one said, helping me out. "Safe journey home."

I often smile when I think about that moment: commuters watching a police car pull into the station concourse, an officer stepping out, and helping a decidedly merry gentleman from the back seat... before bidding him goodnight.

Not the most dignified ending to a career lunch, but utterly unforgettable.

My Mummy's special friend

Writing the computer system for the Middlesex University Alumni Association meant I spent a lot of time with their assistant administrator, Laura.

There was no lightning bolt, no Hollywood slow-motion moment across a crowded office, but there *was* an ease. We laughed. We worked well together. And slowly, almost without realising it, we simply grew on each other.

Whenever she phoned my office and got put through, Neil and Alex, who shared the space with me, would immediately start singing *"Tell Laura I Love Her."*

It became a running joke, and Laura found it endlessly amusing.

At the time, I only had one photograph of her, dark bobbed hair, that sweet, open face. I kept it tucked in my wallet. One day, when the sandwich van pulled up outside the Alumni Office, I handed her my wallet to pay.

She said nothing when she returned with the change. But her expression told me she'd seen the photo.

Months later, when I went to collect her from her flat, I noticed a framed picture of *me* on her bedside table. Reciprocity confirmed.

Laura was a single mum, separated from her husband, with a young son, Jamie, five or six at the time. Bright, cheeky, overflowing with energy.

Our friendship shifted gears over two consecutive weekends.

The first came after an alumni committee meeting. Laura was in the kitchen washing up cups and saucers. I stepped in behind her, put my arms around her waist, and murmured, "Can I give you a hand?"

"You certainly can," she said, turning her head toward me.

We kissed. Not a sweeping, cinematic kiss, just gentle, certain, unmistakably more than friendship.

The following weekend, we were at a party in Highgate hosted by another committee member. We arrived separately, but when Laura saw me, she walked straight over, kissed me on the cheek, and slipped her house keys into my pocket.

"You can keep these safe," she whispered. "You'll need them later."

And indeed, later, after the party wound down, I drove her home.

She invited me in. The details, I'll leave tactfully behind a discreet curtain.

After that, we found our rhythm. Every other weekend together, usually when Jamie was with his dad, and nightly phone calls in between. Eventually Laura decided it was time for me to meet him.

Jamie was a lovely lad, bright and inquisitive, and we hit it off surprisingly quickly.

Which brings me to the moment burned forever into my memory.

One Saturday the three of us were out shopping and stopped for lunch at McDonald's. This was in the days when indoor smoking was allowed, and each table had a little metal ashtray.

Laura went to get our meals. Jamie and I found a table. As bored small boys tend to do, he picked up the ashtray and began tapping it rhythmically against the surface.

Tap. Tap. Tap-tap-tap.

After a minute, I said, "Jamie, please stop doing that."

Tap-tap-tap.

"Jamie," I said, slightly firmer, "stop doing that."

Tap-tap-

Two elderly ladies at the next table turned around, smiling indulgently.

"Now, Jamie," one said, "do as your *Daddy* tells you."

Jamie looked up at them, then at me... then delivered his line with the clarity and projection of a West End performer: "He's **not** my Daddy; he's my **Mummy's special friend!**"

Silence.

Dead. Absolute. Silence.

The ladies turned back to their apple pies with enough disapproval to chill a room.

My face went crimson.

Laura, having clearly heard every word while balancing a tray of burgers, raised one eyebrow in a way that managed to say both *I told you he was cheeky* and *good luck getting out of that one*.

We ate in silence, the three of us, each processing the moment in our own way.

Not quite the idyllic family outing I'd pictured, but, looking back, still one that makes me smile. Every time.

The Brummie taxi driver of Charleroi

When Jan's brother Richard announced he was working in Belgium, just outside Brussels, it didn't take long for the plan to form: **that's where we'd go for Jan's stag weekend.** Easy, cheap flights, plenty of beer, and a built-in local guide. Perfect.

Early on a Friday morning, I met up with Jan and two of his rugby teammates at London Luton Airport. We were flying EasyJet, still a novelty back then, and there was that unmistakable sense of smug anticipation: a weekend of beer, banter, and questionable judgement awaited.

We naïvely assumed that since we were flying from **London Luton**, we would naturally land in something equally convenient, like **Brussels Central International Airport**.

Well... that was our first lesson in low-cost geography.

The flight was uneventful, but as we descended, it became obvious we were not, in fact, approaching a European capital. Fields, warehouses, motorways, yes.

Grand boulevards and elegant architecture, absolutely not.

Charleroi, we discovered, is a good **35 miles south** of Brussels.

And to add insult to distance, the airport doesn't have a train station. At all.

So, feeling only slightly foolish, we opted for a taxi.

We piled into the nearest cab. I remembered Belgium had two main languages, Flemish and French. Flemish, I reasoned, was similar to Dutch, so I thought I'd give it a go.

"Kunt u mij naar de Grote Markt in Brussel brengen, alstublieft?" I asked.

The driver turned, blinked twice, and gave me a shrug that said, *I have absolutely no idea what you're talking about.*

One of Jan's teammates switched to French.
"Pouvez-vous nous emmener au centre de Bruxelles, s'il vous plaît ?"

Another shrug.

Then the driver turned back again and said, in a thick **Brummie** accent:

"Sorry lads, I don't speak Dutch or French - but my English is pretty good!"

There was a brief moment of stunned silence before the taxi erupted into uncontrollable laughter.

"In that case," Jan said, wiping his eyes, "take us as close to the Grand Place as you can."

"No problem, mate," the driver grinned, and off we went.

An hour later, after a tour of half the Belgian road network, we finally rolled into Brussels and met Richard in the Grand Place. It really was spectacular, all gilded façades and cobblestones, the sort of square where you half expect a film crew to step out from behind a pillar.

We did the essentials:

- **Manneken Pis** (much smaller than expected),
- **Royal Palace** (disappointingly drab compared to Buckingham Palace),
- **Heysel Stadium** and the **Atomium**, because apparently you can't bring rugby lads to Brussels without showing them a giant stainless-steel molecule.

And then the sightseeing portion of the weekend came to an abrupt and predictable end.

The rest of the trip dissolved into a golden haze of Belgian beer. Lager, wheat beer, Trappist ale, if it came in a glass and wasn't on fire, we drank it.

One moment stands out. Late one night, on a nearly empty Metro train, someone (possibly me) started singing *Swing Low, Sweet Chariot*.
Within seconds all of us had joined in.

Then we segued into *Jerusalem*, booming it down the carriage like a slightly bedraggled cathedral choir.

Our fellow passengers looked on with a mixture of confusion, pity, and, in one or two cases, amusement. A couple even joined in for the second chorus. As stag-do travel choirs go, we were surprisingly tuneful.

By Sunday night we were running on fumes, caffeine, and the vague memory of solid food. Monday morning hit like a freight train, and I think it's fair to say every single one of us returned to work with a hangover that could have qualified as a medical emergency.

But it was everything a stag weekend should be: chaotic, hilarious, and utterly unforgettable.

A memory held between friends

There are moments that settle in the mind like an old photograph on a mantelpiece, not dramatic, not posed, just quietly present. A small square of time you never intended to frame but somehow did.

The morning before Jan's wedding is one of those for me.

Jan was, in every way that mattered, my brother. We'd been through exams, heartbreaks, hangovers, and the kind of ridiculous student antics that make you wince and grin in equal measure. That morning, in his hotel room, we were easing the nerves with a couple of beers, the two of us half-dressed and surrounded by the calm-before-the-ceremony stillness. Outside, the world was lining up its music, flowers, and formalities.

A soft knock came at the door.

Cathy stepped in.

We'd known her since our university days, mischievous, funny, and brilliant in ways that only become clearer with hindsight. She wasn't the carefree student anymore; she carried herself with a mature confidence now, but the spark in her eyes was unchanged. She perched on the edge of the bed, accepted a beer, and the conversation rolled the way it always had with her: easy, warm, familiar.

Then came a sentence from Jan that shifted the air in the room without fanfare, like a curtain catching a breeze. "Well, Keith and I need to leap in the shower."

Cathy raised an eyebrow, the corner of her mouth lifting. "Room for a little one? Remember the naked conga?" she teased.

And just like that, the moment unfurled, natural, unforced, and oddly gentle.

Within a minute we had all lost our clothes. There are things in life that don't need deep analysis. They simply are.
What happened was not wild or reckless or fuelled by anything other than friendship and affection. No drama. No awkwardness. No ulterior motives. Just three people, linked by

years of trust, finding themselves in a fleeting, human moment, innocent in its way, intimate without being complicated.

It passed almost as quickly as it came.

Laughter, warmth, water, then the quiet shift back into the day ahead.

We dried off, exchanged small smiles, and drifted back into the rhythm of preparation. Cathy sat calmly on the bed, fastening silk and lace with her usual effortless composure.

"Zip me up?" she asked, turning slightly.

I did, leaning forward to kiss the nape of her neck.

"Thank you," I whispered.

She tapped my nose lightly. "I could tell you needed that," she said with a knowing smile.

Jan straightened his collar, caught my eye, and grinned. "Right then, wedding time."

Cathy pinned white carnations to our lapels. Then, with a soft kiss on each of our cheeks and a little wink, she said:
"That was fun, a perfect reminder of old times. But let's keep it ours. No one else needs the details."

And we did. For years.

It became a quiet thread woven into the fabric of our friendship, unspoken, undramatic, held with respect. When Jan died, and later Cathy too, the memory shifted from a mischievous secret to something much more delicate. A pressed flower between pages. A moment to be held gently.

I tell it now for one reason only: because it mattered.

Not as scandal. Not as confession.

Just as truth, one small, human moment in a life made up of many.

Some memories aren't meant for an audience, but they still shape you.

They don't diminish love or loyalty.

They simply sit quietly alongside them.

That morning will always stay with me: the soft laughter, the warmth of old friendship, the sound of running water, and the feeling that sometimes the most meaningful moments are the ones that never make it into the photo album.

When the world changed shape

Although I'd already lost Nan, Auntie Dollie, Aunt Nell, and Uncle Jim, nothing prepared me for the blow that came when Mum died. Losing older relatives is never easy but losing a parent... that's a different kind of grief. It hits somewhere deeper, somewhere you didn't even know existed.

Mum had always been relatively fit, but around August 1989 she started complaining of pain in her back. Tests were done, nothing showed, and our GP gently suggested it was probably "just wear and tear."

By the end of the year, she was noticeably worse. She spent most of her time in bed. That really wasn't like Mum, but she stayed cheerful, and Roger, Dad and I took turns looking after her. Most evenings I'd lie next to her on the bed, the two of us watching television and talking about nothing in particular. Those simple, soft conversations, they stay with you.

Then came January 1990. The diagnosis.

Bone cancer.
Terminal.
No cure.

From that point on, the doctors focused on keeping her comfortable, and the Macmillan nurses visited every day. Every single one of them was extraordinary, kind, patient, calm in a way that made you feel safe even when nothing else did.

By May, Mum had taken a definite turn for the worse. The doctors advised that she be admitted to King Edward VII Hospital in Midhurst. She didn't want to go. She wanted to stay home. Deep down we all knew, and she knew, that once she was admitted, she wouldn't be coming home again.

But she agreed.

At first, strangely, she improved a little, perhaps the constant care, perhaps the medication. I had to travel to Jersey that week to oversee a software installation, so I spoke to her about it.

"Go," she said.

"I'll still be here when you get back."

So, on Monday morning I drove to Heathrow as I'd done so many times, caught my British Airways flight, and got to work.

Each evening, I rang home.

"Mum's fine," Roger or Dad would say.

Until Thursday.

I heard it in Roger's voice before he'd even said the words. "Mum's not so good," he said quietly. "I think you should come back."

I rang British Airways. There was one seat left on the Friday 4 p.m. flight. Expensive. Didn't matter. I booked it instantly. From that moment until I reached the hospital, everything blurred.

When I arrived, Mum had been moved into a side room, never a good sign. Roger, Roy, and Dad were already there. Dad's eyes were red. I'd never seen my father cry. He was from a generation that didn't.

I took Mum's hand. She looked so small, so fragile. Her eyes were closed, drifting in and out of consciousness. Within minutes, her breathing quietened and then stopped. Roy checked for a pulse and called a nurse.

Moments later, a doctor came in, examined her gently, and said the words I'll never forget:
"I'm sorry. She's gone."

We cried quietly. No drama, no big sobs, just that deep, heavy grief that sits in the chest and refuses to move.

We were shown into the relatives' room while the doctor completed the paperwork. I felt hollow. Mum wasn't just my mother; she was my best friend. She always knew what to do. She gave advice freely and loved me unconditionally, whether or not I actually followed it.

After a while, Roy said he'd drive Dad and Roger home.

"You go," I said. "I just need a bit of time. I'll follow later".

And suddenly I was alone. Really alone.

Sad. Angry. Lost. It wasn't fair. None of it was fair.

I kicked out at the coffee table in the middle of the room. It felt strangely good. So, I kicked it again. And again. The wood splintered. The table collapsed.

I took a deep breath, walked out, and found a nurse.

"Who do I speak to if I want to make a donation?" I asked.

"Oh, you don't have to do that," she said kindly.

"I do," I replied. "I've just kicked the living daylights out of your coffee table."

She poked her head around the door and winced sympathetically.
"Oh. I see what you mean."

She disappeared for a moment and returned with a compliments slip, names and phone numbers written on it.

"This one's the donations office," she said, pointing.

"And this one is our emotional support team in case you need someone to talk to. They're here twenty-four hours."

"Thank you," I said.
"And... I'm really sorry about the table."

She gave a soft smile. "Don't worry, love. We've all been there."

I walked out to the car park, got into my car, and drove home. A long, quiet journey into a life that had suddenly changed shape.

A chapter I never chose, but one I had no option except to live through, one day at a time.

Reflection: The Quiet After

Grief has a way of hollowing out the world.

The voices become quieter, the rooms feel bigger, and even the familiar becomes strange. In those first days after Mum died, I found myself moving through life as if it were a corridor full of closed doors, each one marked "before," while I stood firmly in the place called "after."

But loss also sharpens the edges of what matters.

I learned that the world doesn't stop for you, but people do, the nurse with the compliments slip, the friend who checks in, the family who sit with you in silence because words aren't needed.

And somewhere in all of that, in the mess and the ache, you start learning how to live with a different sort of love, one that doesn't vanish, just changes shape.

Eurovision, flat-screen TVs and the road to Harare

Probably the biggest business trip I ever took, and certainly the furthest, was the one to Zimbabwe and South Africa. One of our major clients, Standard Chartered, was opening a new satellite office in Harare, supporting their main hub in Johannesburg.

I was scheduled to spend a few days in each location, smoothing out IT issues, meeting the local teams, and then heading down to Cape Town to explore potential opportunities. Our company was toying with the idea of expanding into Sub-Saharan Africa, and I'd been tasked with a bit of reconnaissance. Essentially: shake some hands, meet some agents, and see whether there was money to be made.

My trip began the usual way: a taxi to Gatwick. The driver was chatty, as they often are, and I found myself explaining that this was my first proper long-haul business trip. UK and European travel had become routine by then, but this felt different, bigger, bolder, and with just the faintest whiff of adventure.

At the Air Zimbabwe desk, I noticed something unusual.

Alongside the normal suitcases and duty-free bags, dozens of passengers, black, white, families, couples, business travellers, were checking in brand-new 24-inch flat-screen TVs in neatly taped cardboard boxes. I later discovered why: Zimbabwe had no domestic supply of TVs at the time. People brought them from the UK, sold them on arrival for a handsome profit, and offset half their airfare in the process.

If only I'd known... I would have squeezed one between my shirts and socks.

It was Eurovision night, and every departure lounge in Gatwick was tuned in. Terry Wogan's commentary drifted through the air like a familiar comfort blanket, interrupted every few minutes by yet another Tannoy announcement. Each interruption was met with a chorus of groans from the travellers.

It was strangely unifying, hundreds of strangers collectively annoyed that they'd missed half a chorus of a slightly off-key Balkan ballad.

Then came the inevitable announcement: **"Flight delayed."**
Two hours.
Not ideal.
It was close to midnight before we finally boarded.

I was meant to be met at Harare Airport by Gavin, one of Standard Chartered's local managers, but with the delay I had no way to tell him. I just hoped he'd be checking the arrivals board.

The plane was half-empty, which made things more bearable. I watched a film, then an episode of *The Brittas Empire*, a surprisingly fitting choice considering I was heading to a country where British cultural remnants still lingered, sometimes charmingly, sometimes absurdly.

Later, I discovered that Zimbabwean TV showed not just *The Brittas Empire*, but also *Dad's Army* every night. I've often wondered whether viewers there genuinely believed that was still the state of the British military.

We landed early the next morning. I followed Gavin's advice from his last email: find a customs official, declare any foreign currency, and insist, politely but firmly, on getting a "B3" form signed and stamped. He'd warned me they might try to wave me through to avoid the paperwork. He was right. The customs officer sighed heavily, counted my dollars twice, and reluctantly stamped the form, as if I'd just ruined his entire week.

Out in arrivals, no Gavin.
I scanned the line of people holding signs. No sign of "Mr Budden."

Eventually I found an airport information desk.
The assistant smiled, reached under the counter, and handed me a handwritten note.
It read:
"Get a taxi to the hotel. Relax today. See you in the morning. Cheers, Gavin."

The taxi rank was a museum of British cars long since extinct back home. My taxi was held together by optimism and rust.

After loading my luggage, the driver shut my door, then padlocked it shut.

Seeing my expression, he said, "Passengers sometimes run away without paying."
"I won't," I replied.
He chuckled. "That's what they all say."

The drive into Harare was surreal, old cars, dusty roads, and wide, sunlit streets. The hotel was an imposing twenty-storey tower. The fare was twenty US dollars. I tipped him five, not sure of the custom.
His face lit up. "Thank you, sir. Very kind."
Clearly, I'd tipped above the local rate.

A porter swept my luggage away as if afraid it might escape. The moment I stepped into the lobby, the cool blast of air-conditioning felt like heaven.

Up in my room on the twelfth floor, I handed the porter another tip and his eyebrows shot up.
"If you like, sir," he said, "I can press your shirts and trousers. No extra charge."
Who was I to argue?

He returned an hour later with my clothes looking like they belonged in a fashion shoot. I don't think I've ever looked that sharp before or since.

Standing by the window, I noticed a strong draught. One of the floor-to-ceiling windows was open by a good twelve inches, held in check only by a small metal safety panel. I closed it most of the way. If I'd had today's balance issues back then, it could very well have been my last view.

Later, I asked a poolside waiter why the TV didn't work.
"It does, sir," he said. "But only from five o'clock to ten. People are at work before then."
Perfect logic, really.

The next morning, Gavin appeared in reception, fresh as a daisy.
"Good flight?" he asked.

I smiled. "Educational," I said.
And so the African chapter began.

Tipping points

If my first night in Harare had been a lesson in polite persistence, padlocked taxis, and tipping mishaps, then the weeks that followed were a masterclass in adaptation. Zimbabwe didn't shout its lessons; it delivered them quietly, almost politely, often when you weren't paying attention. And just like that, you'd realise you'd learned something without ever feeling taught.

On my first full day, Gavin and I visited Standard Chartered's city-centre office, a gleaming, glass-fronted building that wouldn't have looked out of place in Canary Wharf. Inside, we mapped out my itinerary: meetings, site visits, and the wider exploration our company hoped would lead to a move into the Sub-Saharan market.

"Tonight," Gavin announced with a grin, "I'm taking you to the Colonial Club. Tomorrow, we'll get you settled in your new accommodation. Saturday, safari. And next weekend you're coming to Lake Kariba with my family."

It was the kind of schedule you don't argue with. And as it turned out, every moment was unforgettable.

That evening, Gavin collected me from the hotel. As we drove, I asked about tipping etiquette. "Generally, yes," he said. "If someone gives good service, you tip. How much did you give the hotel porter?"

"Five dollars," I said.

"About right," he nodded. "Zim dollars, I assume?"

"US dollars."

He nearly drove off the road laughing. "That explains the perfect ironing! You've just tipped him more than he earns in a day.

Don't worry, I'll get you sorted with some Zim dollars tomorrow."

The Colonial Club was like stepping into an Agatha Christie novel: deep leather armchairs, ceiling fans, immaculate waiters in crisp white jackets. A string quartet played softly in the corner. It quickly became my favourite haunt in Harare, though I didn't notice, or didn't question, the obvious divide at the time: every guest white, every staff member black. Back then it somehow felt "normal." Now, looking back, it's impossible not to see the imbalance staring you in the face.

On the way back, Gavin gave me one final piece of advice: "Never discuss politics in public. Walls have ears."

Sounded melodramatic at the time. It wasn't.

Back in the hotel I flicked through the two available TV channels: one showing The Brittas Empire, the other state news. A report claimed US jets had bombed Rotterdam, footage so obviously fabricated it made Dad's Army look like a modern documentary. I realised most viewers wouldn't know that. Then an uncomfortable thought hit me: how sure was I that *our* news was always accurate? A small seed of doubt, but a healthy one.

The following day Gavin drove me to my new accommodation: a spacious two-bedroom bungalow with polished floors, a veranda, and a separate outbuilding.

"There's your maid's quarters," he said casually. "She and her husband live there. She'll take care of the cleaning and ironing. Don't try to do it yourself, she'll be offended."

"My maid?" I spluttered.

"Welcome to Africa," he said.

Later, I met her, Bernadette, who insisted on "Berni." "This is my husband, Jake, and our son, Bri," she said warmly. "What shall I call you, sir?"

"Keith," I said.

"Kith," she replied. Close enough.

Over the weeks, Berni ran the household with gentle efficiency. Clothes were washed and ironed before I'd even realised they were dirty. Meals appeared as if conjured. And when I eventually left Zimbabwe, I handed her a ten US dollar tip and a bouquet of flowers. She hugged me so tightly I nearly toppled backward.

Then came the safari weekend, dusty tracks, huge skies, and animals I'd only ever seen in David Attenborough documentaries.

Our guide told me he feared rhinos most: "Bad tempers, long legs, and more stamina than a Land Rover," he said. Comforting.

We encountered a baby elephant standing completely alone.

"Where's its mum?" I whispered.
"Close," he replied. "Very close."

I don't think I've ever looked around a clearing so quickly.

Lake Kariba was pure magic, water shimmering like molten silver under the sun, the low hum of cicadas, and the soft crackle of a campfire. One night I spotted two glowing red dots floating across the dark water.

"What's that?" I asked.

"Crocodile," Gavin said cheerfully. "Probably sizing us up."

He burst out laughing. I laughed too, slightly later and slightly less convincingly.

Back in Harare, the streets were full of hawkers selling everything from hats to carved wooden animals. One particularly committed seller followed me for a full fifty yards, shouting prices in pounds, then dollars, then rand, then, in sheer desperation, "Fine, you bloody South Africans, you never buy anything!"

One of the last lessons Zimbabwe taught me came at the airport.

A large American man ahead of me was having a heated exchange with customs.

"Your B3 form?" the officer asked.

"Don't have one."

"Then these nine hundred US dollars are forfeit."

"You can't do that!"

"There's a phone over there if you'd like to call your embassy," the officer said calmly. "Your flight leaves in an hour. And I have your passport."

I clutched my own B3 form like it was Willy Wonka's golden ticket.

Moments later, I was airborne, bound for Johannesburg, wiser, humbler, and carrying a suitcase full of crisply pressed shirts, memories of crocodile eyes on dark water, and a sense that the real adventure was only just beginning.

The trip that changed my compass

The descent into Johannesburg could almost have been the descent into any major European city. No gentle rural sweep like Harare. Instead: motorways, office blocks, endless housing estates, and then, suddenly, the unmistakable patchwork of townships, corrugated iron roofs, dust roads, and clusters of tiny buildings pushed up against the sprawling modern city centre.

It was 1993. Apartheid was being dismantled in real time, Mandela was not yet president, and the country felt like it was standing on a fault line, not quite past its past, not quite ready for its future.

You could feel it in the air.

Customs at Johannesburg International was a masterclass in organised chaos. Lines that snaked, officials who wandered, and a general sense that no one was entirely sure whose turn it was next. Eventually, I made it through and found the shuttle into the city.

Looking out of the window on the ride in, the contrast with Harare was stark. Harare had been calm, measured, almost old-fashioned. Johannesburg buzzed. It was a city in a hurry, brash, bold, and determined to outrun the weight of its own history.

My days there passed without incident, which in those days counted as a win. Standard Chartered's Johannesburg office was modern, slick, and decidedly corporate. The meetings were polite, productive, and, if I'm honest, forgettable.
But on my final morning, something caught my attention.

In the hotel breakfast room, CNN was on the silent screens. The subtitles read:

RIOTING IN CAPE TOWN OVERNIGHT.

I was due to land there in a few hours.

"Crikey," I muttered into my coffee.

The flight to Cape Town was smooth, and the passengers were

invited to look out of the windows as we descended. And then there it was, Table Mountain. Majestic, immovable, impossibly flat on top. A landmark that made you feel exceedingly small, in the best possible way.

But as we dropped lower, I saw the townships again. This time with thin streams of smoke rising lazily into the morning sky. A reminder that beauty and struggle often sit side by side in the same frame.

Cape Town itself felt calmer than the news had suggested, though there was still that faint tension hanging in the background, like a note of static you only notice when the room goes quiet. I attended the networking events, met plenty of people, and confirmed what I'd already begun to suspect: South Africa would be a huge market one day, but not yet. It wasn't ready for what we were offering.

Harare, though? I'd go back there tomorrow.

My time in Cape Town was brief, barely thirty-six hours, before I began the long journey home. In hindsight, I should have booked a direct flight to London, but the itinerary had me returning via Harare to catch an Air Zimbabwe flight to Gatwick.

To my surprise, landing back in Harare felt like returning somewhere familiar. Somewhere that had left its mark on me.

We took off for Gatwick on time, the cabin half-empty again. Hours later, the captain came over the intercom.

"Ladies and gentlemen, there is a major thunderstorm ahead. We will be diverting to avoid it and will refuel in Frankfurt before continuing to Gatwick."

As we approached the storm, I could see it from my window, a colossal cloud mass, flickering constantly like a malfunctioning disco strobe. It was mesmerising and unsettling in equal measure.

The diversion turned out to be a gift. We flew over the Alps as dawn broke, the rising sun painting the snow in shades of pink and gold. Even now, decades later, that view remains one of the most beautiful things I've ever seen.

Landing in Frankfurt brought its own small adventure. Because Air Zimbabwe didn't have a fuel account there, we sat on the tarmac while the crew worked out how to pay. For nearly an hour, jokes rippled through the cabin:

"Anyone got a credit card with a high limit?"
"Maybe we could all chip in?"
"Has the captain tried turning the plane off and on again?"

That peculiar camaraderie that only delayed passengers understand.

Eventually, the fuel truck arrived, breakfast was served, and we were airborne once more.

We landed at Gatwick three hours late. I collected my luggage, stepped into the cool English air, and felt that blend of relief at being home and a strange nostalgia for the red dust, warm air, and unexpected lessons I'd left behind.

Africa, I realised, teaches you quietly. And rarely in the way you expect.

The interview that ran for 3 hours

One quiet Saturday morning, while doing what everyone used to do before the internet swallowed our attention spans, flicking through the local paper, an advert jumped out at me.

A systems installer wanted.
Based in Alton.
Nothing flashy, nothing mysterious.

But: **salary 20% higher** than I was on, **plus a company car**. That last part alone was enough to make me sit up straighter. After all, any job that saved me from nursing temperamental second-hand motors was immediately worth a closer look.

The company was in the electronic document management space, which, at the time, felt nicely futuristic without being too sci-fi. I liked the sound of it. So, I dusted off my CV, gave it the full Mr Sheen treatment, and sent it off.

A few days later, I found myself in their office, an old, converted mill building in Alton. It had that unmistakable "Barnardos charity shop meets tasteful heritage restoration" charm. Wooden beams, exposed brickwork, and a mild but persistent scent of old paper. I liked it immediately.

Hugh, the Managing Director, conducted the interview. He was one of those people who seemed cut from solid oak: calm, steady, and entirely unflappable. He explained the company, HRH Business Technology, nothing whatsoever to do with the Royal Family, consisted of four divisions: their payroll bureau (Hugh's personal kingdom), systems management, training, and the electronic document management arm led by one of his directors, Colin.

The interview was surprisingly relaxed, more like two people sounding each other out across a pub table than your standard corporate grilling. At the end, Hugh said I'd be invited back for a second interview, this time with Colin, and if that went well, the job was mine.

A couple of weeks later, I was back.

Colin turned out to be sharp, charismatic, and immediately engaging. What was meant to be a routine follow-up turned into a three-hour conversation that meandered through technology, business, psychology, the future, the past, and the state of the nation, which we fixed at least twice before lunch.

Eventually, he leaned back, smiled, and said, "Well, Keith... I'd like to offer you the job."

My acceptance was instant. No drama. No pretending I needed time to "think it over." I wanted the role, I liked the people, and crucially, I liked the trajectory it hinted at.

And so began my time with HRH Business Technology.

A funny anecdote about Colin, he once told me on a long car journey together. His dad was also called Colin. They had been living in Devon at the time, and one weekend they got into difficulties on their boat and ended up being safely rescued by the RNLI. It certainly proved why you shouldn't give your child your Christian name.

Their local paper printed a photo of the duo, safely back on shore. The caption underneath said the photo shows Colin and his son, Ditto.

(And as for the connection with the royals?
That comes later - and it's worth the wait.)

The foot under the table

Hants One Voluntary Aid Detachment of the British Red Cross Society had been around so long it practically had its own ancestry. Formed shortly after the 1909 regulations, it pulled its volunteers from Winchester, Southampton, and the surrounding villages, nurses, teachers, and sensible women who knew how to keep a cool head and a clean bandage. They trained hard, drilled regularly, and when the call came in 1914, they stepped forward without hesitation.

They worked in military hospitals across Hampshire, tended the wounded in converted manor houses and school halls, and some even went out to France, Malta, and Salonika. When the Second World War rolled round, Hants One stepped up again. That was the kind of organisation it was, steady, dependable, stitched into the fabric of its community.

By the time I came along, the war years were long behind us and the Detachment had evolved into something more everyday but no less important: teaching First Aid, tending sprained ankles at village fetes, keeping an eye on rugby matches, and covering the big annual events like the Farnborough Air Show and the Ken Hall Trophy motocross scramble at Langrish.

Roger had joined first. He always had one foot in community service, and the Detachment suited him perfectly. He qualified as a First Aid instructor, rose through the ranks, and eventually became Quartermaster, guardian of all supplies, equipment, and bandages that had lost their will to stick. He took it seriously. Very seriously.

Watching him, I didn't need much persuading. I joined the moment I turned fourteen, the youngest you were allowed. Every Monday night from 7 to 9 we'd meet at the Red Cross Centre on the corner of Readon Close and Love Lane, a building with more stories in its walls than there were plasters in the cupboard.

The ambulance was kept next door in the County Council's landscaping depot, tucked in among lawnmowers and sacks of soil improver. It all felt wonderfully official to a teenage lad. The Detachment was eventually disbanded in the late '90s when the national Red Cross shifted focus to broader humanitarian work. The Centre itself has long since vanished too. A shame. It had been a second home to so many for so long.

Once I was trained and certified, I started joining the duty teams at events. Motocross meets, summer fêtes, school displays, you name it, we covered it. But the crown jewel was always the Farnborough Air Show. We did all five trade days as well as the public ones. It didn't take me long to discover that the freebies handed out on trade days were far superior to anything the general public ever saw. If you wanted a novelty pen shaped like a Harrier jump jet, that was the time to collect one.

After the Shoreham disaster, the Air Show changed dramatically and eventually became trade-only. Times change, and sometimes the fun gets trimmed with them.

We were a good team.

Dave, our Commandant, was a full-time paramedic and an endlessly calm presence. His wife, Diana, cheerful, efficient, blonde curls bouncing with every laugh. Frank (our Deputy Commandant) and Chris both worked at the Post Office. Bob worked in aerospace. Bill, who Dad had known for years, was at British Rail. Heather was a Girl Guide Commissioner, Lesley's husband was a Royal Navy Commander, and Shirley... well, Shirley had been there since the dawn of recorded time.

And then there was Debbie, my age, brown bobbed hair, warm smile, mischievous glint. We got on well. Very well, as it turned out.

A couple of times a year we'd go to County HQ in Weeke, near Winchester. Elizabeth Balfour ran the place, elegant, sharp, with a memory that could shame a computer. Whether you were a new recruit or had medals older than the chairs, she greeted you as if you personally kept the whole Red Cross afloat.

And then there was the annual Christmas do, sometimes a disco at the Centre, sometimes a pub meal. The tradition, without fail, was Roger's song. Every year he rewrote the lyrics to a popular tune, wove all our names into it, and sang it with a sincerity far greater than his ability to hold a note. Dogs howled. Cats made for the door. We loved it.

One particular Christmas stands out. Roy and I were running our own disco at the time, so we provided the music. The mood was high, the dance floor full.

And Debbie... well.

She turned up in a white blouse and skirt. Harmless enough. But we had a mauve/ultraviolet lamp, the sort that makes white clothes glow and, apparently, turns certain fabrics transparent. Mid-dance, everyone dropped into a crouching frog move (don't ask - it made sense at the time). Debbie caught my eye, smiled, winked... and crouched.

Her blouse, skirt, and underwear lit up like an X-ray.

I was seventeen. You can imagine the effect.

Life carried on after that, as it does. I went to university, drifted away from the Detachment, and years passed before Roger persuaded me to attend their annual dinner as a returning guest.

It was lovely, familiar faces, warm nostalgia, a lovely chance to dip briefly back into a younger version of myself.

Midway through the meal, I felt something tap my ankle.
Then stroke.

Then rest firmly against thigh. Then stroke.

Then a little higher. Then stroke.

A foot. Definitely a stockinged woman's foot.

Now, given her previous... illuminated performance... Debbie was my prime suspect. But Ruth, Stuart's sister (both were sitting opposite me), was a possibility. She wasn't a member, but she had a friendly sparkle about her.

Before I could politely, or impolitely, investigate further, the meal ended, and Roger announced we had to head off. He was on an early shift the next day.

I was left wondering who the mysterious foot belonged to.
But, as you'll see in the next chapter, I didn't have to wonder for long.

Closed for lunch: a turning point

By the Thursday after the Red Cross dinner, life felt like it was finally lining up in my favour. I was starting my new job with HRH in just over a week, I'd been fiercely productive all morning, and, most impressively, I'd participated in zero procrastination activities by lunchtime.

Unfortunately, the downside of productivity is forgetting to eat.

At 2:15pm my stomach staged a small rebellion.

Asda? Absolutely not. Not three weeks before Christmas.
KFC? Already ticked that box earlier in the week.
Chip shop? Closed. Their fryer was probably still cooling.
Fridge? A barren wasteland echoing with disappointment.
Then inspiration struck like a beacon from the culinary heavens:
Spud-U-Like. Aldershot. A jacket potato with cheese. Job done.

So off I went.

I wandered into the shop, already picturing that glorious mound of cheese, and walked straight into a happily familiar face.

Behind the counter, tall, slim, blonde hair tied back neatly... Ruth turned around.

"You took your time," she said, smiling like someone who knew *exactly* what she'd done at the Red Cross dinner, and who'd done it on purpose.

And suddenly, just like that, the mysterious Red Cross footsie incident had a protagonist.

"Er... hello," I said brilliantly, the very picture of suave sophistication.
"What can I get you?"
"Jacket potato. Cheese. Please."
"Coming right up."

As she prepared it, she glanced over her shoulder.
"Haven't seen you in here before."
"I don't usually come in," I said. "But I might start now."
She smirked and handed over the tray.

When I reached for my wallet, she stopped me.
"On the house."

And then came *The Line*. The one that shifted the axis of the afternoon, and, if I'm honest, the trajectory of the next couple of years.

"How long have you got for lunch?"
"About forty minutes," I said, trying not to sound heroic.
"Good. When you're finished, come out the back with me."

Now, you try eating a hot jacket potato with dignity when you know you've been summoned to a back-alley rendezvous behind a potato shop. I did my best.

When the last customer left, Ruth flicked the sign to **Closed**, locked the front door, took my arm, and whispered:
"Follow me."

We slipped through the prep area, out the fire door, and the moment it clicked shut behind us she turned, smiled... and kissed me.

Not a polite peck.
Not a maybe-someday kiss.
This was a full-on cinematic, *oh-so-that's-where-we-stand-now* kiss.

And right there, behind a potato counter, I had the single clearest thought of my life:
I'm very much looking forward to getting to know you better.

🥔 A Proper Romance (with Comedy Along for the Ride)

Over the next two months, we were inseparable. We graduated to proper dates, restaurants, cinemas, bistros, and then discovered the late-night coffee bar in Chelsea. That became *our place*.

Every Friday:
work → home → change → pick up Ruth → Chelsea → bistro → West End → coffee until midnight.

Then Saturdays.
Then occasionally Sundays.
Then it just became a thing.
A good thing.

And then came *The Night of the Broken Car*.

We'd eaten at a nice bistro in Chelsea. On the way back to the car I spotted a small patch of something suspicious underneath. Oil? Coolant?

A mild sign from the universe to behave?

Who knew?

"I'll get it looked at on Monday," I said.

We got in. The engine started smoothly. Crisis averted.
We drove toward Covent Garden for the theatre.
Almost made it.
Almost.

The engine shuddered like it had been shot and died in the middle of London. I coasted us to the kerb.

"Looks like we might miss the show."
Ruth sighed but stayed serene.

I, on the other hand, was brick-through-a-window levels of frantic.

I called the AA.

"If you've had a coolant leak," the operator said, "you'll need towing. But… it's Saturday evening in central London. Could be a couple of hours."
And then I had a stroke of genius the AA operator still probably talks about.

"Could the tow truck… pick us up at eleven fifteen? We've got theatre tickets."

There was a pause.
"...We can do that."

So, we walked to the Palladium, saw a brilliant show we now absolutely cannot remember, and stepped out onto the pavement at exactly 11:15pm...
...just in time for our tow truck to pull up.

Lights flashing like the world's least glamorous chauffeur service.

We climbed into the cab, laughing like teenagers, and as we rattled home down the A3 I thought:
Sometimes fortune favours the bold.
Sometimes the cheeky.
And sometimes, if you're really lucky, it favours the ones sitting next to the right person.

Twin rooms and turning points

Ruth had decided it was time for us to have our first proper weekend away.

Not a day trip.

Not a late-night coffee in Chelsea.

A *whole night* somewhere far enough away to feel exotic and exciting, but not so far we'd need passports or survival rations.

"Where should we go?" she asked.

I thought for a moment, adopting the expression of a man about to say something wise.

"Harrogate," I pronounced.

Ruth blinked. "Harrogate?"

"Yes," I said, warming to my theme. "It's in North Yorkshire, which is practically foreign. And I know all the good spots."

She grinned. "Alright then. Harrogate it is."

And just like that, our first romantic pilgrimage was set.

The Hotel and the Delicate Question of Bedroom Logistics

I rang the Grants Hotel, my old haunt from my Digital Dynamics days.

"Hello, Keith!" the receptionist said, as if we were lifelong friends and she'd been waiting by the phone since my last visit. "Haven't seen you in ages. How's the new job?"

I gave her the abridged version, then added, "Actually, I'm calling because I'm bringing my new girlfriend for the weekend."

"Aww, wonderful!" she said. "Would you like a double room or a twin?"

Ah. The moment.

Ruth and I were very much *romantic*, but as yet not *romantic-overnight-arrangements romantic*.

I didn't want to assume anything. I especially didn't want to appear as though I had purchased champagne, satin sheets, and a neon sign reading *Tonight's the Night*.

"A... twin," I said. Sensible. Respectful. Entirely lacking in swagger.

No problem, she booked it and promised to put wine and flowers in the room "because you're one of our favourite regulars."

I liked Grants Hotel.

Harrogate: A Grand Tour (Led by a Man Who Definitely Belonged There)

Saturday morning, I arrived at Ruth's flat at 6:15 a.m.

She was already at the gate, bag in hand, practically glowing. The drive was long, full of chatter, laughter, and occasional sing-alongs that would have made Gyrating Jeff proud.

We reached Harrogate around 11:30, checked in, admired the wine and flowers (thank you, Grants Hotel), and set off on my "Grand Tour" of the town, a tour I delivered with the confidence of someone who had personally founded Harrogate in 1771.

"This is Betty's," I said proudly.

"This is the restaurant where I once saw a man sweat so much during a spicy meal that I wondered if he was melting."

Ruth lapped it up, linking her arm through mine.

Betty's Tea Room and the Italian Job

The queue for Betty's was out the door, but we waited. You don't take someone to Harrogate and *not* go to Betty's.

Ruth loved it, the tea, the scones, the feeling of being somewhere proper and civilised.

Later, at the hotel, we collapsed on the bed (separate beds, remember) and watched a bit of TV until it was time for dinner.

"Where are we eating?" Ruth asked.

"Pinocchio's," I said immediately. "Best Italian in Harrogate."

We dressed, walked up the hill… and found it packed.

A waiter appeared.

"No table for at least an hour," he said regretfully.

Before I could apologise to Ruth for my utter lack of foresight, the manager, Jose, spotted me.

He gasped dramatically.
"MR KEITH!"

He rushed over, kissed Ruth's hand like she was Italian royalty, and said, "No booking? No problem. For you, always a table."

He marched straight to a table where a couple had just sat down, jackets still on, menus barely opened.

"So sorry," he said firmly. "This table is reserved for Mr Keith." He gestured at us.

They moved without fuss, though the lady's expression suggested we were both lucky her cutlery hadn't become a projectile.

Ruth stared at me.

"Do you realise," she whispered, "I'm dating a celebrity in Harrogate?"

"Yes," I said modestly. "It's my natural charisma."

Merlot, Moonlight, and One Very Significant Shirt
Dinner was perfect, pasta, wine, laughter, the works.

We strolled back to the hotel hand in hand, caught between romance and a food coma. Occasionally stopping for a kiss, just because we could.

Ruth squeezed my hand.

"Thank you for booking a twin room," she said gently. "I'm ready to sleep in the same room... but not quite ready to sleep with you. Soon though. I promise."

I nodded, genuinely touched.

It felt honest. Respectful. Right.

We each sat on our beds.

I headed to the bathroom in my boxer shorts for a quick shower.

When I came back out, towel-drying my hair, Ruth was lying on *her* bed wearing nothing but *my shirt*.

She looked up and smiled.

"I hope you don't mind. It smells of you."

Mind? I was trying not to trip over my own eyebrows.

If I'd been any happier, I would've floated.

We turned out the lights.

Ten seconds later, she was asleep.

I lay there, heart full, thinking:
Life is perfect.

The Morning After (In the Best Possible Way)
Breakfast was lovely.

We walked through Harrogate's formal gardens, I showed her the Majestic, the conference centre, even the old Welcom office.

Then we drove home, content and gently tired.

When I dropped her at her flat, she gave me a slow smile.

"That was perfect," she said. "Let's do Paris next."

And with those five little words, I knew:
This wasn't just a romance.
This was the start of something real.

Three capitals, one love story

It was the May Bank Holiday weekend, and Ruth declared it was high time we had "a proper adventure."

Planning, in our relationship, was always a philosophical exercise rather than a practical one. Our preparations for a three-country road trip went like this:

1. **Check the company car was insured for Europe.**
2. **Book a ferry from Dover to Calais.**
3. **Assume the rest would sort itself out through optimism and hope.**

And that was the entire strategy.

So, at some ungodly hour on Saturday morning, we threw bags into the boot, high-fived the spirit of spontaneity, and set off.

The drive to Dover was smooth, the ferry crossing even smoother, and before we knew it, we'd rolled off the ramp into France, that magical moment where, purely because the road signs look different, you suddenly feel exotic.

Paris became our first target, largely because it was the only place we'd actually mentioned aloud.

Paris: The City of Love... and Absolutely No Available Hotel Rooms
By the time we reached Paris, we realised a tiny oversight.

We hadn't booked anywhere to stay.

Ruth marched in and out of hotel lobbies like a determined estate agent doing viewings. Each time she returned, she shook her head:
"Complet. Complet. Complet."

Finally, on the fourth attempt, she came running out with the energy of a Lotto winner.
"They've got a room!" she beamed.
"It's in the basement... but it's clean!"

When someone says, "basement room," you imagine a dungeon.

In truth, it was... well, still a dungeon, but a clean one. There was a bed, a kettle, and a TV attached to a table that wobbled every time you breathed near it.

Still, it was *our* dungeon.

I eyed the bed, a double.

Ruth caught my expression and smiled gently.

"It's OK," she said. "I want this. I want you."
Reader: I nearly melted through the parquet flooring.

We explored Paris hand-in-hand, ate a beautiful dinner, skipped the Louvre because even love has limits when faced with that queue, and on the way back Ruth bought a bottle of champagne.
"For later," she said with a grin that could power the Eiffel Tower.

That night was... well, magical. Passionate. A turning point. The kind of night that makes you think, *Ah. This is what all those songs are about.*

Brussels: Mussels, Romance, and Ruth's Sudden Inspiration

Over breakfast the next morning, I asked, "What do you fancy doing today?"

Ruth thought for half a second.

"Let's go to Brussels."

Of course. Why not?
Who needs a plan when you have enthusiasm?

I pulled out my AA European Road Atlas, which by modern standards is the equivalent of navigating Europe with a treasure map drawn in crayons.

"It's doable," I said.
And that was that.

We drove to Brussels, strolled through the Grand Place, found delicious mussels, and even managed to look cultured for a couple of hours.

Then, as we stood admiring the views, Ruth turned to me with the same look she'd used when she bought the champagne.

"Let's go to Amsterdam."

I laughed. "You're mad."

She shrugged adorably. "Three European capitals in one weekend, that's romantic."

I kissed her forehead. "You win."

Amsterdam: The Scenic Route (All 490 of Them)
We reached Amsterdam at dusk, checked into a surprisingly delightful hotel, dumped our bags, and decided to head out for dinner.

This, and I say this with love, was the moment I made the stupidest decision of the entire trip:
I decided to take the car.

If you've never driven in Amsterdam at night, imagine navigating Venice... but with road markings and 200% more cyclists glaring at you.

Ruth dashed into a charming little restaurant to check for a table.

She returned triumphantly.
"They can fit us in! Five minutes. Park the car and meet me inside."

Easy, right?
Ha.
Ten minutes later:
I was lost.
Twenty minutes later:
I was *really* lost.
Thirty minutes later:
I had achieved a level of lostness normally reserved for biblical characters wandering the desert.

Every single bridge looked identical.
Every canal looked like the one I'd just driven past.
Every cyclist looked like they were judging me personally.

Eventually I sighed, turned off the radio for dramatic effect, and prepared to accept that my relationship, and possibly my life, was over.

And then I heard it.
"**KEITH!!!**"

I slammed the brakes so hard the hazard lights nearly came on by themselves.

In my rear-view mirror, I saw Ruth sprinting towards the car like a blonde streak of salvation, arms waving, laughter streaming behind her.

She flung open the door.
"I thought you'd abandoned me!"
"Never," I said. "I was... doing reconnaissance."

She laughed so hard she nearly slid off the seat.

"Let's go back to the hotel," she said. "Before Amsterdam actually kills us."

I didn't argue.

Dinner at the hotel was simple, warm, and perfect.
We fell asleep curled up, equal parts exhausted and utterly content.

Heading Home - And the Twist in the Queue
We were up early the next morning and drove back toward Calais. The return ferry queue was long, but we didn't mind.

Ruth took my hand, squeezed it gently, and said:
"I've decided... I'm going to move in with you."
Just like that.

No fanfare.
No hesitation.
Just certainty.

Three capitals in one weekend.
One great love unfolding.

And one utterly ridiculous misadventure in Amsterdam I will never, ever live down.

But looking back...
I wouldn't change a single wrong turn.
Not even the 400 incorrect ones.

The M3 Changing Room: A love story (with tights)

By the time Ruth and I had been living together a couple of months, life had settled into that comfortable, domestic rhythm where you know exactly whose turn it is to make the tea, exactly which side of the bed they prefer, and exactly how many seconds of eye contact will tell you whether they want a cuddle or a biscuit.

Every morning if I was working in the office, I'd drive her to Spud-u-Like in Aldershot, drop her off in her green apron, then head to the HRH office in Alton. But as charming as the world of jacket potatoes is, Ruth was starting to get restless.

"Too predictable," she said. "I want something more exciting."

Given her love of mischief, drama, and occasional theatrical eyebrow raises, it was no surprise that the job advert she fell in love with was:
STORE DETECTIVE - WOKING.

Yes.

My sweet, funny, gentle Ruth had decided she wanted to fight crime between the lingerie aisle and the frozen peas.

She filled in the application form, sent her CV, and a few days later rang me at work.

"Hi, darling. Any chance you could sneak off early this afternoon?"

"Why?" I asked, fully prepared for an answer involving coffee, shopping, or a sudden emergency involving a cat stuck in a tree.

"They've called. They want to interview me for the detective job. At four."

She paused dramatically.
"My car's at home. If I wait until three to finish here, I'll never make it."
"What do you need me to do?" I asked, already knowing the answer would involve some sort of mild chaos.

"Could you go to the flat, grab my interview outfit, the cream chemise you like, my white blouse, grey skirt, and a pair of tights, not the thick woolly ones, and meet me out back? I'll just... get changed in the car."

I laughed. Of course she would.

Ruth could probably perform a full costume change during a parachute jump and still come out looking immaculate.

I checked with my boss, Colin, who waved me off like a benevolent uncle.

So, Operation Fetch-The-Outfit commenced.

The Wardrobe Expedition
I arrived home, opened the wardrobe, and immediately forgot every item Ruth had listed.

"Cream chemise... white blouse... grey skirt... wait, which grey skirt? The dark one that looked black? The short one? The long one? The one that has a belt? Why does she own so many grey skirts?!"

I grabbed two. And two pairs of tights. And the deodorant. And the lipstick.

And possibly a packet of mints because you never know.

I crammed it all into a holdall and raced to Aldershot.

At 3:10, Ruth appeared at the back entrance of Spud-u-Like, apron off, hair neat, excitement glowing off her like a furnace.

"You remembered everything?" she asked.

"I think so," I said, which was technically a lie but delivered with confidence.

The M3: Britain's Most Inappropriate Boudoir

We hit the motorway.
After a while, Ruth checked the clock.

"Right," she sighed. "I'd better get changed."

She unzipped the holdall and glanced inside.

"You got my deodorant! And my lipstick!" she said, beaming. "Brownie points for you."

Then the changing began.

And let me tell you: the interior of a moving car is *not* designed for a full wardrobe transformation.

But Ruth?

Ruth transformed it into a backstage dressing room at the Royal Opera House.

Off came her socks.
Off came her green Spud-u-Like trousers.
Underneath? My favourite blue satin knickers, which were frankly a hazard to road safety.

"Eyes on the road!" she laughed.

"I'm trying," I protested. "But you're practically a one-woman cabaret."

On went the tights, in one fluid, balletic movement that defied gravity, physics, and modesty.

Off came her blouse.

On went the cream chemise.
Then the white blouse.
Then the black skirt.

"Where's the grey one?" she asked, narrowing her eyes.

"Ah," I said bravely. "About that…"
"Typical," she muttered, but with a grin.

Then she frowned at her reflection.
"This bra is all wrong."

Before I could reply, she performed The Move.

Every woman knows it. Men talk about it with reverence.

The unhook-bra-through-the-sleeve technique.

I swear I saw a faint puff of smoke from the frictions of the universe recalibrating itself.

"That's better," she said, smoothing her blouse. "Almost there."

"Good," I said. "Because we're here."

The Detective Is Hired
She dabbed her lipstick, fluffed her hair, turned to me, and asked:
"How do I look?"

"Like a detective who's about to solve all the crimes in Surrey."

She kissed me, hopped out of the car, and strode towards the building with absolute confidence.

Almost an hour later, she came back, practically glowing.

"Well?" I asked.
"I start in four weeks!" she squealed, throwing her arms around me.

We celebrated with a bottle of wine on the way home.
And as I watched her grin and chatter away, I realised:
Not many men can say they've helped their girlfriend become a store detective by providing a high-speed mobile dressing room on the M3.

Frankly, I deserved a medal.

The Liverpool Weekend

It was supposed to be a simple, sensible, grown-up weekend.

A practical road trip.

A responsible expedition.

Translation: *we were doomed from the start.*

James was moving from his flat in Liverpool down to Alton, and I'd volunteered to drive up on Friday, pack across the weekend, and head back Sunday with two cars and absolutely no drama whatsoever.

Which, obviously, is when HRH intervened.

Because at HRH, even "helping a mate move house" somehow becomes "a travelling circus with more subplots than an EastEnders Christmas special."

By Friday lunchtime, our two-man mission had evolved into a four-person misadventure.

Clayre and Justine decided Liverpool sounded far more interesting than whatever they'd planned originally (likely laundry and mild resentment).

"Fine," James said, shrugging. "But don't complain if you're squashed between boxes all the way home."

Clayre just grinned. "Depends on what I'm squashed against."

Always a good omen.

☘ The Drive North - Three Teammates, One Chauffeur
After work I collected Clayre, then Justine. They slid into the back seat like two schoolgirls on a field trip, immediately whispering, giggling, and plotting something almost certainly ill-advised.

We hit the motorway.

Music on.

Takeaway coffee fumes filling the car.
A gentle hum of tyre noise and questionable conversation.

Somewhere near Birmingham, the giggles escalated into full-blown hysteria.

"What are you two scheming back there?" I asked.

Clayre spoke up cheerfully, too cheerfully.

"I told Justine I'm going to get James into my bed this weekend."

"I thought you only had eyes for me," I said.

"My eyes, yes," Clayre replied. "But my fanny wants James."

Justine choked on her latte.

I nearly drove into the central reservation.

By the time we reached the M62, morale was dangerously high.

Arrival at Albert Dock
We rolled into Liverpool late that night.

Albert Dock glowed beautifully in the dark, historic brickwork, iron columns, reflections on the water... very atmospheric, very stylish...
...and entirely wasted on the four of us, who mainly wanted dinner and a loo.

James's building was a converted warehouse, exposed brick, industrial lighting, tall windows overlooking the dock.

Imagine *Not Going Out* meets *Dragon's Den* and you're close.

Sleeping arrangements were sorted diplomatically:
- **Girls** in the spare room.
- **James** in his room.
- **Me** on the sofa, which was wide, comfy, and blessedly free of romantic complications.

We ate James's surprisingly good dinner, opened a bottle (or two) of wine, stuck something on TV, and relaxed into the evening.

For a "practical" weekend, things were going suspiciously well.

⭐ The Morning... and a Brief Episode of Nudity

I woke to the sound of James clattering about the kitchen.

"Coffee's on," he said.

"Good night?" I asked.
"Not bad," he grinned, which, with James, could mean anything from "slept well" to "discovered a new religion."

He asked if I'd go wake the girls.

In my boxers, naturally.
When has that ever-caused trouble?

I knocked.
"Come in!"

Clayre was in a silk dressing gown tied more in hope than security.

Justine was fully dressed and looking like she'd been up since dawn doing Pilates.

"Breakfast is ready," I said.

Clayre yawned, stretched, and very nearly breached broadcasting regulations.

We sat down together.

I was still in my T-shirt and boxers.
Classy.

After breakfast I stood and said, "I'm grabbing a shower."
"Don't use all the hot water," Clayre said. "I'm after you."

Ten minutes later I stepped into the hall wearing nothing but a towel.
Clayre was scrolling through her phone.
She looked up.
Gave me a wicked little grin.
"Go on then... give us a flash."
"I will if you will," I said automatically proving men lose 80% of their IQ when addressed by a woman in silk.

And with that, I dropped the towel.

Clayre froze for half a beat, assessing the situation, then let her dressing gown fall open and slip to the floor like a dramatic stage exit.

We stood there for a moment, naked, amused, and slightly impressed with ourselves, two perfectly sensible adults having an entirely irresponsible moment.

Pointing, well I guess you know where, Clayre giggled, "He's waving at me".

Then she turned away, retrieved her towel, and said:
"Right. Shower time. And… shhh."
That conspiratorial "shhh" sealed it.

A shared secret.
A mischief pact.
A "yes, this happened, now let's pretend we're grown-ups again."

⭐ The Big Night Out
While James and I packed boxes all afternoon, the girls went exploring. They returned with shopping bags, stories, and, in Justine's case, a fridge magnet shaped like a guitar.

That night we hit the town:
James's local, then The Cavern Club.

We danced, we sang, we attempted harmonies we had no business attempting.

By midnight, we were gloriously dishevelled and ready for bed.

Then we reached Albert Dock's main gate.
Locked.
Empty.
Guardhouse deserted.

"Fantastic," James groaned. "My access card's in the flat."

"There's a gap underneath," Justine said. "We can crawl through."
James went first.

Then each of us in turn, wriggling like commando trainees who'd taken a wrong turn at Boot Camp.

By the time we emerged on the other side, we were dusty, breathless, and laughing like idiots.

It was *exactly* the kind of thing friends remember forever.

Final Secrets and One Last Cuddle

Back at the flat, we poured a final drink.

Clayre slipped into James's room behind him, turning to give us a wink as she closed the door.

Justine looked at me and said gently,
"You can share my bed if you want. No funny business, just a cuddle."

I smiled.
And we did exactly that: a warm, simple, friendly cuddle.

Sometimes that's all you need at the end of a perfect, chaotic day.

The Final Punchline

Next morning we loaded the last boxes and drove to the gatehouse to return James's pass.

The guard grinned.
"Thanks for the entertainment last night."
James frowned. "What entertainment?"

"Oh, we were watching from the south gatehouse," he said cheerfully.

"You four crawling under that barrier... honestly, you looked like contestants on *It's a Knockout*.

If you'd buzzed the intercom, we'd have just let you in."

Silence.
Processing.
Realisation.
And then we absolutely *howled*.

It was the perfect end to a weekend that had veered off schedule in all the best possible ways:
chaos, friendship, flirtation, farce, and more laughter than lifting boxes.

Exactly how HRH weekends tended to go.

The one where I bail out Jan at 3am (because that's how we roll)

You'd think that by this point in my life, I would have learned that friendship, real, proper, you-might-need-a-spare-kidney-one-day friendship, does not keep sensible hours.

But no.

At three o'clock in the morning, just as I was entering that delightful phase of sleep where your brain plays avant-garde jazz, the phone rang.

Ruth answered it, because apparently, she has quicker reflexes when it comes to ringing phones and impending doom.

A moment later she jabbed me in the ribs with all the subtlety of a trained assassin.

"Ow! What was that for?"

"It's Wood Green police station," she said. "They want you."

Nothing wakes you up faster than that sentence.

Not coffee.
Not a fire alarm.
Not even stepping barefoot on a LEGO.

I grabbed the phone.

"Mr Budden?" an officer said in that polite-but-firm tone police reserve for late-night stupidity.

"We've been given your number by a Mr Jan-"

"Yes," I sighed. "Is he alright?"

"Oh, he's fine," the officer replied cheerfully, always a bad sign, "just a little... merry."

Merry.

The universal code for *absolutely plastered.*

"He's in custody for the night," the officer continued. "We need someone to stand bail until his magistrate hearing."

Marvellous.
My best friend: a one-man crime wave powered by lager and poor decisions.

"How soon can you get here?"
"I'll leave now," I said. "Should be there in two hours."

"No rush," the officer said brightly. "He's certainly not going anywhere."

⚜ The Hero's Journey (Featuring: My Car and Several Motorway Lorries)
Ten minutes later I was dressed, slightly awake, and explaining the situation to Ruth.

"So, he's in trouble and I have to go to North London."
"At three in the morning?" she said, blinking.

"Well, apparently crime waits for no man, so neither can I."

I grabbed a coffee for survival purposes and set off along the M3, accompanied only by lorries, road signs, and the creeping suspicion that my life choices needed reviewing.

By 5 a.m., I reached Wood Green.

Having lived nearby as a student, I navigated the area like a nostalgic ghost.

Inside the station, a tired-looking constable appeared behind the desk.

"I'm here for Jan," I said, with the weariness of a man who has said this sort of thing before.
"Ah yes," he replied, perking up. "He's sleeping it off in one of our cells."
Sleeping it off.
Of course he was.

I filled in the paperwork, confessed that I'd never bailed anyone out before, and was reassured:

"No charge, just make sure he turns up to court. Otherwise, we'll come looking for you."

Great.
A double-or-nothing situation.

Enter Jan: The Man, The Myth, The Bollard Enthusiast
A few minutes later, a door buzzed open.

Out stumbled Jan.
Bruised, dishevelled, smelling faintly of beer, public toilets, and regret, but grinning like a schoolboy caught climbing the gym roof.
We exchanged our usual man-hug: the kind where you slap each other on the back as if trying to burp a baby.

"So," I said as we shuffled toward the car, "what on earth happened?"

And thus began the saga.

It had started innocently enough: a reunion with his old rugby mates.
Pints, laughter, nostalgia.
Then, inevitably, chaos.

After leaving the pub crawl, Jan popped into a public loo on Tottenham High Road… and emerged to discover he had absolutely no idea where he was or where everyone else had gone.

He began walking.
And walking.

Until he reached the A10 dual carriageway.

Where he apparently decided, in that special drunken logic, to *sit down for a rest on a traffic bollard.*

A passing police car saw a lone man perched on a bollard in the middle of the A10 at 1 a.m. and, reasonably, assumed something was amiss.

One officer approached.
"Sir, are you alright?"

And Jan, bless him, responded with a few colourful expressions that did not appear in the police handbook under "cooperative behaviour."

Seconds later, he was under arrest for being drunk and disorderly, plus "assaulting an officer," which apparently referred to Jan flinging his arm out in an attempt to steady himself and accidentally making contact.

"Look on the bright side," he said as I stared at him. "you rescued me. And it could've been worse."

"Worse? How exactly?"

"Well," he said, sheepish, "when I went into the loo… I couldn't figure out the lock. So, I just kicked the door through."

"Probably leave that out of your court testimony," I suggested.

"Fair point," he nodded.

✦ Back Home, the Aftermath, and a Sandwich
We got back just as Ruth was leaving for work.

"What happened to him?" she asked, eyeing Jan like a fragile archaeological discovery.

"I'll explain later," I said, kissing her goodbye.

Jan collapsed on the sofa and immediately fell into the sleep of the righteously exhausted drunken idiot.

I worked from home that day, partly because Jan required occasional monitoring, and partly because I felt if left unattended, he might try to make toast and set fire to something.

By mid-afternoon, he emerged from his slumber, human-shaped again.
"Do you mind if I grab a sandwich before you take me to the train station?"

"Only if you promise your next arrest happens before 9 p.m."

He grinned. "Deal."

When I dropped him off, he clapped me on the shoulder.

"Thanks, mate. You're a legend."

"Please don't do it again."

"I won't," he promised.
(Reader: he probably did.)

The birthday I came home early

I honestly couldn't tell you the exact moment I started suspecting Ruth was having an affair.

It wasn't a dramatic *"lipstick on the collar"* moment.

More of a gentle, creeping "hmm..." that settled on my shoulder like a nosy parrot.

She was working more late shifts as a store detective.
Some stores weren't exactly local, the London suburbs one night, Southampton the next, so her rolling in around 10 or 10:30 p.m. wasn't unusual.

Then came the occasional "girls' night."
Which slowly evolved into "girls' night but I'm staying over" nights.
Which, if I'm honest, evolved into "girls' weekend but don't wait up" weekends.

Individually, nothing.
Collectively, suspicious.

But I'm not the confrontational type.
I'm more the *"maybe it's fine, maybe I should have a biscuit"* type.

Our life together had settled into a rhythm, not the fireworks-and-champagne stage, but the comfortable stage.

Sunday mornings were our 'time' together, half a night in the week if we weren't exhausted, the sort of domesticity where you know what brand of cereal the other person prefers.

Then came one particular Saturday.

A whisper of instinct nudged me.
So I drove past the house where Ruth said she'd be.
No car.
No sign of life.
Just me, my suspicions, and the sound of my dignity deflating like a slow puncture.

"They've probably gone out," I told myself, loudly, firmly, desperately.

Confrontation, again, not my strong suit.

She arrived home at 1:30 a.m. I pretended to be asleep, as one does in healthy adult relationships.

One eye open, I watched her in the mirror as she unzipped the green dress I'd bought her.

No underwear.
Interesting.

She climbed into bed and wrapped her arms around me.
"You're cold," I whispered.
"Freezing outside," she murmured.
We slept.
Or rather, she slept. I lay there wondering whether frostbite had reached her knicker drawer.

Weeks passed. Things went back to normal. Or seemed to.
Perhaps I *had* added two and two and made five.
Or made nine. My maths isn't great under emotional strain.

⚜ My Birthday Surprise (The One That Backfired Spectacularly)

My birthday arrived on a day cursed by the scheduling gods.

A huge meeting with Boots Pharmaceuticals landed smack on it, and every attempt to move it failed. So, off I went to Nottingham, resigned to spending my birthday with a Premier Inn kettle and a sad sachet of instant coffee.

An hour up the M1, my mobile rang.

"Happy birthday, Keith!" chirped one of the Boots team.

"Also, really sorry, two of us are sick. We'll have to reschedule."
I nearly kissed the steering wheel.
A birthday reprieve!
A surprise return home!
A romantic gesture in the making!

I turned off at the next junction and headed back, determined to walk through the door like a hero in a rom-com.

I didn't text Ruth, the element of surprise, I thought, would make it sweeter.
Oh, the irony.

Her car was in the car park.
Odd, but fine.

I opened the flat door.
Voices.
Bathroom to the right.
Spare room next.

"Hi, darling!" I called, trying to sound jaunty.
"Don't come in!" she replied instantly, the fastest response she'd ever given me.
"I'm dyeing my hair!" she added. "I wanted to surprise you tomorrow!"
"Lovely," I said, "I'll just get changed."

But my Suspicion Parrot had returned, now wearing a trench coat and holding a magnifying glass.

I stepped quietly into the spare-room doorway.

Waited.
Listened.
Then it came.

"Quick," Ruth whispered urgently, "just put your pants on and do the rest on the landing. Go out now, while Keith's in the bedroom."

The bathroom door opened.
Out slipped a young man in nothing but wet hair, wet pants, and the face of someone who has spectacularly misjudged his life choices.
"Oh," he squeaked.
"Out," I said, very calmly for a man watching his relationship pirouette off a cliff.

He stammered about needing his shoes.
I grabbed them, opened the door, and tossed them down the stairs like a disappointed parent returning a boomerang child.

Ruth emerged wrapped in a towel, crying.

"It's not what it looks like," she said, which is universally recognised as "It's absolutely what it looks like."

"You weren't supposed to be here," she sobbed.

"Well," I replied, "I wasn't expecting to find you in the bath with your lover, but here we are."

I told her I was going to Roger's.

She needed to be gone by 10 p.m., belongings and all.

We were both crying.

Shock, betrayal, humiliation, the full emotional buffet.

⭐ A Birthday to Forget, Except You Never Do

Roger opened the door.

"Happy birthday," he said gently.
"Is it?"
It didn't feel like one.

Later, Ruth texted saying she'd gone to her mum's and hoped we could be friends someday.

Back at the flat, the silence was enormous.

Wardrobe open.
Make-up gone.
Bedside table stripped.

I sat on the hallway floor and howled like a man being exorcised by grief.
"How could she?"

A question with no useful answer.

I eventually drifted into the lounge.

The landline was off the hook. I put it back on.

Weeks later, when the bill arrived, I discovered an additional injury: £70 to the speaking clock in Australia.

Because heartbreak apparently comes with international timekeeping fees.

I rang her mum's house:
"Is Ruth there?"

"She's at work. Shall I take a message?"

"Yes," I said. "Tell her... tell her never mind."
(The version in my head was decidedly shorter and extremely unprintable.)

🌼 The Door That Slammed... and the One That Opened
That relationship ended with a thud, a towel, a stranger's footsteps, and a phone bill.

But heartbreak is funny.

Not "ha-ha" funny, more "ah, so that's what soul-depth renovation feels like" funny.

At first, it hollows you out.
Then, slowly, it gives you room to rebuild.

You start hearing your own thoughts again.

Start liking your own company again.

Start remembering that you existed before someone else chose not to.

One day, quietly, without ceremony, you realise you're ready for whatever door opens next.

And, as it turned out, the door that eventually opened for me wasn't just better.

It was built to last.

The one where my cars suffer more trauma than I do

Considering the number of miles I've driven in my life, enough to circumnavigate Earth, woo the Moon, and possibly deliver post to Mars, I've actually had remarkably few crashes. Whether that's down to divine protection, superior skill, or sheer dumb luck is still a matter of vigorous pub debate.

Only one of those accidents ever left me injured, which is less "proof I'm a great driver" and more "proof engineers deserve awards."

Anyway, here is the full saga of My Greatest Hits: Car Edition.

Crash #1: The Cortina Catastrophe (a.k.a. Learning to Drive, Learning to Swear)
Picture this: Dad's Ford Cortina, our entire family crammed inside, and me, still a learner, driving us toward Havant Hypermarket like a responsible young man.

Back then, before the A3 bypass existed, Petersfield was a vehicular torture chamber: miles of traffic, misery, and overheated engines all queuing politely for a chance to move six feet forward every twenty minutes.

We crawled to a halt.
I slowed, braked, even put the hazard lights on.
Then:
BANG.

The car behind us, presumably driven by someone who believed hazard lights were decorative, smashed straight into the back of us.

We were fine, just shaken, which might explain what happened next.

I got out, absolutely fuming, and marched to the offending vehicle.
"How did you NOT see me? Has your car NOT GOT BRAKES?" I shouted.

Then the passenger door opened, and a man stepped out.

"Don't you speak to my wife like that!" he barked.

"Oh believe me, on my menu of rudeness, I'm still on the Canapes!" I snapped back.

Not my finest moment.

But in my defence, I was 17 and had just had my adolescence jolted through my spine.

Luckily, a passing fire engine stopped.

Even more luckily, one of the firemen knew Dad.

They radioed the police, cleared the road, and ushered us off to safety with the efficiency of men who'd clearly seen worse on a Friday.

The next day the insurer wrote off the Cortina.

Dad was philosophical.
"It wasn't your fault, son. That could've happened to me."

A miracle.
I wasn't grounded.
I lived to tell the tale.

Crash #2: The One That Was Actually My Fault
Foggy morning, junction outside Liss, me feeling confident.
Confidence was misplaced.
I misjudged the distance, pulled out, and we collided.
Not dramatically.
No explosions.
No slow-motion Hollywood roll across the bonnet.
Just a small *crump* followed by the sound of my dignity leaking onto the tarmac.
Both cars were still drivable.
My bumper bent.
Their tempers less so.

Lesson learned: fog is rude and should be avoided.

Crash #3: The Fox, The Swerve, The Very Expensive Mistake

Driving onto the A3 one evening, minding my own business, when a fox appeared.

A beautiful fox.
A majestic fox.
An "I must protect this Disney creature at all costs" fox.

I swerved.
This was, in retrospect, idiotic.

I hit the kerb with enough force to destroy the suspension.
The fox, meanwhile, walked away without even saying thank you.

The AA man shook his head as though he'd been summoned to rescue a toddler who'd shoved crayons up his nose.

Crash #4: The Big One - Featuring Airbags, Adrenaline, and a Lorry Driver with Hero Tendencies
This one wasn't my fault.

Which is handy because it was dramatic enough for both of us.

It was quiz night in Alton.
Our HRH team had just lost (probably; it's statistically likely), and I set off home in torrential rain.

Fifty miles per hour felt fast enough.
Visibility was terrible.

Up ahead, a car approached on the opposite carriageway.
I dipped my headlights.
He did not.
Then his lights vanished completely.
"Odd," I thought.

Then they reappeared.
Sideways.

He had spun across the central reservation and was now parked at a jaunty 90-degree angle across my lane.
No time to think.
Only time to react.
I aimed for his rear quarter.
Braked.
Took my hands off the wheel at the last second (a tip I had

thankfully learned from somewhere sensible).
And-
CRASH.

Airbag exploded into my face.

Bonnet flew upward like a trebuchet malfunction.

I honestly thought it was about to re-enter through the sunroof like some sort of automotive boomerang.

Somehow, it landed neatly beside the car.

My knee was in agony, but adrenaline carried me out onto the road.

The other driver was alive, dazed, and presumably reconsidering every life choice that led to this moment.

A heroic lorry driver pulled up, blocked the road with his truck, switched on every light he owned, and called 999.

When the ambulance arrived, the paramedics cut my trousers open.
"Bit swollen, bit bloody," one said. "You'll need X-rays."

At Frimley Park Hospital, the doctor confirmed I'd torn a ligament, but nothing was broken.

Then the police officer arrived, breathalyser in hand.
"All clear," he said after the test.
"Well... I did only have one pint three hours ago," I said, trying not to sound smug.

But the real miracle happened next.

The Surprise Rescue (Because My Friends Are Apparently Psychic)

My phone was lost somewhere in the wreckage.
I had no way home.

Then the A&E doors swung open dramatically, and in walked Heather from the quiz team.
She'd driven past the accident, recognised my car, and traced me to the hospital.

"You'd better not have crashed just to get out of next week's quiz," she said, hands on hips.
"I can neither confirm nor deny," I replied.

She took me home, where the real challenge awaited:
six flights of stairs to my flat.
On crutches.

Heather half-carried, half-shoved me upwards, laughing the whole way.

At the top, she straightened up, dusted herself off, and declared: "You are *not* coming into work tomorrow. I'll tell Colin myself."

And that was that.
Quite a day.
Quite a crash.
Quite a reminder that my cars, like my love life, have survived mainly through humour, luck, and the timely involvement of other people.

The Last Job

I didn't know it at the time, but what I'm about to describe turned out to be the last time I would ever work for someone else.

(I feel this should come with a drumroll but imagine instead a kazoo. More fitting.)

It all began one otherwise innocent evening when I arrived home, slightly hyper, slightly terrified, and picked up the phone to call Steve.

"Hello mate," he said cheerfully, as if I were phoning to ask whether he wanted chips with his burger.

"I've done it," I blurted, still on an adrenaline high. "I've managed to get Colin to sack me. So, you'd better be good to your word, because I am now officially unemployed and there is absolutely no universe in which he gives me a reference."

Steve laughed, the relaxed, carefree laugh of a man who has *not* just detonated their own career on purpose.

"Fear not," he said. "Take a couple of days off. I'll swing by Monday morning, pick you up, and your career with Baker Woodrow will begin."

Just like that, my new life was set in motion.

No fireworks, just a promise, a BMW, and the knowledge my old boss was probably somewhere writing my name on a dartboard.

✦ Monday: The First Day of the Rest of My Bank Balance

Monday morning arrived with that strange energy you get when you're doing something life-changing but also mildly reckless, like bungee jumping, or assembling flat-pack furniture without reading the instructions.

I stood outside my flat waiting for Steve, who soon appeared in a silver-grey BMW that looked like angels had polished it. We set off for Epsom, chatting half about work, half about nothing, until I said:
"Your car looks cleaner than normal."

"I should hope so," he said. "I had it valeted for you on Saturday."

"For... me?"

"Oh yeah," he said casually. "This is your car. I'm getting a new one. You'll keep this until your Renault Laguna arrives."

I must have looked like a child being told Christmas would now occur twice a week.

My salary had doubled, I now had a BMW with a car phone *and* a CD jukebox, and suddenly my life felt like an upward arrow with very few breaks in the line.

Happy days indeed.

My New Office: The Glass Aquarium of Destiny
After the usual paperwork and the proud handover of my newly claimed BMW keys, I was shown to my office.

It was a glass cube, approximately four metres square, which made me feel like a rare zoo exhibit that visitors could stare at but not feed.

My cubemate was Oscar, the Head of Marketing: jovial, sharp-witted, and blessed with the ability to make even the dullest Monday morning feel like a pub quiz.

We became instant allies.
Which was fortunate because I was about to need allies.

Day Three: *Operation Hide Keith*
Three days into my shiny new career, Steve appeared at my door with a face like a man trying not to laugh at his own prank.
"You need to go upstairs to Meeting Room 5," he whispered, "and stay there until I come to get you".

"Why?" I asked.
"Because Colin is in reception."

My stomach dropped.
Colin, my recently former boss, had not taken my exit well.
In fact, he'd reacted as though I'd run off with the crown jewels.

"He's here to meet Gerald and me," Steve continued, "and he's still furious. Gerald doesn't want a scene. So... hide."

So up I went, laptop in hand, like a man fleeing across rooftops in a spy thriller, except my version included an awkward lift ride.

An hour passed. Then Steve reappeared wiping tears of laughter from his eyes.

"All clear," he said. "Also... Colin is convinced you've run off to one of his clients. He's been ringing around trying to track you down".

I wasn't sure whether to be flattered or mildly concerned that I might need a disguise and a fake passport.

⭐ The Job Itself: A Buffet of Random Tasks
Life at Baker Woodrow was good.

Busy, varied, unpredictable.

One minute I'd be doing technical support, the next writing something for marketing, the next programming, and occasionally performing tasks so random they defied category.

But the rhythm was brilliant.
Fridays, for example, were... flexible.

By which I mean:
At 12:30 we all went to the pub.
Those who drove had soft drinks.
Those who didn't... well, let's just say productivity levels varied. It was relaxed, warm, human, everything a workplace should be but rarely is.

⭐ Swindon: Where Everything Changed
Six months later, I was sent to Swindon for a four-day pensions training course. (Lucky me).

By Wednesday lunchtime, just as I was finally understanding annuities without wanting to cry, my mobile rang.
"Keith," said one of the receptionists, sounding tense, "you need to come back to the office straightaway."

I frowned. "Really? I'm back Friday. Can't it wait?"

"No. Steve and Gerald insist."
Now *that* got my attention.

I packed up, drove back, and arrived at an office that felt like the aftermath of an evacuation drill: empty car park, empty desks, strange security guard.

"Mr Budden? They're waiting for you in the boardroom."

Up I went.

Steve stood grinning. Gerald looked like a man about to drop an important plot twist.

"We've been bought out by one of the Big Four," he said.

Just like that.
Boom.
The end of the company as we knew it.

They'd made a tidy sum, both were leaving *that day*, and the rest of the staff were being invited to relocate to central London or Birmingham.

"Oh," Gerald added, "and I think most people have already gone to the pub."
Classic.

Birmingham: Where Hope Went to Die
A few days later, I drove up for my "reassignment interview."

The area was... bleak.
Concrete everywhere.
Grey pavements.
Tired shopfronts.
It felt like someone had drained all the colour and left only the bits you avoid after dark.

The interview itself was worse.
I waited half an hour before a man called Mike strode in looking like he'd rather be alphabetising envelopes.
He hadn't read my file.
He clearly didn't want to hire me.

The entire thing felt like a blind date arranged by someone who hated both parties.

So, I cut to the chase.
"Look," I said, "let's be honest. This isn't happening. The commute is impossible, the role doesn't exist, and neither of us wants to drag this out. Why don't we just agree terms?"

Mike actually sighed with relief.

"We'll honour your six months' notice," he said. "Just make the car available for collection in a month."

And that was it. No drama. No row. No farewell party.
Just me, driving home thinking:
"Well... now what?"

✦ The Blank Page
I had six months' pay.
A company car for a few more weeks.
And, for the first time in my adult life:
Total freedom.

Scary, yes.
But exciting.
I realised something that day, something that had probably been bubbling beneath the surface for years:
I didn't want to work for other people anymore.

Their moods. Their decisions. Their politics. Their surprise sales.
Their Birmingham office blocks with the personality of a morgue.

No thanks.
It was time to build something myself.

Because in the end, one truth had risen above the chaos:
If it's fun, it gets done - and I was ready to start having fun on my terms.

I went on holiday - and came back with a limited company

After the surprise ending of my time at Bacon & Woodrow, which felt a bit like being politely escorted out of a party I didn't realise I'd already left, I decided to treat myself to two weeks of doing nothing.

Sun. Sangria. Sleep.

A three-step mental health programme, courtesy of Valencia.

And for the first few days, it was bliss. I sat in the sun doing absolutely nothing, which, for someone who once scheduled bathroom breaks between client meetings, felt almost illegal.

Then my phone rang.
It was Chris.
Chris and I went back a bit. We'd both survived Welcom Finance, which forged a certain brotherhood, like war veterans or people who've accidentally attended the same awkward wedding.

"Alright, mate?" he said, breezy as ever.
"How's things?"
I told him my latest news, suddenly unemployed, currently in Spain, trying to work out whether my future involved a new employer or a life of petty crime.

"Well," he said, "perfect timing. I've been offered a high-paying contract. Want to buy my business?"

I blinked at the phone.
What I'd expected: sympathy.
What I got: a pitch.

Still, it was intriguing.

"Let's meet when I'm back," I said, trying to sound calm while my brain was already calculating things like projected revenue, overheads, and how many more sangrias I needed before this felt like a sensible idea.
   Holiday Mode: Cancelled

For the rest of my "relaxing break," I found myself doing more business analysis than sunbathing. Chris emailed me his client list, three main contracts. Two finance companies and a no-win-no-fee firm dealing with road traffic accidents.

I made notes.
I researched.
I pretended the man at the hotel pool bar was my PA.

By the time I flew home, I was technically still unemployed but mentally halfway through running an empire.

The Deal

Back in the UK, Chris and I met up. He was true to his word, he wanted out, and he wanted out *fast*.

We shook hands on the spot:
50% upfront, 50% in six months.

No drama. No lawyers. No corporate fuss.

Just two blokes in a café making life-changing decisions between sips of lukewarm tea.

All I needed now was a company.
A small detail, really.

Just the legal existence of the thing I was apparently about to run.

How to Start a Company (Step 1: Panic)

I had absolutely no idea how to form a limited company.

Fortunately, in those days, *Computer Weekly* was the holy writ for IT folk. And tucked away in the back pages, next to ads for printer ribbons and "gently used" modems, was an advert for an accountancy firm in Hampstead offering same-day company formations.

Perfect.
I rang them. They said, "Come tomorrow."

Sorted.

Hampstead, the Birthplace of Destiny

I sat in the accountant's office the next day feeling a bit like a child pretending to be an adult. He handed me a huge folder filled with hundreds of pre-approved company names.

"Pick one," he said, as if choosing the name of a company was no different from choosing a sandwich.

I flipped through the list, looking for something that sounded... well... like a business run by someone who knew what they were doing.

Then I saw it.
Concepta Designs Ltd.
It jumped out at me.
It sounded clever. Professional. Slightly mysterious.

Like I might design software, build satellites, or possibly run an art gallery in Monaco.

"That one," I said.

And just like that, with one finger jabbed confidently at a piece of paper, I became the Managing Director of my own limited company.

No ceremony. No champagne.

Not even a balloon.

The tube back to Waterloo, then the train home, felt surreal. Everything looked the same, yet nothing was the same.

I wasn't waiting for a job anymore.
I wasn't hoping someone else would give me an opportunity.
I'd created my own.
And just like that...
self-employment had begun, with sunburn, a folder full of company names, and absolutely no idea what I'd got myself into.

The Password Is 'Mary'

A contract we won, working in partnership with Steve and Kerry at Echelon, was for a project to oversee the introduction of electronic document management for the National Criminal Intelligence Service (NCIS).

NCIS itself no longer exists, having since been merged into the Serious Organised Crime Agency (SOCA).

I still remember Steve and I visiting their head office, an anonymous-looking office block not far from Vauxhall Station in London. We sat in reception until we were called into a committee room where four members of the NCIS team waited for us, one in uniform and the others in civilian clothes.

We knew we were up against two of the big four consultancies, PCW and KPMG, so we were definitely the underdogs.

At one point during the interview, one of the panellists said, "Obviously you're a much smaller organisation than the others we're talking to. So why should we be working with you?"

I paused for a moment and replied,
"Well, of course, we can't compete with them on resources but being small means we're more agile. And with Steve and my organisation working together, we have tremendous cohesive synergy."

When we left the building, Steve looked at me with a grin. "What on earth was that 'cohesive synergy' bit about?"

"I haven't the faintest idea," I admitted. "Even as it was coming out of my mouth, I was thinking, *please don't ask me to explain that.*"

As it turned out, they didn't. Thinking back, I suspect it was a real case of The Emperor's New Clothes. Possibly none of them understood what I meant either, but they each assumed the others did and didn't want to look foolish in front of their peers. So, they all nodded sagely.

Whatever the reason, it worked. We won the contract. It kept me busy for much of 2001, three days a week at their offices, two working from home.

I can't share much about the project itself, given the Official Secrets Act, but a couple of moments stand out.

The first was when I was sent to one of their satellite offices in the City of London. Like all NCIS locations, it was discreet, this one hidden above a working pub. The difference was that the landlord was an NCIS employee, and all the bar staff had to pass Home Office vetting.

The people I were meeting worked on the three floors above the pub. My instructions were clear:

"Enter through the front doors, order a soft drink, and ask, 'Is Mary working today?'"

That was the trigger phrase that would unlock the door to the stairwell.

I arrived early, walked into the bar, a handful of city types scattered around, some with laptops, some with pints, and went to the counter.

"A diet coke, please," I said. "And is Mary working today?"

The young barmaid nodded. "Yes, she'll be upstairs in five minutes. Would you like ice with that?"

"No thanks," I replied.

"That'll be £1," she said, then nodded discreetly towards the far corner. "The door you want is over there."

Sure enough, as I approached, the lock buzzed and clicked open. I slipped through the door and up the stairs to the meeting room, still half expecting George Smiley to be waiting for me with a file marked Top Secret.

I remember thinking, did anyone who was a regular in that pub ever realise what was happening above their heads?

And then, of course, there was September 11th, 2001 - 9/11.

I was working from home that day. I was on the phone to someone at NCIS when he suddenly said,
"Have you got the television on?"

"No," I replied. "Why?"

"There's been a dreadful accident in New York. An airplane's crashed into the World Trade Centre."

"I'll call you later," my NCIS contact said. "Everyone here's glued to the screens."

I walked through to the living room, picked up the remote control and switched on the TV. Smoke poured from one of the Twin Towers. Then, as I watched, the second aircraft flew into the other tower.

"This is no accident," I thought. "Something sinister is going on."

Like millions of people around the world, we sat glued to the screen for the rest of the day, the Pentagon strike, the note passed to President Bush, the news of the fourth plane crashing in Pennsylvania.

It's not often you can say you lived through a day when the world changed.

But 9/11 was one of them.

From the Majestic to the missing kettle

For someone who never set out to be an international man of mystery, I've spent a suspicious amount of my life in hotels. And like a Craig Revel Horwood review, they've ranged from **"fab-u-lous, daaahling"** to **"Oh dear God what *is* that stain?"**

Let's begin with the fabulous, because optimism is cheaper than therapy.

THE MAJESTIC, HARROGATE - OR THE FIRST TIME I PHONED MY MUM FROM A BATH
The Majestic Hotel in Harrogate (now a DoubleTree but still looking as if it could boss a parish council meeting) is the undisputed queen of hotels in my personal history.

Grand Victorian building.
Sweeping staircases.
Chandeliers so large they require planning permission.
Carpets deeper than most philosophical thoughts.

I first stayed there in my twenties, arriving early for the Digital Dynamics/Welcom Christmas party, partly out of excitement, partly because I wanted maximum time pretending to be posh. I checked in, went to my room, opened the door... and nearly passed out.

A *suite*.
A full-blown, honest-to-goodness suite.
Sofa. Coffee table. French doors. Balcony.

I half expected a footman to appear and offer me a sherry.
I made a coffee, stepped onto the balcony in freezing December wind, and soaked in the view like a man who wasn't sure if he'd ever be allowed back.

Then came the bathroom.
Lights that came on automatically.
Thick towels. Two robes. A flannel (the international sign of civilisation).

And next to the toilet... another bowl.

"Marvellous!" I thought.
"Two people can go at once!"

Reader, it was a bidet.

I'd never seen one.

I briefly considered testing it by pressing random taps, but I liked my eyebrows too much.

Then I noticed a telephone mounted beside the bath.
A *bath phone*.

This was pre-mobile days, remember, so the idea of phoning someone from the tub felt indecently luxurious.

Naturally, I did.
"Mum," I said.
"Oh hello love," she replied. "I'm cooking tea. You got there alright? There's a bit of an echo"
"Yes. That's probably because I'm ringing from the bath."
Silence.
The kind of silence only mothers can deploy.

"Yes, very funny," she said, clearly imagining I was calling from a bathroom floor somewhere in Sheffield.
To this day, I don't think she believed me.

THE MANCHESTER BOUTIQUE HOTEL & THE GREAT GLASS WALL INCIDENT

Years later, I found myself staying in a chic boutique hotel in Manchester with my colleague Beth, separate rooms, I should add, before you get too excited.

We'd driven up for an awards evening.
After check-in I lay down "just for a moment" and instantly fell asleep, because that's what men do when left unsupervised.

A knock at the door woke me.
"Keith? It's Beth. Are you alive?"

I opened the door to find her in a full evening gown, shawl, handbag, and the look of a woman who'd dressed up for the Oscars only to discover she'd brought a man who couldn't remain conscious.

"You look great!" I said.
"You don't," she said.
Fair.

She sat on my bed while I jumped in the shower, separated (I thought) by an opaque glass wall.
"Can you see me?" I shouted.
"Just a shadow!" she called back.

Then I noticed a small silver button.
And, because I am a man, I pressed it.

The glass instantly turned transparent.
Beth shrieked like a Victorian lady confronted by a squirrel.
"Turn it *off*! My eyes!"

I slapped the button like it was a nuclear launch abort key. My nerves meant I pressed it rapidly repeatedly, like *Naked Attraction* meets *Peep Show*.

Thankfully, finally, the glass fogged back up, though I'm fairly sure the damage to her retinas was irreversible.

I asked her to pass me my boxers, "They're in the left-hand end of my overnight bag". Her hand appeared round the bathroom door, clean boxers dangling from her finger. I'm not sure why she didn't come in, it's not like there's anything she hadn't had engraved on her retina by then. Once I had my suit on, she fastened my bow tie, called me "Big Boy" in a tone that suggested she was winding me up for sport, and we headed out.

We didn't win the award, but we *did* dine out on that story for years.

THE GLASGOW PREMIER INN - WHERE HOPE GOES TO DIE
Now, I like a Premier Inn.

Dependable. Purple.
Mattress like a friendly hug.

But the Premier Inn at Glasgow Airport?
That was... something else.
The hotel was "open during refurbishment," which is corporate speak for:

"We apologise in advance for absolutely everything."

Check-in took so long that I grew a beard.

Tall potted plants attempted to hide the construction work, failing spectacularly. I was tempted to do my David Bellamy impression but restrained myself.

I got to my room. Keycard in. Switch on. No ceiling light.
Just two wires hanging down, like a warning about my electricity bill. One night. I will live with just the wall lights.

Dinner didn't help.

Lukewarm Guinness.
Fish and chips that took an hour to appear, I was beginning to wonder if it was freshly caught from the Clyde.

I asked to speak to the manager.
He arrived looking like a man who'd been assaulted by fifteen complaints and a rogue ceiling tile.

"Would now," I said loudly, "be a good time to order breakfast?"

The restaurant erupted in laughter.

He turned the colour of salmon and apologised like he was reading from a hostage statement.

The next morning at breakfast I was treated like royalty, as if they feared I'd call head office and say the words:
"I have photos."

THE GLASGOW HOTEL WITH SEASONAL HEATING POLICIES

Another Glasgow stay:
Mid-October.
Freezing.
"The heating doesn't work," I told reception.
"Oh aye," she said.
"You're from the South, aren't ye?
We don't turn the heating on till November."
She handed me a blanket like it was a family heirloom.
I slept fully dressed.

THE HOTEL THAT WOULDN'T PROVIDE KETTLES FOR FEAR OF THEFT

Then there was the Birmingham sporting-pub-slash-hotel.

Rooms accessed via a door beside the bar, always a promising sign.

My room had:

- No kettle
- No mugs
- No tea
- A carpet stained with what I pray was coffee

"Can I get a latte?" I asked at the bar.

"Tea or coffee?" she replied.

"Coffee."

She handed me a pint mug of it, filled *to the brim*, clearly the cause of every stain on the stairwell.

As I trudged upstairs, I thought:
"Towels, toiletries, maybe even the odd bathrobe - sure, people steal those.
But kettles?
What is going on in Birmingham?"

TRAVEL LESSONS LEARNED (THE HARD WAY)

1. **Pressing mysterious buttons never ends well.**
   Especially if your colleague is on the other side of the glass.

2. **Hotel stars are suggestions, not promises.**

3. **If a hotel hands you a blanket instead of fixing the heating, leave. Immediately.**

4. **Bidets are not tandem toilet facilities.**
   (Not even in an emergency.)

5. **Always check for a bath phone.**
   Not because you need it, but because calling your mum

from the tub is a memory you'll treasure forever. Even if she doesn't believe you.

Even with the best laid plans, hotel bookings can go wrong, as you will discover in the chapter where I venture into Germany for a Scandinavian adventure.

When in Europe do what the Europeans do

Following my "sell-out" talk at the Document Management Show in London, and yes, *sell-out* is technically accurate, because all 100 chairs the organisers put out were indeed occupied (mostly by people guarding the free pastries), I received an invitation from Optika to speak at a conference in Leipzig.

There was only one small logistical hiccup: you can't fly from Southampton to Leipzig unless you sprout wings or hijack a migrating goose.

So, the plan was simple. I'd fly to Frankfurt, and Sonja, representing Optika, would pick me up and drive me the rest of the way. She lived in Frankfurt, so for her it was nothing more than a pleasant Tuesday. For me, it felt like being chauffeured by a Scandinavian diplomat.

I drove to Southampton Airport, constantly checking that I had all of the paperwork in my jacket pocket, mostly to ensure I hadn't left my passport on the kitchen worktop, in the glove compartment, or in the fruit bowl (all known previous hiding places).

This was my first time flying Lufthansa and, in the most German way possible, the aircraft rolled into the arrivals gate at Frankfurt **to the second**. I swear the pilot had the smug air of someone who times his dishwasher cycles.
Pre-Brexit German customs were the usual spectacle:
300 passengers...
3 customs officers...
and a level of "just wave them all through" that made you wonder why they even bothered with booths. One guard looked at my passport for roughly **two nanoseconds,** just long enough to confirm I wasn't carrying a pitchfork, and waved me through.

I stepped into the arrivals hall and spotted her instantly:
A blonde woman holding a placard that read **"Kieth"** as if she were meeting a rock star instead of a workflow consultant.

"Keith!" she called, waving enthusiastically. "You look exactly like on Skype. Taller, obviously."

"Thank you," I said. "You look exactly like on Skype too. Considerably less pixelated."

We hugged, or rather, *she* hugged, and I attempted the awkward British response to a European greeting. She kissed both cheeks. I was prepared for one, forgot the second, and we had a brief but intimate collision of noses.

"By the way," I said, nodding at the sign, "you spelled my name wrong."

She blinked. "Did I? In English it is always 'i' before…" She paused. "No, that is German. In German we use twenty letters and an umlaut where six letters would do. It is a personality trait. Even our language sounds like we are arguing with furniture."

I decided that debating this would require a rewrite of the Treaty of Versailles, so I simply nodded.

"This way," Sonja said brightly. "And by the way, I am allowed to make jokes about German efficiency. I am Danish."

That explained a lot. The calmness. The confidence. The dry wit. The ability to make a decision without a committee meeting.

She took my overnight bag before I could protest and carried it with the effortless authority of someone who secretly lifts men for sport, then strode through the airport. People parted for her like she had diplomatic immunity. I followed behind her, trying not to look like a toddler being escorted to school by his Scandinavian au pair.

Her car was a new Volkswagen in "Midnight Black," which she explained was chosen because "the cream interior hides dog hair."

She opened the boot, revealing her bag… and a towel that smelled faintly of a Danish fjord.

"Don't mind the smell," she said as I got in. "My dogs were swimming. I forgot to valet the car."

"I can't smell anything anyway."

She glanced at me sharply. "Nothing? At all?"

So I explained the Marfan's, the Lymphoma, the whole biological circus.

Sonja nodded thoughtfully.
"In Denmark we would call that… 'a bit inconvenient.'"
"That's one way to put it."

We left Frankfurt behind and headed towards Leipzig, the landscape opening out into the rolling green hills of the Rhöngebirge. I told her it reminded me of the South Downs. Conversation flowed easily, clients, legislation, the strangely cosy world of document workflows (don't judge me), and the ways British people can apologise for things that aren't their fault.

We stopped for coffee halfway.
I immediately regretted drinking mine.

"I'll need a loo when we get there," I said. "Coffee goes straight through me."
Sonja nodded with that Scandinavian bluntness I'd come to appreciate.
"Yes," she said. "With your conditions, everything seems to go straight through you."
"Charming."
"It is why you like me," she deadpanned.

And annoyingly… she was right.

We rolled away from the service station caffeine stop and continued toward Leipzig, the German countryside blurring past in strips of green and gold. Sonja drove the way only Scandinavians and rally champions seem able to: calm, precise, and entirely confident that the rest of us will keep up.
By the time we reached Leipzig, the daylight had given up entirely, slipping into that early-autumn darkness that makes everything look vaguely mysterious and slightly haunted.

We visited the exhibition centre first to inspect the setup. The stand looked immaculate, symmetrical, clean, not a cable out of place. The sort of thing that would make a German engineer weep with patriotic pride.

Then we headed for the hotel.
And that's where the **comedy of international logistics** really kicked in.

We checked in. The receptionist tapped her keyboard, frowned, tapped again, frowned harder, the sort of frown that suggests someone has accidentally booked a camel into the system.

"I'm afraid," she said, "we only have one room reserved for you. A twin."
Sonja blinked. Slowly.
"A twin?" she repeated. "Our admin office booked two singles."
"Yes," said the receptionist. "But… everything is full. Exhibition week. Maybe you can share?"

She said this with the apologetic tone of someone handing you bad news and a free biscuit.

Sonja turned to me.
"Well," she said matter-of-factly, "we are both grown-ups, yes?"
"Technically," I replied.
"Then we share the twin. And do not worry," she added with a raised eyebrow. "I am too tired to murder you in your sleep."
"Comforting."

The receptionist, mortified, handed us two complimentary spa passes "to make up for the inconvenience."

Which, honestly, was the most European solution imaginable: *"We have messed up your accommodation. Here, have a sauna."*

Upstairs, the room was cosy, warm, and, as advertised, contained two single beds placed about twelve inches apart. The hotel's idea of optimism.
Sonja dropped her bag onto one of them.
"Well," she said. "We will eat. Then we will sleep. We will manage."

We walked to the restaurant, grabbed a quiet table, and ordered.

I had Guinness, she had gin and tonic, and the conversation loosened further. Sonja had that brilliant Scandinavian quality of saying outrageous things in a perfectly calm voice, leaving you to decide whether to laugh or apologise.

After food, we returned to the room.

And then it began
I closed the door behind us, automatically, flicking the little security latch into place.

Sonja raised one eyebrow.
"You lock us in," she said, amused. "How very British."
"Reflex," I said. "I lock hotel doors the way other people breathe."
"Well," she said, hands now on her hips, "that brings us to the topic."
"What topic?"
She pointed between us.

"This topic. We are sharing a room. We will be showering. Changing. We will see each other naked anyway. It is better to remove the awkwardness now."

"Oh," I said. "Now?"
"Yes," she said, with the bluntness of a woman who grew up comfortable in saunas.
"You go first."
I hesitated. Not because I was shy, I've had more medical staff see me naked than most naturists, but because I'm British. No one trains us for this.
Still, I agreed.
"Fine," I said. "But no laughing."
"I *will* laugh," she replied. "But politely."

I sat on my bed, removed my socks. She nodded approvingly as though grading technique.
Then came the jumper and T-shirt.
"You have good shoulders," she observed. "Not bad for a man whose organs try to escape twice a year."
"Touching."

Then the jeans.
"You undo those like a man who has done it many times."
"I have indeed removed trousers previously." I confirmed.

She laughed loudly, a warm, Danish laugh that made the room feel safer.

Then I needed a wee.
"Oh, hang on, I need a wee" I said.

I went into the bathroom. I left the door open, there didn't seem much point in closing it. I flushed the loo.
"All clear!" I called (no idea why, nerves probably).
"I admire a man who inspects his own plumbing," she replied.

Then, with one decisive motion, I slipped off my boxers.
Sonja examined me clinically.
"Turn around."
I did.
"Very nice bum," she said. "Firm. Only slightly surprised for your age."
"And that's high praise?"
"For Denmark, yes."

She paused, then pointed downward.
"He saluted."
"He does that."
"He is waving. Like a happy dog." She laughed so much she snorted.
"Your turn," I said quickly.

The Danish method of undressing
Sonja stood in the centre of the room like a lecturer preparing to give a talk entitled "Nudity: A Practical Guide."
"Blouse or skirt first?"
"Blouse," I said.
She unbuttoned it with the serene precision of a woman unbothered by life's nonsense. Underneath was a simple chemise.
"This does not match," she said. "But I dress for laundry day, not for men."
Skirt next, slipping effortlessly to the floor.
Then the chemise, followed by her bra, tossed onto the bed with the relief of someone who had been politely fighting it all day.
"Ohhhh... I feel like a boiled potato escaping its skin." She said.
"You have very... Scandinavian.... shoulders," I said carefully.
"Yes. Built for chopping wood and carrying men."

Then she paused.
"Knickers next?" I asked, then immediately winced at how eager that sounded.
"Yes," she said, entirely unfazed.
She removed them in one smooth, completely unapologetic motion, folded them, then removed her stockings and suspender belt with the calm competence of someone assembling IKEA furniture by instinct.

"Well?" she said, turning around.
"Very symmetrical." I said.
She giggled, "My mother will be thrilled."

She placed her hands on her hips.
"There. Now we are equals."
"Well... almost."
She glanced down.
"He is still waving."
"Apologies."
"It is fine. In Denmark we see this every day. Usually at breakfast."

Then came the shower.
"Since we are already naked," she said, "it is illogical to shower separately. Waste of water. Bad for planet. We shower together."

I blinked.
"That's... logical?"
"It is Danish logic."

In the bathroom, she turned on the shower and stepped in. I followed, trying not to trip over my own feet.

In the shower, steam rising around us, she handed me the shower gel.
"Soap your front," she instructed. "I will do your back. Then we swap. You do mine..."
"You start," she said. "British men like to feel useful."
I soaped her back, carefully, respectfully.
She soaped my back, the last time I'd had a back massaged that well I'd paid a chiropractor a day's wages for it.
It worked surprisingly well, efficient, practical, oddly sweet.

When it came to rinsing her back, I lifted the shower head from its holder.
"You are tall," she said. "Useful. You can reach all the places."
She turned around to let me rinse her front.
The inevitable happened.
"Oh look," she said cheerfully. "He salutes."
"It's just gravity."
"No, it is enthusiasm," she corrected, tapping it once with her finger.
"Behave."

I nearly died laughing, mainly because she did it with the exact tone you'd use on a naughty puppy.

We dried off, still naked, still casually chatting about workflow software. Only in my life could nudity feel more natural when discussing ISO compliance.

"Tell me, Keith," she continued, "is this the part where British people get shy?"
"Oh, that happened ten minutes ago."

The nights that followed
The next two days were a warm blur, saunas, shared humour, deadpan teasing, the kind of gentle closeness that didn't need to cross lines to mean something real.

Being naked in our room became the norm. The moment we were in the room after dinner, off came the clothes. We shared the bathroom, brushed our teeth naked next to each other. We chatted about clients and what we had seen at the conference that day as though this was all perfectly standard workplace procedure (It probably was if you're Danish).

We climbed into our separate beds, politely ignoring the foot wide "No Man's Land" between them both of us warm, clean, and remarkably relaxed.

"Goodnight, Keith."
"Goodnight, Sonja."

"You British," she murmured in the dark,
"You make nudity more dramatic than funerals."
"And you Danes treat it like returning a library book."
"Exactly."

We fell asleep.
Nothing happened, nothing needed to.
The intimacy had already happened, in laughter, honesty, ridiculousness, and trust.

By the time she dropped me off in Frankfurt after the conference, we were laughing like friends of decades.

We hugged and kissed, on the lips this time, a kiss between two good friends, reassuring rather than passionate. I can't pretend

I wasn't tempted to kiss her more passionately, but Sonja had been right all along:
Some lines don't need crossing to mean something.
Some intimacy isn't physical.
Some closeness doesn't need labels.

What mattered was the trust, the honesty, and the warmth of knowing we could be unguarded humans in each other's company.

For two days we had simply been two humans,
unarmoured, unembarrassed, unfiltered.
And in its own quietly ridiculous way,
that was enough.

"Text me when you get home to let me know you got there safely," Sonja said.
"OK, I called back as I walked towards departures with a skip in my step. It had, I thought to myself, been a great trip, most of the time it felt more like a holiday than working.

I drove home, made myself a cup of tea, kicked off my shoes, and let the normality of home settle around me.

And then I remembered, I should text Sonja, let her know I was home safe.
After the last forty-eight hours, it felt not just polite... but right.

Keith:
Home safe ☺
No delays, no drama, no one saw me accidentally saluting any passers-by.
Thank you again for a brilliant few days. x
Sonja:
Good. I was worried you might get arrested on the plane for "waving."
Denmark would have understood.
UK... maybe not.
Keith:
In fairness, you did tap him like a naughty Labrador, so he's still confused.
Sonja:
It was gentle discipline.
In Denmark this is called "corrective guidance."
You British call it "flirting."

Keith:
Oh, is *that* what we were doing?
I thought it was protection.
Sonja:
Yes.
Protection... of your modesty.
Keith:
You didn't protect *my* modesty.
You dismantled it like flat-pack IKEA.
Sonja:
Only because you looked like you needed the help.
Also, you have a good bum.
Danish verdict: 8.5/10
Could be 9 with more squats.
Keith:
I'll add that to my New Year's resolutions:
   1. Survive.
   2. Squat.
   3. Avoid being disciplined by naked Scandinavians in hotel showers.
Sonja:
You forgot:
4. Buy waterproof phone.
In case I must FaceTime you next time for... supervision.
Keith:
Supervision?
Or quality control?
Sonja:
Both.
And next time we share a room, I am choosing the playlist.
Something with rhythm.
Your shampoo technique needs work.
Keith:
HEY.
British men have been shampooing people badly for centuries.
It's tradition.
Sonja:
Exactly why we must modernise you.
Consider me your EU directive.
Keith:
I'd better comply then.
Sonja:
Good boy. See you next time you come to see us at Optika.
Sleep well, Keith.
Thank you for being... uncomplicated company.

It is rare.
x
Keith:
Night, Sonja.
Thank you for being... wonderfully complicated company.
xx

Sonja and I had created a memorable moment in our lifetimes.

That, in its own way, was intimacy enough.

Stars over Crystal River

I've only crossed the Atlantic three times, which feels criminal given how much I enjoy American breakfasts.

The first trip was to a business conference in Colorado Springs. And I use the word "Colorado Springs" generously, because the only part I actually saw was the road between the airport and the hotel. The conference *and* the accommodation were in the same building, creating a three-day loop of: **bed → breakfast → conference → dinner → bar → bed → repeat**.

For all I know, Colorado Springs might be stunning.
Or it might be a giant car park with a moose in it.
I'll never know.

But the *second* trip? Oh yes. That one was memorable.

The Florida Business Trip That… Became Something Else Entirely
At the time I was running *e-magineit*, my new trading name for Concepta Designs, and we were selling a clever little Belgian invention called the iKey: part cybersecurity device, part internet nanny, and a big hit with worried parents everywhere.

My friends Mike and Richard loved the product, and Richard had a contact in Crystal River, Florida who thought we could make a splash there.

So off we went: three British men heading to Florida, armed with optimism, a product nobody had heard of, and absolutely no plan beyond "Richard will drive."

Orlando airport welcomed us with heat like someone opening an oven door.

We grabbed the hire car, and Richard (the only one comfortable driving on the right) took the wheel.

The journey to Crystal River was a blur of banter, palm trees, and me nervously trying to remember which lane Americans die in if they get it wrong.

Our host, Audere, greeted us at her bungalow, a sprawling

Floridian house that looked like it had been designed by someone who thought windows were optional.

She was warm, funny, and disarmingly charming.

Richard knew her already, so after introductions he promptly abandoned Mike and me and disappeared to stay with another friend, leaving us in the care of this fascinating, free-spirited Englishwoman who'd adopted Florida as her homeland.

The business part went swimmingly.
The personal part… even more so.

My First Time Driving in America (and the Americans' Aversion to Walking)
I drove a US car for the first time, all the way from Crystal River to Sarasota.

I kept muttering,
"Right side, right side, right side,"
like a man trying to hypnotise himself out of causing an international incident.

We spent our downtime lounging by the hotel pool, strolling the coastline, and observing America's unique approach to walking:

In nature:
They'll walk for miles, often in khaki.
In retail parks:
They'll drive 30 metres to the next store rather than cross a car park.
It was astonishing, like watching gazelles who refused to run unless it was for a clearance sale.

The Redneck Bar, and an Unexpected Invitation
One night, Audere took Mike and me to a redneck bar, proper sawdust-on-the-floor stuff.
Check shirts everywhere.
A band that looked like they'd escaped from a country-music dream sequence.
People line-dancing with alarming precision.

After a while, during a slow number, Audere pulled me close and whispered:
"Come to my room tonight."

It was said in the tone of a woman who absolutely meant it.

I smiled, very flattered, but declined.
Not because I didn't want to, oh, I wanted to, but because it didn't feel right sneaking off while Mike was still in the house.

She looked a little disappointed but not defeated.

"Next time, then," she said, with eyes that meant business. "Don't leave it too long."

Reader: *I did not leave it too long.*

Three Months Later: The Shoeless Immigration Saga
Three months later, I flew back, alone this time.

The moment the immigration officer learned I was staying at a friend's house rather than a hotel, his face tightened like he'd found a suspicious sausage roll at a crime scene.

"Sir, come with me."

I was escorted to a waiting room where he said the immortal line:

"And your shoes, please."
"My shoes?"
"We don't want you running."

"Trust me," I said, "I can barely run for a bus."

He stared.
Not a flicker of amusement.
Americans take shoe-related security extremely seriously.

An hour later, Audere burst in, waving my shoes triumphantly.

"Come on," she said. "Let's get you out of here before they confiscate your trousers as well."

A Week of Magic, Mischief, and Stars
That week was... wonderful.

Warmth, laughter, long talks, gentle teasing, chemistry that didn't need defining.

It was uncomplicated, unhurried, and unlabelled, grown-up

connection at its best. Sex, yes, but oh so much more.

On our last night, Audere borrowed a boat and we motored out into a quiet bay.

Audere cut the engine, and the world fell silent except for the water nudging the hull.

The sky above was ridiculous, a Milky Way so bright it looked like someone had dusted sugar across the heavens.

Then she said, with the grin of a woman who collects memories the way others collect luggage stickers:

"Let's get naked.
Not for swimming, just to feel alive."

So, we did.
Two people lying under the stars, entirely unbothered by modesty or gravity.

It was one of those perfect moments life hands you rarely, a little pocket of peace, joy, and clarity, wrapped in warm night air and starlight.

We Both Knew It Was Temporary, and That Was the Beauty of It

We weren't destined for the long haul, and we knew it.
But not everything needs to be permanent to be meaningful.

Some relationships are novels.
Some are short stories.
Some are beautiful poems that fit on a single page.

Ours was a poem.

She visited England later.
We stayed close for a while.
Then life took us in different directions, gently, without drama.

But she remains a golden little chapter in my life, the kind you never rewrite, because it was perfect as it was.

And Me?
I learned this:

Travel changes you.

People change you.
Being open changes you.

And sometimes, it takes flying halfway across the world, surrendering your shoes to a humourless immigration officer, and lying naked under the Florida sky to realise who you're becoming.

Not bad for a business trip.

Driving in circles - and loving every lap

I should have known the trip was going to be interesting the moment Nick, our team principal at Eagle Motorsport, said the magic words:
"Do you fancy joining us in Spain for winter testing?
You'll have to pay for your own flight, but everything else is covered."
Lovely, I thought. Sun, circuits, and someone else footing the hotel bill.
What could possibly go wrong?

Well... as it turned out: **me driving the team minibus.**
Across Andalucía.
At night.
On mountain roads.
With four mechanics and absolutely no sense of direction between us.
And Nick *forgot* to mention this tiny detail until we landed at Málaga Airport.
"By the way," he said, as casually as if he were asking me to pass the salt,
"You're driving the minibus."
I blinked. "What?"
"Yeah, none of the lads are old enough."
He said it proudly, like he'd masterminded a brilliant logistical strategy rather than condemned us all to an early death.

Also unmentioned: **Guadix is 115 miles from Málaga.**
Up a mountain.
And also unmentioned: **Granada airport is 30 miles away.**
But why fly there when you can accidentally recreate a Top Gear special?

We threw our bags into the van, and I climbed into the driver's seat, silently praying the mechanics valued their lives enough not to distract me.
The first few gear changes were... experimental.
You know the sound a gearbox makes when it's thinking,
"Oh dear God, what is he doing?"
That.

But eventually we found a rhythm:
I drove, the lads navigated, and we all pretended we weren't terrified.

As we climbed into the Sierra Nevada foothills, the temperature dropped, and the road signs became more like riddles. Spanish road planners, I realised, operate on the principle of:
"Why warn people about a tight bend? It'll be more exciting if they find out by surprise."

By the time we reached the hotel car park, it was dark, moonlit, and I was emotionally ready for a long lie down or a stiff drink. We chose the drink.

The Circuit, the Speed, and the Foam Seat of Destiny
The next morning was motorsport heaven, spotless cars, crisp winter air, and two exceptionally talented young drivers: Danny Watts and a polite, baby-faced Finn named Heikki Kovalainen.

Motaworld had brought a young Scottish driver too: **Susie Stoddart**, later Susie Wolff, and even then, she had the quiet confidence of someone who absolutely knew she belonged in a race car.
I watched her on track and thought,
She's going places.
(Spoiler: she did.)

Then came the part I still grin about; Nick told me I could drive one of the Formula Renaults.

Now, this was the year 2000.
I was slimmer, sprightlier, bendier.
Nowadays I'd need a shoehorn, a tub of Vaseline, and possibly a small crane to get into a single-seater cockpit.
But back then? Oh, I was game.

First step: **seat fitting.**
This involved me sitting in the cockpit while a mechanic poured fireproof expanding foam into a black plastic bag stuffed behind my back.
It felt like being slowly embalmed but in a cheerful way.
Then they loaned me the proper drivers' race suits.

If you've never worn someone else's balaclava, let me tell you... it's intimate. You learn a lot about a man from the shape of his helmet padding.

Out on track, the first sensation was:
"Good grief, I'm practically sitting *on* the tarmac."

The second was discovering that a racing helmet, which weighs almost nothing in your hands, weighs approximately *16 tons* when you take a corner at speed.
I did five laps.
Smooth, steady, brave ish.

The timing sheets later confirmed I was ten seconds off the proper drivers' pace, but I told everyone this was deliberate "to preserve the tyres."
No one believed me.

Susie, the Trailer, and a Very Professional Strip-Down
Later that day I was chatting in Motaworld's trailer with their team boss Alan when Susie walked in, fresh from a testing run, unzipped her race suit, and got changed right beside us.

White bra. Tanga briefs. Zero fuss.
Total professionalism.

Alan kept talking like nothing unusual was happening, and I nodded along pretending I was absolutely not having a religious experience.

Motorsport may have been male dominated, but Susie had such confidence you couldn't help but admire her. No nonsense, no preening, just focus.
I thought,
That woman is going to absolutely run the show one day.
(Spoiler: correct again.)

Heikki's Crisis of Blonde Faith
The next morning at breakfast, Heikki sat next to me with the expression of a man who'd just solved, or possibly broken, the Da Vinci Code.
"Keith," he said, gravely, "I am confused."
"What's up?"

"In Finland, all the girls are blonde," he said. "But last night... the barmaid... when she took her clothes off... the curtains did not match the carpet."

I nearly choked on my croissant.
"Heikki," I said, "sometimes women *dye* their hair blonde."

He nodded slowly, digesting this revelation.
"Ahhh," he said, relieved. "Now I understand."
I've never seen enlightenment happen so fast.

Another Surprise from Nick (Because of Course)
Midway through day two, Nick approached with the same innocent expression that had doomed me to a three-hour mountain drive.

"Keith, good news! Another team's taking our mechanics back tonight."
"Right…"
"And I need you to drive back to Málaga to pick up a new driver, Tim, and his sister, Natalie."

I stared at him.
"You're joking."
"No," he said cheerfully. "Didn't mention it earlier, you'd have said no."
He handed me €110.
€80 for fuel.
€30 for food.
Not one penny extra for trauma.

At Málaga Airport, I wrote TIM AND NATALIE on a card, feeling like the world's least glamorous chauffeur.

When they arrived, I nearly dropped it.
Tim looked like an Ayrton Senna tribute act.
Natalie looked like every woman Hollywood has ever cast as "mysterious beauty with her own soundtrack."
"I'll sit in front with you," she said, smiling.
We talked all the way back.
She was smart, funny, a dressage rider, and the sort of woman who could turn ordering a sandwich into a cinematic moment.
I remember thinking:
Some families get all the gene upgrades.

The Departure That Definitely Wasn't Optional
On the last day, I made a decree:
"We leave at 4:20 a.m. sharp. If you're not in the minibus, I'm leaving without you."
At 4:10, I was ready.
At 4:15, Tim and Natalie were in the van.
At 4:20… the mechanics were still faffing with the truck.

So, I rolled the bus forward.
"WAIT FOR US!" they shouted, running after us like extras in *Benny Hill*.

"You were warned!" I called back.
They made it. Just.

And That Was Spain
The flight home was full of snores, elbows, and triumphant exhaustion.
It had been a week of unexpected jobs, unexpected driving, unexpected nudity, unexpected Finnish confusion, and that warm glow that only comes from feeling utterly part of something.
I loved every minute of it.
Life with motorsport was never neat, never calm, never predictable.
But it was always, beautifully, hilariously, **alive**.

What happens in Guadix

I was destined to return to Guadix a couple more times, but one particular trip stands out, the one with a young driver we'll call "Abi".

Abi was one of those rare people who make you feel instantly brighter just by walking into the room. Direct, quick-witted, fiercely talented, and utterly allergic to nonsense. She was preparing for the Formula Renault Winter Series, six races over three weekends, and driving for a team I'd been helping with marketing work.

At the same time, I was trying to launch "iKey" under our brand-new E-magineIT label, and I had a dream, a very businesslike, professional, completely sensible dream, of seeing our logo plastered on the side of a race car.

The team principal and I struck a deal:
- I'd do three months' work free of charge,
- he'd stick our logo onto Abi's engine cover,
- **and** he'd give her a 30% discount across the season.

It was the rarest of things: a true win-win-win.

I got exposure, he got marketing, Abi got much-needed support.

Before long, Abi and I had become firm friends. She'd pop by my flat in Holybourne for tea and talk motorsport in a way that made you want to go out and win a championship yourself. She'd raced at Spa-Francorchamps, my favourite circuit on earth, and the way she described flying up Eau Rouge made even *my* spine tingle.

So, when she invited me to join her for a weekend testing session in Guadix, I didn't need asking twice.

This time, I was wiser:
we flew to Granada, not Málaga, thus avoiding the traditional "Keith accidentally drives a minibus up a mountain" experience.

We picked up a hire car, one of those tiny ones that always feels like it would sulk if you asked it to go uphill, and drove to the hotel, Abi in the passenger seat acting as a cross between a co-pilot and a driving instructor who couldn't help but give helpful commentary.

We'd booked separate rooms. Professional. Civilised. Mature. *(I was learning.)*

Dinner with the team was lively, full of gossip and good humour, and after a nightcap we headed to bed early.

Saturday - Speed, Talent, and Telemetry Magic
Abi was flying.

Two to three seconds faster than the development drivers she was mentoring, and when she leaned over their shoulders explaining telemetry traces, braking points, and throttle curves, even I understood what she meant, which is saying something.

I felt proud watching her. She *deserved* chances, and she took them, later racing in Germany, the UK, and even the USA.

That evening, I fell into conversation with the team principal, a chap who later went on to a senior Formula 2 role. We chatted business and racing for ages, until Abi gently tapped my shoulder.

"I'm off up to my room. When you're done, pop in, I need your help with something."

I assumed she needed help with her laptop, or to look over a sponsorship doc, or something equally harmless.

How wrong I was.

⭐ The Shoulder Situation
About forty-five minutes later I knocked on her door.
"Come in!" she called, half-watching Spanish TV.

She was dressed in her sports bra and black Lycra shorts, pretty standard race-driver attire between sessions, and explained she'd rubbed her shoulders raw wearing the wrong bra under her race suit.

"Can you have a quick look?" she asked. "Just tell me if it needs dressing."
Completely reasonable. Totally fine. I nodded in a professional, medically sounding manner despite having no actual medical

qualifications bar my Red Cross training 20 years ago which now barely stretched to sticking plasters on my own scrapes.

She turned around, and I gently checked the sore patches. "Nothing terrible," I said. "Bit of dressing, bit of after-care, you'll be right."

Then came request number two.

"Can you help me with my neck-strength exercises? Dad normally holds my legs steady so I can use my helmet as a weight."

So, there we were: Abi doing neck exercises on the floor, fireproof balaclava on, race helmet wobbling slightly, me holding her ankles like some kind of motorsport personal trainer.

We lasted about two minutes before descending into hopeless laughter.

"Right," she said, wiping her eyes, "let's be serious."
We tried again.
More laughter.

Then she tugged off her sports bra so I could place a dressing on her shoulder properly.

Again, all very matter of fact.
Completely unselfconscious.
The way racing drivers often are.

At one point she pulled the balaclava and helmet back on, still topless, looked in the mirror and said:
"Good grief, I look like a rubbish Marvel superhero."
We both collapsed.

And somewhere between the comedy, the closeness, and the quiet of the Spanish night, the mood softened. There was a brief, warm, impulsive moment, affectionate, tender, unplanned, the kind you don't analyse or define, just accept.

It wasn't dramatic.
It wasn't life changing.
It was simply... human.

Sunday - Back to Normal
The next morning at the circuit she was 100% professional again, focused, fast, analytical.

No awkwardness. No weirdness.
Just two friends, smiling occasionally at the shared secret of the night before.

On the drive to the airport, she glanced at me with that mischievous glint of hers.

"About last night," she said. "It was lovely...
...but you do know you're twenty years older than me, right? You're basically Dad-aged."

"Wonderful," I said. "Romance isn't dead after all."

She laughed and nudged my shoulder.
"Let's just agree it's a good memory."
"Perfect," I said.
She grinned.

"What happens in Guadix stays in Guadix."

A Note to You, Dear Reader
I still have enormous respect for her, her drive, her talent, her courage, and this is one chapter where, for obvious reasons, names have been changed to protect the innocent, the guilty, and the easily blushable.

Some memories stay gentle, private, golden...
and this was one of them.

The day I discovered freedom

You know how every adult documentary starts with a soft-voiced narrator saying:
"Keith never expected his life to change that afternoon…"

Well, this was *that* afternoon.

My Holybourne flat had **one thing** my previous homes didn't: a private garden just big enough for a sunbed and far enough from civilisation that, with the right angle, I could pretend I owned a villa.

The only person who could see me was my upstairs neighbour, and only if she leaned so far out of her window, she'd need to file a flight plan.

At first, I sunbathed like a normal man:
shorts, T-shirt, respectable British modesty.
Then one day, lying face-down, the sun warming my back, a single thought crept across my mind with the elegance of a drunk fox:
"You know… the shorts are holding the whole experience back…"
And so, ladies and gentlemen of the late-night schedule…
I slid them off.
No underwear.
No regrets.

Just me, my sunbed, and the kind of breeze that should really take a man out to dinner first.

And then, emboldened by silence, sunshine, and the realisation that nothing terrible had happened, I rolled over.

Let's just say there was… **animation.**
Not a full salute, but definitely a "good evening" rather than a "good afternoon."
But after a moment, everything calmed.
Returned to factory settings.
And I lay there thinking:
"Well, THIS is bloody marvellous."
That was the moment I officially joined the naturist community.

Unofficially. In my garden. With no membership card.

Before long I was doing everything naked out there:
reading, eating, sunbathing, contemplating life, contemplating lunch, contemplating why I hadn't done this sooner.

Then came the curiosity.
The forbidden whisper:
Studland...
Official naturist beach...
Field research, really...

So, one sunny Saturday, off I went, like a man embarking on an erotic pilgrimage.

Sandbanks ferry.
Diet Coke in the cool box.
Nerves jangling like loose change in a washing machine.

I passed the families. The topless sunbathers. The people pretending not to look at the topless sunbathers.

Then I saw the sign:
"Beyond this point, you may encounter naturists."

Encounter.
Like Pokémon.

I stepped forward, removed my T-shirt and shorts, and, BOOM, I was free-range.

The breeze hit me like a spiritual awakening.

Suddenly I understood every Greek statue ever carved.

Within minutes I was walking along the shoreline, letting the waves kiss places waves normally don't get invited to.
It was glorious.

Until, of course, I passed a group of stunning young women splashing in the sea.
My body reacted with the enthusiasm of a Labrador hearing a biscuit tin open.
I froze.
"Not now," I whispered internally.

But the beauty of naturist beaches?
Nobody cares. Nobody looks twice. They just splash harder.
Crisis averted.
Blood pressure normalised.

I laid out my blanket, cracked my Diet Coke, and basked, a man reborn.

Until-
"Hello Keith - fancy seeing you here!"

I opened my eyes.

It was a receptionist from one of my client offices.

Completely naked. Not a stitch. Freshly shaved. Sun catching the curve of her breasts.

Smiling like we'd bumped into each other at Tesco, not on a beach where my bits were making their public debut.

For one mad second, I considered covering myself, but honestly, the towel was miles away and dignity had left the chat long ago.

So, we chatted. As we are innocently chatting she placed her hand on my thigh, nowhere naughty, nonetheless my body chooses that moment to salute her. "Great", I think to myself, "she's attractive, I'm trying to play it cool, and my body is behaving like an excitable Labrador puppy."

She looks down, turns to me and with a cheeky grin said "Well someone's pleased to see me."

I blushed. "I'm sorry" I said.

"Don't worry about it" she said with a grin, "It's just nature, and I'm flattered."

From there on it was just two naked professionals discussing work deadlines while she brushed sand off parts of her body I'd only ever seen on *late-night cable TV*.

Eventually she stood, smiled, and said:
"See you soon - either at the office or here."

Well... she certainly put the "meetings outside office hours" in a new category.

She never told a soul. I never told a soul. Until, of course, now, where you're reading it and probably laughing into your tea.

As the sun set, I packed up, dressed, and drove home feeling relaxed, liberated, and slightly smug.
That day marked the beginning of many summers at Studland, each one a masterclass in sunshine, serenity, and strategic towel placement.

10/10.
A life-changing experience.
Strongly recommended - after 11pm.

My brother from another mother

Some friendships feel accidental.

Mine with Jan felt like destiny, or at least like the universe looked down at the two of us and thought,
"Oh yes. These idiots belong together."

We were more than best mates.
More than brothers.
We were a two-man comedy double act with a telepathic link and absolutely no off-switch.

We'd be sitting in the Wolverton pub, beer in hand, and one of us would lift an eyebrow and the other would already be laughing, and poor Carrie, Jan's future wife, would sit there watching the pair of us dissolve into hysterics over absolutely nothing.

"Come on, boys," she'd plead. "What's the joke?"
But that *was* the joke.
And of course, the more she said it, the harder we laughed.

Sometimes she'd roll her eyes, grab the car keys, mutter "marry *each other* then," and drive home. Jan and I would watch her go, pause... and then erupt again.

We weren't being unkind.
We were just... us.

Beams, Chips, and One Unplanned Knockout
The Wolverton pub had low ceilings with big, dark, medieval beams, the kind old buildings love to show off as if to say,
"Look at me, I'm historic."

Well, they certainly made history with my forehead.
Every time I visited, I'd smack my head on one of them hard enough to make the beer taps vibrate. It got to the point regulars would wince before I even reached the bar, like watching someone approach a glass door they definitely weren't going to see.
Maybe that's how my skull evolved into the armour-plated model it is today.

But even armour has limits.
One night, after a few too many pints, Jan and I stopped at a fish and chip shop. The doorframe was, and I still maintain this, illegally low. I stepped forward, misjudged it, and WHACK.
Lights out.
Keith down.

I came to staring up at the universe, or possibly at the "Open Late" sign. Hard to tell.
Jan stood over me, deadpan as ever.
"Well," he said, "I guess we're not getting our chips then."
The man should've been a stand-up comedian.

An ambulance came, loaded me up, and Jan joined for the ride, making the paramedics laugh the whole way. At the hospital, the doctor told me I had mild concussion and needed to stay overnight. Jan gave me one of our legendary man-hugs, the kind that meant more than words, and left to meet Carrie.

The next morning, she picked me up from Milton Keynes Central.
"Say thanks to Jan," I said.

She gave a small smile.
"Oh, trust me - he was worried sick."
It was nice, that. Warm. Real.

Mud, Muskets, and Two Blokes in One Sleeping Bag

Before all that, in our Middlesex Polytechnic days (which became Middlesex University halfway through, like a Hogwarts upgrade), Jan invited me into one of his favourite hobbies: English Civil War re-enactment.

Think the Sealed Knot... but without the rulebook. Or much of the accuracy.

One weekend stands out, Cheriton, near Winchester. It rained so much you'd think we'd offended the weather gods personally.

The journey was already ridiculous.
We travelled across London, on the Tube, mind you, in full 17th-century battle gear, with canvas rucksacks stuffed with tent poles, sleeping bags, and possibly the hopes and dreams of two very wet, very naïve young men.

Commuters stared. Rightly so.

We arrived in Winchester, discovered we'd missed the last bus, and ended up trudging miles through the downpour before collapsing into the Percy Hobbs pub, soaked, muddy, and smelling like damp historical reenactors (a niche perfume line that never took off).

The landlord took one look and asked, "…Where are you two off to?"
Jan, ever the performer, bowed slightly.
"To the Battle of Cheriton, sire."
A burly local at the bar snorted into his pint.
"You're walking? In this?"
"Yes," Jan said nobly. "We missed the bus."
"Well, you're not missing a lift," the man said, Bill, our damp hero,
and drove us the rest of the way in his mud-caked Land Rover.

We tried to buy him a pint. He refused. Decent bloke, Bill.

Re-enactors, Dung Cannons, and Improvised Finance
Jan's group took authenticity very seriously.

Some slept under canvas sheets strung between branches.

We, being soft, had a tent. And thank goodness, it rained all night.

Breakfast was a skillet over the fire: bacon, eggs, and the ingenious trick of burying foil-wrapped pies in the embers so that dinner cooked itself over eight hours.

Our weapons?
Real muskets firing pyrotechnic flashes.
And a cannon that fired cannonballs made from hardened cow dung and straw.
Safe enough unless some bright spark wrapped theirs in newspaper.
Flaming dungballs across the battlefield.
Historical accuracy: *zero*.
Entertainment value: absolutely *priceless*.
The Royalists always won Saturday.
The Parliamentarians always won Sunday.

Tradition.

We celebrated Saturday's victory in the marquee bar, where we discovered a lucrative sideline:

£1 deposit on plastic pint glasses.
So we collected abandoned ones, stacked them neatly, and returned £10 worth at a time.
We were business geniuses.
Damp, muddy, slightly tipsy business geniuses.

The Coldest Night of My Life (But Not Without Warmth)

Going back to the tent that night was like walking into a fridge with pretensions.

Everything was soaked. Everything. Including our underwear.

There's only one solution in such circumstances:
body heat.

So, we stripped, hung our clothes to dry, zipped our sleeping bags together, something we'd done once before, and spooned for survival.

Nothing romantic.
Nothing sexual.
Just two mud-covered warriors clinging to warmth and dignity by the thinnest thread.

Sunday, we lost the battle on schedule, Dad collected us, and Mum made us strip down to our boxers before stepping into the house.

She took one look at us, bedraggled, muddy, exhausted, and said,
"Oh, for heaven's sake. Clothes off. Porch. Now."

There's something humbling about standing in your childhood home, dripping mud in your underwear while your mother judges your life choices.

We laughed about it then. I still laugh about it now.

Those trips weren't glamorous. They weren't sensible. They weren't dry.

But they were glorious because they were with Jan.

Some friendships aren't just chapters.
They're the heartbeat running through the whole book.

When fate knocks twice

There's a theory I've mentioned a few times in this book, my personal law of cosmic nudges:

- If someone appears in your life once, that's coincidence.
- Twice, that's chance.
- Three times or more?
  That's the universe shaking you by the shoulders going, *"Oi. Pay attention."*

Which brings me neatly, and somewhat dramatically, to Enma.

Roy, Hazel, and the Open Secret No One Discussed at Christmas

My brother Roy was married to Hazel, and they had the kind of marriage that survives everything. Arguments, boredom, routine, even, apparently, Enma.

Because Roy and Enma had been conducting an "on-and-off… but mostly on" affair for years. The kind of family secret everyone knew, nobody mentioned, and which hovered over gatherings like an unwanted balloon.

For Roy, Hazel was home.
For Roy, Enma, was… well, let's say "after-hours entertainment."

Enma had two faithful companions apart from Roy:
Cigarettes and vodka.

She battled alcohol dependency the way some people battle weeds, sometimes it looked under control, sometimes it came roaring back stronger than ever. One tiny emotional bump and she'd tumble.

At the time, my own life wasn't exactly a victory parade. Concepta Designs had gone under.

I was living like a well-organised hobo on a camp bed in Roger's lounge.
Everything I owned was stuffed into Roy's lock-up or one of his many sheds.

(If Roy could've hidden the moon in a shed, he would've.)

Roy was due in hospital for a few days.

"If you take me in," he said, "you can use my car. Just keep an eye on Enma. Cigarettes or vodka when she asks."

Not exactly Florence Nightingale, but fair enough.

Day One: Cigarettes, Vodka, and the Window Tap
Enma lived in a neat ground-floor flat in Readon Close, the sort of place where the curtains were always drawn but the welcome was warm enough.

She texted:
Could you get me cigarettes and vodka and pop round? Just tap the window.

The great romance of our age.

I went. Tapped. She opened the window like a transactional fairy godmother, took the bag, said thanks, and that was that.

Easy.

Day Two: "Come Keep Me Company"
The next day, another text, this time just vodka.
When I arrived, she didn't hand-wave me away.

"Come in for a bit," she said. "Keep me company."

She was tucked up in bed watching a murder mystery, smoking like someone had stolen her last match.

"Do you mind?" she asked, holding up the cigarette. "It's your flat," I said. "I'm just the delivery boy."

"Want a drink?" "I don't drink vodka." "Make yourself a coffee then."

And that was us.

TV murmuring.
Coffee steaming.
Two people talking late into the night like the world outside didn't exist.

At eleven I stood up.

"I'd better go. Roger will think I've been kidnapped."

I leaned in and kissed her cheek, a simple, friendly goodbye.

Except it didn't quite feel simple.

Day Three: The Kiss That Lasted Too Long
Night three, she greeted me with a kiss before I'd even sat down.

We talked for hours again, the conversation the kind that drifts where it wants to go, memories, regrets, hope, fear, laughter, the odd deep breath.

When I finally stood to leave, she held my hand.

The kiss... lingered.

Then she said the words that froze the room:

"If you walk out of that door tonight, you'll never see me again."

Not angry. Not dramatic. Just truth.

One of those universe-shaking-your-shoulders moments.

And that was the night everything changed.

"Roy Will Swing for You"
The next day I told Roger, "I'll be staying with Enma for a few days."

He blinked.
"Roy will swing for you."

"I know. But I think this is where I'm meant to be."

The "few days" became a few weeks.
Then months.
Then three years, right up until the moment life took her far, far too soon.

Michelle's Entrance: A Daughter, A Threat, and a Truce
One early afternoon I was lying next to Enma, not asleep, just drifting, when the door opened and in walked Michelle, her grown daughter, holding a Tesco bag.

"Hi Mum, I-"

She stopped. Saw me. Assessed the situation.

"And who is **he?**"

"This is Roy's brother Keith," Enma said. "We're together now."

Michelle blinked once. Raised an eyebrow that could cut glass. Then headed for the kitchen.

"I'll help," I said, following her like a nervous apprentice.

She closed the door behind us. Quiet voice. Utterly calm.

"If you make my mum happy, that's fine by me.
But if you ever treat her like your brother has…
you'll be spending the rest of your life singing an octave higher."

I believed her. Anyone would.

I nodded. "I'd never hurt her. I hope we can be friends."

She paused.
Nodded slowly.

"We'll see."

And that was the moment I knew:
this wasn't just a detour.
This was a real chapter, one full of mess, sweetness, pain, laughter, and a woman who'd become part of my story in a way I never expected.

Sometimes the people you're meant to meet don't arrive with fireworks. Sometimes they tap on a window.

And sometimes…
you tap back.

The great escape

Enma's mum, Emma, had the kind of backstory that deserved its own Netflix mini-series.

She'd fled Spain with Enma near the end of Franco's rule, real historical drama, only to spend her later years in a nursing home in Southsea, where her life became... well, more *Benny Hill* than *Ben-Hur*.

By the time I knew her, Emma had early-onset dementia. But please understand: this didn't stop her from living her best life. If anything, it seemed to supercharge her talent for mischief.

Because Emma, dear reader, was an **escape artist**.

Not occasionally. Not accidentally. Not "once during a full moon."
No, *regularly*.

Every so often we'd hear a knock at our door, look up... and there she was.

Tiny Spanish woman. Little handbag. Big grin.
Absolutely no idea how many buses she'd taken or whose garden she'd walked through to get here.

I'd have to gently coax her back into the car, and off we'd go to the home like a mismatched detective duo. Sometimes Enma came with me, and they'd chatter away in Galician Spanish, all rolling r's and laughter, like two birds singing in a dialect only they understood.

Emma's English...
Well.

Let's say it was **highly strategic**.

When it suited her, she understood everything perfectly.
When it didn't?

"¿Qué?" Shrug. Head-tilt. Innocent eyes.

She could've replaced Manuel in *Fawlty Towers* and no one would've spotted the swap.

The Southsea Incident

But nothing, *nothing,* prepared me for the famous L'Escargot affair.

It was a cold December afternoon when my phone rang.
Portsmouth number.
Didn't recognise it.

"Hello," said a polite female voice. "Is that Keith?"

"Yes…" I replied, already bracing myself. "Who's calling?"

"This is L'Escargot restaurant in Southsea."

Now, nothing wakes you up like the words *restaurant* and *Southsea* when you aren't in one.

"We have Emma here," the woman continued sweetly, "and she's had a three-course lunch with us. And a couple of glasses of wine."

Of course she had.

"When we brought her the bill, she said, 'It's fine, call Keith. He'll pay.' So… it's £31.95. If you've got a card handy, I can take payment now."

I froze.

There are moments in life when you feel two emotions at once. This was equal parts outrage and admiration.

The cheek of it. The brilliance of it. I paid.

"What about Emma?" I asked. "Do I need to come get her?"

The woman laughed.

"No, one of our staff recognised her - her mum's in the same home. We'll take her back."

Of course.
Emma knew *everyone*.

"Thank you," I sighed. "And if she escapes again and ends up with you…, could you just run her straight back?"

"We'll do our best," she said, the voice of someone who already knew this was not going to be the last Emma-related episode of her career.

Whether Emma ever returned to L'Escargot, I'll never know. They never rang again...

Which means one of two things:

1. **She found a new restaurant to charm.**
   or
2. **Southsea collectively decided I had suffered enough.**

Either way, she lived life exactly the way she wanted, with mischief, laughter, and a well-timed "¿Qué?" whenever the bill arrived.

A weekend of water, warmth and quiet joy

Enma's mobility was always a sort of negotiation with gravity. Indoors, she moved with the regal precision of someone conducting an invisible orchestra, one hand on a doorframe, one on the back of a chair, a little shuffle here, a little pivot there. Outdoors, it was the wheelchair and me, her faithful chauffeur with questionable pushing technique.

But swimming, ah, swimming was her escape hatch.
Once a week, if she felt up to it, I'd help her into her swimsuit, drape loose clothes over the top, and wheel her down to the leisure centre. It became our ritual.

I'd get her settled in the disabled changing room (which, frankly, felt designed by someone who'd never undressed another human being in their life), then hand her over to the pool attendants. Off she'd go, gliding through the water.

I'd nip to the gym, gently pretend I knew how treadmills worked, then return to collect her, dry her, dress her, wheel her home, and help her in the shower.

Some days it went smoothly.
Other days I needed the strength of a forklift and the dexterity of a ninja.

South Devon: The Weekend of Sun, Spa, and Surprises
Breaks were rare, but one year we managed a long weekend at a holiday park in South Devon. Accessible cabin. Nice pool. Spa. The holy trinity.

We arrived Friday lunchtime, just the two of us and the suitcase that weighed suspiciously like it contained the entire contents of Boots.

On Saturday morning we treated ourselves to the spa.
Sauna first, hot enough to roast a small turkey, then a couples massage. Two beds, two masseuses, soft music that sounded like someone rubbing a wind chime. It was oddly romantic. Enma reached across the gap between our beds and took my hand.

Just a small touch, but lovely.

Later, she wanted to swim, and I was desperate to try the archery, I'd decided it was time to see whether I still the Robin Hood of my university days or whether I'd evolved into Friar Tuck.

The holiday park changing room was a revelation - a *proper* changing table.
"Why can't our leisure centre have one of these?" she said.

I nodded. "Because that would be useful, helpful, and logical, three things they avoid at all costs."

On poolside, the hoist awaited. Enma tolerated it the way a cat tolerates being placed in a bubble bath.

"It makes me feel like a whale," she muttered. "Now imagine David Attenborough narrating this."

We laughed. She splashed blissfully. I went off to dangerously brandish arrows.

When I returned, she was being hoisted out, tired but glowing. Back to the cabin. She napped. I sat beside her watching the world's quietest television.
We'd needed this.

Sunday: Roast Dinners and Reckless Decisions
Sunday was slow and peaceful.
Lie-in. Breakfast. A roast lunch so good I nearly proposed to the chef.

After a few lunchtime drinks, Enma decided she wanted another swim.

I hesitated. She'd had... let's call it *a generous amount* to drink.

But when Enma made up her mind, resistance was as effective as trying to hold back the tide with a pot noodle.

So, off we went.

I wheeled her down, helped her change, handed her over to the pool team, then nipped to the gym. When I got back, she was freshly hoisted and ready to be dried and dressed.

We reached the changing room, the nice one, thank heavens,

and I helped her onto the table.
Swimsuit came down to her waist. I moved to the end to slide it off fully.

I turned to fetch her clothes.

When I turned back...
she'd shuffled herself down the table, legs dangling, elbows propped behind her, mischief sparkling in her eyes like someone about to break every rule in the handbook.

"Make love to me," she said.

"Of course," I replied. "When we're back at the cabin."

She reached forward and in a move Houdini would have been proud of, tugged my shorts and boxers down to the floor. I swear I never saw her hand move.

"No. Now."

I laughed nervously. "Enma... we can't do that here."

And then, Lord help me, she deployed **the nuclear option**: "If you don't," she said sweetly, "I'll pull that red alarm cord. And when they come in, I'll tell them you assaulted me."

Under normal circumstances I'd assume she was joking.
But tipsy Enma did not bluff.

I pictured the newspaper headline:

"Local Man Arrested in Changing Room Chaos, Swimsuit Still at Scene."

"You win," I sighed. "But you have to be quiet."

(If you've been paying attention, you'll know: Enma was *not* a quiet woman.)

Was it romantic? Not in the cinematic sense.
Was it... memorable?
Oh yes. Unforgettably so.

Afterwards, she kissed me cheerfully.
"Right," she announced, "get us dressed. I'm sleepy."

"And by the way," she added with a grin as I packed her bag, "I absolutely would've pulled that cord."

"I know," I said. "That's why I surrendered."

Walking out, I avoided eye contact with every living human.
If anyone heard anything, they never mentioned it.
I never asked.

Heading Home
The rest of the weekend was wonderfully normal.
TV. Tea. Gentle kisses. Peace.

On Monday morning, as we loaded the car, Enma squeezed my hand.

"That was a good weekend," she said.

And she was right.

It had been warm, ridiculous, tender, chaotic, funny, exhausting, and utterly ours, which, in its own way, made it perfect.

The longest goodbye

New Year's Day 2005 felt like stepping onto a brand-new page.
Enma and I were engaged. We'd just had approval on our first proper home together: a two-bedroom bungalow in Liss.

After three years squeezed into a one-bedroom flat in Petersfield, a charming little shoebox where you could make a cup of tea *and* turn the bed down without taking more than two steps, the bungalow felt like Buckingham Palace.

We got the keys on 1st February.
My friend Mike helped me move. No removal men, no chaos, no broken furniture, just two blokes, a hired van, and enough coffee to keep a small army alert.

I remember walking to the van hire in Bedford Road that morning.

Crisp winter air, pale sunlight, that delicious "new life is starting" feeling bubbling somewhere under my ribs.
It all went perfectly, van collected, van returned, furniture arranged, kettle unpacked, and by nightfall we were officially in.

Twenty years later, I'm still here.
The longest I've ever stayed in one place.
Funny how life roots you when you're not looking.

Settling In, and the First Signs

February was all about boxes, paint swatches, and debates over appliances.

Enma insisted, *insisted,* that we buy a Bosch washing machine.

"It'll last forever," she said confidently.

I wasn't convinced, but she was.

And in fairness, the thing lasted fifteen years, outliving several relationships, a car, and two microwaves.
Never doubt a Spanish woman with a strong opinion and a catalogue.

But by early March, something didn't feel right.

Enma was having more "bad days" than good ones.
She stayed in bed longer. Curtains closed. Appetite low.
I urged her to see Dr. Ellis, our lovely GP, the kind who always looked like he'd just stepped out of an advert for sensible jumpers, but she brushed me off.

Then, one morning, I opened the curtains and sunlight poured across her face.

Her eyes… were yellow.

Not "tired yellow." Not "winter light yellow." **Jaundice yellow.**

Under the artificial bulb of the bedside lamp, I hadn't noticed. But the daylight told the truth in one brutal flash.

I rang Dr. Ellis immediately.

He came that afternoon, gentle, calm, professional as ever, but his face tightened as he examined her.

"Enma," he said softly, "you need to be in hospital. I'm calling an ambulance."

Then he walked me to the door and dropped his voice.

"Keith… she's extremely ill. I think her pancreas and liver are failing. Prepare yourself. She may not come home again."

The words felt like stones landing on my chest.

I packed her a small bag, nighties, toiletries, her favourite moisturiser, the little things she liked to have nearby.

The ambulance came. Blue lights flashed.

I followed in my car, praying the A3 would stay clear.

The First Night
Hours passed at QA Hospital.
Hours filled with the sterile smell of disinfectant, bad coffee, and that anxious pacing you only do in hospital corridors.

Eventually a doctor appeared. I followed him to her bed.

She was weak, but conscious. We talked a little.
I stayed until her breathing slowed and she drifted to sleep.

Later, they moved her to a side room.
The moment I stepped in, a memory slammed into me, Mum's final hours in a similar room.
Whenever I visit that same hospital today, as I have many times, I still can't look up at the window of that room.

I told Enma I'd return in the morning.

Her eyes fluttered open.

"Please don't go, darling," she whispered. "I need you."

So, I stayed. Sat beside her. Held her hand. Watched her sleep.

Before leaving, I kissed her hand.

"Bye bye, darling. I'll be back in the morning."

3 a.m.
I made it home just before midnight. Made a mug of Horlicks. Told myself I'd call Michelle in the morning.

At 3 a.m., the phone rang.

"Mr Budden? I'm afraid Enma has taken a downturn. You should come at once."

The A3 was a ghost road at that hour.
I don't think any of the traffic cameras caught me, if they did, they were merciful.

A nurse met me at the door.

"She doesn't have long," she said softly.

I sat beside her again. Held her hand again.
No drama. No suddenness. No last words.
Just the gentlest slipping away, like someone blowing out a candle.

I felt her hand go limp.

"I think she's gone," I told the nurse.

She checked, nodded, fetched the doctor.

"I'm so sorry," he said.

I stayed. Talked to her. Cried. Thanked her for every day we'd had. Told her I was glad her pain was over.

Telling Michelle
I drove home in a fog.
At 7 a.m., I phoned Michelle.

"Michelle..." I said softly. "I've got some really bad news."

Her voice broke. She came later that morning. We talked. We cried. We tried to make sense of something that never really does.

The Farewell
The weeks that followed drifted past in slow motion.

We arranged a Roman Catholic funeral in the small wooden church in Liss.

I'd never been to a Catholic service, all incense, rhythms, and responses, so different from the Church of England ones I grew up with.

Enma's son, Richard, wasn't sure he could face it, but he arrived just in time. I hugged him and said, "You won't regret coming."

The burial at West Liss Cemetery was quiet and peaceful. Later, at the Spread Eagle, we shared stories, funny ones, tender ones, the kind that remind you someone's life was full, even if their years were too few.

A year later, Michelle and I chose the headstone.
We joked about engraving:

"KEITH... YOU LITTLE SHIT, GET HERE NOW!"

(It was her favourite command.)

But we chose something more traditional.

Gentler. More Enma.

Twenty Years On
Two decades later, I still live in the bungalow.
Still open the curtains where the sunlight once showed me the truth. Still feel her presence in the quiet corners of the house we never quite finished decorating.

And Michelle is still in my life - not as a reminder of what I lost, but as a continuation of what Enma gave me.

A little adopted family. A little legacy. A little love that didn't end.

Enma hasn't faded.
She's woven into every room, every memory, every quiet evening in this house we built together.

Some loves don't vanish. They just change shape. And stay.

The year that wouldn't behave itself

If 2005 had been a polite, well-mannered year, it would have tapped me on the shoulder, apologised for the mess so far, and promised to do better.

Instead, it leaned in, whispered *"hold my beer,"* and carried on.

Enma's passing had hit me harder than I admitted to anyone, including myself.

Silence settled over the bungalow like a heavy quilt. Too heavy. Too quiet. Too full of reminders.

The Bruises I Didn't Notice
One warm day in April, after a few hours attacking weeds in Michelle's garden that refused to die, I was sweating like I'd run a marathon.

"Mind if I use your shower?" I asked.
"'Course not," Michelle said. "You know where everything is."
She handed me a towel with that domestic efficiency she'd perfected long before marriage.

I pulled off my T-shirt and she frowned.
"What are those bruises under your arm?"
I turned to the mirror.
She was right, faint purple blotches, nothing dramatic, but definitely there.
"No idea," I said. "Maybe I'm sleepwalking into furniture."
I shrugged it off. Michelle didn't.

A week later, while shaving, I noticed the left side of my neck was swollen. Firm. Uneven. A bit like someone had glued half a golf ball under my skin.

And, like most men, I thought:
I'll get it checked one day.
When it grew bigger, noticeably bigger, I finally rang the out-of-hours GP.
He took one glance and declared confidently,
"It's mumps. Go home, rest, two weeks."

Two weeks later: no change.
If anything, the swelling had ambitions for promotion.

Michelle's voice tightened when she saw it.
"Daddy, please. See Dr Ellis."
Dr Ellis, the man who had treated Enma with more care than some people give their own family, took one look at me, and gave me his famous "why-do-you-make-my-job-harder" stare over his glasses.
"It's not mumps," he said. "I'm referring you to oncology at St Mary's."
Then he handed me a sick note for three months.
Three months.
Either he expected a long wait...
or he expected something else entirely.
I wasn't left wondering for long.

Fast-Tracked
The next morning, St Mary's called.

"Mr Budden? We'd like to see you tomorrow morning."
Tomorrow.
That was when my stomach did the kind of slow gymnastic roll that only unwelcome news inspires.

At the hospital, they drew blood and told me results would take a couple of hours.
A text from Michelle.
"How's it going?"
"Given blood," I replied. "Not seen doctor yet."

I tried to drink coffee, but my hand trembled, giving the cup the personality of a nervous hamster.

Eventually, the doctor called me in. And I knew. I knew from the way he closed the door. From the way he sat. From the way he didn't blink quite enough.

"I'm sorry to have to tell you this," he said gently, "but from your symptoms and blood results, we believe you have cancer. Likely lymphoma."

He talked about biopsies, scans, staging, treatment plans.
He finished with: "Try not to worry."
I actually stared at him.
Try not to worry? You've just told me my body is staging a coup, and your advice is *don't fret*?
Doctors are incredible people, but sometimes their optimism is written in a language the rest of us don't speak.

The Call
I phoned Michelle that evening.

"They think I've got cancer," I said.

Silence. A breath. Then, softly: "Oh my God... I'm coming over."

She arrived, hugged me tight, and we sat together, talking, not talking, eating without tasting anything.

When she left, she hugged me again at the door.
I stood alone in the bungalow, the word *cancer* sitting beside me like an uninvited guest.

For the second time that year, life had changed direction without warning. And this time, it didn't whisper. It roared.

The day my life hit pause (but the hospital hit play)

The next few weeks of my life were basically the medical equivalent of a pub crawl, except instead of beer, there were scans, needles, blood tests, and the faint smell of antiseptic.

St Mary's, QA, Southampton General, Salisbury... by the end of it, I could've led guided tours.

"On your left, the waiting room where I lost all feeling in my backside. On the right, the vending machine that stole my pound *every single time*."

The Scans: A Symphony of Beeps and Banging
The CT and MRI scans were strangely fascinating, like being slid into a giant mechanical doughnut with the personality of an irritable drummer.

The CT was quick and civilised.
The MRI, however, sounded like someone was trying to break out of the machine with a sledgehammer.

They gave me headphones and piped music, which was adorable, really, because the machine simply turned up the volume and shouted:
BANG-BANG-BANG-BANG-BANG
like it was auditioning for a heavy metal band.

But the best bit?
The Scottish lady.
Every CT scan I ever had, Portsmouth, Guildford, Southampton, the same voice drifted into my ears:
"Breathe in... hold your breath... breathe normally."
After the third hospital I remember thinking:
"She's everywhere. She's like the Morgan Freeman of radiography."
And then it hit me.
She wasn't teleporting between counties, she was **pre-recorded**.
Still, she was excellent company.
7th July 2005 - The Day London Stopped, and My Life Tilted on Its Axis

The morning of my diagnosis began with me pulling on my shirt while Sky News reported "possible power faults" on the Underground.

By the time I reached the oncology department, every screen showed chaos.
Bombs. Sirens. Confusion. The whole country frozen with fear.
Oddly, having that on the screens calmed me.
My brain went: "Well... at least everyone's day is going badly."

Then the nurse called out:
"Mr Budden?"
And in I went.

Meeting Dr Ann O'Callaghan, the Calm in the Storm
She had a warm smile, steady eyes, and on the wall behind her was a wonderfully inappropriate cartoon:
A plane falling out of the sky, engines on fire, and a passenger yelling into a phone,
"You bastard, you said I'd die of cancer!"

I liked her immediately.

Then she told me the news:
Diffuse Large B-Cell Non-Hodgkin's Lymphoma.
A tumour in my chest. Cancer spread to my neck, armpits, groin.
But still contained in the lymphatic system. Treatable. Urgent.
Aggressive plan.

R-CHOP chemotherapy, every two weeks.

A pharmacological alphabet soup.
She gently listed the side effects.
I heard about three of them.
Then she said, "hair loss" and suddenly my brain switched back on like someone had hit Ctrl+Alt+Del.

Sitting beside her was Becky, the loveliest oncology nurse ever to walk the earth.
She handed me a card with all her numbers.
"Call me any time. Day or night."
And I believed her.
Walking back to the car, the radio was still full of terrible news from London, but somehow, listening to that was easier than thinking about the word I'd just been handed:

Cancer.

"Why me?"
Michelle came over that evening.

And I broke. Properly broke. The kind of crying you only do when you've run out of brave.

"Why *me*?" I said.
"I've never smoked. I hardly drink. I eat properly. Why the hell should *I* get cancer?"

I looked upward, in the general direction of God, heaven, fate, or the ceiling plaster, and said:
"Go on then. Hit me again."

Michelle wrapped her arms around me.
"Hey. You'll beat this," she whispered.
"You've got strength, and humour, and stubbornness... and me. Always me."

And in that moment, in that quiet, fragile space, I decided:
"Cancer, you can fuck right off."
And that was the beginning of the fight.

The day I donated my future to Salisbury Hospital

One of the many side effects of chemotherapy, Dr Ann O'Callaghan explained, was infertility.

She said it kindly, professionally, but with the firmness of a woman who had given this speech to hundreds of hopeful dads-to-be and the odd startled bachelor.

I was forty. Widowed. Exhausted. And, frankly, in absolutely no rush to revisit the world of romance.

Still, she recommended, strongly, that I go to Salisbury Hospital and freeze a sample.

"Insurance," she said.

"You don't know what the future holds," Michelle echoed later. "You might not want children now... but you might one day. And once you start chemo, that choice is gone."

When two determined women give you the same advice, the wise response is to nod and do as you're told.

So, one sunny July morning in 2005, I drove to Salisbury Hospital, armed only with directions that sounded like they'd been written by someone who didn't believe in road signs.

The Waiting Room of Destiny
Inside the fertility clinic, the air hummed with an atmosphere I can only describe as *hopeful tension*.

Couples everywhere. Handholding. Nervous smiles. Whispered conversations about ovulation, hormones, appointments.

And then there was me. Solo.
Holding a letter that essentially said:

"Dear Mr Budden,
Please arrive at 10:30 a.m.
Abstain for 48 hours beforehand.
Best of luck."

I'm fairly sure several people wondered what sort of experiment I was participating in.

My name was called, and a cheerful clinician led me to a consultation room.

"This is the jar."
"Here are the tissues."
"And here is... the library."

She handed me a specimen jar like it was the Holy Grail.

Then she opened a tall metal cupboard with the reverence of someone unveiling treasure.

"In here," she said, "is a selection of... publications to help with the process. Most are adult. Some are... alternative."

She paused.
Completely straight-faced.

"We did have a copy of *Horse & Hound*, but someone stole it."

I don't know who that man was, but I salute his courage.

With that, she showed me the sink, the discreet paper bag, the lock on the door, and left me.

"No time limit," she said. Which is possibly the most unhelpful thing to say before such a task.

A Solo Mission with an Unwanted Soundtrack
There I was. Just me. My jar.
And a room whose walls were thinner than human decency deserved.

Every time I approached... well... the moment of inspiration, someone would walk past, cough, or drop a clipboard, and everything inside me would slam on the brakes like a learner driver approaching a roundabout.

But eventually, eventually, the stars aligned, the corridor fell silent, and mission success was achieved.

I sealed the jar like it contained state secrets, tidied up, washed my hands with the thoroughness of a man who wanted absolutely no misunderstandings, and walked out to reception trying to look casual.

The receptionist took the bag.
"Take a seat while I pop this to the lab."

She returned a few minutes later with a warm smile that blended medical professionalism and faint amusement.

"Good news, Mr Budden. Your sample is perfectly viable."

I thanked her, resisted the urge to salute, and walked out into the sunshine feeling oddly relieved, and profoundly grateful that I'd never have to do *that* again.

Insurance policy for life

While I'd already made that first donation of stem cells for future generations of my family, I now needed to make one for *me*. Insurance for later, as Dr Ann O'Callaghan put it, and when Ann gives advice, you take it. She's got that calm, reassuring manner that makes you believe she could probably land a plane if needed.

Given how far my Non-Hodgkin's Lymphoma had advanced, she recommended I undergo a stem cell extraction. The idea was simple enough: under sedation they would draw bone marrow and blood from the back of my pelvis, right at the top of the hips, harvest the stem cells, freeze them, and keep them ready for a future transplant if things got worse. Because they were my own cells, the rejection risk would be lower. A tiny chance existed that the lymphoma had already mutated some of them, but the odds were so small it was barely worth a mention.

In short: very sensible science. An easy decision. I agreed.

They wheeled me into the treatment room, dressed in the standard hospital gown that never quite covers what you hope it would. This time they didn't even bother fastening it properly at the back, the doctors would need full access to my pelvis anyway, so modesty wasn't going to make the guest list for this procedure.

A cheerful, middle-aged woman introduced herself as my anaesthetist. Warm smile, calm voice, the kind of woman who could tell you your house had exploded and somehow still make you feel better about it.

She explained the plan: sedation through a face mask, and I would hold her hand throughout. If the pain became too much, I was to squeeze. She would increase the sedation, maybe give an epidural. And if all else failed, they could always knock me out completely.

"You'll be fine," she said. "You're a big, strong boy."

That should have been comforting.

It wasn't.

Then, right before we started, she said, "Let me see your fingernails."

I held my hands out. She examined them, sighed, and started filing them like a manicurist on minimum wage.

"Why are you doing that?" I asked.

"Because" she said matter-of-factly, "when it gets really painful and you squeeze my hand, I don't want your nails puncturing my skin."

"How painful are we talking?"

She didn't hesitate.
"For a man? Probably the closest you'll ever get to childbirth."

I gulped. Hard. Suddenly a full anaesthetic sounded like a terrific idea.

But the mask was already over my face, the gas was flowing, and by the time the doctor said, "Ready?" I was floating somewhere between relaxed and "do what you like, mate."

He numbed my left hip. No problem. Then he inserted the needles.

Still fine.

Then the needles reached my pelvis.

Not fine.

NOT fine.

The pain was like nothing I'd felt in my entire life, not stabbing, not burning, not crushing, but all three fighting each other to see who could make me swear first. My body jolted. Instinct took over. I squeezed the anaesthetist's hand so hard I'm amazed she didn't sue me.

She increased the sedation quickly, and the pain eased from "kill me now" to merely "this is absolutely appalling."

Ladies, if childbirth really is anything like that, I bow down to you. No wonder you mock us when we have man-flu. You've earned that right. Frankly, you should get a medal.

The extraction eventually finished, and the stem cells were

stored away like a biological rainy-day fund. Fortunately, I never needed them, but as someone told me years later:

"You don't insure your house hoping it burns down."

Quite right.

Chemo, chaos and the day I told a stranger I didn't give a shit

So began my journey with chemotherapy, a journey no one asks for, but if you're stuck on the ride, you may as well buckle in and make sarcastic comments.

Session One began in the day case ward, where I discovered the glamorous truth: chemo isn't pre-mixed like a cocktail at a hotel bar.
It's custom-made in the hospital pharmacy, tailored, fresh, expensive, like artisanal poison delivered straight to your veins.

Becky popped her head around my curtain, all sunshine and competence.

"How's it going? Any pain? Any dizziness?"

"No," I said. "Just tired. And starving."

"Good," she smiled, rifling through my giant paper bag of medication like she was checking my shopping list. "Remember: if you need me, any time, day or night, call."

You always believe Becky.

By mid-afternoon I was home, on the sofa, telling myself I'd rest "for a minute."

I woke up three hours later, face down, drooling slightly. Excellent start.

⭐ Steroids: Because Cancer Isn't Hard Enough Without Hunger Pangs
The first fortnight was surprisingly manageable, except the steroids. Oh, the steroids.

They made me hungry enough to eat my own curtains.

One day I prowled the kitchen like a bear emerging from hibernation, found nothing appealing, and decided the only reasonable solution was Tesco.

Unfortunately, half of Petersfield had the same idea.

No parking spaces anywhere.

The steroids whispered:
"Park there. PARK THERE. You NEED cheese."

So, I parked in a residents-only spot on Hylton Road.

Twenty yards down the pavement I heard the dreaded:

"EXCUSE ME!"

A woman pointed at my car like I'd keyed her Ferrari.

"You can't park there."

I smiled the calm, serene smile of a man fuelled by pharmaceutical-grade appetite.

"I'm sorry," I said.
"It appears to be a case of mistaken identity."

She blinked, confused.

"You," I continued sweetly, "have mistaken me for someone who gives a shit."

I wished her good day and carried on to Tesco.
Steroids: 1. Manners: 0.

🏆 By Round Three, Things Got... Weird
Six weeks in, the pain ramped up. The co-codamol might as well have been Smarties.

Becky arranged for Dr O'Callaghan to see me.

She came over, radiating calm authority.

"What seems to be the bother?"
(A question that usually meant she was about to prescribe something potent enough to knock out a small rhino.)

"I'm prescribing Oramorph," she said.
"Morphine, but drinkable. It will constipate you. And you may hallucinate."

She was right on both counts. Oh yes. She was right.

🏆 The Hallucinations: A Three-Act Fever Dream

Act I: The Frogs
I glanced into the toilet bowl and discovered six vivid green frogs staring up at me.

"Watcha," one said.

Cheerful little things.
I laughed and thought, *This could be fun.*

Act II: The Giant Teddy Bear
Washing up one day, I looked out the window and saw a blue-and-yellow teddy bear the size of a house walking down the street.

It stepped over roofs. It squashed a car. It waved.

I phoned Michelle, panicked.

"Michelle! There's a giant teddy bear walking down the road!"

A pause.

"Keith... have you taken your morphine today?"

I looked at the bottle.

"Yes."

"Weeellll... that explains it."

We laughed until I nearly dropped the phone.

Act III: The Pigeon That Wasn't
This one wasn't funny.

I walked into the kitchen to find a pigeon on the floor eating crumbs.

I could hear it. Smell it.
I opened the windows.
I flapped a tea towel at it.

It flew, then dissolved into pixels mid-air like a video game glitch.

That one chilled me.

Morphine dreams are not for the faint-hearted.

⭐ Goodbye Hair. And Eyelashes. And Eyebrows. ALL of it.

I'd expected the head hair to go.

Fine. I shaved it. Looked like Ross Kemp's slightly taller cousin.

But the rest?

Gone. All of it. Every last follicle.

Pubic hair? Missing in action.

Eyebrows? Evaporated.

Eyelashes? History.

I discovered, painfully, that their primary purpose is to keep rain out of your eyes.

A raindrop directly to the eyeball feels like God flicking you.

⭐ The Pond, the Ducks, and the Shift

Most days, I walked to the duck pond in Newman Collard Park.

I sat. Read. Thought. Listened to water and wind and the quiet hum of life happening around me.

And slowly, something shifted.

I stopped asking:

"Why me?"

And one day, without fanfare, the question changed to:

"Why not me?"

What made me so fucking special that it shouldn't be me?

What made me exempt from life's randomness?
Who was I to expect immunity?

In that moment, tiny, silent, monumental, everything in me realigned.

I stopped feeling like a victim.

I started to feel like a survivor.

And from that day on, dear reader…

There was absolutely no stopping me.

Three weeks, three tattoos and a bum flashing world tour

So, chemotherapy ended, or rather, staggered to a halt like a drunk crossing the finish line.

The good news? It had worked.
The secondary tumours in my neck and groin had vanished. Poof. Gone.

The less-good news?
One stubborn lump still clung to my armpit like a drunk hanging onto the last bus home, and the mediastinal mass in my chest, although dramatically reduced, was still decidedly *present*.

Dr Ann O'Callaghan didn't hesitate.
"Three weeks of radiotherapy," she said.
"Every weekday. We start soon."

I agreed. Because what else do you do? Politely decline?

✨ Pins, Needles, and the Joy of Permanently Numb Toes
I mentioned the pins and needles, the numbness creeping across my fingers and feet like frost.

Ann nodded, the nod of a woman who'd seen neuropathy a thousand times. "Peripheral neuropathy," she said. "Gabapentin will help."

Then she updated my notes and calmly removed Oramorph from my prescriptions.

I almost saluted.

If Ann said I didn't need morphine anymore, I didn't need morphine anymore. End of discussion.

✤ CT Simulation: A Glorified Photo Shoot Where You're the Hairless Model

A few days later, I reported to QA Hospital for "CT simulation." I didn't know what that meant, but it turns out it's medical-speak for:

"Please remove your dignity and put on this gown."

I was given one of those classic hospital gowns, knee-length, backless, bum-liberating, and asked to remove all clothing and jewellery.

I handed my bracelet and engagement ring to the nurse, who smiled as if she received patients' valuables daily, which she probably did.

When I re-emerged, she tied the back of my gown for me.
In truth, this became a *daily ritual*.

My coordination is... enthusiastic but unreliable at the best of times, and with neuropathy in my fingers, trying to tie those strings was like trying to thread a needle wearing oven mitts.

✤ The Tattoo Parlour Nobody Warned Me About

The simulation room was stark white, bright, clinical, humming with machines and the low chatter of masked staff in protective gowns.

I lay on the table and was told they'd create *three tattoos* to ensure my body lined up exactly the same every day.

One dot between my pectorals.
One dot on each side.
Of course, I secretly hoped for a dragon, or a small romantic something, or even an arrow labelled *"Insert Radiotherapy Here."*
But no, three purple dots.

Minimalist. Functional. Very NHS chic.

✤ The Mask: A Cross Between Hannibal Lecter and a Tight-Fitting Colander

Because they were treating my neck too, they needed a custom mask.

They warmed a sheet of perforated plastic, pressed it over my face, and held it in place while it cooled.

"If you get claustrophobic," one nurse said kindly, "just keep your eyes closed."

I closed them so hard I accidentally crossed them.

The mould hardened. They lifted it off.
That mask and I would soon be very well acquainted.

✴ Three Weeks. Fifteen Sessions. Endless Fatigue.
Monday to Friday:
Arrive. Change into gown. Have nurse tie gown because my fingers were now ornamental. Lie down. Get strapped in. Mask down.
"Hold your breath."
Boomph.
Done.

The treatment itself lasted seconds, but the exhaustion lasted all day.

By week three, I wasn't really living, just rotating between:
Hospital → Home → Bed → Repeat
I was awake long enough to eat, travel, get zapped, and collapse again.
That was my world.

Even now, I've never fully regained the same energy I once had. It changed me. Quietly. Permanently.

✴ But the radiotherapy worked. Completely.
It destroyed the remaining tumours. Shrank the mediastinal mass further.

And although that stubborn chest lump has kicked up a fuss a couple of times over the years, I've never needed more radiotherapy.
Long may that happy streak continue.

The night I met Marfan

One of the many glamorous perks of chemotherapy, right up there with morphine hallucinations and baldness, is that your immune system packs its bags and takes a long holiday.

So, whenever a virus so much as *looked* in my direction, I was done for.

And one particular evening, I felt it coming.
The fever. The shivers. The "oh hell, here we go" moment.

I called Roy.
Roy arrived fast enough to qualify for the British Touring Car Championship, took one look at me, and phoned the oncology support team himself.

Within minutes, the verdict was in:
"Bring him in. Isolation room. 24 hours. Minimum."
Brilliant. A mini break at QA Hospital. Just what every man dreams of.

The Isolation Room with the Wide-Open Door
Roy dropped me off, wished me luck, and I was shown to my isolation room, my own private suite with a bed, a drip stand, and the ambience of a mildly disappointed dentist's waiting room.

The nurse explained the plan, took blood, and carefully peeled off her PPE like she was in a medical version of Strictly Come Dancing.
Then she left. Door wide open.
"Doesn't that defeat the point of isolation?" I asked.
"Oh no!" she said cheerfully.
"As long as *we* wear PPE, *you're* fine."

I nodded, though secretly I wasn't convinced. It felt like putting a tiger in a cage and leaving the door open because the *keeper* was wearing gloves.

Enter: The Oncology Registrar with the Big News
Two hours later, a man in a white coat appeared.
"Mr Budden? I've got your results."
"You have a minor infection," he said, "We'll start antibiotics and keep you overnight."

Then he paused.
"I have two questions:
1. Why is your door wide open?
2. Has anyone ever mentioned *Marfan's* to you?"

Because of the fever and the fact that my brain was operating at 23% capacity, I misheard him. "Martians?" I repeated.
He laughed. "No, Marfan's. With an F."

"Oh," I said. "In that case, no. No one's mentioned it. What is it, and why do you think I've got it?"
He explained:
"It's not a single symptom. It's a combination of physical features. And you... fit the profile."

I smiled. He looked confused.
Most people apparently don't smile at the suggestion they might have a genetic condition.
"I wasn't expecting that reaction."

"Well," I said, "nobody's mentioned *long-term* anything to me in months. Honestly, I'm delighted you think I *have* one."
He chuckled. "Fair enough. Let's get you tested."

Tests, Letters, and Genetic Surprises
The infection settled. I went home.

A week later, Southampton General's Genetics Department summoned me like Hogwarts inviting a new student, only without the owl.

They examined me, measured me, checked joints, heart, eyes, history, everything short of reading my palm.

Diagnosis confirmed:
Marfan Syndrome.
Tall? ✓ Long limbs? ✓ Flexible joints? ✓
Aorta with an attitude problem? Potentially ✓

I was given new rules:
- Annual scans of my heart and aorta.
- No high-impact sports. (As if I'd been planning a career in rugby.)
- No unnecessary strain on the heart.
- And lots of monitoring, for life.

They recommended testing my brothers, Roger and Roy, and my nephew, Grant.

Thankfully, all three emerged Marfan-free, leaving me as the family's genetic lucky dip winner.

Southampton asked if I wanted to know whether the mutation came from Mum's or Dad's side. I declined. They were both gone by then. Knowing wouldn't change anything.

I did inform Uncle Ben, Mum's brother, so he could choose whether to get tested himself. He appreciated the warning.

A Problem for Later
Marfan's would go on to be a big part of my story in the years ahead, sometimes dramatically so.

But at that moment, in the thick of cancer, chemo, radiotherapy and isolation rooms with inexplicably open doors, it barely registered on my mental priority list.

Oddly enough, I was grateful for that.
One life-altering diagnosis at a time was quite enough.

The Queen, the cancer and the housing association

They say things come in threes.
In 2005, life said, "Challenge accepted."

First, I lost Enma. Then came cancer. And just when I thought the universe might give me a moment to breathe, a letter arrived from my landlord, Radian Housing.
The tone was cold enough to chill a bottle of Pinot Grigio:

"As the tenancy was in Miss Enma -'s name and she has now passed away, you have no legal right to remain in the property.
As a compassionate organisation, we will allow you eight weeks to grieve."

Eight weeks.
Imagine grief coming with a Best-Before date.

I was tempted to write back:
"Thank you for your compassion. I'll ensure my mourning concludes promptly by the second Tuesday next month."

But the sensible voice in my head, the one I rarely listen to, suggested I sleep on it and visit Citizens Advice the next morning.
Surely, *surely*, they couldn't just throw me out.

"They can throw you out."
The advisor at Citizens Advice was kind, sympathetic... and devastatingly direct.
"Yes, they can legally evict you."

"But I'm having chemotherapy," I said, as if that might somehow add +10 to my tenancy defence score.

"I understand," she said gently, "which is why you need a solicitor."

I was sent to Burley & Geech in Petersfield, a firm that sounded like the legal equivalent of Wallace & Gromit.
A kindly solicitor listened to everything, Enma, the engagement, the will, the whole heartbreaking year.

Then he exhaled the way professionals do when they're about to give bad news with a biscuit.

"Sadly, a tenancy isn't something she *owned*. But... we do have arguments. We can push for an extension. And we can insist they help rehouse you because of your medical condition."

He added, delicately, that as a single man I should "prepare emotionally for the possibility of... a bedsit."

Nothing screams "fresh start" like a single-room flat that smells faintly of chips and disappointment. Still, it was something.

When your MP can't help, try the Queen
A few days later, I wrote to my MP, Michael Mates.

His staff rang to say he'd contact Radian personally. Good, I thought. Hope!

Then the letter arrived. House of Commons embossed paper.
Very official. Very encouraging.
And yet... not.
"Regrettably, Radian is a commercial organisation.
There is nothing further I can do."
Translation: *I tried. They ignored me. Best of luck with all that.*

I sat there stunned.
Homeless, ill, grieving.
It was too much.
Then an idea arrived, either genius or delirium:
Write to the Queen.

Yes, *that* Queen.
Why not? When life is on fire, you may as well call the fire brigade with the biggest hat.
I found the address, wrote a respectful letter, and sent it Special Delivery. And then... nothing. For two weeks, silence.

Then one morning: a cream envelope.
Royal crest.

On Her Majesty's Service.
My heart did a full somersault.
I opened it carefully, half afraid it would dissolve if touched too eagerly.

✿ "Her Majesty was sorry to learn…"

The letter was warm, kind, unmistakably formal, exactly as a royal letter should be.

But then came the sentence that nearly knocked me off my chair:
"Her Majesty has instructed her Private Secretary to write to the Deputy Prime Minister, Right Honourable John Prescott MP, and ask him to take an interest in your case."

I just stared at the paper.
The Queen.
The actual Queen.
Had personally escalated my housing crisis up the political food chain.

I walked straight to Burley & Geech with the letter.
The receptionist beamed like I'd just handed her a winning lottery ticket.
"We don't often get letters from Buckingham Palace to photocopy," she said. No, I imagine not.

The solicitor read it, eyebrows climbing towards the stratosphere.
"Well done, Keith. That was a bold move."

✿ Prescott Enters the Chat

A week later, a letter arrived from John Prescott's office.
He'd contacted Radian.
Asked a minister to "encourage them to listen to reason."
I imagined him thumping his desk, muttering,
"Give the poor man a house, for heaven's sake."

And then, one crisp morning, my solicitor phoned.
"How are you feeling today?" he asked.
"Not too bad," I said, my default answer for everything from sniffles to existential despair.

"Well… I think I'm about to make you feel a whole lot better."
He paused, long enough for my heart to do a tap dance.
"Radian have dropped the eviction.
They're issuing you a brand-new tenancy. Your home is secure."
I sat there, stunned.

"We did it!" He laughed. "Yes, we did."

A Forever Home (By Royal Appointment)
The next morning, I walked into his office carrying a bottle of champagne and a massive box of chocolates. I couldn't really afford either right then, but it felt necessary. Ritualistic. Right.

And that, dear reader, is how this bungalow became my forever home.

Was it John Prescott? Was it the solicitor's legal precedent? Was it the Queen giving the nudge only a monarch can?
I'll never know.

But twenty years later, I'm still here, and every time I put my key in the lock, a tiny voice whispers:
"Thank you, Ma'am."

This is as good as it gets
Like hell it is

The day started completely normally.
I'd set aside the day to deliver leaflets for the next local election. Target: about 300 houses on my estate.

I had:
- A rucksack full of leaflets
- A water bottle
- My walking stick
- And my usual level of stubbornness

Thanks to the peripheral neuropathy, I already needed a stick and a sit-down after every half-dozen houses. But it was warm rather than boiling, so perfectly doable.

My estate sits on a steep hillside.
The houses at the top are about 60 metres higher than the ones near the entrance.
You *feel* it.

I also had house rules:
- No houses with "Beware of the dog".
- No houses with letterboxes near the floor

I've delivered enough leaflets to know that low letterboxes are a chiropractor's retirement plan.

The morning went fine. I popped home for a sandwich, then headed back out. A couple of times I had little dizzy spells, just a few seconds, nothing spectacular. I'd been having them for a few weeks.

The pharmacist had suggested "possibly a weird type of migraine" and said if they got worse, I should see my GP.

"Mmm," I thought, "I really should book that GP appointment."

I finished my round. Went home. Made a cup of tea. Food. Sat for a bit.

Then I got ready to walk over to see my friend Andrea on the Greenfields estate across the main road.

My estate is mostly 1950s. Greenfields is very 70s/80s. When I was a kid, it was all fields, and you could walk from our side nearly all the way to Liss Forest. Now, it's all houses and cars and people who "didn't see the sign, officer".

Between us is Rake Road. Officially 30 mph. In practice... let's call it "aspirational".

I walked down past the allotments, reached Rake Road, and got ready to cross.

Looked right. Looked left. Saw a lorry coming, but far enough away. I stepped off the kerb.

And that, dear reader, is the last thing I remember.

How To Rupture Your Brain in Stereo
Everything from that step to waking up is blank.

According to the driver, I collapsed like a jelly in the middle of the road. No attempt to save myself. No outstretched hands. Just... down.

He later told the police he thought he'd just watched me die.

What I didn't know, and couldn't possibly have known, was that thanks to Marfan syndrome, three blood vessels in the right side of my brain had ruptured.

And because I never do anything by halves, when I fell, I cracked the *left* side of my head on the kerb and picked up a bleed there too.

Double points.

Andrea came running when she heard. She lived on Greenfields and later told me I was at least partly conscious when she arrived. She asked if I wanted her to ride in the ambulance with me.

Apparently, I said no, I'd be fine.

I have **zero** memory of any of this.
Next stop, for me: complete darkness.

Waking Up on Wednesday (Apparently, I Missed Tuesday)

The next thing I remember is waking up in a hospital cubicle.

For a while, I thought it was a dream.
I was opposite the nurses' station. A nurse looked up, saw my eyes, and called down the ward:
"Doctor, Mr Budden is awake!"

"Maybe I'm *not* dreaming," I thought.
A young doctor appeared.

"Hello, Mr Budden. Welcome back to the world. Do you know where you are?"

"Please call me Keith," I said. "I hate formality. I'm in hospital. No idea which one. Given where I live, I'd guess QA in Portsmouth or Royal Surrey in Guildford."

He smiled. "That's good. You're speaking coherently and you've got good awareness. Do you know what day it is?"

"The last thing I remember is crossing Rake Road on Monday evening," I said, "so... Monday? Maybe Tuesday?"

"Close," he said. "It was Monday. It's now almost lunchtime on Wednesday."

Wednesday.
What on earth happened to Tuesday?

"How are you feeling?" he asked.
"Well, I've got a headache like a herd of elephants dancing on my skull," I said, "and I'm really hungry. Otherwise... fine."

He asked me to move my arms.
If I stared at them and concentrated, I could. Sort of.
"Good," he said.
Not "brilliant," just "good." Which in doctor-speak means "could be worse, could be better."

"And your legs?"

I hadn't even thought about my legs. I tried to move them.
Nothing.

When he lifted the sheet and touched my foot, my shin, even my thigh, there was... nothing. No sensation at all.

"Right," he said. "Please don't touch your head. It's all a bit vulnerable at the moment. You've got stitches on both sides. Now that you're awake, we'll get you an MRI and move you to the ward."

"Where am I now?" I asked.

"You're in the Medical Assessment Unit. We've been monitoring you. Your next of kin were here Monday night and yesterday, but we didn't know when you'd wake, so we sent them home to rest. We'll let them know you're back with us."

I nodded, as if any of this was remotely normal.

Life on the Neuro Ward
The next couple of weeks were a blur of scans, beeping, and trying not to drop my dinner.

I was moved to the neurosurgery ward.

Four of us in the bay.
One of us didn't make it.

Every few days they trundled me off to the MRI scanner to see how much blood and fluid was still pressing on my brain. The answer, for a long time, was "rather a lot."

With physio and the stroke rehab team, I slowly got some movement back in my arms. Eating became... performance art. More food on my bib than in my mouth, but I celebrated like I'd won MasterChef when they finally removed the nasal feeding tube and let me try solids again.

As things stabilised, the full damage report began to emerge.

- The right side of my face is basically frozen. Eyelids and eye muscles still work, but the rest doesn't really move. Most people never notice unless I point it out.

- I've lost the ability to wink. I can blink both eyes, and open both, but one at a time? Not on the menu.

- My sense of smell went AWOL, and my taste took early retirement.

- Worst of all, I lost heat and cold sensation in my lips and fingertips.

Early on, I repeatedly burned the inside of my mouth. Now, I test hot food on my cheek and blow on everything like a pensioner with soup.

On the plus side, my fingertips are now so numb I can pick roast potatoes straight off a baking tray. It's become my slightly disturbing party trick.

Most of this book is dictated because if I tried to type the whole thing, you'd get volume one around 2087.

The good news: the bleeding in my brain had stopped.
The bad news: there was still too much fluid.
The solution, according to the surgeons, was "simple."
"We'll drill a small hole in your skull," the consultant said. "It'll relieve the pressure. I've done hundreds."
Easy for him to say.
I signed the consent form. Nil by mouth. Outwardly calm.
Inwardly thinking:
What if this goes wrong?

Then I looked at my current reality:
- I couldn't move my legs.
- My arms worked only if I watched them.
- I couldn't smell, barely tasted.
- I was incontinent.
- My memory had potholes you could lose a bus in.
- I was having convulsions several times a day.

Could it get much worse? Probably not.
So, I slept.
They wheeled me down. Usual anaesthetist patter:
"Count down from ten."
I think I made it to seven.

I woke in recovery with an oxygen mask on my face.
Back on the ward, the surgeon appeared.
"The op went well," he said. "We've significantly reduced the cranial pressure. Just don't touch the top of your head for a few days."
I laughed.

He looked puzzled. "What's funny?"
"These days I have real trouble consciously touching anything," I said.
He grinned. "Fair point."

Within a day or two, I felt different. Not amazing. But *better*.
I could push myself upright in bed. Still no legs, apart from the odd flicker, but something had shifted.

The seizures continued, but I started getting an "aura" before they arrived. A strange internal warning. I'd say, "I'm going," and apparently my eyes would roll back, and I'd vanish for about thirty seconds.

The neurologists wired me up to capture one of these episodes. The results: inconclusive. The current theory: **non-epileptic epilepsy**.
Because of course I couldn't just have the standard version.

They started me on Phenytoin.
"Will it stop them?" I asked.
"Probably not completely," the neurologist said. "But hopefully fewer. And you'll need to take it for life."
I mentally added it to my growing personal pharmacy now big enough to meet the needs of a small village.

"This Is as Good as It Gets"
One evening, my consultant came and sat on the end of my bed.

The ward was quiet. Her face told me this wasn't going to be a chat about the weather.
"Mr Budden," she said, "I'm terribly sorry... but this is as good as it gets."
I'll never forget that sentence.
This is as good as it gets.
In my head, a voice shouted back:
Like hell it is.

She asked if I had any questions.
"Just one," I said. "It's about my private parts."
"Would you prefer to speak to a male doctor?" she asked gently.
"No," I said. "You know me best."
I explained that I was incontinent. I needed bed baths. And when the nurse washed my genitals, I felt... nothing. No sensation. No response. Not even when I tried to think of old girlfriends and particularly memorable evenings.

"Is that permanent?" I asked, terrified.
"It may return a little from time to time," she said, placing her hand on mine. "But I'm afraid it's unlikely to come back fully. I'm so sorry."

She left. I cried. Not a few tears. Proper, silent, ugly crying.

Then something in me hardened.
No. Not like that, more like this:
When life gives you a hundred reasons to cry, show life that you have a thousand reasons to smile.

And I prayed. Not a polite, churchy prayer. A raw, no-filter one. "Father, if this really is it for the rest of my life, then take me now. I don't want it. But if there's anything else You still want me to do here, then I need Your help, because I can't do this on my own."

When I woke the next morning, I was still there.
"Right," I thought. "Time to think."

The 48-Hour Rule
I listed my biggest problems:
1. I couldn't walk.
2. My memory was a mess.
3. I couldn't concentrate and my dreams were vivid and confusing.
4. My "bits" didn't work.

I decided number 4, however annoying, could wait.
If I was going to get better, **when** I was going to get better, I needed more brain space.

I did remember that quote from Martin Luther King:
"You don't have to see the whole staircase, just take the first step"

So, I invented my **48-hour rule**, which I still use today:

It's very simple:
- I only think seriously about the next 48 hours.
- Anything *before* that? I can't change it. It doesn't deserve my energy. Never be a prisoner to your past - it was just a lesson, not a life sentence.
- Anything *after* that? Might never happen anyway.

That doesn't mean I don't have plans. Of course I do. I just refuse to be a slave to them.

And here's the thing: since adopting that rule, despite everything, I haven't had a single night in over a decade where I haven't slept well.

Sleep better → make better decisions → sleep better.
A virtuous circle.

I'd accidentally hacked my own mental health.
With that in place, I felt like I'd finally got a bit of my head back.

"I'm Going to Walk Before My 50th"
Next up: legs.

Physio came every day to exercise them, keeping the muscles from wasting away entirely.
One day I said, "I'm going to walk again. And I'm going to do it before my 50th birthday in five weeks time."

She gave me the "that's adorable but insane" look.
"We'll see," she said.
"No," I replied calmly. "We won't see. I will."
She held my gaze for a long time.
"Oh my God," she said quietly. "You actually mean it, don't you?"
I nodded.

"Right," she said, shifting gears. "Then we work to a plan. But I don't want to give you false hope. If you walk again, it will almost certainly be with a frame. You're a big chap. We'll need two of us and we still might not catch you if you fall."

"Walking with a frame," I said, "will feel like winning the London Marathon."
She smiled. "We start tomorrow."

The next day they hoisted me into a wheelchair and took me to the physio gym. Just sitting up and leaving the ward felt like a day trip to the seaside.

In the gym:
Parallel bars. My physio. Her colleague Graham, built like a brick shithouse.

They got me on my feet. For the first time in eight weeks, I was vertical. My head span. My feet looked miles away. I couldn't feel them, but the view from up there was glorious.

"You're safe," my physio said. "We've got you. One tiny step. Move one leg if you can."
I poured everything into it. My right leg shuffled a couple of inches.

I cried.

"Good," said Graham. "Now the other foot."
Nothing.

"That's enough for today," my physio said gently. "Back to the chair. More tomorrow."

Fast-forward a few weeks, I'll spare you every wobble and swear word, and I was walking around the ward with a Zimmer frame. Slowly. Awkwardly. But walking.

Before my 50th.
My consultant was genuinely delighted.
"I didn't think you'd manage it," she admitted. "But I'm proud you proved me wrong."

I got back little bits of independence. I could walk to a proper toilet instead of using a commode. Still incontinent sometimes. Still in adult nappies (not the sexiest look, but fabulously practical). But moving under my own steam.

The nurses and I christened my Zimmer frame **Polly**.
"Where's Mr Budden?"
"Oh, he's taken Polly for a walk."
I still have Polly. We've been through a lot together.
Indoors I mostly "wall-walk" and "furniture-surf." Outside I use a rollator. I still fall over occasionally. I used to be embarrassed. Now I just check for broken bones and carry on.

Rebuilding a Life in My Head
Then there was my memory.

I told my consultant about the dreams. Hundreds of faces flickering past, some I knew (Enma, Michelle, Ruth), many I didn't.

She explained:
"Your brain is trying to rebuild its filing system," she said. "Imagine a big box of photos. It's holding up each one and asking, 'Is this important?' If you react, it keeps it. If you don't, it bins it."

"How long will it take?" I asked.
"No idea," she said. "You've got nearly fifty years of memories to sort."

Oddly, that helped. I can put up with most things if I understand the mechanics.

The bit that scared me was the day Michelle brought my grandson Davy to visit.
I looked at him and *knew* he was my grandson. I recognised his face. But his name... nothing. Completely gone.
I didn't want to panic Michelle by saying, "Sorry, who's this?"
So, I waited, silently praying she'd say his name.
In the end, the tea trolley saved me.
"Tea for you, tea for Michelle," said the lady.
"What would you like, Davy?" asked Michelle.
Davy.
Of course.
After they left, I cried. That one rattled me.
If I could forget my grandson's name, who else might disappear into the fog?

The Vicar, the Pulse, and a 3am Pacemaker
By now, I'd stopped asking when I'd be going home. I decided one day someone would just appear and say, "You're off," and it would be a lovely surprise.
One afternoon, I heard a voice at the nurses' desk.
"That sounds like Chris Williams," I thought. Our vicar.
I was not what you'd call a regular churchgoer. Weddings, funerals, Christmas, Easter, Remembrance Sunday, which was about it. So, I was surprised when he appeared at my bedside.

"Stay put," he said. "I'll find a chair."
We talked for hours.
About Liss. His family. My situation. Fate. God. All the big stuff.

I remember saying, "Given the brain bleed, the injuries, the fact I asked God to take me but I'm still here and walking again...

I've concluded that whatever I'm here to do, I clearly haven't done it yet."

He paused.
"Have you considered," he said, "that this might be it? Your determination, your humour, the way you keep going. You are, quite simply, an inspiration."

I teared up.
"I mean that," he added.
"I know," I said quietly.

He glanced at his watch. "I must go, or my dinner will be in the dog."
We laughed. He prayed with me. It helped.

Later, my consultant arrived with a final-year doctor and asked if she could examine me as part of her training. I was told to answer as if it was my first exam and not to volunteer extra information.

Halfway through, an aura hit.
"I'm going," I said, and disappeared for thirty seconds.
Afterwards, my consultant asked the junior doctor, "Notice anything?"

"Yes," she said. "During the episode I couldn't find a pulse. Not in his wrist, neck, ankle… nothing. Then he jerked, and it came back."
They left. I called my consultant back.
"No one's ever mentioned my pulse during a seizure before," I said. "Could this be cardiac?"
"We'll investigate," she said.

The next day, they wired me to a 24-hour heart monitor.
"If there's anything worrying," the cardiac doctor said, "we'll be in touch within 48 hours."

At 3am that night, a nurse woke me.
"The doctor needs to see you."
A man appeared. "Hello, Mr Budden. I'm Dr Cole, one of the cardiac surgeons."
"What time is it?" I croaked.
"Just after three in the morning," the nurse said.
"We're taking you to the cardiac lab," he said. "We think we know what's wrong. You need a pacemaker."

"When?" I asked.

"Now," he said, as if we were discussing a car service. "Porter's on the way. I'm off to scrub in. We'll pop it in, stitch you up, and you'll be back in time for breakfast."

Of all the times I've heard the phrase "pop it in", that one was the most surreal.

They wheeled me down, wired me up to more machines. Beep, beep, beep. I joked I felt like an extra in *Holby City*. The nurse smiled.
I don't remember much after that.

When I woke, I was in a side room on the Cardiac Care Unit, cables everywhere.
"If you want the loo," the nurse said, "ring the bell. We'll come and take you, and the monitor."
"But Polly will think I'm being unfaithful," I said.
"Polly?" she asked.
"My Zimmer frame," I explained.

She laughed. "I'm Anna," she said. "Anything you need, ask."
She was in her early twenties, wavy hair, friendly smile. I didn't fancy her, but she was a ray of light. She understood my jokes. She liked my stubborn positivity. She treated me like a person, not a chart.

That evening, while I was eating, the rhythm on the monitor changed. Nurses sprinted over, moved my tray, flattened the bed.
"What's wrong?" I asked.
"Your pacemaker's stopped," a doctor said. "We're taking you back to theatre."
Back down I went.

Next thing I remember? Waking in Intensive Care feeling like I'd been mugged by a rugby team.
"Your heart stopped in the lab," the nurse said. "They had to shock you several times with the pads."
"That'll explain why I feel like I've been kicked by an elephant," I replied.
I stayed in ICU about 36 hours, then returned to Cardiac Care. And to Anna.

One quiet night shift, I asked her, "If money was no object, what would you love to do?"

"Honestly?" she said. "Skydiving. But I'm scared I'll die."
"Here's the thing," I said. "We're *all* going to die one day. It's the only guarantee in life. And when you're close to it, I can promise you, you don't lie there thinking, 'I wish I'd spent more time at work.'"
She laughed.
"Do it for charity," I said, "and I'll cover the cost."
She did. Raised £3,000 for Lymphoma Action. I paid the jump fees.

That felt like a perfect trade: she got her adventure, the charity got money, and I got the joy of being part of something life-affirming instead of life-threatening.

Turning 50 (With Cake, Banners, and Dutch Lunatics)
And then, somehow, we got to my 50th birthday.

Roy, Roger, and Michelle came in that morning. Roy put a big **Happy Birthday** banner across the window. The nurses brought cake. I felt ridiculously loved.

That afternoon, I heard two more familiar voices at the nurses' station. "That sounds like Rolf and Arjo," I thought. From Fotovoordelig in the Netherlands.

They had:
- Driven from the Netherlands to Calais
- Taken the tunnel.
- Driven to Portsmouth

All in one day, just to see me.
"We can only stay an hour," Rolf said. "We're on the Eurotunnel back tonight."
"But we brought cake," added Arjo. "We've given it to the nurses. They're finding plates."

We talked about business, life, nonsense. Then Rolf told me about their car park adventure.

"The machine only takes sterling," he said. "We only had euros. Arjo asked if there was a bureau de change. Of course there wasn't. So, I left the car outside the entrance, put 300 euros and my keys on the reception desk and told security: 'We drove all this way. We have one hour to see our friend who is terribly ill and then we drive back. You now have my money and my keys. If this is a problem, *you* move it.'"

I laughed so hard I almost fell out of bed.

Too soon, they had to leave. We hugged. I wanted to walk them to the door, but I don't think the NHS insurance would have covered it.

After they left, I lay down with a book and thought, *Fifty's not a bad innings. And I'm still here.*

"You're Going Home"
From there, the trajectory was up.

No more beeping monitors.
Fewer seizures. More walking. Slightly less falling.

Then one day, Anna walked in with a grin that made me instantly suspicious.

"Good news," she said. "Social services have finished your house adaptations. Wet room, handrails, all signed off. Doctors are happy. You'll have outpatient appointments, but… you're going home. I've called your friend Elwyn. He's on his way. So, let's get you dressed."

I must have been beaming.
"That," she said, "is the biggest smile I've ever seen on you."
"I'm going home," I said. "I'm actually going home."

"You are," she said. "Let's get those pyjamas off, get you washed and dressed, and you can go."
"Could you shave my face?" I asked. I'd grown a full beard in hospital. I hated it, even if it did wonders for my David Bellamy impression.

"Of course," she said. "It would be my pleasure."

By the time Elwyn arrived, I looked like me again.
"You've lost the beard," he said. "You look well. You look like Keith."

"Let's go home," I said. And we did. Not to the life I'd had before. That life was gone. But to a new one, stranger, messier, wobblier,
and, as it turns out, still very much worth living.

"The past is behind you, learn from it. The future is ahead of you, prepare for it. The present is here, live it."
— Thomas S. Monson

The day that didn't let up

It was the day of Uncle Ben's funeral.

I'd been feeling a bit off for a day or two, nothing dramatic, just that vague "am I coming down with something or is life simply being life again?" feeling.

And funerals... well, they stir more than memories.

Ben's service was at The Oaks Crematorium in Havant, one of those rare crematoriums that actually feels peaceful. Big windows looking out onto woodland. Light. Calm. Gentle even. If I ever needed to be cremated The Oaks would be my pick.

When I'm cremated though I already know what I want my exit music to be while everyone is filing out. A classic by Johnny Cash:-

I fell into a burning ring of fire
I went down, down, down and the flames went higher
And it burns, burns, burns, the ring of fire, the ring of fire

There are two reactions to that - either you've got a big smile on your face, maybe a chuckle or too. That's ok, it's allowed, you are 'my tribe'.

or you're sitting with your head in your hands thinking "Only Keith could say that" - don't worry, you're not quite totally in my tribe yet. Treat this book as an initiation ceremony, by the end you'll either be in my tribe or asleep - I don't mind, either way I'm happy.

Anyway, back to the plot. We were halfway through a hymn when the wooziness hit. Like the floor shifted slightly. I sat down quickly, telling myself it was emotion. Ben was Mum's last surviving sibling. Her generation, gone. Sometimes grief sneaks up wearing the disguise of dizziness.

Roy had driven me there. After the service he asked, "Off to the wake?"
"Could you drop me home first? I'm not feeling great."
"Of course," he said. As I got out: "And if you're still rough in a day or two, see your GP."

Inside, I called Shona.
"You're back early," she said.
I told her I'd felt faint. She already knew I'd been "a bit off".
"I think you should see your doctor tomorrow," she said.
"You're probably right," I said. "Cheese on toast, telly, early night. That's me done."
"Well, you know where I am if you need me. Love you."
"Love you too."

I flopped down with the TV. And then the ache started.

Left arm. Dull. Nagging.
Rubbed it. It eased. Came back. Spread into my shoulder.
My Red Cross training nudged me.
"I think I might be having a heart attack."

I phoned NHS out-of-hours. The call handler listened, asked questions, and then delivered the classic line:
"It's *probably* nothing… but I'm sending paramedics to assess you."
Translation: It's absolutely *not* nothing.

She told me to unlock the door. She stayed on the phone, chatting calmly until I heard the ambulance outside.
The paramedic walked in, took one look at me, and said, "Okay. Aspirin," handing it over like holy water. A few questions. A blood pressure reading. Then:
"I think you're having a heart attack. Would you like to pack a few things?"

Amazing how practical you can be in a crisis.
Pants. Pyjamas. Wash bag. Phone charger. Meds.
If I'd had a clipboard, I'd have ticked items off.
"Think you can walk to the ambulance?"
"I think so."
Once on the stretcher, she wired me up.
"What have you been up to today?" she asked.
"Uncle Ben's funeral."
Her face softened. "I'm so sorry. Quite the day."
"You could say that."

The journey blurred by. Bright lights. The crash room. A voice calling "suspected heart attack." A doctor leaning over me.
"Mr Budden, can you open your eyes?"
I did.
"Do you know where you are?"

"QA Hospital."
"Good. Try to stay awake."
I wanted to sleep more than anything.

Blood tests. CT scan. A cubicle opposite the nurses' station.
"Can I have a drink?" I asked.
"Not yet. Possible operation."
She moistened my lips with something wonderful. Amazing how much comfort can fit on a cotton bud.

Then a cardiologist appeared in scrubs.
"We're taking you to the cath lab," he said, already pushing the trolley toward the doors.

"Cath lab," I thought. "Odd name. Sounds like somewhere you neuter a tomcat."
"If you're planning to neuter me," I said, "you're far too late."

He paused… then laughed.
"Oh, I'll be using that."

In the cath lab, which contained no cats, he explained the plan:
Stent. Groin incision. Sedation. Awake the whole time.

"You can watch the stent travel to your heart on that monitor," he added, like someone offering me the window seat on a flight.
He handed me the consent form.

"I haven't got my glasses," I said.
A nurse fetched them and settled them gently on my face, the way you do with someone you're determined not to break.
Midnight arrived as I signed.

The procedure was surreal, watching a thin tube thread its way inside my own body, calmly, purposefully.
Humbling, really, seeing science take over where willpower and stubbornness can't compete.
Afterwards, back on the ward, the nurse placed my glasses and overnight bag exactly where she'd promised.
I lay back.
Time for sleep, I thought.
Quite a day.
Even by my standards.

Four stops, zero arrests, (A driving career in review)

Considering I've driven well over half a million miles in my life, enough to circumnavigate the planet twenty times or, more impressively, enough to get from Liss to Newcastle **without once stopping for a wee,** it's genuinely surprising that the police have only stopped me four times.

Now, dear reader, I don't want you to think this is because I was an impeccable driver.
I was not.

Did I occasionally break the speed limit?
Absolutely.

Did I perhaps glide through the odd red light with the confidence of a man who believed in miracles?
I couldn't possibly comment.

But four stops... that feels practically angelic.

1. The Night Shift, The Bend, and the 40mph I Definitely Wasn't Doing

I was still a fairly new driver, still winding down windows by hand, still owning cars with more rust than paint. Could've been the Marina. Could've been the FSO. Hard to tell; both drove like they resented being alive.

It was late, around 11:30pm, and I was heading back to Liss along the A325. No traffic. No streetlights. Just me, a dark road, and the youthful belief that speed limits were "suggestions."

Approaching Bordon, the 40mph zone began. Ahead: green traffic lights. Behind me: a car that had appeared without ceremony.

I rounded the bend doing 55-60mph.
Crossed the lights doing 50mph.
Thought, *I'll slow down in a minute.*

Then:
Bee-bah, bee-bah. Flashing blue lights.
Ah.

Pulled over. Officer approached.

"Do you drive this road often?" "At least once a week."

"And the speed limit?" "40mph."

"And where does it start?" "Just before the fire station."

He nodded, impressed.
"So if you know all that... why did I just follow you across the junction at 50?"

Quick as lightning, I said: "I didn't see the fire station."

He actually chuckled.
"Good answer. Don't make a habit of it."

He left.
I waited until he was out of sight before moving an inch.
You could've balanced a cup of tea on my accelerator foot on the drive home.

2. The Red Light, The Crawl of London, and the CCTV That Never Blinks

Most of my driving life unfolded in Central London. I wouldn't claim "The Knowledge", but I had *a knowledge,* the shortcuts, the secret subways, the weirdly helpful ramp by Waterloo Bridge.

But familiarity... ah, it breeds contempt. Or, at minimum, carelessness.

One morning, the traffic was crawling.
I was thinking about cut throughs and beating the lights.
Cars moved. I followed.

Then, once again,
Bee-bah. Bee-bah.

Police pulled me over. Two wheels on the pavement, trying to look cooperative.

"Step into the patrol car," the officer said.

Never a promising start.

He pointed to the fuzzy CCTV screen.
There I was. My car. Bright red light.

"Banged to rights," I sighed.

Two options: Fixed penalty and points, or court and a bigger fine.

Reader, I took the points.

Not the best start to a working day. HR were delighted.

3. The Missing Tax Disc and the Most Stressful Game of Hide-and-Seek

Ironically, I'd spent the whole day at the Metropolitan Police Trading Service. You'd think that'd buy me some goodwill.
It did not.

I stopped at traffic lights in Wandsworth.
A policeman stared at my windscreen like he'd spotted the Holy Grail.

Lights turned green. Pulled off. Police van waved me into a layby.

"Sir, can you explain why your vehicle isn't displaying a tax disc?"

What?

I *knew* I had one. But the windscreen was blank.

"Produce it at a police station within 24 hours," he said, handing me the dreaded notice.

I went home and searched everywhere. No disc.

Next morning, I continued. Then I saw the faintest sliver of blue, wedged deep under the dashboard like it had fled to a parallel dimension.

It took forty minutes and long-nosed pliers to rescue it.
When it slid free, I actually kissed it.

At the police station, the receptionist doubled as a one-woman West End show, she laughed the entire time.

Crisis averted. Barely.

4. The Hogs Back, The Ice, and the Slide of Shame

The final time was pure bad luck.
Weather-induced humiliation.

Snow had been falling. Roads looked passable.
I headed up the Hogs Back, thinking "It'll be fine."

Reader, it was **not** fine.

Near the Puttenham turn-off:
Police car. Flashing lights. Officer signalling to stop.

I gently applied the brakes. Nothing happened.

I glided, gracefully if unintentionally, straight past him.
His headshake communicated disappointment on a spiritual level.

Another officer caught up with me.

"The Hogs Back is closed, too icy."
"I noticed," I said, apologetically horizontal.

He smiled, guided me in reverse to the slip road, and suggested the Aldershot Road.

Made it home safely.
Hindsight, as they say, is the only exact science.

And so, ends my record:

Half a million miles. Four stops. Zero arrests.
And a lifetime of stories from behind a steering wheel that has seen more drama than most soap operas.

The best? Overrated
The first? Now that's a legacy

My father didn't hand out life lessons very often.
In fact, if you blinked, you might've missed one.

But the few he *did* share were like quiet little time bombs, you don't realise they've gone off until decades later, when suddenly you're standing in a council chamber, or behind a microphone, or producing a GDPR podcast, thinking:
"Ah. So *that's* what he meant."

I remember one afternoon as a teenager, sitting with him, awkward limbs, big dreams, hair doing whatever it liked, and I said the sort of earnest thing teenagers specialise in:
"Dad, I don't know what, but one day I want to be the best at something. The best there's ever been."

He didn't laugh. He didn't wince. He just gave me a small smile, the kind that meant he was about to drop something quietly profound.

"Son," he said, "don't bother trying to be the best at something. Being the best feels good for a bit… but someone better can always come along."
He paused, let that settle, then added:
"Instead, focus on being the *first* at something.
Because no one can ever take that away.
There can only ever be one first."

At the time, I nodded as if I understood.
I didn't.
I probably went back to thinking about girls or cars or what sandwich Mum had packed for lunch.

But somewhere deep inside, the seed had been planted.

And looking back now, I realise:
it was one of the most quietly brilliant pieces of wisdom I've ever been given.
So - what "firsts" have I managed in my lifetime?

Let's have a little roll call:

- **The first in my family to go to university**
  (well... polytechnic initially but still counts).
- **The first in my family to serve as a councillor**
  parish or district. Mum would've been proud. Dad would've told everyone in the pub.
- **The first Chairman of Liss Parish Council from our family**
  and, at the time of writing, still the only one.
- **The first person EVER to hold that Chairmanship for more than eight years**
  (my backside still remembers those chairs).
- **The first, and if reorganisation goes ahead, likely the *only*, person to serve more than one consecutive year as Chairman of East Hampshire District Council**
  ...a record no one asked for, but there it is.
- **One of the first four people to introduce Electronic Document Management to the UK**,
  back when the word "metadata" made people squint.
- **The first person to present and produce a UK podcast dedicated solely to GDPR**,
  a sentence that 20-year-old me would never have believed.

There are probably a few others buried in the attic of my memory, but honestly, that's not a bad list.

And every one of them, every unexpected left turn, every job, every project, every title, traces back to that one piece of simple, quiet wisdom my father handed me all those years ago.

Not: "Be the best."
But: **"Be the first."**

Because the best is temporary. But the first is forever.
And, dear reader, if you take anything from this chapter, take that. Not the titles. Not the list. Not even my dad's understated genius.
Take the truth at the heart of it:

The world remembers the first more than the flawless.
So dare to be the first.
And let someone else chase being the best.

The Burglars, the Insurance, and the Sunroof Escape

I've been fortunate in life.

For all the extraordinary things that *have* happened to me, cancer, brain bleeds, pacemakers at 3am, serious crime has never really been one of them.

But like most people, I've had my fair share of... let's call them "criminal inconveniences."

Little reminders from the universe that even when you're minding your own business, thieves occasionally aren't.

The Camberley Bedsit Burglary
It started in Camberley, in my very first bedsit, a charming euphemism for "small room with big dreams."

The house had been chopped into multiple flats, each with its own lock, although the front door had the unhelpful habit of being left open as if inviting guests... or burglars.

One Thursday night, after visiting Dad and Roger, I came home to find my bedsit door slightly ajar.
And not the "gentle breeze" kind of ajar.
The "someone-kicked-this-in-like-an-audition-for-The-Bill" kind.

Inside:
- TV on the floor
- Video recorder gone.
- Laptop gone.
- Drawers systematically opened.
- And in the sink... a stubbed-out cigarette.
   A calling card, of sorts. Or unbelievably bad manners.

The police came quickly. Nice lads.
"You're lucky," one said.
I looked at the broken door.
"Define lucky," I thought.
"They were professionals. They didn't trash the place," he continued.

He pointed out their "methodical approach," opening drawers bottom to top to avoid tipping.

I admired the craftsmanship.
Didn't make me feel better.

A locksmith arrived, the door was secured, and I spent the night in the classic "I know they won't come back but what if they do?" state. Within weeks, I moved out. No contest.

Luke From Insurance, and Keith from 'Not Having It'
Then came the insurance claim.
A six-week masterclass in bureaucracy, delays, and a man called Luke whose job title must have been "Professional Avoider of Responsibility."

Every time I called:
"It's being processed." "We're looking into it." "Shouldn't be long now."

Then came the day I asked to speak to his manager.

"Mrs Ferguson is not in until Monday," he told me.
I thanked him politely, hung up, took a deep breath... and then rang the main switchboard.
"Hello, can I speak to Mrs Ferguson please?"
"One moment, putting you through."
And there she was.

"Mrs Ferguson?"
"Yes."
"Excellent. From your desk... can you see Luke?"
A pause.
"Yes..."
"Well, he's just told me you're not in until Monday."

Two days later, my cheque arrived.

Amazing how quickly processes speed up when the manager discovers her staff are auditioning for the role of "Person Most Likely to Be Thrown Out of an Open Window."

Cars, Crimes, and the Great Sunroof Escape
There were other minor incidents:
- A stolen CD jukebox from my BMW, back when a CD player was practically a status symbol. To add insult to

injury they removed all of the CDs and left them in the car footwell - speaks volumes for my taste in music.
- A bungled break-in on my Cavalier that broke the door mechanism so thoroughly the door only opened if the ignition was turned on. (A fun party trick, less fun at petrol stations.)

Which all led to this absolute gem:
I had given my car to a hotel valet.
Ten minutes later, the concierge appeared looking... embarrassed.
"Mr Budden... we have a situation."
The valet had managed to lock himself inside my car.
And couldn't figure out how to get out.

Despite being a grown adult. Despite being a professional valet. Despite, presumably, many years of door-opening experience.
In the end, he climbed out through my sunroof.

I repeat:
He climbed. Out. Through. My. Sunroof.

I received a £50 refund for "cleaning costs" because he'd got muck from his shoes on my interior.

Honestly? Worth every penny.

Small Crimes, Big Lessons

Looking back, none of it traumatised me.
None of it made me fearful.
Just a little more aware. A little more amused. And every time, a tiny bit wiser.

I learned:
- **Always check locks twice.**
- **Always challenge incompetent insurance handlers.**
- **Always expect the unexpected from valet parking.**
- And always, *always,* keep your sense of humour nearby.

Life throws small tests at you sometimes, just to make sure. you're still paying attention.

And occasionally, it throws you a valet climbing out of your sunroof.

Both, as it turns out, can be educational.

Did the Earth move for you too?

I can already hear the giggling from the naughty ones at the back.

But no, this is *not* that kind of "Did the Earth move for you?" story.

This is the night of **20-21 October 2022**, when the earth genuinely moved, and I happened to be in Manchester minding my own business.

I'd gone up to deliver a GDPR training session the next day, glamorous, I know, and arrived late Thursday afternoon by train. Checked into a hotel near Piccadilly, one of those modern ones where the décor is trying a bit too hard to look casual. Not unpleasant, just… very Manchester.

I had a relaxed dinner in the restaurant, then drifted into the bar for two pints of Guiness. Nothing dramatic, nothing wild, nothing involving shots, karaoke, or poor decisions.

At 10:30pm, I decided to be responsible, took the lift up to my room, and settled into bed.

A bit of telly, lights off, asleep by 11:30.
Perfectly ordinary.
3am: The Not-So-Ordinary Bit
Around 3am, I woke with a jolt.
Not a gentle *stirring* or a confused *where-am-I?*

No, it felt like someone was physically shaking the bed.
There was a low, distant rumble.
Thunder? In October? In Manchester maybe, but still unusual.

The room itself looked still and undisturbed. No rattling glasses, no flickering lights, no poltergeist activity. So, I assumed it was a vivid dream, rolled over, and went back to sleep.

I've survived cancer, brain bleeds, and pacemakers, I wasn't about to lose sleep over imaginary thunderstorms.
7am: The Reveal

Wake-up call came at 7.

I reached for the lamp, sat up... and something felt subtly wrong.
Both pictures on the wall were crooked.

Not dramatically, just noticeably.

I stared at them.
"They definitely weren't like that when I went to sleep," I thought.

I'm many things, but I'm not *so* messy that I dislodge hotel artwork in my sleep.

Still, I shrugged it off.
Coffee, shower, shave, clothes on, ready by 8.
Downstairs, the breakfast bar TV was on.

And there it was, in bold letters at the bottom of the screen: **"EARTHQUAKE RECORDED IN LANCASHIRE OVERNIGHT."**

I stared at it, then at my toast, then back at the TV.

"Right," I thought. "So, I *did* feel the earth move. Excellent. And not a single person to boast to."
Honestly, it felt like a missed opportunity.

Some people get dramatic stories of natural disasters.
I get a slightly wobbly bed and two wonky pictures in a Premier Inn. Still, another unusual event to add to the list.

And, for once, the earth really did move for me.

Dad, dementia and Danny Boy

Dad's dementia didn't arrive with fanfare.
It crept in quietly, like an unwanted houseguest testing the back door.

At first it was insignificant things, forgetful, almost harmless.

He'd forget what he'd had for lunch.
He'd miss the odd appointment.
He'd mix up names.

Roger, who was living with him, would mention it when I visited.
And I, ever the optimist or ever the avoider, depending on your angle, shrugged and said, "Well, he is getting on a bit."

A sentence capable of covering a multitude of sins.
But then the forgetfulness got... stranger.

He'd go for a walk and someone from the village would have to escort him home because he'd forgotten which way "home" was. Sometimes he couldn't even remember where *home* was supposed to be.

And then there were the little moments that punched you harder than the big ones.

One day I opened the microwave to heat something up.
His slippers were inside.
That was the moment we all knew the "getting on a bit" excuse wasn't going to cut it.

The Budden Brothers Summit
Roy, Roger, and I held what we dramatically called a "family conference."

It made us sound like the Dingles from *Emmerdale*, but really, it was just three middle-aged men trying to work out what to do with their increasingly muddled father.

Roy, the only one with any mental-health training among us, said Dad was showing classic signs of dementia. Which type? Impossible to say without tests.
But he was clear about two things:

1. **Dad needed to see the GP.**
   This was tricky. Dad only saw doctors for Mum, the kids, or livestock. Never himself.
2. **We needed a Lasting Power of Attorney.**
   Dad could no longer manage finances safely. Roger volunteered for that one.

And so, we set about making the house safer, better locks, small precautions. Night wandering was becoming a real risk.

I managed to get a GP appointment within days, a miracle achievable only in the late 1990s, and went with him.

The GP didn't hesitate.
Urgent hospital referral. Social services.

Enter **Teresa**, the social worker every family hopes for: kind, human, and someone Dad took an immediate shine to.

But dementia has its own momentum.
Over the next few months, Dad worsened.
Teresa eventually said the words we'd all been avoiding:
"For his safety... he needs residential care."
It felt like being punched in the chest.
We knew that once he went into a home... he wouldn't be coming out again.
But the alternative was terrifying, wandering off unnoticed, getting lost, leaving the gas on.
We had no choice.

Operation Cover Story
Getting him to agree was the next challenge.
In the end we used the classic family tactic: **a polite lie.**

Roger had to "go away for a weekend."
I was "working in Scotland."
Roy's house was "having building work done."
Just for a few days, Dad.
Just until everyone is sorted.
He accepted it completely.

Teresa collected him on Friday and took him to the home on Portsdown Hill.
Beautiful place. A lounge with panoramic windows over Portsmouth harbour.

She told him he'd be "going home on Tuesday."
And somehow... he believed it.

"Three Years I've Been Here, Son!"
A month later, I visited.
I braced myself for:
"Are you taking me home now?"
But it never came.

He proudly took me to see his room. His bits and pieces artfully arranged. A couple of paintings on the wall.

"This is nice," I said. "Settling in, okay?"

"Settling in?" he said. My stomach lurched, here came the moment.
"Settling in?" he repeated.
"I should *bloody well hope so*. I've been here three years!"

I burst out laughing with sheer relief.
Then he added, with classic Dad attitude,

"The only thing I don't like is that everyone here's old. Wish they'd get some younger people in."
He was 80-odd at the time.

The Harrow Incident
He spent about eighteen months there, until the home closed, and he was moved to Steep House in Petersfield, closer for us, more familiar for him.

Too familiar.
He recognised the area, so his attempts to "go for a walk" multiplied.
He didn't see it as escaping, he was just "nipping to the pub."
Once, he actually made it.

By sheer coincidence he found himself at **The Harrow,** his old haunt, which served Gales HSB, his favourite pint.
He ordered one.
No money, of course.
But fate had put my friend Paul behind the bar that day.
Paul recognised him instantly, poured him a pint "on the house," and phoned me.

"I've got your dad here," he said.
"You sound like Chris Tarrant on *Who Wants to be a Millionaire*," I replied.
He laughed. "No, Keith, I literally have your dad. In the pub."
Steep House collected him shortly after.
It turned out to be the last proper adventure he ever had.

The Last Visit
A couple of weeks later, dementia accelerated into its cruellest stage.

I visited one Saturday. He looked up from his bed.
"My name's George," he said. "Are you new here?"
My heart cracked.
He didn't recognise me at all.
"I'm Keith," I said gently.
"I used to have a son called Keith," he said. "Haven't seen him or the other two in years. But I don't mind. I've got lots of friends here."

I didn't correct him.
What would be the point?
Truth, in that moment, would have been cruelty.

I left after twenty minutes and cried in the car park.

From there I drove to Michelle's.
"How was your dad?" she asked.
"Not good," I said. "I think I've seen my dad for the last time."

The Phone Call
Two days later, I arrived back from a meeting. The answerphone light was flashing. I pressed the play button.

"Mr Budden," a voice said quietly. "Steep House here. I'm sorry to have to let you know that your dad passed away during breakfast. Please call us when you can."

I made a cup of tea. I sat down to call Steep House, my hand trembling.
The matron at Steep House answered the phone.
"Hello Mr Budden", she said, "thanks for calling back."
"What happened?" I asked.
"It was sudden," she said. "George finished breakfast, pushed back his chair, and collapsed. We don't think he knew anything about it."

Somehow, that helped.

Danny Boy
The funeral two weeks later was a blur.
The only part etched into my memory is Roy.
Dad always had his own... unique way of singing *Danny Boy*.
Not quite tuneful. Not quite in time.
But heartfelt.

Roy stood up and sang it solo, completely unaccompanied.
He sang it *Dad's* way.
That was *the moment* I cried.

When he finished, everyone clapped, a rare thing at a funeral.

I remember thinking,
"Dad will be sitting up there loving this."

Twenty-four years later, at my 60th birthday, Sue asked Roy to sing it again. He did. Just as moving, Just as Dad.

Thank you, Roy.

The Christmas we didn't see coming

It was one of our quiet little Budden traditions, no pomp, no ceremony, just the three brothers gathering a Sunday or two before Christmas to swap presents. A bit of tea, a bit of chat, a bit of affectionate mockery. Nothing extravagant. Just... us.

By 2024 the pattern was set: meet at Roger's flat in Southsea; Roy would drive up to Liss, collect me and the gifts; then we'd head down together sharing bad jokes and stories we'd each told a hundred times before. Familiar. Comfortable. Almost festive.

That year it was Sunday 15th December.

Roy arrived right on cue. We loaded the gifts into the car, congratulated ourselves on remembering everything, and set off.

The journey down was lovely, quiet roads, gentle winter sunshine, and the two of us chuckling at our own brilliance. By the time we pulled up, we were in full Christmas spirit.

The flat looked lived-in: kitchen light on, the soft glow of what looked like a Christmas tree behind the lounge curtains.

But no answer on the buzzer.

We tried again. Nothing.

"He's probably popped out," Roy said. "Forgot the time."

"Maybe," I said, "but he never leaves the blinds up after dark."

We stood there debating when another resident arrived and let us in. We knocked. No response. Roy bent down and called through the letterbox.

After a pause, a voice we knew well replied, "Oh. Hello."

A minute later the door opened. Roger sat in his wheelchair, looking his usual slightly rumpled self, except for the dried blood around his nose.

"What are you two doing here?" he asked, genuinely puzzled.

"We're here to swap presents," I said. "We arranged it weeks ago on Zoom."

Inside, something felt off. The lounge was dim, his speech slow. I sat down and immediately realised the armchair felt... damp. I made an excuse to fetch a towel from the bathroom.

On the way, I saw the dark dried patch on his bedroom carpet.

Blood. A lot of it.
I signalled Roy. He went to look. Came back. Quiet nod.
Definitely blood.

Meanwhile, Roger was making tea.
"Milk, no sugar," I called.
"Didn't catch that," he said.
"No sugar!"
"Too late," he replied matter-of-factly. "Already in."
Almost funny. Almost.

We sat with him for a while. Roger, normally a chatterbox, barely spoke. His answers were clipped, distant. He wasn't himself.

"You sure you're alright?" I asked.
"Just tired," he said. "Didn't expect visitors."

We took the hint, exchanged gifts, his unwrapped, ours in bags, and left quietly.

Roy lit a cigarette the second he shut the car door.
"Something's not right," he said.
"I know," I replied. "I'll call NHS Direct in the morning."

Monday: The Call
I rang 111 first thing.
The nurse listened carefully, then asked,
"Would you be willing to introduce me on a three-way call? People often respond better if they hear someone familiar."
"Of course," I said.
She patched Roger in.
"Hello?" he said cautiously.

"Hi Roger, it's Keith. This might sound strange, but I've got someone from NHS Direct on the line. We were a bit worried last night."

"Well, this isn't your usual number," he replied, dry as ever, which was oddly reassuring.

The nurse asked if he'd like me to stay on the call or if he'd like to talk privately.

"Privately," he said.
I hung up.

Ten minutes later she called back.
"Mr Budden, we suspect your brother may have had a TIA, a mini stroke. We've arranged a GP visit this afternoon."

I thanked her and called Roy.
"Good," he said. "He'll get looked at properly."
For a moment, I felt hopeful.

The Knock at the Door
That evening, after a Parish Council meeting, Paddy gave me a lift home. I let myself in, took off my coat and headed to the kitchen to make a cuppa.
A knock at the door.
"Paddy again," I thought. "Left my phone in his car."
It wasn't Paddy.
It was a uniformed police sergeant.
"Mr Keith Budden?"
"Yes," I said. "What's happened?"
"May I come in?"
"Of course."
"I'm very sorry to tell you... we found your brother, Malcolm Roger Budden, deceased at his flat earlier this evening."

The words floated above me for a moment, as if addressed to someone else entirely.

"Sorry... what?"
He repeated it gently.

A friend had gone to play chess with Roger, their usual Monday-night tradition.
No answer.
He'd looked through the window and seen a body.

Fire brigade forced the door.
Paramedics confirmed Roger had died.
I stood there in stunned silence.
And then, without meaning to, I smiled.

If there *is* a heaven and Roger's watching, he would have been delighted with himself: fire brigade, ambulance, *and* the police all in one night. Only the coastguard missing.

"Is he still there?" I asked quietly.
"Yes, until forensics finish their work."
Then came the surreal part.
Because Roy and I had been the last known visitors, we were "persons of interest."

"You'll be interviewed under caution," the sergeant said. "You're not under arrest, but we need a statement. Due to your disability, we can conduct the interview here. My colleague will be round about 1:30am."

"Tonight?" I asked.
"Yes."
I nodded, numb.
"Fine. And I can ask for a solicitor at any point?"
"Absolutely."

I phoned Michelle.
"Are you sitting down?" I asked her.
"Why?"
"It's Roger. He's gone. And the police are interviewing me under caution."
"What? Tonight?"
"Yes."
"Call me afterwards," she said. "I'll wait up. You're not going through that alone."

I hung up and sank into my armchair.
The same one I'd sat in the night before, laughing with Roy.
Now I sat in silence. And waited for the police.

The interview at 1:30 am

There was a knock at the door.

For half a second, my brain tried to pretend it might be a neighbour. But of course, it wasn't. Nobody pops round at 1:30 in the morning unless they're drunk, desperate, or in uniform, and this knock had "police" written all over it.

"Mr Budden?" he asked.
"Yes," I said. "Come in."

Years of being a councillor kicked in automatically. I could've been on the doorstep in a high-vis vest discussing blocked drains.
"Can I get you a tea or coffee?" I asked.
"Coffee, please. Milk, no sugar."

I led him into the lounge. He unpacked a small forest of recording equipment while the radiator hummed away, and my neat little towers of Christmas presents stared at us like witnesses. I handed him his coffee and lowered myself into my usual armchair.

"Before I start recording," he said, "do you have any questions?"

"Yes." I cleared my throat. "Your colleague said that if at any point I want to stop and speak to a solicitor, I can."

"Absolutely," he said. "If that happens, we'll pause the interview and continue at the station."

I nodded. He pressed record.

He read the caution. Hearing it out loud, *You do not have to say anything,* made the room suddenly colder. Smaller.

"Right," he said gently. "In your own words, tell me what happened when you visited your brother on Sunday."

So, I told him everything.
The blinds still up. The dried blood on his carpet and nose. The sugar in my tea I hadn't asked for. The distance in his eyes. The feeling, the gut certainty, that something in him wasn't right.

It took more than an hour.
When he finally pressed stop, he packed up quietly.
"Thank you, sir," he said. "And for the coffee. Try to get some sleep if you can."

I managed a faint smile.
"I'm a councillor," I said. "I've done election counts. Sleep is optional."

He chuckled, said goodnight, and disappeared into the glow of his patrol car.

I watched the taillights vanish. Then I rang Michelle.
"How did it go?" she asked softly.
"I told him everything. They'll know more after the post-mortem."
"Do you want me to come over?"
"No," I said. "I'm exhausted. I'll see you tomorrow."

Clearing the Fog
The next few weeks blurred together, calls, emails, waiting, more waiting.

The post-mortem confirmed Roger had died of natural causes.

When the officer phoned to say Roy and I were no longer under caution, I exhaled for what felt like the first time in days.
Even when you *know* you've done nothing wrong, being officially told you're innocent is a different kind of relief.

Roger had worshipped with the Salvation Army in Southsea for years, so Roy and I met with their captain. They were extraordinary: calm, compassionate, practical. They offered to conduct the funeral free of charge, provide the hall for the wake, even supply the catering. We donated, of course, but the kindness was real.

On the day of the funeral, I wasn't sure how I'd react. When Mum died, I'd cried with anger. When Dad died, it had been a quiet sadness. But with Roger...
When the hearse arrived, a single tear escaped, just one, and Michelle gently rubbed the middle of my back in that instinctive way she has.

The service was simple. Honest.
Very Roger.

The Flat
Because the post-mortem delayed things by several weeks, I decided to start clearing Roger's flat before the funeral. I knew he hoarded, we all knew, but I wasn't prepared for the scale.

By the time I'd hauled the 120th black bin bag to the big communal bins, I realised I was operating at professional decluttering level. Those bins were taller than me, emptied daily, and I was filling them at exactly the same rate.

Some things made me pause, a photo, a card, an old Red Cross badge. Others made me wince, like the dentures I discovered in his bathroom cupboard.

"Well," I thought, "I didn't know he wore dentures... but good dentures are supposed to be invisible."
And into a bag they went.

Michelle helped for a couple of days. The rest was just me, and Roger's unique filing system, which seemed to consist entirely of the words "I might need this."

Roger's Last Joke
At the wake, a man I didn't recognise approached me.
"Jim," he said, shaking my hand. "I'm the friend who found him. Chess night."
I thanked him, sincerely, and we chatted a bit about Roger.

Then he asked, "Did you find a set of dentures in the bathroom?"
"Yes," I said, relieved to provide useful information. "I did."
"Excellent," he said. "They're mine."
I blinked. "Sorry... what?"
He grinned sheepishly.

"Roger baked a cake every week. One in particular, his Dundee cake, was frankly inedible. Lovely attempt, dreadful execution."
I laughed already. I knew exactly where this was going.
"So, I'd always ask, 'What cake tonight, Roger?' If he said 'Dundee,' I'd nip to the loo, pop my dentures out, hide them in his cupboard, and when he handed me a slice I'd say, 'Oh dear, Roger, forgot my teeth. I'll take it home.' I didn't want to hurt his feelings."

He paused.
"That last Monday, chess ran late. I had to catch the final bus. Left the dentures behind."
I swallowed.

"Well... Jim... I didn't know. I assumed they were Roger's. I'm afraid they've... gone."
Thrown away. Bag number 114, if memory serves.
Jim burst out laughing. "Ah well," he said. "He'd like the joke."
He absolutely would.

One Last Favour
Surprisingly, clearing the flat never felt like a chore. Roger had always been good to me. In a strange way, sorting through his life felt like my final act of loyalty. My last job as his brother. When the final bag was dragged out, and I closed the door behind me for the last time, I rested my hand on the lock and whispered,
"Rest in peace, dear brother."

Because he deserved that.
And more.

Welcome to Liss, Home of the White Elephant

Long before I dipped my toes, or, let's be honest, my entire body, into local politics, I was just a man with too much time and a regular habit of reading the *Petersfield Post* from cover to cover. It was cheaper than therapy and more entertaining than daytime television.

One weekend, an article caught my eye. Liss was getting a youth centre. In a retail unit. Near the station. The one by St Mary's Church and the surgery. The conversion alone was going to cost tens of thousands, funded by a cocktail of the Parish Council, East Hampshire District Council, Hampshire County Council, and presumably anyone else who had a spare fiver and didn't mind seeing it vanish.

And Hampshire County Council were even throwing in a full-time youth worker.

My cynical eyebrow performed a perfect Olympic-level arch. I'd seen similar ventures come and go. Many had lasted about as long as a snowflake on a bonfire. Yes, we had the odd bit of anti-social behaviour, but nothing serious, and certainly not the sort of thing that would be solved by giving the culprits somewhere with beanbags.

So, I did what any sensible, mild-mannered, reserved Englishman would do.

I wrote a sarcastic letter.

Its title?

"Welcome to Liss, Home of the White Elephant."

I expected nothing.
The *Petersfield Post*, however, printed the whole thing in glorious black-and-white.

It was, as the young people say, a vibe. Some villagers loved it. Others were ready to hold a community bonfire in honour of my head. Marmite would've been proud.

Ten Years Later...

Fast-forward a decade. Somehow, despite that letter, or possibly because of it, I was Chairman of Liss Parish Council.

And into my inbox arrived a very polite invitation to the **Crossover Centre's Tenth Anniversary Dinner**.

Yes.
The very same youth centre whose early obituary I had so confidently written.

At the dinner, the Chair of Trustees stood to speak. And of course, of *course,* he reminded the entire room of my now-infamous "White Elephant" letter. There was a ripple of laughter, the kind you get when everyone is secretly delighted you're about to eat humble pie.

Then he invited me up to say a few words.

As I stood, I remembered something I'd learned at my very first public speaking event, courtesy of a wise CBI speaker:

"Always keep your words soft and sweet... because one day you might have to eat them."

So, I stepped up to the microphone and said,
"Well, now that you've all been reminded of that letter, I'd like to begin by saying: those words are *delicious.*"

The room erupted, laughter, clapping, even a few cheers.

"I'm genuinely delighted to have been proven wrong," I continued. "Thanks to the incredible hard work of Georgina, Georgie to most of you, and every single trustee, volunteer, and supporter, the Crossover Centre has become a tremendous success. So please join me in a toast... to the next ten years!"

Everyone stood. Glasses were raised. What could have been awkward turned thoroughly heartwarming.

It was, in its own strange way, one of the most satisfying moments of my life in public service.

And Georgie...

I should mention Georgina, Georgie, properly. Even though she later moved on, she remains a friend to this day.

Lively. Gifted. Whip-smart.

Famous for her trademark Rastafarian hairdo, her drumming skills, and her alter ego on the roller hockey rink: **Harold Bashup** of the Portsmouth Roller Wenches.

Yes. Really.

Only in Liss, ladies and gentlemen. Only in Liss.

The €65 Snack Run

It was one of those evenings that begin perfectly innocently and end with you questioning every life choice you've ever made.

I was in Rotterdam on business, due to meet Herman the next day, and with my flight back to the UK looming, I decided to nip out from the hotel to buy a few snacks. A simple plan. Sensible. Frugal. Airport prices being what they are, I thought I'd save myself a small fortune.

Reader, I did not.

The corner shop was only a short stroll away. I wandered in, grabbed a few bits, paid my €4.50, and mentally awarded myself the "Thrifty Traveller of the Year" award. Snacks secured, wallet intact, mission accomplished.

I stepped outside, turned towards the hotel, and ambled along the quiet street until I reached a pedestrian crossing. The little red man was lit. I looked left. I looked right. Nothing. Not a car, not a bike, not even one of the Dutch pigeons, who I swear operate under their own cycling proficiency code.

All clear.
So, I crossed.

Halfway across, a piercing whistle split the air.
I turned to see a police officer striding towards me with the purposeful energy of a man who had been waiting his whole career for this exact moment. He gestured for me to return to the pavement. I did, fully expecting some friendly Dutch advice about being careful in the dark.

Nope.
He launched into rapid Dutch, which might as well have been Klingon in that moment.
"I'm sorry," I said, hands up in full surrender, "I'm English."
He switched to English so flawlessly that I momentarily wondered if I'd misheard the Dutch. And then he delivered the news:
"You have committed the offence of crossing the road while the signal was red."
Jaywalking. In Rotterdam. At night. On an empty road.

I tried, very politely, to explain:
"There were no cars." "There was no danger." "I'm British - we do this all the time."
He was unmoved.

Out came what I assumed was a notebook. Wrong. It was his fixed penalty pad, and he wielded it like Thor's hammer.

Name. Address.
Then: "Your passport number, please."

Which, of course, was not in my pocket. It was safely tucked away in my hotel room like a responsible adult.

"Do you have a photo of your passport on your phone?" he asked.
"No," I said.
"In that case," he replied, perfectly calm, "I will accompany you to your hotel so you can get it."

And that is how I ended up being escorted through Rotterdam by a police officer at 10pm because I had dared to cross an empty road slightly too enthusiastically.

We reached the hotel. He waited in reception while I fetched my passport, and then he carefully wrote down every tiny detail before handing me my notice.

€65.
For crossing a road. A road with more tumbleweed than traffic.
I stared at the ticket. Then at him.
There really wasn't much to say.

On the way back to my room, the maths hit me:
Snacks: €4.50
Fine: €65
Net result: €69.50

I could have had a three-course meal and a glass of wine for that.
I sat on the edge of my bed, shook my head, and muttered the only conclusion possible:
"Well done, Keith. More fool you."

The Dutch chapter - where business became family

Some of the most important relationships of my career didn't start in boardrooms, Zoom calls or conferences. They began in hire cars, print factories, late-night kitchens, and with glasses of wine at 3am. My whole Dutch chapter began that way, almost by accident, with a trip that turned colleagues into friends, and friends into something much closer to family.

Pixami had a long-standing European client in the Netherlands, Icnia BV, better known as Fotovoordelig. When Herman suggested I fly to Rotterdam, two days, one extra client meeting, then two days with the Fotovoordelig team, I assumed it would be a bog-standard consultancy trip. Systems, processes, plans. Tick the boxes, shake the hands, back home by Friday.

I had absolutely no idea what was coming.

Day One: All Business

That first day was textbook: productive, tidy, professional. I met Rolf, Arjo, and their developer (whose name I've shamefully forgotten). We analysed the system, agreed timelines, made lists, ticked boxes. Good people, good brains. A solid day.

Day Two: Everything Changes

The next morning, Herman was supposed to join us for the drive up to Groningen, three hours north, to visit Fotovoordelig's print partner. Something urgent came up, so it ended up being just the three of us in the car.

And that's where the turn happened.

You know those long drives that start with polite chat about work... and end, hours later, with you sharing stories about childhood, heartbreaks, daft mistakes, family, ambition, the stupid things you've done, the things you dream of doing?

That was us.

We got into the car as business contacts.
We got out as friends.

The Print Factory That Made NASA Look Sloppy

When we arrived at the printers, my jaw nearly hit the floor. Decades of business process engineering had not prepared me for this operation.

Rolls of paper taller than me were forklifted onto machines with the precision of a space launch. I assumed this was stock for the week.

"Oh no," our guide said. "This will all be gone tomorrow. We run on two hours' buffer."

Two hours.

I practically wept with admiration. It was a cathedral of workflow perfection.

Over lunch, I had to laugh at the irony. I'd spent years evangelising electronic document management, reduce paper! Eliminate paper! and there I was in a factory that ate paper by the truckload. The universe really does enjoy a joke.

The Offer

Driving back, we stopped at a quiet coastal restaurant. Simple. Beautiful. We ate, drank, watched the sun drop behind the dunes.

Then Rolf turned to me.

"We've been talking," he said, nodding at Arjo. "We're impressed. Would you consider going into business with us? A third share. And we'll pay you twenty percent more than Pixami."

One of those fork-in-the-road moments. Rare. Weighty. Full of possibility.

I didn't say yes instantly. But if you'd checked my brain at that moment, you'd have found it already packing its suitcase.

By the time we pulled back into Rotterdam, we were booking the follow-up meeting for contracts.

I flew home quietly buzzing... and carrying a guilty little secret: I hadn't told Herman. Yet. My logic was simple, get the paperwork done first; do the explaining (and apologising) second. Asking forgiveness is so much easier than asking permission.

Staying With Rolf - Where Friendship Really Began

On my next visit, Rolf asked if I'd stay at his house instead of a hotel. He was separated, the kids only there at weekends, and I could use his daughter's room. Practical. Easy. And without realising it, it was the start of one of the warmest friendships of my life.

I still remember that first night.

Dinner out with Rolf, Arjo, and Rolf's partner, Chantal. Lovely meal. Lovely people. Then back to the house. Arjo left. Chantal went to bed. Rolf and I sat at the dining table and talked.

And that's when we met... **the light fitting**.

A gorgeous hanging lamp positioned at *exactly* the height of my forehead. Over the next few years, I smacked my head on it so many times we could have sold tickets. It became a running joke:
Budden vs. The Lamp
(The lamp remained undefeated.)

Eventually we moved to the sofa, floor-to-ceiling windows looking out onto a canal, reflections rippling on the water. We talked until 3:30am. Not business, life. Hopes. Fears. Regrets. It was like discovering a brother you didn't know you had.

Then came the moment I've told countless people since.

There we were, side-by-side in the bathroom, toothbrushes in hand. Me in my boxer shorts. Rolf in white cotton briefs so tight they needed their own postcode... with Mickey Mouse on the front and Minnie Mouse on the back.

"If you've never brushed your teeth in your boxers next to a man wearing Disney underwear at four in the morning," I told him, "You haven't lived."

We dissolved into hysterics, hugged, and then crept off to bed like naughty schoolchildren terrified of waking the adults.

That's when you know a business partnership is going to work, when the foundation is affection, not spreadsheets.

The Years That Followed

We built things. Good things. Clever things. We produced charity projects, Dakar Rally books, 24 Hours of Nijmegen books. We supported others. We made a difference. We became woven through each other's lives.

Arjo passed away too young. A good man. A kind man. Missed deeply.

Rolf, though... Rolf is one of the strongest threads in the tapestry of my life.

And then... The Coaster Incident

Now we get to the part where I wished the ground would open and swallow me whole.

The Dutch speak English terrifyingly well. But of course, in meetings with Dutch clients, the conversation would drift into Dutch. Over time, I learned to follow the gist. Not perfectly. Not enough to join in. Just enough to nod convincingly. Speaking Dutch myself was hopeless; Dutch men have throat muscles the rest of us can only dream of.

Still, I'd tried to learn basic phrases: hello, goodbye, thank you... and what I believed to be the Dutch word for a *drinks coaster*.

One evening in a restaurant, everyone else had a coaster. I did not.
"No problem," I thought. "I've got this."

The waiter approached. I delivered my carefully practised sentence.

Rolf and Arjo immediately burst into laughter. The waiter stared at me as though I'd asked him to adopt me.

So, I repeated it.

Louder.

Slower.

Because of course, that always helps.

Now half the restaurant was watching the strange Englishman apparently demanding something deeply confusing.

Rolf finally composed himself enough to ask the waiter for a coaster in proper Dutch. The waiter nodded, fetched one, and repeated the correct word.

The first half sounded *just* like what I'd said.
The second half... absolutely nothing like it.

I checked the note on my phone. Spelling correct. Pronunciation exactly as learned. So, what had gone wrong?

"What did I actually say?" I asked.

Rolf put a hand on my shoulder, tears of laughter still in his eyes.

"Mate... you didn't ask him for a coaster. You kept asking the waiter for a small fishing boat."

And that was it, I started laughing too. Because once you know, you know.

Every chilli has a silver lining

I've mentioned before about the loss of sensation in my face. It's not all bad news.

One evening at our local curry house, I was out with a couple of friends when a group of lads at the next table started taking the mickey out of me. I'd been blowing on every forkful of food before eating it, old habits die hard, and I'd burnt my mouth enough times since the brain damage to know that caution is a lifestyle choice.

What they *didn't* know was that one of the great, unexpected perks of my facial numbness is this:
I can eat ridiculously hot chillies without even blinking.

(Though, as I've learned the hard way, I *can* still feel them when they make their grand exit the next morning. Nature has balance.)

Anyway, I decided to have a little fun.
I asked the chef to bring us six different chillies, lined up from "respectable curry heat" to "call an ambulance."

The lads huddled like they were choosing a gladiator. Eventually, one brave volunteer stepped forward. The wager was simple: £10 for the first chilli, rising in £10 increments as we worked our way to the hottest.

The first two? A doddle for both of us.

The third? A single bead of sweat appeared on his forehead. I smiled sweetly and asked, "So... when do we start on the hot ones?"

The whole restaurant cracked up. Chairs scraped. People came over to watch. We had an audience now.

Number four made him wobble.

Number five made him stop entirely. He stared at it. Looked at me. Looked back at the chilli. Then quietly put down his fork. "Nope. I'm out."

The watching crowd cheered. Then a voice called out:

"I know you're getting £60 from these lads. Tell you what, if you eat that last one, the hottest one, I'll give £100 to a charity of your choice!"

Well. You can't turn that down, can you?

"Challenge accepted," I said, and without hesitation, picked up the final chilli.
Nom, nom, nom.
Gone.

The place erupted. Cheering, applause, someone high-fived me like I'd just won MasterChef.

The lads tried to give me the £60, but I told them to put it towards our bill. The kind chap with the donation pulled out his chequebook there and then, £100 straight to Lymphoma Action.

So yes, every cloud has a silver lining.
Or, perhaps more appropriately… every chilli does.

My motoring life

I've mentioned my love of motor racing, so it seems only right to include a tour through the many cars (and occasional mechanical catastrophes) that made up my driving life, before my brain injury in 2014 brought it to an abrupt end. The after-effects meant the DVLA declared me unfit to drive, and fair play to them, they were right. But I still managed to cram an impressive number of vehicles into my thirty years on the road.

The first car I ever drove was my dad's Ford Cortina MkIII: British Racing Green, brown vinyl roof, and those infamous faux-leather seats that could peel the skin off your legs if you wore shorts in summer. Driving it wasn't just transport, it was dermabrasion.

Next came **a Morris Marina**, white, amiable enough in a straight line but treated corners as optional suggestions. Especially in the rain. After that was the mighty **FSO Polonez**, built like a Cold War tank, with cloth seats and a boot release that felt positively futuristic.

The FSO once spat out an entire spark plug halfway up Stoner Hill. I lifted the bonnet to find it dangling like a Christmas bauble. Yet the stubborn thing still got me home. They really *don't* make them like that anymore.

Then came the corporate years:

- A beige **Vauxhall Cavalier** (drab but dependable),
- A white **Peugeot 405** whose dashboard tried to collapse into my lap,
- A red **Ford Orion**,
- And then my absolute pride and joy: a British Racing Green **Renault Laguna**, sleek, comfortable, and years ahead of its time.

My move to HRH landed me a red **Renault 11**, memorable because it had… a *car phone*. Not a mobile, a full-size, hard-wired, battery-in-the-boot beast. It felt like piloting Air Force One.
Then another Laguna. Then another. (I was in a committed relationship with Renault by that point.)

Eventually I graduated to a silver **BMW 5 Series**, then wandered back to Renault, before self-employment budget realities nudged me into a modest white **Ford Fiesta**. It leaked oil, and the radio only worked for five-minute intervals, like it needed regular union-mandated breaks. But it got me around.

Then came a **Suzuki Swift**, perfectly pleasant until its clutch died on a hill in Four Marks.

Business picked up again, and I treated myself to contract hire: first a sleek **Mitsubishi Gallant**, then a **Mercedes C180**. For the first time we I felt like a Proper Business Person.

When the company closed, the car disappeared overnight like Cinderella's coach. I was carless again.

My next attempt at motoring glory was a second-hand **Vauxhall Carlton** in Horndean. Lovely thing, until the MOT revealed it was actually two cars welded together. A "cut and shunt," the mechanic said, in the kind of tone normally reserved for breaking unwelcome news to distant relatives. Back it went.

Finally, I settled on a white **Rover 75**. A little tired. A little frayed around the edges. But then again, so was I. It carried me where I needed to go, and that was enough.

And that, dear reader, was the end of my motoring story.

I don't regret much about the health challenges that followed, but I *do* miss driving-the freedom, the independence, the sheer joy of pointing a car at a horizon and going.

Still, I know I'm one of the lucky ones. And as I often say:
I never lose. I either win, or I learn.

Keeping the sea on your left

I've made countless trips to Europe over the years, some by air, some with the car on the ferry from Dover, but one journey stands out like a lighthouse warning you that you've absolutely taken the wrong turning.

A late-night run to Breskens in the Netherlands.

The plan was elegant in its simplicity:
- Take the 9 p.m. ferry from Dover to Zeebrugge
- Disembark
- Drive along the coast with the sea on your left.
- Forty kilometres later: Breskens. Job done.

What could possibly go wrong?

Everything at Dover went perfectly. A peaceful meal on board, a smooth crossing, and customs at Zeebrugge waved me through with the relaxed air of people who'd seen it all before. Soon enough I was out of the town, the moon bright and full, the sea glittering loyally on my left.

Ten kilometres in, I expected signs to Breskens.
Instead?
Bruges. Bruges, the famous inland city. Bruges, which famously does *not* sit forty kilometres up the coast.

But the sea was still on my left, so my logic insisted I must be fine.
Then a lorry lumbered across a bridge to my left.
I followed it.
A few metres later came that sinking, Oh-you-idiot realisation:
That wasn't the sea.
It was a canal.
A canal masquerading as the North Sea.
No wonder the road signs were staging a mutiny.

Do I laugh? Do I cry? Do I abandon the car and adopt canal life?

I chose "reverse direction" and headed back to the tiny petrol station I'd passed earlier. If fate had any sense of humour, it would be closed and staffed by a man who only spoke Flemish. Mercifully, fate was in a generous mood.

The attendant spoke flawless English, produced a road map like a magician unveiling a rabbit, pointed out exactly where I'd gone wrong, and folded the map neatly to my corrected route. I bought it instantly.

Breskens was twenty kilometres away, not the scenic coastal hour I'd imagined.

From that night on, I travelled with a map in the passenger seat. Lesson learned.

The Calais Youth Group Caper
That wasn't my only memorable Channel crossing.

For a few years I helped with the local youth group, and one summer we took twenty teenagers by coach to Calais. It was a brilliant day, sunshine, French cafés, GCSE-level French used with worrying enthusiasm.

One lad proudly ordered steak... only to discover later he'd accidentally ordered horse.
He ate it anyway, because teenagers are indestructible.

The trouble arrived on the journey home.

Four of the boys, fifteen, full of confidence and absolutely no sense, had gone wandering alone and returned with items that customs officers work hard **not** to find:
- beer
- penknives
- adult magazines

I briefly considered confiscating the knives and discreetly throwing them overboard. Tempting... until I remembered ferries now have CCTV. The last thing I needed was to be caught on camera chucking sharp objects into the Channel like a serial killer disposing of cyclists with a hint of garlic about them.

So, we needed a plan.
Once on the ferry, we ushered the kids upstairs. When we reached Dover, just before the customs officer boarded, we issued our calm, professional instruction:
"Everybody pretend to be asleep."

It made no sense whatsoever, but in the strange logic of youth work, it was the only plan we had.

Amazingly, it worked.

The officer walked up the aisle, counted passports, glanced at twenty allegedly slumbering angels, and waved us through.

Just as he stepped off the coach, one bright spark piped up at full volume:
"IS IT TIME TO WAKE UP YET?"

The officer turned, gave a wry smile, that perfect mixture of "I heard everything" and "I'm choosing to let this slide," and waved us on our way.

Phew.

Soft and sweet

People who know me now would probably struggle to recognise the me of years ago.

Not physically, although yes, I've developed what polite doctors call "a generous build." That's what happens when chemotherapy gives you steroids by the bucketload. One minute you've got cheekbones, the next minute you've got a neck like a Christmas turkey that's been overfed.

But the biggest change hasn't been weight.
It's confidence.
Especially with public speaking.

Back then, I barely said *boo* to a goose.

Now, if you give me a room of three people, ten people, two hundred, or even four thousand, I'll stand up and talk like someone's paying me by the syllable.
(I know I can do it. Because I *have* done it.)

Was it courage?
Not really. Courage implies heroism. This was survival. Because, as I discovered, being "first" at things is pointless if nobody knows you exist.

If a tree falls in the forest and nobody hears it, philosophers get excited.
If your business launches and nobody hears it, the bailiffs get excited.

Networking forced me into speaking.
That 60-second pitch? Oh yes, that's public speaking. Even though no lift on earth actually lasts 60 seconds. If one did, I'd assume it had broken down, or the hamster powering it had gone on strike.

The Roadshow on the Back of a Fag Packet
My first real plunge into speaking came when I was part of the tiny handful bringing Electronic Document Management (EDM) to the UK. There were four of us nationwide. We could've held our national conference in a lift. (A 30-second one).

After an industry event, a few of us ended up in the pub. Pints of London Pride in hand, ideas started bouncing around. Back when indoor smoking was legal, and "ventilation" meant opening a small window and hoping for the best.

Mal smoked. Handy, because we needed the back of his fag packet for brainstorming. Back then, all corporate strategy documents were either on the back of a fag packet or typed by someone who had definitely *been smoking*.

"What if," one of us said, "we do a five-city UK tour... in a week?"

Five cities.
Five days.
Ten presentations.

A plan drawn up with the precision of a military operation... if the military had three pints and access to a packet of B&H.

We booked:
- a man with a van
- an executive minibus and driver (if we were doing all of those miles, we were doing them in comfort)
- a telesales team
- five venues
- and a frankly impossible schedule

Skype meetings followed (Zoom's Neanderthal ancestor).
The telesales team sold the sessions *before* we'd written a single slide.
We were committed.
Game on.

Rotating Floors & Innocent Victims
Leeds... oh Leeds.
The venue had a rotating floor. Yes, really.
The audience sat stationary in the middle while the floor rotated us around like some kind of low-budget Bond villain lair.
Mal's alcove lit up.
Then the lights went out, the floor rotated, and Gary's alcove lit up.
Then rotation again, and my spotlight came on like the world's slowest magic show.

Afterwards I thanked the DJ/sound man. He told me his favourite prank was to rotate the floor when someone nipped to the loo. They'd come out and find the room layout completely changed, assume they were losing their mind, and stagger back into the toilet.

I laughed so hard I nearly needed the toilet myself.

Cardiff was packed. Standing room only.
I thought we'd cracked the Welsh market.
The venue manager said:
"Oh, people are only here because *nothing* comes to Cardiff. You're exotic."

I've never been exotic before or since, so I'll take it.

What's New, Pussycat?
We chose our walk-on music.
I chose Tom Jones' "What's New Pussycat?"
Don't ask me why, I genuinely don't know. But it works.
To this day, the second I hear those opening bars, "Presenter Keith" clicks into gear and "Normal Keith" sods off for a coffee.

Years later, I told Brad Burton that I struggled when venues couldn't play it.
His solution?
"Put one AirPod in and play it to *yourself*. They don't need to hear it."
Genius.
Infuriatingly obvious.
Like discovering you could have used the dishwasher all along instead of handwashing your pots like a Victorian servant.

Soft and Sweet - Words to Chew On
My first *big* audience - 400+ people - was at a CBI conference at IBM's South Bank centre.
They were *paying me*.
£400 for twenty minutes. In 1998. £900-ish in today's money.
I was pacing behind the stage like a caged tiger who'd only just remembered he left the gas on.

A seasoned speaker approached me.
"Nervous, laddie?"
I nodded.

"Golden rule: always keep your words soft and sweet. Because you never know when you might have to eat them later."
That line has stayed with me for thirty years.

And probably saved me from being punched in the car park more than once.

Walk-on music. Switch flick. Out I went. And nailed it.

My "Script" (or Lack Thereof)
If you give me a script, I sound like a bored hostage reading demands off a cue card.

Give me six bullet points on a postcard, and suddenly I turn into someone who knows what they're doing.

At a major conference, with a full film crew, the producer begged me to repeat my rehearsal "word for word" for camera cues.

I handed him my postcard with six vague scribbles.

He looked like a man realising he'd boarded the wrong flight.

But I've learned: trust what works.

The Mosque Speech
As Chair of East Hampshire District Council, I was invited to the opening of the new Ahmadiyya Mosque.

I prepared a polite two-minute speech.
Then our guide casually said:
"His Holiness asks that you keep it to ten minutes."
TEN.
I scribbled like a lunatic in every spare bit of white space.
Then Dominic Grieve MP spoke before me… and proceeded to use *all* my material. Every line. Every anecdote. Every fact I'd stolen from the leaflet.
By the time I walked on, my notes were more crossed-out than a teenager's first diary.
And then a shaft of sunlight came through the dome.
That was the spark.

"Before I say anything, turn to the person beside you, shake their hand, tell them your name, and let them know how glad you are they're sharing this moment with you."

The whole room lit up like someone had plugged joy into the mains.
I spoke for my remaining minute.
People stood. They applauded.

His Holiness took my hands and said:
"Inspirational speech, my man. Inspirational."
I smiled, thinking:
"If only you knew..."

Jalsa Salana - The Big One
Then came the big invite:
Speak at Jalsa Salana.
30,000-40,000 attendees.
Michelle dropped me as close as she could.
"Go! You're on in 45 minutes!"

Backstage felt like the set of Strictly Come Dancing:
• microphones everywhere
• sound techs
• someone powdering my forehead, so I didn't blind the audience.

I peeked out, maybe 1,000 people, I thought.
Then I reached the lectern.
OH.
Not 1,000.
Not 10,000.
Tens of thousands.

AirPod in.
Tom Jones in one ear.
Switch flick.
And somehow... it worked.

One of my best talks ever.

Afterwards I thought:
That was a once-in-a-lifetime moment.
And I meant it.

The Brad effect

I first met Brad Burton at a business seminar in Southampton in 2010.

He was the headline speaker, loud, energised, swaggering around the stage with the confidence of someone who had absolutely nothing to hide and absolutely no interest in hiding it. His message was simple: **Get Off Your Arse.**

I liked him immediately.

No jargon. No corporate waffle. No pretence.
Just Brad, being Brad, in all his blunt, caffeinated glory.

After the talk, I bought his book and tucked it under my arm, feeling rather inspired… and slightly exhausted. A couple of hours later, I spotted him again in the coffee bar and thought, "Why not?" So, I wandered over.

"Hi Brad," I said. "Great talk earlier. Really looking forward to the book."

We chatted politely for a minute or so. Then he asked:
"You got a business card?"

Now at the time, I'd just had a brand-new batch printed, glossy black with silver lettering. The sort of card that practically winked at you. I thought they were the dog's bollocks.
So, feeling quietly smug, I handed him one.

Brad took it.

Held it up. Turned it over. Looked at me.
Then announced, in the same tone one might use to describe a wet fart:
"Well, that's a piece of shit, isn't it?"
I froze.
"…Why?" I managed.
He shrugged.
"I was going to write some notes about you on the back. But I can't. Because the back is glossy black. Nothing will stick. So, it's useless."

And there we have it, the most perfectly delivered, unexpected business lesson of my life.

I muttered something like, "Fair point," and tried not to look like a child whose sandcastle had been kicked over by a passing giant.

When I got home, I ordered new business cards with a plain white back.

Lesson learned. Painfully.

Years passed. I kept a distant, intrigued eye on Brad's work. Bought his second book, *Get Off Your Arse Too*. Life moved on.

Our paths didn't cross again until Spring 2020, the year we all learned how to use Zoom, forgot how to use trousers, and lived through the global phenomenon known as Clubhouse.

I was hosting a *Rebuild the High Street* session when a familiar name popped up in the room.
Brad Burton.
I smiled, invited him up to the virtual stage, and sure enough, he accepted. For a few weeks, he became a regular fixture, bringing his trademark blend of energy, bluntness, and cheerfully weaponised truth-telling.

Then he messaged me.
"Keith, you need to come to one of my online networking groups."

He gave me the details, told me someone would be in touch, and sure enough, a few days later, I got a call from Yiannis Charalambous. Friendly, fun, overflowing with enthusiasm, the kind of person who could make a two-hour Zoom call seem like ten minutes.

He told me about a group called **Team 1Nclusive** and invited me to join a meeting.
"It's free," he said. "Come and see if you like it."
So that Friday, I logged in.
Within minutes, I was hooked.
The energy.
The humour.
The kindness.
The complete lack of pretentiousness.

It was the first, and only, business networking group I've ever joined after attending *one* meeting. That's how certain I was that I'd found something special. Something that wasn't just about business but about belonging.

That decision shaped the next several years of my professional life. It changed how I networked, how I collaborated, and, more importantly, how I looked at people.

With 1Networking and Team 1Nclusive, I didn't just make business contacts, I made true, genuine, friends.

Meeting Brad Burton didn't just introduce me to a new way of networking.

It introduced me to a new way of thinking.

And all because of a business card that really was, as he quite rightly put it...
...a piece of shit.

Networking, Glocks and Pippa hugs

I've always said networking brings people together, but even I wasn't expecting it to introduce me to Pippa, a police firearms unit, and a full English breakfast in the same morning.

Through Brad, I ended up deeply woven into the worlds of **4Networking** (now run by the networking superstar Caroline) and **1Networking** (now guided by the fabulous duo of Jen and Matt).

Now, Jen, bless her, is to rowing what my mum was to knitting: **oarsome**.

Matt is a man of many talents too, chiefly guitar-playing and proudly displaying a genuine 1980s Speak & Spell on his wall. I once saved my paper-round money for weeks to buy one of those. Back then, for tech nerds like me, they were the height of sophistication. You weren't clever unless the Speak & Spell told you so.

But here's the thing: Brad may have built the empire, but no man builds a business alone. For Brad, her name was **Pippa**.

Now Pippa... where do I start?
She's got everything.
(Lee, if you're reading this, mate, you absolutely punched. Massively. Be grateful.)
She has a personality so vibrant it could power half of Birmingham.
She has a smile so bright aircraft could use it for final approach on a foggy night.
She lights up every room she walks into.
She's got a lovely figure.
And, she gives **the best hugs known to mankind**.
(If they ever get their own Saturday-night TV show, I'll be first in the queue for tickets.)
But above all, Pippa is the **administrative powerhouse** that keeps planets spinning.

She could answer the phone with one hand, cook dinner for Lee and the girls with the other, while her feet simultaneously reply to emails and fold meeting agendas into perfect thirds. If normal humans are a Google search, Pippa is **ChatGPT on steroids**.

And I wouldn't have met her without networking.
Put Pippa together with my PA from EHDC, Kim, and the two of them are probably responsible for half the UK's GDP. Excuse the finance reference, it's Budget week and political nerds like me watch the Chancellor with the kind of intensity Attenborough reserves for a rutting wildebeest.

Anyway, back to the plot. (If you've lost the plot, don't worry. Michelle will happily confirm that I lost mine years ago.)

At the end of Covid, Brad announced a one-day networking roadshow at **Aston Villa Stadium**.
(You will find the hotel review elsewhere in this book. Spoiler: it involves confusion, questionable décor, and a shower with the water pressure of a French kiss.)

It was my first exhibition in years. I ordered new materials. I set up my stand the night before.
I got my mandatory Pippa hug, which should pretty much be available on the NHS.
Next morning: bright and early. Breakfast in the bar. No buffet. Just a Full English or nothing.
Vegetarian? Vegan?
There's a patch of grass outside, help yourself.

I set off from the hotel toward the stadium, mind wandering, brain in neutral, thinking through the day ahead. It might have been Birmingham, but it could've been anywhere. I was not paying attention.

And then it happened.
Screech of brakes.
Two cars boxing in a third BMW.
I assumed car accident.
Until I saw four police officers jump out with **Glocks** drawn.
One officer pointed directly at me.
"Armed police! **Stand still!**"
And let me tell you, when someone's pointing a gun at you from six feet away, you don't argue.
You don't even breathe.
You just grip your rollator like it's your emotional-support pension scheme and hope for the best.

The other officers yanked two men from the BMW. The driver's window wasn't so much opened as "removed by force via Glock."
Once the suspects were dealt with, the officer nearest me lowered his weapon.

"Sorry, sir, we just needed you to stay put. Can you tell my colleague what you saw?"

What I *wanted* to say was:
"Mate, when you say, 'stand still' while pointing a firearm at me, I'm not planning a conga line."
What I *actually* said, when his colleague got his notebook out, was:
"Well... I saw two black cars pen in a blue BMW, then you all got out with Glocks drawn."
He seemed satisfied.
Apparently my observational skills were enough to categorise me as "harmless pedestrian," not "international drug baron."
They released me back into the wild.

I walked into the exhibition hall... and my stand was gone.
Vanished. Vaporised.
I wondered if I was having another episode of Leeds revolving-floor syndrome (see earlier chapter; keep up, dear reader).

Then I spotted Pippa.
She saw my face and immediately opened her arms.
Never, and I mean **never,** has a Pippa-hug been more necessary.

"My stand... it's disappeared," I said, half expecting her to tell me I'd imagined it.

She laughed. "Keith, your stand looked so good that Brad and I moved it.

We put it right by the public entrance. It's the first thing people will see."

Well.
That will do nicely.
Coffee first, naturally.
Then...
What's New Pussycat?
Let the show begin.

Serial Huggers, Cat Rescuers & Other Networking Legends

Networking has taken me into more Zoom rooms, hotel bars, and questionable conference buffets than I can reasonably count, and along the way I've met so many incredible people that if I listed them all, this book would turn into one of those *Build Your Own HMS Victory* magazine series.

You know the ones, £1.99 for Issue 1 (comes with a free cannon!), then by Issue 10 it's £5.99, and by the time you're halfway through you've spent more money than it would cost to fly first class to Portsmouth, have a weekend at the Holiday Inn, and buy the fully-built model already sitting proudly in the Dockyard gift shop.

But hey, you've come this far, you may as well finish the bloody boat.

Anyway, I digress. (I know. Shocker.)

I can't possibly include everyone, but a few people absolutely *demand* a mention — partly because they're brilliant, partly because they'd kill me if I didn't.

Stacey Calder

If networking had a Nigella Lawson, it would be Stacey. Charismatic, organised, unflappable, and capable of running more Business Success Network groups at once than seems legally permissible. Somewhere out there is probably a BSN group for left-handed Peruvian basket weavers, and Stacey will still have it running on time.

Then there's the legendary BSN Awards Night. I was lucky enough to be a finalist one year. The event. The afterparty. The photos. The sore head the next morning. The fact that I found glitter in my shoe three days later. That after-party which almost became an after-morning with Stacey, Pippa, and the Oarsome Jen.

And then there's Choppers, Stacey's daughter, with more

confidence at 16 than I had at 40. That girl is going places, probably with Stacey shouting encouragement and carrying a clipboard.

But most importantly, Stacey is simply a lovely human. She's seen me laugh, she's seen me cry, and she always knows exactly what to say. Stacey, thank you.

Laura Jewell

The undisputed goddess of Utility Warehouse.
Her giggle is so infectious that even COVID would back away saying, "Nope, too contagious for us."

A joy to know, a delight to listen to, and if laughter really is the best medicine, Laura is a walking NHS pharmacy.

Yiannis (Surname Redacted for the Safety of Spellcheckers)

I'm not even going to attempt his surname. It's Greek. That's all you need to know.

Yiannis is the only man I've ever seen manage to sell someone a van, walk across hot coals, and juggle crockery *at the same time*, the most Greek multitasking imaginable.

Suzii Fido

Suzii lives in Greece and has rescued more cats than I've had hot dinners.

Honestly, her cat sanctuary is so famous I've heard rumours of Turkish cats attempting the crossing in tiny inflatable dinghies with little feline paddles.

She is sunshine in human form, with fur on it.

Tina Gillies

Fiery red hair, warm heart, sharp mind.
Looks fierce, acts gentle.
Tina is one of those people you meet, chat to, and suddenly an hour has vanished and you have no idea where it went, which is

pretty much the ultimate networking compliment.

t'other Keith - Keith Blakemore-Noble

Mindset Maestro.
Tell him your problems and he'll rearrange the furniture in your brain until everything makes sense again.

If 99% of our troubles are in our head, Keith is the bloke who brings the broom, the bin bags and the sparkle spray.

Tony Edwards

If it has chips and a screen, Tony can fix it.
Honestly, I think he's one wand short of being admitted to Hogwarts. Computer viruses evacuate the premises the moment he enters a room.

Even his shadow can troubleshoot a printer.

Ben (BJK Entertainment)

Ben can't walk, but that doesn't stop him running a thriving entertainment business.

Need a disco? A party in a box? A night to remember?
Ben's your man.

He proves something I've said all my life: your body might limit you, but your mind never has to.

Rachael Chiverton

My long-suffering VA.

Rachael is powered by caffeine, spreadsheets, and pure magic. Her entire office is magnetic, not just the fridge. *The wall.*
I wouldn't be surprised if eventually she magnetises the family dog, Leo, and uses him to file paperwork.

If I ever run for Prime Minister, Rachael is the only person I'd trust to run the country.

⭐ Caroline Jane Andrew - CEO of 4N, Human Megawatt

Leather trousers. Platinum hair. Laser eyes.
Caroline walks into a room and before she's even taken off her jacket, 20 people are already networking like they've trained for the Olympics.

She took 4Networking by the scruff of the neck and breathed fire, structure, and brilliance into it.

A force of nature, but the warm kind, not the hurricane kind.

⭐ Matt Richardson & Jody Fletcher

Promo legends.

If you can print it, wear it, stick it, or hand it out at a conference, Matt and Jody can supply it.

I've had tote bags.
I've had piggy banks.
And now I've planted the idea of a turbo-charged camouflage camel. God help us all.

⭐ Wayne Trice - Magician, Mind-boggler, Legend

He performed at my 60th birthday and people in Liss *still* talk about it.

Wayne is so respected in the magic world that even the Magic Circle twitches nervously when he walks past.

Hire him. Trust me.

⭐ And finally... Paul Newton

Paul was unique, the hat, the humour, the heart.
He could read minds, charm rooms, and once performed for the British Army and walked out with the nuclear codes (well... allegedly).

Taken far too soon, but never forgotten.

His hat alone could fill a room with stories.

❦ In Closing...

Networking brought me clients, yes. But more importantly, it brought me people, the accidental family that forms when you spend half your life in Zoom boxes, conference halls and hotel lobbies.

Every one of them added something to my journey.
A moment. A laugh. A hug. A spark.
And this chapter is my little thank you.

(Though if you weren't mentioned, don't worry. Knowing me, I'll forget someone vital and have to release a second edition by Tuesday.)

For all the laughter, the silliness, the inside jokes and the daft moments I'll forever cherish, here's the truth: these people, every single one of them, held me up in ways they'll never fully understand. Through the health scares, the heartbreaks, the losses, and the messier chapters of my life, they showed up. They didn't need to, but they did. And that's the thing about real connection, it arrives disguised as a networking event and ends up becoming a lifeline.

"If networking has taught me anything, it's that life is less about who you meet... and more about who insists on hugging you before you've finished your coffee."

The pilot has landed us in the car park

In other chapters I've talked about my long-haul adventures to Zimbabwe, South Africa and the United States, but over the years I've also clocked up more modest miles across the UK, Ireland, France, Belgium, the Netherlands, Denmark, Germany and Spain.

Most flights were completely unremarkable, the kind where you land, stretch, and instantly forget everything that happened in the sky.

But a handful have stayed with me.

My First Time in the Air
Like many people of my generation, my first flight felt like a rite of passage. We never travelled abroad as a family, though my brother Roger had been to Israel, which gave him bragging rights for decades, so there was a special nervous excitement about boarding that first British Airways flight from Heathrow to Glasgow.

Back then you still got a complimentary newspaper as you boarded, which made me feel terribly sophisticated.

I remember the plane taxiing to the runway, the engines spooling up, that strange pushback into my seat, and then the sudden, smooth lift as the ground dropped away. I knew intellectually that we must be going fast, but my senses simply didn't buy it. I became convinced we weren't going quickly enough, the pilot had misjudged it, and we'd fall out of the sky within seconds.

We didn't. Obviously.

But try telling that to twenty-something me as we climbed through the clouds.

Landing was worse, my ears felt like they were being vacuumed inside-out. No one had taught me the trick of holding your nose and swallowing to equalise pressure. These days, I don't even think about it. Back then, I thought my skull was going to implode.

After that first trip, Glasgow became a regular commute. I flew so often that the novelty wore off and I became one of those travellers who barely looks out the window, more interested in the crossword than the clouds.

But one flight did break the monotony.

The Glasgow-to-Heathrow Odyssey
It was classic Glasgow weather, rain, wind, more rain, and the hint of yet more rain. At the airport we learned that high winds in the south might delay the flight. They did. When we eventually boarded, the pilot warned that we might be diverted to Birmingham or Bristol if Heathrow became too gusty to land.

"We'll arrange coaches," he said cheerfully, which is airline-speak for: *You're not getting home anytime soon.*

Forty minutes later he returned to the intercom.
"Good news, ladies and gentlemen, we're heading to Heathrow after all."
A ripple of relief spread through the cabin.

Then, as we approached the runway at London Heathrow, the engines suddenly roared, and the nose lifted sharply. Missed approach.

"Apologies," the pilot said, still calm. "That landing wasn't safe. We'll try again. If we can't get in, we'll divert to Bristol."
He couldn't.
So off to Bristol we went.

That landing was silky smooth, and the cabin erupted in applause, the sort that isn't polite, but heartfelt. British Airways were on the ball: coaches waiting, engines running, drivers ready. An hour later we were heading back down the M4 to Heathrow.

Not the homecoming I'd hoped for, but memorable all the same.

The Funniest Safety Announcement Ever
Another standout flight was an EasyJet hop from Gatwick to Edinburgh, also in high winds. The head steward was one of those rare people who could do comedy without trying.
"Ladies and gentlemen," he began, "welcome aboard this EasyJet flight to Edinburgh. The next announcement will be of

interest to the person sitting next to you."

Instantly, everyone looked up.

Then, of course, he launched into the standard safety briefing, but for once, the entire plane listened.

Landing in Edinburgh was... spirited. Lots of bumps. A few gasps. A couple of nervous prayers.

Once safely on the ground, he picked up the microphone again: "Ladies and gentlemen, thank you for flying EasyJet and welcome to Edinburgh. It's wet and windy outside, so I hope you've brought your coats... and judging by that landing, I think the pilot's put us down in the car park."

The whole cabin erupted.
Give that man a BAFTA.

The Smallest Plane I've Ever Been On
The final flight worth mentioning was a tiny regional hop from Amsterdam to Maastricht, by far the smallest passenger aircraft I've ever boarded. Dual propellers, sixteen seats, and no door between us and the pilots. You could see every switch, every movement, every coffee sip.

I was in the front row, practically in the cockpit, enjoying a level of legroom that felt almost decadent. At times I was tempted to stand up and look over the pilot's shoulder like an overexcited child, but I thought better of it.

Still, it was a fascinating peek into the skill and serenity required to fly something so small.

That flight didn't just get me from A to B - it gave me a new respect for the people who make aviation look effortless.

The Day I Attempted the Heathrow Grand Prix
By this point in my life, I'd flown to Glasgow, Edinburgh and Jersey so often that airport security were practically on a first-name basis with my luggage bits. Domestic flights had become as routine as catching a bus, except with fewer pensioners and slightly better snacks.

So, when a client asked if I could fly to Stuttgart, I thought, "Easy. How different can it be?"
(Those words never end well.)

The trouble began on the M25, as all good British disaster stories do. A crash had snarled up traffic, leaving me inching forward with all the urgency of a constipated tortoise. I eyed the clock. I did some mental maths. I swore under my breath. *Long-stay parking?* Not a chance.

Short stay it was. My wallet winced.
"Well," I reasoned, "I'm only away for the day. How bad can it be?"
(Another phrase destined to age badly.)

I dashed into the terminal and joined the queue for British Airways check-in, casually surveying the hall like a man.

pretending to be calm while silently dying inside.
Then I saw her, two people ahead of me, a perfectly ordinary woman... except for the very *extraordinary* object in her hand.
A passport.
My brain halted.
A passport.
A PASS. PORT.
The thing *I* did not have.

I'd been flying domestic for so long that my brain had switched to "bus mode." Glasgow doesn't require a passport. Edinburgh doesn't require a passport. Jersey barely does.
Stuttgart, however, very much does.

I began a frantic mental calculation that would've impressed Carol Vorderman.
If, *if,* the roads were clear, and, *if,* I drove like Lewis Hamilton after three Red Bulls, I could get home to Farnborough, grab the passport, and get back to Heathrow with about 15 minutes to spare.
Pre-9/11, 15 minutes was basically a fortnight.

So off I sprinted, back to short-stay, £20 already lost to Heathrow's parking gods and I hadn't even left the country yet.

I leapt into the car and hurtled out of Heathrow like a mouse whose backside had landed on a hot ring and was now on fire.

M4. M25. M3. I drove with the speed of Nigel Mansell and the eyesight of an eagle with a mission.

Home.
Up six flights of stairs.
Front door.
Passport sitting in the fruit bowl, *of course it bloody was*. Why wouldn't it be next to the bananas?
Is it in date?
YES.
Hallelujah.
Back to the car.
Reverse the route.
M3. M25. M4.
Short stay again. First available bay. "Premium Parking," it said. That's Heathrow for "We will charge you enough to make you reconsider all your life choices."

Into Heathrow. Back to BA check-in.
I arrived sweating, panting, slightly vibrating.
"My flight—!"
"Yes," the BA agent said, "it's boarding. Follow me."
What followed was not walking. It was not even brisk walking. It was Olympic speed-walking, BA-staff style, the kind where their legs move like sewing machines while they somehow speak full sentences without pausing for breath.
She barked instructions into a radio while I jogged behind her like an asthmatic Labrador. I swore that if I could walk that way, I wouldn't need talcum powder.

Through security.
Through departures.
Through the gate.
She practically shoved me onto the airbridge where the flight attendant greeted me with the sort of smile usually reserved for naughty schoolchildren.
"You must be Mr Budden," she said.
Translation: *You're the one we've all been waiting for.*
"I'll take that," she added, snatching my laptop bag before I could drop dead. "Just find your seat, please, we're closing the doors."

Brilliant. A full plane. Every single passenger staring at me like I'd just eaten the last Rolo. And naturally, of course, my seat was by the window.

I apologised to the aisle passenger, a man who looked like he ironed his socks, and squeezed past him. He sighed the sigh of a man whose life's work (the Bayeux Tapestry, presumably) had just been undone by the fraying thread of my existence.

Seatbelt on. Heart still racing.
"Cabin crew, doors to manual."
I'd made it.
Alive.
Just.
My body began whispering,
"Coffee... now..."
with the urgency of a caffeine addict who'd been clean for 24 hours.

I leaned back, closed my eyes, and thought:
"If this is how the *outbound* flight went... God help me on the return."

The business that didn't fly (and the pigs arse incident)

It would be easy to read this book and assume that everything I've touched in business turned to gold or at least gave off a respectable shimmer for a few years. And yes, I've had some wins.

But not everything worked.
One of the more memorable misfires? **SaveWithCDC**.

I'd spent years watching the rise of cashback platforms like Quidco and TopCashback. And one day it hit me:
Why wasn't anyone doing this for *businesses*?

Companies spend fortunes on insurance, broadband, card processing, energy, all of which run through affiliate deals. Why not let *them* earn cashback too?
It seemed obvious.

And I'd been in affiliate marketing long enough to understand the backend, tracking, databases, conversions. I could build the engine. All I needed was someone to make it look nice.

Thanks to my networking circle (which has rescued me more times than I can count), I found a designer. Not cheap. But excellent value, and those two things are often confused.
We ran beta tests. Feedback was 90% positive. We had an MVP, Minimum Viable Product, good enough to launch.
So, launch we did.

We booked a stand at **The Business Show at London ExCeL**.

Branded piggy banks with our logo printed on the side and a QR code linking straight to the sign-up page. Inspired, I thought. And to be fair - it *was*.

People loved them.
They took photos.
They scanned the code.
They laughed. They queued. We handed out every single pig.
Four hundred sign-ups in two days.

Brilliant.
And then...
Tumbleweed.

Not *no* traffic. Just not *enough*.
People visited the site.
They clicked around.
And then they drifted away like bored tourists.

We ran diagnostics.
Session recordings.
Explainer videos.
Tweaked onboarding.

Spent five figures on marketing.
We got more traffic.
More sign-ups.
More... nothing.

Email campaigns? Silence.
After a year, I made the only sensible call:
We shut it down.
Was it painful? Yes.
Was it the right decision? Definitely.

Lesson learned:
Sometimes, when no one else is doing something, it's not a gap in the market.

It's a gap because *nobody wants it*.

🐷 Enter Lord Sugar... and the Piggy Bank Incident
Yes, he was there at ExCeL, walking the aisles like the Ghost of Business Present. I spotted him heading our way, at precisely the same moment I was admiring the neat little regiment of piggy banks I'd lined up with OCD-level precision.

He stopped. Turned. Walked right back to our stand.

"Is this your business?" he said.
"Yes," I replied, proudly.
"And who lined up these bloody pigs?"
"That would be me."

He pointed down the line of pigs.

"If I walk from *that* direction, all I see are faces. That's good, faces attract people."
So far so flattering.

"But if I walk from *that* direction," he said, pointing the other way, "all I see are **pigs' arses**. Not so good, is it?"

He shook his head.
"Put them in a bloody semi-circle, for God's sake."

Then he turned and marched off, job done.

Naturally, I rearranged the pigs into a semi-circle.
He was, annoyingly, absolutely right.

The day I joined the beautiful game

I was standing on the platform at Liss Station waiting for the 10:02 to London. One of the perks of not commuting daily is that you can pick the quiet trains, the ones where you can sit down without performing gymnastics worthy of Cirque du Soleil. It was a cool morning, and I was early. Ten minutes to spare.

My phone rang.
Unknown number.
I had my AirPods in, so I tapped.
"Hello?"
"Hello," came a woman's voice. "Is that Keith from Ensurety?"
"It is," I said. "How can I help?"
"This is Kimberley from **Blackburn Rovers Football Club**. We've got a GDPR issue, and we've been told you're the man to speak to."

I blinked.
Blackburn Rovers?
Was this real, or was this Roy winding me up?

She carried on, perfectly serious. "Legal want everything tightened up, policies, procedures, training… the lot. I mentioned it to a contact, and they gave me your number."

Right, then. Not a prank.
I quickly Googled *where* Blackburn actually was (north… further north… keep going… stop).

"Well," I said, "this sounds like something best sorted face-to-face."
"Do you charge for that?"
"No charge for my time," I said, "just travel expenses. I'm based in Hampshire, and on longer journeys I usually go first class, legroom and work space."

"Not a problem," she said. "Let me know your train times, I'll pick you up from Blackburn Station. You might need to stay overnight; we can put you in the B&B next to the ground."
She sounded so matter of fact that I half expected her next line to be: *And bring boots, we're short a right winger.*

"My train's arriving," I said. "I'll email you from onboard."

The train arrived; I boarded, stowed the rollator, found a seat. Kimberley had already messaged her email and landline; the landline matched the official club switchboard. This was definitely happening.

I sent my availability. Ten minutes later: booked. Then another: room confirmed. I booked the trains: Waterloo → Euston → Manchester Piccadilly → Blackburn.

Arrival in Blackburn
The day came quickly. The journey was smooth, and when I reached the booking hall, Kimberley spotted me instantly. We'd had a few Teams calls; we recognised each other's faces before we even waved.

We exchanged one of those awkward professional hugs, the kind where you both hesitate mid-air like malfunctioning majorettes.

"Can I take your bags?" she asked.
"If it's no trouble."
She eyed the rollator. "That's... probably going on the back seat."
"No problem."

We drove to the B&B, a pub with rooms. Clean. Quiet. Slight hint of fried onions in the corridor. The usual.

"Breakfast is 7 to 9:30," said the receptionist.

"And tomorrow," said Kimberley, "just cross the road, turn left, follow the wall, that's the back of the stand. At the end, you'll see some old black railings. Looks locked. It isn't. Slide the bar. Head in. Reception's right there."

"Got it," I said.

Room was simple: shower, TV, kettle. All the essentials for a travelling consultant. I ate in the bar under the gaze of a dozen framed Blackburn shirts, then called it a night.

The Stadium
Morning. Crossed the road. Followed the wall. Gave the gate a shove worthy of a Viking raid.

Inside, I was hit with the sight of a *large* staff car park. Two hundred cars at least. I hadn't expected that scale.

I reported to reception, who called Kimberley.
"We'll take the lift," she said. "What time's your train back?"
"3:45."
"Right, we'll aim for 3:15."

Then came two hours of touring the behind-the-scenes world of Blackburn Rovers:

- Football Operations
- Commercial
- Marketing & Comms
- Ticketing & Matchday
- Retail
- Finance
- Facilities
- Broadcasting
- Community
- HR
- Player Care

It was like wandering through the backstage of a West End show, except with more filing cabinets and far fewer sequins.
"So," she asked at the end, "is this a project you think you can get your teeth into?"
"Oh, definitely," I said.

(And silently: *If only we still did electronic document management, half this building would be my Christmas bonus.*)
"Lunch next," she said, "then a stadium tour, then we'll head up to the Executive Box. A few department heads want to meet you."

"Perfect," I said.

Lunch was surprisingly good, and the stadium tour, even as a non-football person, was impressive. I took photos from the stands, feeling that odd spark of admiration for a place that clearly holds history, hope, and heartbreak in equal measure. The meeting in the Executive Box was one of those magical ones, easy, productive, full of laughs. No egos. No corporate nonsense. Just people doing their jobs well.

Final Whistle
Kimberley drove me to the station.
"So," she said, "how was the tour?"
"Fascinating," I said. "But then I had a wonderful guide."
"I'm flattered," she replied. "But I'm more interested in your quote."
I laughed. "I'll send it by Monday."
I caught my train, made it home, sent the quote, and, miracle of miracles, it was approved without fuss.
A rare win
.
So no, I'm still not a massive football fan.
But I can say this:
For one day, I got to see the beautiful game from the inside, and I rather enjoyed it.

The London Triathlon (without the medals)

I was a member of Richard Wood's Million Dollar Sprint business development programme, a community I'd happily recommend to any established business owner who feels like they've stalled somewhere between "coasting" and "what the hell am I doing?"

If that's you, drop me a message via the contact details in this book and I'll introduce you to Richard myself.

Most of the programme ran online, but every few months we had **Sprint Days** in Central London, live, in-person gatherings full of ideas, energy, and caffeine, with a social afterwards that usually resulted in at least one story no one should repeat in polite company.

The venue?
The Union Jack Club.
Right across from London Waterloo.
Ideal for someone coming up from Liss on the direct line.
Well... ideal-ish.

Because while the Union Jack Club *has* disabled access, it's the kind of access that makes you wonder whether the designer had ever actually met a disabled person, or whether they thought accessibility was simply a theoretical concept, like time travel or a polite taxi driver in London.

Still, all seemed promising from the outside: a run of steep steps... and beside them, a vertical platform lift. A familiar sight. Roll in, press the button, hold it (never forget to hold it), and up you go.
And miracle of miracles, I remembered to keep my finger pressed down.
Victory.

Inside, I approached reception.
"Ah yes," the receptionist said, "your event is in the **conference suite, in the basement**."
Of course it is.
"How do I get there?" I asked.

She leaned over the counter, eyeing my rollator the way a cat eyes a vacuum cleaner.

"You'll need to go to the lift at the end of that corridor. Take it *up* a level. Straight through the double doors is our restaurant. Ask one of the staff to direct you to the rear service lift. That'll take you down to the conference floor."

So off I went. Corridor. Lift. Pressed the button. Nothing.

Classic. Someone upstairs had left a lift door open. These lifts are more temperamental than a teenager denied Wi-Fi.

I waited.

Eventually, an elderly gentleman in a suit appeared at the top of the stairs.

"Excuse me, sir!" I called.

He looked around like a startled meerkat.

I waved.
He spotted me.

"Could you check the lift door on your left?" I called. "Open and close it firmly?"
"I'll do one better," he said in a clipped, authoritative tone. "I'll *ride it down to you.*"
Of course he would.
Royal Navy, I guessed, turns out I was right.

He stepped in. The door shut with a slam that made me worry for the structural integrity of Waterloo Station.
"You learn to shut a door properly at sea," he said.

He pressed the button.
Nothing.
"You need to press and *hold* it," I said.
He did. The lift moved.
"Ridiculous contraption," he muttered.
When it arrived, he gallantly held the door.
"Need me to shut it for you?"
"No, thank you," I said, keen to avoid a second sonic boom.

Up I went. Out. Door latched. Onwards.

Through the double doors into the restaurant, a spacious room mid-setup for lunch. In the middle stood a young waitress, laying cutlery with the precision of a neurosurgeon. Her black-and-white uniform looked like something from the 1950s. She even bore a momentary resemblance to my granddaughter Bethany.

"We're shut," she said without looking up.

"I know," I replied. "I'm trying to find the conference suite. Reception said you could point me to the rear lift."
She sighed lightly, set down her knives and forks, and said, "Follow me."

As we walked, I said, "You've clearly been doing this a while, very precise."
"I've been here two years," she said. "It takes practice."
"Would be a great job for someone with OCD."
She blinked. "OCD? Is that a pop group from the eighties?"
I paused.
Considered a correction.
Decided, nope. Leave it.
"I don't think so," I smiled. "But I'll check when I get home."

We reached a set of plain double doors and stepped through into what looked like wartime London, peeling grey paint, squeaky lino, lighting last updated during Churchill's second term.

She led me to a heavy sliding service lift with a metal concertina gate.
"In you go," she said. "Close both doors. Go down one floor. Turn left. Keep going. You'll hear them."

I thanked her, descended, admired the exposed masonry of the lift shaft (lift nerds unite), and arrived at...
...steam.
A wall of steam.
I had walked straight into the dish-washing area. Plates and mugs zoomed along a conveyor belt like the world's least practical rollercoaster. I half expected Wallace & Gromit to appear in hairnets.
I pushed on.
Another set of doors.

Another blast, this time from the laundry room. A woman operating an enormous trouser press looked up, startled. She removed an earbud. "Can I help you?"
"I'm looking for the conference suite."
"You're close. Two more doors. Someone should've come with you, you know."
"I'm beginning to understand why," I said. "Feels like I've been on a bushtucker trial."
She laughed. "I like that one."
"Take it," I said. "All yours."

Finally, carpet. Wood panelling. Signs. Civilisation.

I entered the conference suite. Richard looked up.
"Keith!" he said, hugging me. "You're a bit damp, was it raining outside?"
"No," I replied. "I've just completed the London Triathlon to get here."
He blinked. "Ah. Right."
"Coffee?" someone asked.
"Yes," I said, collapsing into a chair like I'd crossed the finishing line at the Olympics.

Later, I pulled aside a staff member and asked:
"Is there an easier way out?"
"Oh, yes," he said brightly. "We'll open the fire exit for you. It goes straight onto the street opposite Waterloo."

So, when the day ended, that's exactly what he did.
Beep. Beep. Beep.
Door opened.
Out I rolled, directly onto the pavement, ten seconds from the station.
Some days, dear reader, fact is stranger than fiction.
And occasionally much funnier.

Sometimes it's the small things

Given my love of railways, and my habit of drifting toward anything even vaguely community-shaped, it was probably inevitable that when the East Hampshire Rail Partnership was formed, I'd end up involved. Honestly, they barely got the name out before I was waving my hand like an overexcited contestant on *The Price Is Right*.

So, onto the stakeholder committee I went, delighted to finally combine my affection for trains with my affection for, well... meddling helpfully.

🔔 What Community Rail Partnerships Actually Do
Contrary to public belief, CRPs don't just hang up floral baskets and hope for the best (though if there were a National Hanging Basket League, we'd win).
We do things like:
- helping nervous first timers understand ticket machines ("Yes, it *will* eventually spit the ticket out, no, don't hit it").
- running "Try the Train" days because some people really *have* avoided trains since 1987.
- explaining that yes, you *do* have to press the button to open the doors, they're not psychic.

We also speak in schools about railway safety, particularly vital down here where the third rail is powered 24/7. This surprises some people. Electricity tends not to take weekends off.

Most of our magic is achieved by volunteers, with a couple of salaried officers funded entirely by South Western Railway, which means every penny we raise goes into community projects rather than someone's sandwich budget.

🛍 Free Shop Friday (and Its Extended Family)
One of our proudest projects is **Free Shop Friday** at Petersfield Station, an initiative run from what used to be a dusty storeroom and is now basically Santa's Grotto for adults.

It's not a food bank. It's simple:
Walk in. Bring a bag. Take what you need.
Pop something in the donation tin if you fancy it.

No forms. No judgement. No interrogation about your last three electricity bills.

It's been so successful that we now have Free Shop Thursday, Free Shop Saturday, a school uniform exchange, and a Winter Warmer that hands out coats, scarves and gloves.

Someone once found a coat just like the one her father wore. She cried all the way home. I don't cry often, but that one got me right in the chest.

✨ "Keith, Would You Mind Being Chair?"
Eventually I ended up as Chair of the East Hampshire Rail Partnership, which later expanded into the **Hills to Harbour Rail Partnership**, covering everything from Guildford to Portsmouth Harbour. I also now chair the **Wey Valley Rail Partnership**, which covers Guildford-Alton and Guildford-London Road.
At this rate, I fully expect to wake up one morning as Chair of the Trans-Siberian Railway. Stranger things have happened.

🚤 The Hovercraft Chapter I Never Saw Coming
We also forged a partnership with Hovertravel, the UK's *only* scheduled hovercraft operator, who run the Southsea to Ryde service. I've watched those hovercraft my entire life, buzzing along the Solent like giant hairdryers with ambition.

But until last year, I'd never actually been *on* one.

I mentioned this casually over lunch. Just conversation. Nothing more.

Then, as we disembarked back in Southsea, the Managing Director approached with the calm poise of a man about to ruin me emotionally.

He handed me a framed certificate.
"Keith Budden - First Hovercraft Flight."

I nearly cried.
Over a certificate.
For riding a hovercraft at the age of sixty.
It was the sweetest, simplest gesture, no speech, no fanfare, just a warm smile that said, *We thought this might mean something to you.*

And it did. Far more than they knew.

And that's the heart of it
Rail partnerships are built on small acts of kindness, tiny improvements, and gestures that seem insignificant until you realise, they mean the world to someone.
Sometimes, it really is the little things,
A folded map,
A fresh coat,
A friendly nudge onto a train,
Or a certificate you didn't know you needed.
Those are the moments that stay with you.

And before I close this chapter, here's one last tale that absolutely deserves its moment in the spotlight.

You'll have read earlier about **Free Shop Friday,** the little community idea that exploded into something so popular it practically needed crowd control and an air-traffic controller. Well, success has side effects... and at Liss Station, we discovered this the hard way.

We installed these lovely **community bookshelves** in the waiting room. Cute idea, very wholesome:
take a book, leave a book, read it on the train, return it someday (preferably the same decade).

At first, it worked perfectly. A delightful mix of crime thrillers, gardening guides, old cookbooks, the occasional Mills & Boon that had clearly been read more times than the Bible, you know, village classics.

But then... the donations *changed*.

It started gradually. One copy of *Fifty Shades of Grey*. Fine. Adults read on trains too. Then a second copy. Then three. Then a mysterious spin-off I'm still convinced was printed on someone's home printer called *Fifty Shades of Beige*.
Within a month, the shelf looked less like a community library and more like the back room of Ann Summers.
And here's the thing:
there is **only so much erotic literature one small Hampshire village can absorb** before the Parish Council starts to worry about the moral fabric of society.

In the interests of public safety, and, crucially, **the eyesight of unsuspecting younger commuters,** we decided the bookshelves had to go. Or at least be sanitised with industrial bleach and a priest.

The next morning they were quietly removed.

Somewhere, I swear, the entire village breathed a sigh of relief... though a few disappointed faces told me not *everyone* was against the Fifty Shades franchise continuing its hostile takeover of the Petersfield line.

Footnote:
For the record, South Western Railway denies all responsibility for the sudden surge in erotic literature at Liss Station. Though, between us, if any train company was ever going to inspire the phrase *"transport delays... and unexpected steamy content"*, it was always going to be them.

Actually, given the state of the delays our line has suffered during the signalling upgrade, I'm amazed *Fifty Shades of Grey* wasn't reclassified as "self-help for frustrated commuters."

How I became Mr GDPR

In business circles, if people know me for one thing, it's GDPR.

Not the most glamorous of titles, I grant you. Nobody grows up thinking, *"One day I shall be internationally recognised for my ability to explain lawful bases for processing."* But here we are.

These days, people associate me with:
- my bestselling book *GDPR Made Simple* (now updated for 2025),
- the training programmes,
- the consulting work across Hampshire, Hamburg, Cape Town, and California,
- The GDPR Weekly Show podcast,
- the keynote speeches,
- the radio interviews,
- and that surreal moment I found myself discussing the right to erasure with a Belgian finance minister who spoke five languages and still maintained I pronounced "pseudonymisation" incorrectly. (He was probably right.)

But hardly anyone ever asks the obvious question:
How did I end up in GDPR in the first place?
So, here's the truth.

The Conversation That Changed Everything
I owe a lot to my former mentor, Shaa Wasmund MBE. Brilliant, direct, allergic to waffle. The sort of person who can deliver life-changing advice in a sentence and still get home in time for supper.

One afternoon, I was explaining all the different things I was juggling at the time:

- website development for some clients,
- IT security for others,
- business process reengineering here and there,
- and of course, my ongoing European adventures with Fotovoordelig, ICNIA and Pixami.

Everything was fine. Nothing was spectacular. I had more plates spinning than a circus performer, but none of them were exactly attracting a standing ovation.

Shaa listened patiently, then delivered one of those lines that burn into your brain:
"You need to find your one thing, your niche, and own it."
Simple. Brutal. Correct.

Enter: GDPR
At the same time, a new piece of European legislation was whispering its way across the business world: the General Data Protection Regulation.
It was early 2016. Most people couldn't even say "GDPR" yet, let alone understand it. I didn't know much about it either, but I knew two things:

1. It was going to be enormous.
2. Pretty much every business in the UK and EU would need help.

I spoke to Shaa. She didn't pretend to understand the fine detail, but she understood the opportunity, and I got the green light.

So, I did what any sane person wouldn't:
I cleared the decks and jumped.

Diving Into the Deep End
I wound down my other work and immersed myself in GDPR. And when I say immersed, I mean **fully submerged, breathing through a regulatory snorkel**.

I attended European Parliament briefings.
Sat in on EDPB sessions.
Spoke to people at the ICO.
Lived and breathed data privacy, policy interpretation, legal frameworks, and cross-border transfer mechanisms.
It was chaotic. The rules were changing weekly. One week double opt-in was essential, the next week "no one ever said that." Cookies were a minefield. Data transfers a migraine.
But I stuck with it. And slowly, the fog cleared.

Demand Arrives Like a Tsunami
By mid-2017, while most organisations were still asking, "What does GDPR actually *mean*?", I was ready.

And then came the tidal wave.

Training. Consultancy. Speaking engagements. Interviews. Webinars. Workshops. White papers. Radio panels. Podcast episodes.

From Aberdeen to Arizona.
For the first time in my career, I wasn't chasing demand.
Demand was chasing me.
It was exhilarating. Exhausting. Extraordinary.

The Part Where My Heart Had Other Ideas
But, as you'll discover later in this book, I paid a price for that period of intensity.

By autumn 2025, my cardiologist made things painfully clear:
Reduce your stress or your heart will make the decision for you.

I did the hardest thing I've ever done professionally:
I shut down Ensurety.

I won't pretend it was easy. It felt like stepping away from something I'd spent a decade building. But I've always said:
You never lose - you either win, or you learn.

And in the space that followed, something remarkable happened.
For the first time in years, I had room to breathe.
Room to think.
Room to write.
And here you are, holding (or listening to) the result.

If Life Is a Book of Moments…
…then I hope this chapter, this whole autobiography, becomes one of the golden ones.
Because if GDPR taught me anything, it's this:
Even the driest subjects can change your life if you're willing to lean in.

And sometimes, the thing you never expected to define you, becomes the thing you're most grateful for.

Three listeners and a blue yeti

I've mentioned *The GDPR Weekly Show* here and there, but I've never actually explained how it came into existence. And like most things in my life, it began with three ingredients:

1. **curiosity**,
2. **audacity**, and
3. **me sending an email and hoping the Universe was in a helpful mood.**

It all started at an event run by Shaa Wasmund and Matt Thomas. One of the speakers was a chap called Rob, who, at the time, ran a hugely successful podcast with well over 100,000 regular listeners. Naturally, I made sure to get his business card. *(Always get the card. You never know when it'll turn out to be gold dust.)*

On the train home, I did what any self-respecting business nerd does: I Googled.
There wasn't a *single* UK-centric GDPR podcast.
Another "first" waved at me from across the platform like a slightly overexcited labrador.

So, I emailed Rob.
And let's be honest here, the opening paragraph was shameless flattery. I'd listened to his last three episodes at double speed so I could quote back a few lines. People *love* it when you've genuinely paid attention to their work.

Then I got to my real question:
"I can see the value in a GDPR podcast...
but I have absolutely no idea how to start one.
Could you point me in the right direction?"

My motto: **Don't ask, don't get.**

To my amazement, he replied within a few hours:
"Are you free Sunday evening at 7pm?
I'll jump on Zoom and talk you through it."
Rule number one:
When the Universe opens a door, don't stop to tie your shoelace.
I replied immediately.

How The GDPR Weekly Show Was Born
Our call was brilliant. Rob cut through all the noise and gave me the essentials:
- **Microphone:** Blue Yeti
- **Stand:** vital - no one wants "booming desk noises"
- **Software:** Audacity (free)
- **Future upgrade:** Rodecaster Pro II (expensive, ~£600, but worth it later)
- **Publishing:** Libsyn, which pushes the episodes out to everywhere
- And then...
- **A jingle.**

A *jingle?*
"Absolutely," he insisted.
"If you're serious, you need branding."
He put me in touch with **Music Radio Creative** on the Isle of Wight. I've used them ever since, podcasts, promos, presentations, you name it. Wonderful people.

And that was that.
The GDPR Weekly Show existed.
All it needed now... was me actually recording something.

Episode One: The Week I Became an Audio Surgeon
The first episode took me the best part of a week to edit.
I removed every:
- err,
- umm,
- sniff,
- lip smack,
- breath that sounded even remotely suspicious.

By day three, I could identify an "umm" waveform like a twitcher spotting a rare finch. I had become the **David Attenborough of unnecessary mouth noises**.

Eventually I learned a vital lesson:
It doesn't have to be perfect. It just has to be human.
Cut the long pauses. Leave the rest.
People don't want robots. They want real.
Over time, I produced more than **300 episodes**.
They're all still live.
People still listen.
But eventually the numbers told the truth:

It brought *some* return, just not enough to justify the time.
So, with a sigh and a stiff drink, I stopped.

Will There Be a New Podcast? Yes.
Probably 2026.
But this time:
- **Monthly, not weekly.**
- **Fun, not a chore.**

Because one of my personal commandments is:
If it's fun, it gets done.
If it's a bore, it's a chore.
So keep it fun.

A weekly podcast? Too much bore. Not enough fun.

Should *You* Start a Podcast? Absolutely.
"Why bother?" you might ask.
"There are already 1.1 million English-language podcasts."
Yes... but most of them die before episode six.
People give up far too soon.

My first episode had **three listeners**:
1. me,
2. my neighbour,
3. and my neighbour's dog -
   who, frankly, looked sceptical about my interpretation of Article 17.

By episode 10: around 100. By episode 20: nearly 200. And then, boom.

Once you cross the 1,000-listener mark, the curve changes shape.
At its peak, the show had around **20,000 listeners**.
Not all hung on every syllable, but that's fine.
They listened long enough.

And if you're worried about the crowd? Remember:
There are billions of websites. Did that stop you having one?
Didn't think so.
So don't let 1.1 million podcasts stop you either.

"Once you think you're too small to have an impact, try going to bed with a mosquito in the room." - Anita Roddick

Networking: The long game

I've mentioned business networking a few times already in this book, and with good reason. If you're serious about your business reaching its full potential, networking isn't optional. It's essential.

Over the years I've dipped my toe, my foot, and on occasion my entire body into more networks than I can count without caffeine support:
BNI, First Friday, 1Networking, ONLE Networking, Signal, 4Networking, The Business Success Network, Network B2B, 555 Networking, Peppercorn...

If they had a meeting and a biscuit tin, chances are I turned up at some point.
And here's the truth most people never tell you:
Every network is different.

Some, like **BNI**, run with military precision. A strict format. Attendance rules. Referral quotas. And then, when renewal time arrives, the group collectively decides whether they'd like the pleasure of your company for another year. All that *and* one of the highest membership fees in the game. It always felt a tad Hunger Games to me.

Others, like **4Networking**, live much further along the scale. Still structured, yes, but with a looser, friendlier vibe. Less clipboard, more conversation.

Most networks sit somewhere in between, each with their own quirks, characters, and unwritten rules.
Single-seat networks (BNI, 1Networking) mean you're the *only* person doing what you do.
Multi-seat networks let you have a whole handful of social media consultants, coaches, copywriters or GDPR boffins in one meeting. (Though heaven help the group that tries three GDPR consultants at once. Even *I* would need a lie-down).

Almost all networks let you visit a couple of times for free. **Do it.**
Treat it like a networking buffet: pile your plate high, see what tastes good, and quietly avoid anything that smells odd or looks like it might give you food poisoning.

That's exactly what I did.

Two groups I joined almost immediately were **1Networking** and **ONLE Networking**. The rest I road-tested for two or three sessions each, just like taking a car for a test drive, except with coffee mugs instead of steering wheels.

What Most People Get Wrong
Networking is *not* a quick fix.
This isn't Google Ads where you press "Go" and hope the sales fairy appears.
Networking takes time.
People need to **know you**, **like you**, and **trust you** before they'll risk recommending you to someone they care about.
It can take **nine to twelve months** before a solid referral lands.
Yes, you might get lucky sooner, but don't count on luck.
Count on consistency.

Keith's Two Golden Rules of Networking

1. Turn up. Then turn up again.
Trust grows slowly but dies fast.
Turn up consistently and you become part of the furniture, in the good way, not the dusty way.
Miss too many meetings and people start wondering whether you're serious.

2. Follow up like it matters.
Because it *does*.
If someone gives you a referral and it sits in your inbox untouched, you may as well stand on the station platform watching the train pull away.
Follow up fast.
Be the person others feel confident recommending again.

I could author an entire book on networking.
In fact, I probably will.
Actually, scratch that - I **am**.
So, if you want:

- the strategies,
- the stories,
- the structures,
- the scripts,

- and the mistakes I've already made so you don't have to...

Then keep an eye out for my next book:
How to Be a Master Networker
Arriving on Amazon in early 2026.

(And yes, the title *is* a little tongue-in-cheek. It wouldn't be me otherwise.)

The Hawaiian shirt strategy

You may remember from the last chapter that I talked about public speaking and the importance of getting your message out there.

But there's a flip side to that coin, a lesson I learned years ago thanks to my good friend Stu Morrison, a man whose wardrobe looks like it was curated by Liberace during a sugar rush.

I've always been one of life's natural question-askers.
Asking comes easily.
Answering comes even easier, probably because I've spent too many years in local politics, where you can't sneeze without someone shouting a difficult question at you.

And with my default "why not?" attitude, I've never once struggled to put my hand up.
But the real lesson wasn't about *asking*.
It was about being *distinctive*.

The Hawaiian Shirt Strategy
If I'm going to an event where I want to be remembered, I wear something that stands out.

Not like Stu, whose suits sometimes look like they were designed by a collaboration between Joseph's Technicolor Dreamcoat and a Vegas slot machine.

No, I go for something slightly more subtle...
The Hawaiian shirt.

And yes, I mean a *proper* Hawaiian shirt. Not the tasteful sort.

The sort that looks like a tropical fruit salad exploded.
Why?
Because during any good seminar or conference, I will **always** ask a question.

But while everyone else is busy scribbling notes, I'm doing something slightly different:
I'm crafting a question that makes the speaker look good, and makes me memorable.

Not rude.
Not clever-clever.
Not an ego trip disguised as a question.
And absolutely never one of those "gotcha" questions that trap the speaker either way, like:
"Is this the first time you've ever murdered someone?"

Those questions are cheap, childish, and deeply disrespectful, and they make you look like an arrogant twat.
And if you ever want the organiser to book you as a speaker, trust me... that is *not* the vibe.

The Good Question Formula
I aim for a question that is:
- Pertinent
- Thought-provoking
- Useful
- And answerable

The sort of question that helps the speaker shine *and* quietly signals that I:
- listen properly
- think deeply
- and engage professionally

And here's the magic bit...
Ask a good question in a way that stands out, and suddenly the break-time coffee bar becomes your personal networking HQ.
People find you easily ("Ah! The Hawaiian shirt guy!").
They walk over.
They chat.
They ask follow-ups.
Sometimes they even ask for help.
Sometimes they become clients.
I've won more consultancy work this way than I ever expected.

Why the Shirt Matters
And this, dear reader, is why the shirt does the heavy lifting.
If someone hears your question and wants to talk to you afterwards, they need to be able to find you without playing corporate "Where's Wally?" in a room of navy-blue suits, identical ties, and name badges printed in font size 8.

I want to be visible.
Like a lighthouse.
Or a cocktail umbrella.

Or a parrot that's escaped from a cruise ship.

Because sometimes the simplest advice in life really is the best:
Keep it simple, stupid.
And if in doubt?
Wear the shirt.

How it all began - from resident to councillor

It all started with a plan to build a skate bowl.

Where exactly this skate bowl was first proposed, I genuinely couldn't tell you. Over the years, the idea seemed to migrate across Liss like a lost sheepdog, popping up in every patch of grass big enough to host a wheelie bin. If you owned a garden larger than a doormat, someone probably suggested plonking a skate bowl on it.

And, as expected, out came the nimbies.
"Not in my back yard!"

Although in Liss it was more:
"Not in my village! I moved here for tranquillity, hedgerows, and the ambient hum of the A3."

Now, I'll be honest, I had objections myself.
Not nimby objections (goodness, listen to me, who even says goodness anymore? Apparently, I do. I've clearly been watching too much *The Traitors*).

No, my concern wasn't the *where*.
It was the *how much*.
£50,000 to £75,000.

For a parish our size, that's not insignificant change, that's "take a deep breath before opening the budget spreadsheet" money.

And yes, a group of enthusiastic young people promised they'd use it. But with skate bowls already in Southsea, Petersfield and Liphook, the Petersfield one being the teenage equivalent of Mount Everest, it didn't seem the best investment. Especially when rail travel still worked properly. If you could get to school, you could get to a skatepark.

Then came the public consultation.
"Well," I thought, "if they want consultation, let's give them consultation."

Forty-Two Questions and an Assistant Clerk Named Andrea

I spent an entire weekend researching skate bowls.
Every success. Every failure. Every community revolt.

By Sunday night I had compiled forty-two questions, each one detailed enough to qualify as a short dissertation.

On Monday morning, armed with my questions and the righteous energy of a man who'd had too much coffee, I marched into the Parish Office and handed them to the assistant clerk, Andrea.

Andrea looked at the stack.
Then at me.
Her face said:
"Oh good. A hobbyist."
She said, very politely,
"Well... this is obviously going to take us some time to answer."
"Excellent," I thought. "That's the idea."

(And yes, I had a second set of questions ready at home. You never fire all your ammunition at once, this was community politics, not paintball.)

Whether Andrea raised two fingers behind my back I will never know.
Frankly, I would have applauded her if she had.

Ironically, years later, Andrea, her partner Alan, and her daughter Lucy became some of my closest friends. Lucy and I still wave at each other through the estate agent window like characters in a low-budget sitcom.

The Truth About NIMBYs
I've always said this:
We all have a bit of nimby in us.
Every one of us.
If someone proposed a nuclear waste reprocessing site 500 miles away?
No one bats an eyelid.
Move it to 5 miles?
You'd have petitions, banners, and three Facebook groups before breakfast.
Perspective is everything.

The Bluebell Inn Resistance Movement
Soon, a local pressure group formed to oppose the skate bowl. We met weekly at The Bluebell Inn, a charming old pub that has since been replaced by housing (which, incidentally, nobody protested... funny how that works).

Maybe it was my research.
Maybe it was my enthusiasm.
Maybe it was simply that I'd written the longest list of questions the Parish Office had ever seen.
Whatever the reason, I somehow became the group's de facto spokesperson.

Two public meetings were held at the Village Hall.
I created a **forty-two slide** PowerPoint (of course), and we filled the place.

It was well received, except, naturally, by the supporters of the project, led by Parish Councillor Paddy. Our debates were polite but carried all the warmth of a handshake between two people both convinced the other stole their parking space.

At this point I was still just a member of the public, albeit one who attended meetings with the enthusiasm of a man who believed the council provided free snacks (they didn't).

I even turned up at a District Council meeting to accuse them of "mugwumping," an old Hampshire term meaning having your mug (face) on one side of the fence and your wump (bottom) on the other.
They didn't laugh.
But they also didn't approve the funding.
Call it a win.

"Why Don't You Apply?"
One day, I was in the Parish Office chatting with Dick, the Parish Clerk, when he mentioned that a councillor had resigned.
"Why don't you apply?" he said.
"You spend more time here than most of our councillors anyway."

It was said jokingly, but I considered it.
Then applied.
The interview panel included Howard and Sue.
Possibly Gina.

Definitely *not* Paddy, he'd declared that if I were appointed, he'd resign immediately.
"Whatever," I thought.
He didn't resign.
And now, sixteen years later, I'm Chairman and he's my Vice-Chairman.
If you're ever tempted to believe life doesn't have a sense of humour, Liss Parish Council suggests otherwise.

Welcome to Liss Forest
I was inducted at the next council meeting.
My political career had begun.
My seat covered the part of the parish known as Liss Forest, and let me tell you, Forest residents may technically be part of Liss but tell them that and they'll disown you faster than a teenager disowns their parents at the school gates.

Despite living in Liss most of my life, I realised I barely knew Forest at all, beyond the Temple Inn, the post office, and the butchers. Entire roads like Pine Walk, Warren Road, Mint Road... complete mysteries. Others, like Newfield Road, I'm fairly sure I'd never even driven past.

Then Tony appeared, a friendly resident who insisted on giving me a full tour.
He drove me through every lane, pointed out every landmark, introduced me to half the village, and explained the local politics, the gossip, and which roads flooded if someone so much as sneezed.

Tony has since passed away, and I miss him dearly. He was one of those rare community heroes, the kind you can't replace, only remember fondly.

Reflection
A skate bowl proposal.
Forty-two questions.
A pub-based rebellion.
And I accidentally became a councillor.

Proof that sometimes, community concern leads you somewhere unexpected.
And sometimes your fiercest debating opponent becomes your vice-chairman and one of your closest allies.

Life, as ever, has a wicked sense of humour.

The day "comrades" changed everything

I've mentioned Howard before, my predecessor as Chairman of Liss Parish Council. A good man. Earnest. Enthusiastic. Passionate about community. And a Labour member so committed he probably buttered his toast from left to right.

Just one tiny issue:
Parish councils are meant to be apolitical.

Councillors *can* have party allegiances, of course, but those allegiances stay firmly outside the council chamber. That's why parish councils work. People vote for neighbours, not party colours. (Unless their neighbour has terrible hedges, then all bets are off.)

Anyway, it was about a week after the Labour Party Conference when Howard tabled a motion:
that Liss Parish Council should pay its employees the "real Living Wage."
Reasonable enough today.
In 2012?

It had a faint whiff of party-political aftershave.
Still, Howard *might* have got away with it...
...if he hadn't opened his speech with:
"Comrades..."

You could feel the room seize.
Not just the Conservatives.
Not just the neutrals.
Even people who normally had to check their voter registration to remember their political leaning suddenly sat bolt upright.

"Comrades."
At a parish council meeting.
I was a Labour member myself back then, and even *I* wanted to crawl under the table, tunnel out the fire exit, and start a new life under a false name in Belgium.

The motion was dead on arrival.

I voted for it out of loyalty, political, personal, and pity-based, but it was lost somewhere between the "Com-" and the "-rades."

Paddy Calls with a Plot Twist
A couple of nights later, my phone rang.

Paddy.
"What did you think of Howard's performance on Monday?"

I attempted diplomacy.
"It wasn't... his strongest moment."
Understatement of the century.

"I've spoken to the other councillors," he said. "We want to remove him as Chairman. Vote of no confidence. And we want you to replace him."

Cue my brain doing the mathematical equivalent of falling down a flight of stairs.

First shock: they thought *I* should be Chairman after barely two years on the council.
Second shock: I was being recruited into a coup against the man who'd mentored me.

"I need to think," I said.
"Don't take too long," said Paddy. "Most councillors are behind you."
Most?
Apparently this coup had a mailing list.

Phone-a-Friend: Michelle and Sue
I rang Michelle.
"Should I do it?" I asked.
"If *you* want to," she said. "But don't say yes just because someone asked. You do that too easily."

Which is true.
If someone asked me to officiate their hamster's wedding, I'd probably check my diary before questioning their sanity.

Next, I called Sue, the council's sage, conscience, and database of all historic wrongs since 1974.
"Oh, hi Keith," she said immediately. "I assume Paddy's spoken to you."
Clearly the rumour mill had entered Olympic mode.

She backed me fully.
With that, my mind was made up.
I called Paddy the next day.
"Alright," I said. "I'm in."

Howard's Driving: A Metaphor for What Came Next
That weekend, Howard and I drove to a Labour meeting in Aldershot.

Now, Howard's driving style deserves a paragraph of its own. Imagine:
- the confidence of Lewis Hamilton,
- the spatial awareness of a confused pigeon,
- and the lane discipline of an overly caffeinated shopping trolley.

That's Howard.

We once circled a roundabout *twice* before he realised he'd missed the exit. When someone honked, Howard waved and said:
"It's amazing, wherever I go, someone who knows me always gives me a toot!"

Back in Aldershot, I pulled the local Labour leader aside, explained the situation, and asked for guidance.
"Well," he said, smiling, "congratulations... I think."

His advice:
"If you can persuade Howard to resign before a vote, it's kinder. Cleaner. Better for everyone."
Sound counsel.

"Et tu, Brute?"
Back in the car, Howard immediately asked:
"Why did he wish you good luck? Is it your health?"
"No."
"Then what?"
"I'll tell you later. Let's just get home."
Once parked outside my house, I told him the truth.
"There's going to be a vote of no confidence. They want you to resign."
"It'll be Paddy and two others," he scoffed. "I'll win."
"I don't think you will," I said. "Everyone I've spoken to is supporting it."

He stared at me.

Then:
"Well, at least I can count on *your* vote."
I said nothing.
He inhaled sharply.
"Et tu, Brutus?"
Ouch.
Straight to the Shakespeare.

"I'm sorry," I said.
"And who," he asked slowly, "do they think will replace me...?"
The penny didn't just drop, it plummeted.

"It's you, isn't it?" he said.
"Yes. But I didn't ask for this."
"You'd better go."

He drove off with the delicate gearwork of a man chewing a wasp.

Council Night: The Speech, the Vote, the Aftermath
The next day he arrived to reclaim the political autobiographies he'd given me during chemotherapy.
(Kind gesture. Terrible reading. Not one of them is half as entertaining as this book, I promise you).

For the next week, he gave no hint of his decision.
Then the council meeting arrived.

Howard stood.
"I have an announcement."
He spoke for ten minutes.
It was part resignation speech, part Shakespearean monologue, part therapy session.
Lots of references to loyalty, betrayal, service, and unnamed parties (spoiler: it was me).
"...and therefore, with regret, I tender my resignation as your Chairman."

Motion to accept?
Proposed: Paddy.
Seconded: everyone except me.

Passed: unanimously.
Then:
"I propose Keith to be our new Chairman."
Seconded by Sue.

Vote passes.
Nearly unanimous.
Howard abstains.

I abstain too, until Dick leans over and whispers:
"You *can* vote for yourself, you know."
So, I did.

Another one of those surreal, life-changing moments.
And from that night forward, I've always been either Chairman or Vice-Chairman.

Apparently...
I must be doing something right.

The nightcap that changed everything

I'd always got on well with Andrea during her time as our Assistant Parish Clerk, which is impressive, considering the first proper conversation we ever had involved me handing her a forty-two-point interrogation about the proposed skate bowl.

A lesser woman would have set my trousers on fire.
Andrea merely sighed, raised an eyebrow, and got on with it.

Over the years, we became friends. She was ambitious, smart, and good at her job, sometimes *too* good. She also twigged fairly early on that while Dick remained Parish Clerk (and to be fair to him, he was excellent), there was zero room for her to progress. She was basically waiting for a pair of "dead man's shoes" to free up.
And Dick was stubbornly refusing to die.

On top of that, she'd endured low-level bullying from another councillor. I stepped in where I could, and things improved, but it never fully went away. Some people mellow with age; this particular councillor seemed to think he was maturing like Stilton, except without the charm.

So, when she called one day to say she'd been offered the Town Clerk role at Whitehill & Bordon, I wasn't remotely surprised.

Bigger authority, better salary, more responsibility, and a town undergoing massive redevelopment.

In football terms, it was like being promoted from League Two to the Championship.

There was no "please don't go" speech from me.
Just congratulations, admiration, and genuine sadness to see her leave.
We agreed to stay in touch, and we did. She's still one of my closest friends.

The Bluebell, the Dance Floor, and My Dad-Dancing Shame

We had her farewell drinks at the WhistleStop, a classic Liss send-off: laughter, prosecco, and the sort of speeches where everyone pretends not to cry.

A few months later, I went to Les's 50th at the Bluebell Inn. Packed pub, great atmosphere. I did notice Andrea and Les weren't talking much, but with fifty people trying to hug you at once, you don't always spot the subplots.

Despite my worsening mobility, Andrea practically hauled me onto the dance floor.
To say I danced would be generous.
I looked like a dad who'd wandered away from the buffet and was trying to discreetly realign his hips.

We all laughed. She teased me mercilessly. It was a good night.

We walked most of the way home together. Andrea tripped off the kerb, nothing serious, just enough to remind us both that gravity has a dark sense of humour. Les and his brother walked on the opposite pavement. When they invited me in for a nightcap, I said yes. It would've been rude not to.

Inside, Andrea kicked off her knee-high boots. (I swear she could make an entrance in a room made of carpet and silence.) We had a whisky. Around half an hour later I got ready to leave. Andrea fetched my coat, zipped it up like a mum doing the school run, and walked me to the door.

We shared a slightly tipsy peck; the kind of accidental little kiss two friends give when both of them have had one more drink than intended.

Then I toddled home, warm of heart and head.
Nothing unusual.
Or so I thought.

"Come round tonight. It'll just be me."
A few months later, Andrea called.
"Do you want to pop round tonight? Les isn't here, Alex is away, Lucy's out. We can have a proper catch-up."

"Of course," I said. "I'll bring wine."
Not wanting to risk the wrong choice, I brought red *and* white. She greeted me with a kiss on the cheek, took the wine, and said, "Let's have the red."

We sat on the sofa, TV murmuring quietly like background wallpaper. We talked about her new job, the council gossip, the usual.

When Lucy came downstairs to head out, the atmosphere shifted slightly, not romantic, just... private.
Unfiltered.

"That's better," Andrea said when the door closed. "Now we've got the place to ourselves."
I joked, "That sounds ominous."
"Oh, it is," she said. "I've got news. Les and I are splitting up."
Not a shock. Anyone with functioning ears and eyes could sense the strain.

"There's someone else," she added. "And you know him."
"Do I?"
"Yes. Alan."
"EHDC councillor Alan? *That* Alan?"
She nodded.

Well. I didn't expect *that* plot twist.
Not disapproving, just surprised enough to almost spill my Merlot.

We talked for an hour about the kids, the house, the future, and how she hoped things would stay civil. She also said, giving my knee a gentle squeeze, that she hoped we'd stay close friends.

"We will," I said, kissing her hand. And I meant it.

As 11pm crept up and Lucy was due back, I left. Another gentle kiss goodbye, not romantic, just affectionate. Reassuring. The sort you give someone on the first page of a new chapter.

I walked home thinking of everything she'd told me. Happy for her. A little concerned. Mostly hopeful.
Would Alan mind our friendship?
Would things change?
I needn't have worried.

A New Friendship Triangle (The Healthy Kind)
Fast-forward to today:
Andrea, Alan, and I still go out together five or six times a year. Meals, quizzes, pub nights, the works.

Alan's no longer a councillor, but the three of us slide comfortably between politics and family life like we're shifting gears in a well-maintained car.

Andrea got her fresh start. Alan got someone wonderful. And I got a friendship that didn't just survive a plot twist, it grew because of it.

Funny how life works sometimes.

The buffer stop and the soldier

I've mentioned Tony before, ex-military, razor-sharp, endlessly practical, and the sort of man who could probably build a functioning artillery piece out of three fence posts and a wheelie bin.

In his last posting he'd been one of the commanding officers at Longmoor Training Camp, which meant settling in Liss Forest made perfect sense. He could practically have abseiled to work.

I've also mentioned the Riverside Walk. Before it became part of the national Shipwrights Way, it was the track bed of the Longmoor Military Railway, the Army's own private playground for training railway engineers. From 1903 to 1970, thousands of soldiers learned to operate locomotives there. Steam, diesel, you name it. They even trained engineers in derailments, often by actually *derailing* trains. Imagine Network Rail's reaction if you tried that today.

The line is also something of a celebrity, appearing in films like *The Great St Trinian's Train Robbery*, *The Lady Vanishes*, and *The Bed-Sitting Room*, as well as the 1960s TV series *The Fugitive*. When you own a railway where no one minds if you crash things, Hollywood tends to notice.

When the line closed, hopes were high that it might become a preserved railway. Instead, bits of the track bed were snapped up by local residents, neatly scuppering the plan. That stroke of local opportunism is why we now have the Riverside Walk rather than Hampshire's second heritage railway. Swings and roundabouts, as they say.

At the Liss end of the walk, the old platform shelter still stands alongside a large concrete buffer stop. It's one of those indestructible military structures built to survive anything from runaway locomotives to nuclear winters. It famously stopped a train that once overran and nearly ended up across the road, mercifully with no casualties. The Army didn't do flimsy.
Over the decades, though, the buffer had become rather dismal: graffiti, algae, general sadness. Tony wasn't having that.

"Wouldn't it be nice to tidy it up and make something of it?" he said one day.

"I can probably arrange for it to be cleaned," I replied. "But what else are you imagining?"

Tony's eyes gleamed in that way only ex-military men get when they're plotting something involving heavy machinery.
"A short length of ballasted track. A proper platelayers' trolley welded on top. Something with a real railway feel."

"It sounds brilliant," I said. "But where are we getting all that from? And even if we do find it, there's certainly no Parish Council budget for a miniature restoration project."

"Well," he said, lowering his voice theatrically, "can you find the money for a commemorative plaque?"
"Yes," I replied. "I can twist arms for a plaque."
"Good," he said, grinning like a man with secrets. "You sort the plaque and leave the rest to me. Don't ask any questions."
Wise men know when not to ask questions. I am, occasionally, a wise man.

The Morning the Army Turned Up
A few Sundays later, Tony told me to meet him by the buffer stop at 10am.
Moments later, an Army lorry rumbled into view, HIAB crane mounted on the back, carrying a section of track and a platelayers' trolley.
Behind it? A second lorry filled with ballast.
Behind *that*? A Bedford truck with sixteen soldiers perched in the back.

"Don't ask," Tony said, though the grin on his face said everything.

"Morning, Tony," called the sergeant, hopping down like he owned the place. "Where do you want all this?"

Tony handed over a beautifully precise sketch, the kind that suggested he'd been planning this for days… or decades.
The soldiers got to work. No fuss. No chatting. No tea breaks every fifteen minutes like a civilian team. Just efficient, disciplined graft.

Within a couple of hours, the whole thing was complete, track laid, ballast raked, trolley positioned, every stone perfectly in place. It looked superb, like a little slice of history restored.

We thanked the soldiers, or rather tried to, they were already packing up with military speed, and within minutes they were gone. The walk returned to its usual Sunday quiet, as though sixteen men and three lorries hadn't just transformed it.

A Plaque for Posterity
A few weeks later, the Parish Council installed the commemorative plaque. It's still there today, quietly telling the story to anyone curious enough to stop and read.

The platelayers' trolley has needed the occasional repair thanks to local vandals, the sort of people who see a piece of heritage and think, "Lovely! Let me sit on this until it buckles!" but by and large it's remained exactly as Tony envisioned it.

And every time I walk past it, I smile.
Because it's one of those local legacies that feels personal.
A small moment of history saved.
A friendship honoured.
A job done properly.
I always think to myself:
We did that.
And by "we," I mean "Tony, sixteen soldiers, three lorries, and me holding a clipboard pretending to be useful."

The winter Liss almost went swimming

People often imagine being Chairman of a Parish Council is all ribbon-cutting, tea-drinking, and being asked where the dog poo bins should go. And yes, there *is* a lot of that. But every now and then, the job throws you something a little more… character-building.

For me, in the winter of 2013, "character-building" arrived in the form of water.
A lot of water.
Biblical amounts, frankly, if two giraffes had wandered through the village looking for an ark, no one would have batted an eyelid.

It had rained for what felt like several geological periods. The ground was saturated, the rivers were swollen, and the Western Rother, usually a charming trickle through the centre of Liss, was rapidly developing delusions of grandeur.

Just before the railway level crossing sits the old bridge under Station Road. Victorian, stubborn, and just about wide enough to let the river pass underneath on a **normal** day. This was *not* one of those days.

A Night Out… and a Bridge Doing Its Best Impression of Niagara Falls

It was the week between Christmas and New Year. I'd been out with Andrea and friends at the Spread Eagle, all of us feeling nicely festive. On the drive back, we reached the level crossing, and, in classic fashion, the barriers were down. If you know that crossing, you know its talent for hosting trains back-to-back like it's running a party and didn't want to tell the staff.

There were a couple of cars in front of us, so we stopped on the bridge.
"That's odd," Andrea said. "It feels like something's pushing the car sideways."
I looked out of my window.
Water.
Running **under** the car.
I looked further.

The river, usually several feet *below* the road, was now flowing **over the top of the bridge**.
Never mind Niagara Falls.
We were parked on the edge of *Lake Lississippi*.

Moments later the train thundered through, the barriers rose, and we escaped before we needed lifejackets or an inflatable flamingo.

The Answerphone Messages I Should Probably Have Checked Earlier
Once home, I checked the answerphone. Several villagers had left messages like:
"Keith, do we have sandbags?"
We did not.
And it was almost midnight.
If I rang them back, I'd only have told them what they already suspected: no amount of sandbags was going to fight *that* river.
So, I went to bed.

Dawn Patrol: Chairman vs The Western Rother
The next morning, I pulled on boots suitable for a man about to encounter conditions normally reserved for wading birds, and walked to the village centre.

The sight that greeted me?
The river was *still* flowing over the bridge.
Yorkwood was flooded.
The Crossover youth centre was flooded.
The cycle shop was flooded.
The Riverside surgery was flooded.
Frankly, if we'd had an underground station, that would have been flooded too.

I trudged up Riverside Walk, past the picnic area, only to find the small bridge of railway sleepers had completely vanished. So had the path. The picnic area was now an island. Not a metaphorical island. An actual one. If anyone had been there enjoying leftover turkey sandwiches they would still be there now.

Further along, the river was chewing through the bank like a beaver after three espressos. Tree roots hung out like bad dentistry.

I circled the village: Rotherbank Farm Lane, Forest Road, Mill Road, each showing its own version of chaos. The old mill stream, normally a collection of puddles that only *aspired* to be a stream, was now auditioning for the part of "raging torrent" in a disaster film.

Then I went to Princes Bridge to check on the sewage works. If the river had breached *that*, the entire village would have needed hazmat suits. Thankfully, Southern Water's finest had built a fortress of sandbags around it. It looked like the set of *Dunkirk*, but it was holding.

Chairman vs Call Centre: Round One
Back home, boots dripping, I rang the Environment Agency.
I listened to "Your call is important to us" so many times I almost believed it.
Eventually, a man called Alec answered. He became our case officer. I emailed him all my photos. He took them seriously, reallocated another team of workers to Liss, and asked me to repeat my observations every day until the river behaved itself.

So, I did.
For ten days, I patrolled the village like a damp Batman, minus the cape, plus the wellies.

And finally, slowly, the Western Rother retreated back into its proper home, under the bridge instead of over it.

The Side of Local Government No One Sees
It was a stressful time, not heroic, not glamorous, but real, hard community work. The kind councillors do quietly, behind the scenes, without applause, medals, or even a thank-you sausage roll.

Most people probably never knew any of it happened.
But if you were in Liss that winter, and wondered why a slightly soggy, mud-spattered Chairman kept appearing at random points around the village like a confused heron, now you know.
It was all part of the job.
And no, before you ask, I still haven't forgiven that bridge.

Beacons, flares and best-laid plans

One of the unexpected joys of being Chairman of Liss Parish Council, and later, for two years, Chairman of East Hampshire District Council, is that you suddenly find yourself becoming an unofficial Royal Event Coordinator.

There's something wonderfully British about standing in a muddy field with a brass band, some bunting, a gas cylinder of questionable vintage, and two hundred people who all pretended they didn't check the weather app... then checked it twice more before leaving the house.

Lighting Up for the Queen - The Golden Jubilee
For the Queen's Golden Jubilee, I convinced Liss Parish Council to buy a gas-fired beacon. A proper one. We were joining the nationwide chain of Jubilee beacons, orchestrated by Bruno Peek, the Royal Pageantmaster - a man whose job description must read something like *"Keeper of Flames and General Ringmaster of National Festivities."*

In centuries past, beacons were lit hilltop to hilltop. In the 21st century, the innovative system was:
SMS.

The plan:
- When the previous beacon lit theirs, they'd text me.
- I'd light ours.
- I'd then text Petersfield to light theirs.

A kind of medieval WhatsApp chain.
We tested the beacon the day before. It worked. Marvel of engineering.

The ceremony took place on the playing fields above the primary school, the highest vaguely accessible point in Liss unless you count climbing the longest ladder from Dave at the hardware emporium of Liss, U-Do-DIY.

At the precise moment, my phone buzzed.
Beep-beep.
Text received.

I nodded to the conductor of Liss Band. They launched into the National Anthem. As the drum roll ended, I pressed the ignition.
WHOOMPH.
Up shot the flame.
The crowd cheered.
Children gasped.
The band played triumphantly.
For a moment, the whole village lifted its collective chin in patriotic pride.
Magic.

The Platinum Jubilee - A Glorious Disaster
Ten years later, it was the Platinum Jubilee.
We vaguely remembered that the school had the beacon stored in their loft. After a hunt that probably displaced several frightened spiders, it was found, dusty but intact.

A Gas Safe engineer inspected it.
It failed.
Spectacularly.
We had *days*, not weeks.

Nick, Clayre, and I huddled like a parish council version of Mission Impossible.

Someone, no one is admitting who, had a "brilliant idea":
Three coloured flares (red, white, blue) + a powerful lantern = patriotic smoke beacon.

Nick, ever sensible, ordered *two of each colour* so we could test them in his garden. You know, controlled conditions. Hedge. No wind. Nobody watching.

The test was glorious.
Smoke billowed upwards.
The lantern glowed beautifully through the colours.

We congratulated ourselves as if we'd just solved cold fusion.
Then came the real night.

Conditions:
- Cloudy ✓
- Little wind ✓
- Absolutely no hedge ✓
- Two hundred parishioners ✓
- A completely misplaced sense of optimism ✓✓✓

At the appointed moment, Nick, dressed in a white lab coat, goggles, and wellies, looking like a mad scientist who'd failed the audition for *Time Team,* lit the flares.

The smoke did not rise majestically heavenward.
The smoke drifted horizontally across the field...
...straight towards the exact spot we had *told* people to stand.

Meanwhile, I turned on the lantern.
It shone brightly... into several people's faces.

The disappointment was so thick you could have buttered toast with it.

It was the one time in British history where a crowd collectively wanted to shout, "Was that it?" but was too polite to do so.

They waited until the next morning, then emailed me instead. Sensibly.

Coronation Redemption
Fortunately, by the time of King Charles III's coronation, we'd learned our lesson.

The beacon had been repaired properly.
Liss Band were in fine voice.
The weather cooperated.
I pressed the button.
The flame shot up perfectly.
The villagers cheered with relief.
Normal service resumed.
Reputation restored.
Only minor therapy required.

The Accidental Capability Brown
A quick side note.
In Newman Collard Park's Memorial Gardens, we plant a tree for each major national event.
Lovely idea. Very tasteful.

Every plaque reads:
"Planted by Councillor Keith Budden."

There are now so many that future historians may assume I spent my life striding around Liss with a ceremonial spade and the delusion that I was personally landscaping the South Downs.

If someone ever creates a walking tour based on all my trees, I'll know things have gone too far.

Though knowing Chapplins, they'll try to sponsor it.

If at first, you don't succeed

After a few years on Liss Parish Council, I started to feel that familiar itch.

Not the sort that requires ointment, the sort that whispers: "You should be making bigger mistakes on a larger stage."

Parish work was rewarding, but it's hard to have sweeping influence when your biggest annual controversy is whether the grass cutting rota should be laminated.

I wanted to step up. Become a District Councillor. Do something meaningful. Maybe even make decisions that influenced more than six square metres of verge.
The only question was: *how*?

The Pub, the Pint, and the Political Proposition
One evening in the Whistle Stop, I mentioned the idea to Howard, then Chairman of Liss Parish Council and a man so Labour he probably hummed "The Red Flag" while brushing his teeth.

He looked at me over his beer and said:
"Well, you don't strike me as a Tory.
Why don't you join Labour and stand alongside me?"

It was delivered casually, as if suggesting we enter a pub quiz team together, but with the confidence of someone who had already filled out the membership form for me.

At the time, all three District Council seats covering Liss and Liss Forest were Conservative strongholds.
Deep blue.
Siberian permafrost blue.

You could put a traffic cone on the ballot paper with a blue rosette and it would get elected.

But I thought: *why not?*
After all, I've always believed in learning through experience, preferably someone else's, but mine would do in a pinch.

My Labour Phase: Short, Earnest, Statistically Unsuccessful

I stood twice as a Labour candidate.
Both times:
- I got more votes than Howard (not that we mentioned it too loudly),
- I beat Labour's national polling average for the constituency,
- And Liss... remained Conservative with the unwavering loyalty of a golden retriever guarding a bag of sausages.

After two attempts, I began to question things.
Not my values, just the small detail that the party's national vote share in Liss was roughly equivalent to the number of people who voluntarily choose to holiday in Slough.

With support from Brian and Elwyn, I decided to stand as an **Independent**.

The Independent Era (Also Known As: The Full DIY Campaign)

Standing as an Independent is wonderfully freeing.
It is also the political equivalent of assembling flat-pack furniture using only:
- a spoon,
- blind faith,
- and whatever Allen key you found in the drawer from the last house move.

There was:
- no canvassing team,
- no leaflet designer,
- no campaign manager,
- no printer discount,
- and no party volunteer turning up with three packets of Hobnobs and an encouraging pep talk.

I *was* the entire operation (with help from Brian and Elwyn on the leaflet deliveries).

Still, I finished a solid third, beating Labour and the Lib Dems.
The Conservatives held their seats, of course.

I suspect if they'd run a small border collie wearing a blue collar, the result would've been the same.

But I felt vindicated.
Independence suited me.
I might have stayed that way...
If not for the unexpected events at Judy Onslow's funeral.

Judy, Respect, and the Great Conservative Recruitment Drive
Judy was someone I respected deeply, principled, balanced, and kind.

Her funeral was packed, full of warmth and genuine affection. I was standing outside with a coffee when **Michael Mates**, former MP, approached me.

We exchanged the usual respectful reflections, and then he said:
"Are you planning to stand for the vacant seat?"
"Quite possibly," I replied.
"As an Independent?"
"That was the idea."
"Well," he said, "that would be a shame.
If you stood as our Conservative candidate, you'd be a shoo-in."

A shoo-in?
Me?
In Conservative blue?
I wasn't sure whether to laugh, faint, or check if he'd mistaken me for someone behind me.
But the universe wasn't done.

The Damian Hinds Déjà Vu
Barely an hour later, Damian Hinds, Michael's successor, offered me a lift home.
Free transport is free transport, so I accepted.
Inside the car, the conversation followed the *exact same script*.
Word. For. Word.
"Are you planning to stand?"
"As an Independent?"
"That would be a shame."
"If you stood for us, you'd be a shoo-in."
At this point, I half expected the vicar to pop out from behind a shrub and inform me it was all part of Judy's final wish.
I asked Damian:
"Does Elizabeth know you're saying this?
The chair of the Liss Conservative Association?"
He smiled.
"Oh yes. She's fully supportive."

Which was remarkable, because Elizabeth rarely "fully supported" anything without a risk assessment, a four-page strategy paper, and a committee resolution.

One Night of No Sleep - and a Decision
I went home and lay awake thinking.
Would people say I'd sold out?
Would they think I'd crossed the floor for convenience?
Would Chapplins estate agents start telling everyone I'd "switched sides but still chain-free"?

But the other side of the argument was simple:
- I wanted to serve the community properly.
- I wanted to get things done.
- And I wanted to finally sit on East Hampshire District Council rather than staring at it through a metaphorical window.

By breakfast, I'd made my decision.
I called Elizabeth:
"I'd like to stand as the Conservative candidate."
She was delighted.
"Excellent. I'll pick you up at eleven.
We're going to Penns Place to meet Ferris Cowper."
No escape now.

My First Proper Campaign Machine
Standing for the Conservatives was like suddenly discovering the professional version of everything I'd previously been improvising:
- Leaflets arrived *printed* rather than being held together with hope and a glue stick.
- Canvassers materialised like helpful political pixies.
- I didn't have to design my own posters in Microsoft Word.
- And nobody asked me to personally deliver 1,200 leaflets in the rain.

It was bliss.
But then came the Hustings Incident.

The Hawkley Hustings: The Mistake I Learned From
A public hustings was arranged in Hawkley.

The lineup included:
- Don, a locally famous political maverick

- Howard, my old Labour colleague, who was now fully prepared to say "comrades" into any microphone offered,
- And me.

The party leadership advised me:
"Skip it. They'll use it to call you a traitor."
So, I didn't go.

Afterwards several residents said:
- "We were disappointed you didn't attend."
- "It looked like you were avoiding them."
- "We wanted to hear from you."

They were right.
It stung.

Because politics, like networking, like business, like life, is 80% **turning up**.

It's a lesson I've carried ever since.

A Tie, a Ward, and Nine Votes to Spare

And so there it was: I was now the duly elected councillor for the Hangers and Forest Ward of East Hampshire District Council.

After a lively, door-knocking, shoe-ruining campaign, I squeaked through by a mighty margin of **nine votes**.

Nine.

Enough to fill a minibus, provided everyone sat on each other's laps.

To be fair to Roger, the Liberal Democrat candidate I narrowly beat, if I'd been *him*, I might have demanded a recount. Nine votes could easily be four ballot papers that stuck together, or a gust of wind in the counting hall that shuffled things about like a confused croupier.

But Roger didn't ask for one, proving himself to be a gentleman, a good sport, and, as it later turned out in 2023, perfectly capable of returning the favour by beating *me* in the Liss Ward election.

But that's another chapter.

The Tie Incident (or: My First Lesson in District Council Dress Codes)
I still remember my first full council meeting.
Jacket: on.
Shirt: on.
Trousers: definitely on.
Confidence: medium-high.
Tie: **not on.**

It turned out ties were mandatory, otherwise, apparently, local government collapses into anarchy. Luckily, one of my new Conservative colleagues produced a spare tie from the boot of his car. It didn't match my suit, my shirt, or indeed any known colour palette in existence, but it saved me from disgrace. From that day on I never attended another meeting tieless. I half-expected the dress code to include emergency cufflinks, regulation sock colours, or a pre-approved haircut, but thankfully it didn't go that far.

Seven Years of Meetings, Speaking... and Not Speaking
Another surprise:
Some councillors get elected and then **never speak** in meetings. Not once. Not a peep. Seven years of silent attendance, like a very committed extra on a long-running soap opera.

Maybe they did marvellous work behind the scenes. Maybe they were quietly efficient caseworkers. Or maybe they'd discovered that if you sit very still and avoid eye contact with the Chairman, no one calls on you.

Either way, silence is certainly one way to avoid saying anything controversial.

I preferred the opposite approach. If someone emailed, phoned, wrote, or sent up smoke signals, I answered. Sometimes all I could do was listen. Sometimes all they needed was signposting. Occasionally, the issue was so big it belonged to Westminster, Brussels, or NASA, rather than East Hampshire.

But I always tried. That felt like part of the deal.

Three Parishes, Three Worlds
My ward included **Liss**, **Greatham**, and **Hawkley**, three rural parishes with wonderfully distinct personalities.

Liss - home turf
By then I was already Chairman of the Parish Council, what the world of local government jargon calls *dual hatted*.
It sounds glamorous, like being a spy with a daytime job, but mostly it meant two sets of minutes to approve.

Greatham - democracy with running commentary
Greatham Parish Council operated a unique interpretation of "public participation."
In Liss:
Ten minutes for public questions.
In Greatham:
Public could interject at any moment they wished, including mid-sentence, mid-breath, and on one memorable occasion, mid-sip of my water.

It was chaotic, unpredictable, and absolutely brilliant.

No wonder their meetings were so well attended. People like a bit of dynamic theatre with their local governance.

Hawkley - The Vicar of Dibley with a budget
And then there was **Hawkley**.
If ever a parish council meeting deserved a laugh track, it was that one.
Not because they were incompetent, far from it, but because the topics alone belonged in sitcom land:
- sheep on the cricket pitch,
- a mysterious smell on the footpath,
- and the time someone wanted to report a pothole that turned out simply to be... a puddle.

I used to drive home with tears of laughter streaming down my face, thinking:
"If the BBC ever need a new rural comedy, Hawkley's ready to go."

The Boundary Review: And the Winner Is... Not Me
About a year before the next elections, the Government announced a district-wide boundary review. I opened the report with mild curiosity and a biscuit.

The big headline:
The council would be reduced from 44 councillors to 43.
My first thought:
"Oh dear. Someone's about to lose a seat."
My second thought, reading further:
"Oh dear. That someone is me."

My entire ward was being abolished.
Liss Forest absorbed into Liss.
Greatham and Hawkley shipped off to join a new rural cluster with Ropley.

It was like watching a political game of musical chairs, and discovering the music had stopped while you were still looking for a seat.
I phoned Anthony (our Conservative Association Chairman), and Richard and Julie (our council leadership).

"Don't worry," they said. "There'll be a selection process. You'll be perfect for Liss."

They were right.

At the next election, I was selected, campaigned hard, and was successfully elected as one of the two councillors for the Liss Ward, alongside my brilliant colleague Russell.

New ward.
New boundaries.
Same tie, just in case.

Me, Chair?
No, surely not!

It was March 2019, and the atmosphere at East Hampshire District Council could best be described as **anticipatory with a hint of mild panic**. Richard, our Council Leader, was reshuffling his Cabinet ahead of the May elections.

I'll be honest:
I was quietly hopeful.
Not expectant - just *appropriately optimistic.*

A deputy portfolio holder role, perhaps. Maybe even a Cabinet post if the stars aligned and three other councillors got abducted by aliens.

The process was straightforward:
Richard would ring the chosen ones throughout the day, summoning them to Penns Place for "a conversation," which was council code for:
"Come upstairs and receive your destiny."
By lunchtime, my phone remained quieter than a teenager asked to empty the dishwasher.

Messages were flying among councillors:
"He's just phoned Sarah!"
"Martin's got Planning!"
"Apparently Alison got a two-hour meeting - that means something!"

By 3pm I'd mentally placed myself back on the back benches, ready for another four years of occasionally raising my hand and trying to remember which way up the agenda went.

Then, at half past three, at the very moment I'd accepted defeat and was seriously considering making a cuppa...
The phone rang.
Richard's PA:
"Richard would like to see you at 4:30 at Penns Place."
Game. On.
Guess the Portfolio
I did a quick internal audit of which Cabinet positions were still free. As far as I knew, there were two:

- **Environment**
  or
- **Whitehill & Bordon**

I prayed for Whitehill & Bordon.
The Environment portfolio had been Judy Onslow's, and I vividly remembered her describing her inbox as:
"Mainly complaints about bins and recycling, sprinkled with the occasional person convinced their neighbour is burning tyres."
Important? Yes.
Appealing? Not… quite.

The Meeting
I arrived at Penns Place, walked across the link bridge to the executive suite, and found Richard's office door open. He greeted me warmly, then shut the door behind us, that universally understood political signal of:
"Brace yourself."

"Take a seat," he said.
There was a pause.
A long pause.
One of those *Deal or No Deal* pauses where you half-expect dramatic music and Noel Edmonds to appear from a broom cupboard.

Then he said:
"I'd like you to be Chairman of the Council."
My brain: *Error 404. Thought not found.*
My mouth: slightly open.
My vocal cords: on strike.

"Are you all right?" he asked, laughing.
"Yes," I eventually managed. "Just… processing. I've only been a councillor for two years. I wasn't expecting that. May I ask why me?"

He smiled.
"Simple. The new Council's likely to be mixed, Conservatives, Lib Dems, maybe Labour or Greens. You've chaired Liss Parish Council brilliantly. I want someone who can actually run a meeting."
I took the compliment.
I took the job.
And I left the office trying to look calm and dignified, while inside I was thinking:

"Me? Chairman? Are you sure you've dialled the right Keith?"

May Arrived... and So Did the Chaos
The election came and went (that rollercoaster is covered elsewhere in the book), and Richard turned out to be right: The new Council included:
- Conservatives
- Liberal Democrats
- A couple of Labour councillors
- And one Independent who looked pleasantly surprised to have been elected at all.

And then the big day came:
the first Full Council meeting.
I had a formal briefing with the Monitoring Officer, essentially: "Here's what you can and can't do. Please don't accidentally declare war or dissolve the council."
Then a chat with Richard and Julie about the agenda.

Becoming Chairman
The Council Chamber was packed.
I took my seat next to Anthony, the outgoing Chairman, who delivered his final speech with good humour and only one thinly veiled reference to how heavy the chain is.
Then it was time.

I stood.
Crossed to the centre.
Anthony lifted the Chairman's chain from his shoulders and placed it carefully around my neck.
I braced myself for the weight, people talk about the chain as though it contains at least *one* of Henry VIII's wives, but actually it wasn't too bad. Although anything over a two-hour meeting and it did start to feel like a gym session.

I sat, gavel in hand, and thought:
"Me? Chair? Really? There must be a mix-up in the paperwork..."
But as I looked out across the chamber - a sea of faces waiting for me to begin - it became clear:

It was real.
It was happening.
And somehow...
I was ready.

Chairing, chain gangs and confetti cannons

I called the meeting to order, the first of many now that I was Chairman of East Hampshire District Council.

A surreal moment, really. One minute you're wondering whether you've left the oven on, the next you're wielding a gavel like Judge Rinder on a caffeine high.

I began by thanking Anthony for his hard work and for leaving, as I put it, "large shoes to fill."
(They weren't literally large, size 9s, if memory serves, but metaphorically generous.)
Then came my first address to the full council.
The new chamber was a rainbow of political colours: Conservative blue, Lib Dem yellow, Labour red, and one Independent... who seemed pleasantly surprised to be there at all.

I set out my number one rule:
"I intend to be fair but firm. Everyone will get their chance to speak, but I will not tolerate disrespect for standing orders."
I encouraged everyone to re-read the standing orders, the Nolan Principles, and possibly even the instructions on the fire extinguisher, just to be safe.

Then I added my guiding belief:
"Once we enter this chamber, the election campaigns are over. We may disagree, but let's keep it civil and constructive. We're here to serve the residents of East Hampshire, whether they voted for us or not."

Miraculously, people listened.
Even more miraculously, some followed it.
When the meeting ended, I invited everyone upstairs for wine and light refreshments, flawlessly arranged by my PA, Kim.
Kim and I got on like a house on fire.
Actually, better, a house on fire would cause considerably more stress.
She was calm, efficient, organised, and entirely unflappable.
If Kim ran the country, the trains would run on time and the NHS App would actually work.

The world needs more Kims.

The Chain Gang
Part of the Chairman's job is mingling with the Chairs, Mayors, and Lord Mayors of other Hampshire councils.

We called ourselves, with considerable pride, **"The Chain Gang."**
It sounds like a group of middle-aged men and women who do dodgy DIY in their spare time, but no, these were the keepers of civic order, wielders of ceremonial chains, defenders of proper process and lukewarm buffet food.

We still have a WhatsApp group.
It mainly consists of birthday messages, pictures of cakes, and the occasional mild moan about protocol.

It didn't take long to notice how wildly resources varied.
Some Chairs had entire offices, plush carpets, dedicated staff... one even had **four PAs**.
I had a **hot desk** and **half of Kim**.
Efficiency is fine, but even I sometimes wondered whether EHDC had accidentally put me in a broom cupboard.
Still, value for money, East Hampshire. Tremendous value for money.

Portsmouth: Where Local Government Meets Las Vegas
One of the early joys of the role was attending the swearing-in ceremonies of fellow civic leaders.
Most were modest, dignified, understated.
And then... Portsmouth.

Michelle and I arrived by chauffeur and took our seats near the front of the Guildhall stage.
The Royal Marines Band sat poised, instruments gleaming.
The outgoing Lord Mayor gave a lovely farewell speech and departed to polite applause.
Then the lights dimmed.
Dance music blasted through the speakers.
The master of ceremonies bellowed:
"Everybody please stand!"
From the side doors burst a line of showgirls in blue and gold leotards, pom-poms shimmering, legs kicking.

It was like someone had crossed the Lord Mayor's ceremony with **Britain's Got Talent**, **Moulin Rouge**, and a hen night in Ibiza.
Confetti cannons erupted in blue and gold, showering the first few rows, including us.
I plucked a piece of confetti out of my hair and whispered to Michelle:
"I'd hate to see the bill for this."
After that spectacle, the rest of the ceremony felt almost suspiciously normal.

But it was the beginning of a wonderful friendship with the new Lord Mayor, a man with enough humour, warmth, and mischief to fill several chapters... and indeed, he does. More on him shortly.
But that moment?
Etched in my memory forever.

The Great Prayers Problem
Back in East Hampshire, I faced a more delicate issue.
Tradition held that full council meetings began with prayers. But our new chamber was diverse, Christians, Jews, Muslims, and several councillors whose closest brush with religion was watching *Songs of Praise* by accident while searching for the cricket.

Some councillors admitted prayers made them uncomfortable but had never spoken up.

Legally, the decision was mine.
Option A: End prayers entirely.
Option B: Force dissenters to wait outside in the corridor like naughty schoolchildren.
Neither felt right.
Then, as usually happens, inspiration struck in the shower.
(Not the first time, won't be the last.)
Why not offer a 15-minute "quiet contemplation" room?
Anyone could use it, for prayer, reflection, meditation, or just to hide from other councillors.
The Monitoring Officer approved.
Facilities said fine.
Kim sent the email.
Predictably, the *Herald* ran a slightly dramatic piece.
I received a handful of angry emails ("This is political

correctness gone mad!!!"), but the overwhelming majority either supported the change or didn't care enough to write.
It was the right call.
And the chamber became more inclusive overnight.

Extinction Rebellion & the Climate Emergency Debate

My only real moment of disciplinarian severity came during the debate on whether EHDC should declare a climate emergency.

Extinction Rebellion were planning a demonstration, so we made quiet arrangements for councillors to slip in via a side door if needed, like minor celebrities trying to dodge the paparazzi.

On the night, a dozen or so protestors gathered, loud, colourful, enthusiastic, and carrying more cardboard slogans than a school art cupboard.

I went outside to meet their leader.
"You're welcome in the public gallery," I said.
"But no banners in the chamber.
And if anyone disrupts the meeting, I will suspend proceedings and have them removed."
He nodded, perfectly civil.

The debate began.
Half an hour in, one protestor stood and shouted over a speaker.
"Please sit down," I said. "If it happens again, you'll be removed."
He sat.
For six minutes.
Then he stood and shouted again.
"Meeting suspended," I declared. "Security, please remove that gentleman."

They did, politely, professionally, and the protestors remained quiet thereafter.
After a long, sincere debate, the council declared a climate emergency.
And as I looked around that chamber, I remember thinking:
We can disagree without disgrace.
A rare and precious thing.

And So, Begins the Story of the Lord Mayor...

That dazzling Portsmouth inauguration, the confetti, the showgirls, the pomp, was just the start.

Behind the glitter was a warm, witty, mischievous man who became one of my closest civic allies and whose antics could fill several pages… and will.

But that, dear reader, is a tale for the next chapter.

Confetti, chains and pink slippers

As Chairman of East Hampshire District Council, I soon discovered that civic life has its own rhythm, a sort of ceremonial waltz involving chains of office, buffet lunches, and the constant risk of tripping over a mayoral robe.

Each year, every Mayor or Chair hosts two major events:
(1) a Civic Service - usually in their local church, and
(2) a Civic Day or Gala Dinner - an excuse for dignitaries to gather, eat, drink, and exchange stories about whose chain weighs the most.

With fourteen members in the Hampshire Chain Gang (including the Isle of Wight Chair), that meant *twenty-eight* potential dates. Enough hymns and canapés to last a lifetime.

My own Civic Service
The Civic Services ranged from the intimate to the cathedral-scale, and none more magnificent than the Lord Mayor of Winchester's event in Winchester Cathedral, a building so historic it makes Parliament look like a new-build.

For my service, I returned to my parish church, St Mary's in Liss.
It was a lovely, warm morning, the pews full, Reverend Chris Williams in fine form before he relocated to Florence, leaving Liss for better coffee, superior architecture, and significantly fewer council meetings.

The turnout from the Chain Gang was excellent, though I suspect the real draw was the youth choir from Britain's Got Talent. They sang beautifully. I was the first to stand and applaud.
(If Simon Cowell had been there, he'd have pressed the golden buzzer.)

We ended the morning with drinks and a buffet at the West Liss Pavilion. Sandwiches, speeches, and a lot of chain-jangling when people stood up too quickly.

Civic Days: Where Mayors Play

Civic Days were the fun part of the job, black-tie dinners, Burns Nights with bagpipes, vineyard tours, a vintage bus adventure, even posing by a Spitfire at HMS Daedalus.
Two events are etched in my memory:

1. My Charity Comedy Night
Having previously organised a sell-out comedy evening to raise funds for building the Pavilion, it felt fitting to return to the scene of the fruit of our labours.

We converted the Pavilion into a dining venue for a hundred guests. Cloisters Bistro catered a superb three-course meal, and the comedians had the room roaring from start to finish.
Almost £1,000 raised for my charities, Crossover Youth Centre and Dementia Friendly Petersfield.
A perfect evening: community spirit, laughter, and zero incidents involving collapsing folding chairs.

2. The Lord Mayor of Portsmouth's Gala Dinner
And then there was Portsmouth.
Oh, Portsmouth.
If my event was wholesome, the Lord Mayor of Portsmouth's gala was what you'd get if you crossed **The Ritz**, **RuPaul's Drag Race**, and **Strictly Come Dancing**, then sprinkled the whole thing with confetti, glitter, and a hint of Prosecco.

You will remember him from the last chapter:
openly gay, gloriously camp, and dazzling enough to power the South Coast on sheer charisma alone.

The banquet was held in the magnificently over-the-top Guildhall ballroom. Chandeliers glittering, music swelling, and, naturally, the return of his beloved showgirls in full sequin regalia.
"I'm sure you keep them locked in a cupboard somewhere," I told him.
He clutched his chest theatrically.
"Don't tempt me, darling. I've only just had the locks reinforced!"
The wine flowed, the brandy followed, and by eleven o'clock only a chosen handful of us remained, invited for a **private nightcap in his chambers.**

Into the Lord Mayor's Lair
His chambers were extraordinary: three rooms knocked into one, part civic office, part gentleman's club, part... set for a mildly risqué BBC drama.

He vanished behind his desk, rummaged loudly, and emerged triumphantly holding a bottle of vintage port.
"Now," he said, **"time for the *good* stuff."**

His PA arrived with the glasses.
"Port, whisky, or soft drink?" she offered.
(I didn't hesitate. It was port or nothing.)

We were halfway through our first glasses when he leaned back, eyes sparkling with mischief.
"Fetch... the keys."
His PA sighed the sigh of someone who has fetched many strange things for this man.
Out came the *historic Keys to the City of Portsmouth,* safely stored in his personal safe.
He told us the now-legendary story:
Early in his term, preparing for a visit from the late Queen, he studied the keys and declared them "dreadfully dull."
So he sent them away to be "properly cleaned."
Cue Her Majesty, examining the gleaming keys:
"1845, you say? They're awfully clean, aren't they?"
The room exploded.
That line entered Chain Gang folklore forever.
But the evening was not done.
Not even close.

The Slippers
The Lord Mayor handed the keys back to his PA... then produced a second bottle of port and held one hand mysteriously behind his back.
"And *these*," he purred, **"are my guilty pleasure..."**
Out came a pair of bright pink, fluffy slippers.
The sort of slippers you'd expect to find backstage at a drag revue, not in the chambers of a civic leader.
We erupted.
"The shoes that go with my robes are murder," he explained.
"So when I'm not expecting visitors... I slip into these little beauties."
Then, and this was the pièce de resistance, he kicked off his formal shoes, slid into the slippers, and sighed:
"Oh THAT, my darlings, is simply *divine*."

He then strutted from one side of the room to the other, feathered cuffs flicking dramatically, the ermine robe swirling, pausing to pout like a runway model mid-Vogue.

I laughed so hard I nearly spilled my port.

Somewhere in the middle of the hilarity, I issued a challenge:
"Wear those slippers in a full council meeting, send me proof, and I'll donate £100 to your mayoral charity."

He gasped. He clutched his imaginary pearls. He accepted.

Three weeks later, a photograph arrived in my inbox:
The Lord Mayor of Portsmouth, chain of office gleaming... fluffy pink slippers proudly visible beneath the desk.

I paid up immediately. He earned every penny.

A Final Reflection
Great times. Great people.
And a reminder that civic life isn't all committees and agendas. Sometimes it's champagne, confetti, ancient keys, and a Lord Mayor in pink slippers sashaying across a room like he owns it. Which, technically, he did.

Tea with Titles - and Tales to Tell

One of the quieter joys of being Chairman, first of Liss Parish Council, then of East Hampshire District Council (EHDC), has been the unexpected number of chances it gave me to meet members of the Royal Family.

Although, technically, my *first* encounter with royalty came years before any civic title, during my Red Cross days, and it remains, to this day, one of the funniest things I've ever heard a royal say.
We'll get to that. Trust me, it's worth the wait.

A Princess in Liss
My first official royal engagement was welcoming **HRH Princess Alexandra** to the Crossover Centre in Liss.

Don't feel bad if you just Googled her, I had to as well. She's a cousin of the late Queen Elizabeth II, and genuinely one of the most gracious people I've ever met. The way she chatted with the young people, joined in a game of table tennis, and revealed a rather lethal competitive streak... I decided at once that if the monarchy ever entered the Olympics, she'd be our secret weapon.

That day was also my first proper meeting with **Nigel Atkinson, Esq., the Lord Lieutenant of Hampshire**, Her Majesty's representative in the county. Nigel is the kind of man who could walk into a burning building and politely apologise for the inconvenience. Always charming, always precise, and utterly unflappable.

I'd invited him back to Liss a couple of years later to open the West Liss Pavilion, and once I became District Chairman, we seemed to meet almost monthly. We were practically on nodding terms with each other's diaries.

An Afternoon at the Palace
One of the earliest duties of a District Chairman is to attend a **Buckingham Palace Garden Party,** a once-in-a-lifetime honour. By tradition, once you've been, that's it. No going again. A royal version of "one visit per customer."

My invitation now hangs proudly in my study, partly because it's historic, and partly because it proves to my family that I do occasionally leave the house in a suit.

It was also my first opportunity to use the council's hired limousine, a sleek black Tesla, complete with chauffeur in full livery. We only got twenty or so official uses per year, and thanks to Michelle ferrying me to most engagements in her car, the budget stretched impressively.

As we approached London, the chauffeur abruptly pulled over. I feared a flat tyre, which would have made us the first civic party in history to arrive at Buckingham Palace by Uber.
But no, he'd stopped to attach the EHDC pennant to the bonnet.

I hadn't known we *had* a pennant.

We must have baffled half of Kensington:
A Tesla gliding majestically along, proudly flying a green-and-white flag that looked like we were either representing a local authority... or competing in the world's dullest yacht race.

Inside the Palace gardens, it was glorious. Marquees with proper China teacups, the Grenadier Guards band playing, lawns so perfect they looked ironed.

But wearing the full Chairman's chain in 25°C heat... less glorious. I sweated so much I could've watered the royal rhododendrons.

Then came the moment of inevitability: I needed the loo.

The nearest facility?
Portaloos.

A mobility rollator, a heavy chain of office, and a Portaloo is the holy trinity of poor accessibility design.

Michelle mentioned it quietly to a staff member, who nodded sympathetically and led us through a discreet door... **into Buckingham Palace itself**.

So, there I was, standing inside the Palace, adjusting my chain in front of a disabled loo mirror, thinking:

"This absolutely isn't on the tour map."

After emerging, cooler, relieved, and still faintly dazzled, we rejoined the crowd just in time to see the Royal Family arrive on the terrace.

His Majesty King Charles III, then still Prince of Wales, stopped to shake my hand and share a brief, perfectly mannered exchange.

Three seconds of conversation, but I'll dine out on it forever.

A Duchess with a Sense of Humour

During my term as Chairman, I met **HRH Princess Sophie, Duchess of Edinburgh**, twice, both times through her patronage of Treloar's, an extraordinary institution supporting young people with disabilities.

The first time, she was warm, attentive, charming. We spoke about local issues; she chatted just as naturally with Michelle.

The second time, she was on sparkling form.

She greeted the Chairman of Hampshire County Council and his wife, then turned to me with a mischievous smile that gave the Lord Mayor of Portsmouth a run for his money.

"We had a long chat last time. This time, I'd rather speak with your charming daughter!"

Michelle beamed.
Nigel Atkinson laughed.
I considered retiring on the spot.

Michelle still enjoys reminding me that royalty prefers her company.

A Royal Outburst Behind a Hedge

And now, the story I promised you.

Before politics, before councils, before civic chains, I served with **Hants One Detachment of the British Red Cross**, providing first aid at local events.

One day, I was on duty at a cross-country equestrian event at Tweseldown. One of the riders was none other than **HRH Princess Anne**.

I was standing behind a hedge, as one does, when I overheard her speaking crisply to a member of her protection team.

Apparently, a paparazzo had been following her relentlessly with a long camera lens.

The Princess Royal, in her unmistakable no-nonsense tone, said:

"Please have a word with that damn man with the long camera lens and tell him to *fuck off*."

Not quite the Queen's English I was expecting.
But wonderfully direct.

I have respected her immensely ever since.

Reflections
Looking back, I feel an enormous sense of privilege.

To have met Princess Alexandra's grace, Prince Charles's warmth, Princess Sophie's humour, and Princess Anne's magnificently unfiltered honesty, all while representing the community I love, is something I will treasure forever.

It turns out royalty are human after all.

And sometimes, the funniest moments come not from pomp or ceremony, but from behind a hedge, spoken by someone very much not to be messed with.

Steam, smiles and the Scotsman

Of all the unexpected perks that come with being Chairman of East Hampshire District Council, I never imagined one of the absolute highlights would involve **leaning out of an open railway window like an enthusiastic retriever**, desperately trying to inhale steam I could no longer smell.

Yet there I was at Alresford, boarding the Watercress Line for an incredibly special journey, one hauled by none other than the **Flying Scotsman**, the Beyoncé of steam locomotives.

Step One: Convince Security I Was... Me

Before we even got near the locomotive, Michelle and I had to pass through security.

Despite wearing:

- A name badge reading **Cllr Keith Budden - Chairman**, and
- A ceremonial chain large enough to anchor the Isle of Wight ferry,

...I was still asked to produce photographic ID.

What exactly did they think had happened?

Had I mugged the actual Chairman behind the ticket office, stuffed him in a wheelie bin, stolen his shiny necklace, and thought, *Yes, this will DEFINITELY get me a seat on the Flying Scotsman*?

Still, I dutifully showed my ID. Apparently, I looked sufficiently like myself, so they let me through.

Prime Seating: Coach One, Table Two

Michelle and I took our seats in the second table from the front, close enough that you could *feel* the power of the locomotive and *taste* the steam.

(Not literally. I haven't been able to smell or taste properly since treatment, so I made do with sticking my head as far out of the window as modern safety permits. If health and safety officers had their way, steam trains would come with laminated disclaimers saying: **"Do Not Enjoy Too Enthusiastically."**)

We were joined by:

- **Paula**, Labour group leader,
- **Gideon**, her partner,
- and at the next table: **Damian Hinds** and **Steve Brine**, MPs.

Damian spent more time chatting with us than with Steve, though Steve seemed cheerfully resigned to his fate, the way a man does when he knows he's the least exciting thing in a carriage currently attached to the Flying Scotsman.

Laughter, Steam & The Lord Mayor's Pink Slippers
The moment the train pulled out, the carriage filled with exactly the kind of laughter that doesn't need prompting, or alcohol.

I retold the now legendary tale of the **Lord Mayor of Portsmouth's fluffy pink slippers**, which caused such an explosion of hysteria that anyone passing the window probably assumed we'd polished off several bottles of Prosecco before boarding.

Meanwhile, every station along the line was packed to the rafters. Children, parents, grandparents, railway enthusiasts with lenses big enough to photograph Saturn, all waving frantically.

For a few glorious miles, we were minor celebrities.
Steam royalty, if you will.

A Royal View of Alton… and Zero Chance of Spotting the Grandchildren
As the train approached Alton, it ran along a high embankment that gave us a perfect view of Michelle's house.

Moments later we passed **The Butts**, packed with schoolchildren waving as though the Queen herself was driving the train.

Somewhere out there were my grandchildren Lucy and Davy.

Could we spot them?

Of course not.

The train was moving at a fair pace and all I could see was a sea of limbs and enthusiasm. It looked like a scene from a Where's Wally? book set on fast-forward.

Alan Titchmarsh, Deputy Lieutenant, and National Treasure

At Alton, we disembarked to stretch our legs and admire the locomotive as it ran around the train.

There followed a small ceremony where **Alan Titchmarsh**, Deputy Lieutenant of Hampshire, and Britain's national gardening uncle, unveiled a plaque.

The Lord Mayor of Winchester and I flanked him for photographs.
I'd secretly hoped Alan would join us for the return leg, but alas, his diary did not include "ride home with the Chairman of EHDC while being gently dusted with soot."

Still, he was utterly charming, even if I did look like I'd face-planted a coal bunker.

Return Journey: Full Steam Ahead and Laughter at Maximum Pressure

Back onboard, spirits rose again as though someone had thrown the regulator wide open.

Paula says to this day that she's rarely laughed as much at a civic event, and she was in local politics during Brexit.

It was one of those perfect days:
joyful, ridiculous, historic, warm, funny, and filled with the kind of memories you don't realise are special until later.

Flying Scotsman, national treasure that you are,
thank you for letting a middle-aged council chairman hang out of your window like an excited spaniel.

That day lives with me still.
And always will.

When duty calls (and sometimes drags on)

Being Chairman came with its share of wonderful occasions: civic services, charity galas, comedy nights, grand ceremonies, a surprising amount of cake, and the odd glass of something celebratory.

But it would be an act of outright fiction to pretend *every* event was a delight.

Some were… character-building.

Two, in particular, felt like they had been conceived as **escape rooms**, except without the "escape" part.

The Royal Society AGM: A Journey into Bone Density (and the Limits of Human Consciousness)
The first ordeal was the Annual General Meeting of a Royal Society for a particular medical specialism, bone density and age-related degeneration.

I didn't even know they were headquartered in East Hampshire. I suspect most of East Hampshire didn't either, including possibly the postal service.

But I had made myself a promise:
If invited, I would attend.

Unless I was already triple booked, kidnapped, or clinically dead, I would show up.

My colleagues joked that I seemed determined to be knighted for "Services to Turning Up." They weren't entirely wrong.

I opened the meeting with a short, polite speech, for which the bar was set comfortably low. They clapped warmly. Good. Strong start.

Then came the guest speaker.

A man of tremendous expertise, no doubt. Probably capable of reciting the Latin names of every bone in the human body while blindfolded.

But his voice…

Imagine a dial tone.
Now imagine that dial tone has had a particularly rough day.
Now imagine you are listening to that dial tone through a sock.

By slide **three** (out of **seventy**), my will to live had slipped quietly out the fire exit.

By slide fifteen, I was seriously considering whether anyone would notice if I used a matchstick to prop my eyelids open like a 1940s cartoon character.

Meanwhile, the rest of the audience leaned forward in rapture, nodding reverently as if he were reciting love poetry.

When the final slide eventually, *blessedly,* appeared, the applause was thunderous.

Mine was enthusiastic, too.

Though in my case, the emotion behind it was **relief**, bordering on spiritual renewal.

The Romanian Opera: An Experience I Will Never… Understand
The second trial was… operatic.

Literally.

A village church somewhere in East Hampshire (I won't name it, they were lovely) was hosting an opera as a charity fundraiser.

I asked Michelle if she wanted to join me.
"I'm busy washing… something."
(She didn't specify. I think she just panicked.)

I arrived looking appropriately Chairman-like, took my seat… and waited.

The musicians were excellent.
The singers were talented.
The acoustics were heavenly.

And the entire performance was in **Romanian**.

Romanian.

If they had sung in French, German, or Spanish, I might have clung to the occasional noun like a linguistic lifebuoy.

But Romanian?

For all I knew, they were singing:

"Keith Budden is sitting in the front row and hasn't the faintest idea what's going on."

Ninety minutes later, it ended.

The audience were ecstatic.
I applauded vigorously, partly from relief, partly because my hands needed something to do to stop me drifting into catatonia.

Then came the microphone.

"Ladies and gentlemen, we will now take a thirty-minute interval before the **second** and concluding act."

Act Two?

My soul left my body.

The interval canapés were exquisite, though I suspect they were strategically designed to soften the blow.

The second act lasted forty minutes, though emotionally it felt like several weeks.

When it ended, I was the first person on my feet. Some might say over-eager. I would say **alive**.

The Monday Morning Debrief
On Monday, Kim, my endlessly cheerful and infinitely patient PA, asked brightly:

"So, Keith, how did the opera go?"

I replied:

"Kim... if we ever receive another invitation from that group, please tell them I'll be washing my hair that night."

She dissolved into laughter, practically crying into her paperwork.

"Keith," she gasped, "I *love* you being Chair. You're always a delight to work with."

And honestly?

That summed up public service rather nicely:

- You take the highs with the lows.
- You smile through the baffling bits.
- You clap politely at things you don't understand.
- And sometimes the loudest applause comes not from the grand ceremonies…

…but from the person who organises your diary and keeps you sane.

Schindler's lift

During my time as a District Councillor, and especially in my two years wearing the Chairman's chain (and occasionally nearly toppling forward because of it), I made countless visits to the Havant Civic Plaza, headquarters of Havant Borough Council and, incidentally, one of the few civic buildings that doesn't look like it escaped from the 1970s and survived several rounds of budget cuts.

East Hampshire and Havant shared several senior officers, which meant I was regularly summoned there for briefings, joint committees, and the odd civic occasion where everyone pretended the biscuits weren't the same ones from the last meeting.

The building itself was perfectly pleasant: modern, bright, clean, and, a rarity, logically signposted.

Even better, it had a genuinely decent café on the ground floor. Free Wi-Fi, good coffee, and the sort of flapjack that makes you momentarily forgive local government finances. You don't need to be on council business to use it, a fact I have taken advantage of on more than one occasion.

But despite the café, the real highlight of the Havant Civic Plaza wasn't the council chamber, nor the meeting rooms, nor the wide, airy atrium.

It was the lift. Yes. The lift.

Not because it was fast (it wasn't).
Not because it was large (just big enough to hold six councillors and a political grudge).
Not even because it played gentle music (it didn't - though in fairness, the squeak of the mechanism occasionally hit a melodic note).
No - the magic was in the plaque.
A tidy little brushed-steel nameplate, fixed just above the buttons:

Schindler.
That's right.
Schindler's Lift.

I noticed it on my very first visit. And once seen, it could never be unseen.
Some people find art in cathedrals, others in nature.
I, apparently, find mine in municipal lift humour.

Every time I stepped inside, I smiled.
Some days, I smirked.
Once, I actually chuckled out loud and had to pretend I'd just remembered something amusing from a meeting (which, to be fair, would have been a first).
I often wondered how many thousands of people had ridden that lift without spotting the joke...
and how many, like me, enjoyed the small, perfectly formed piece of unintentional comedy gold.

In politics, you take your joys where you can find them.
Some people seek glory.
Others seek power.
Me?
I found happiness in **Schindler's Lift**.

A reminder, perhaps, that public service doesn't always need fanfare, sometimes it just needs a good pun on the way to the third floor.

Two wins for Liss Forest

During my time as District Councillor, I managed to secure two notable wins for Liss Forest, one within weeks of being elected. Both were triumphs of persistence, creativity, and, in one case, me talking about a mobile Post Office so enthusiastically that even the BBC briefly cared.

The Post Office That Refused to Die
The first issue was the sub-Post Office tucked inside Forest Stores.

The shop was closing, the owner retiring, and the building was set to be converted into apartments, because in Britain, the natural lifecycle of village buildings is:
Pub → Shop → Flats → "Luxury Apartments from £325,000"

Residents were understandably upset.
They could live without the shop, but a Post Office?
That's where livelihoods *and* birthday cards go.
Now, I'm not naïve. I knew the shop itself couldn't be saved. Amazon has decimated village retail so successfully that the next thing they'll deliver is your childhood nostalgia.
But the Post Office... perhaps?
And then, in the shower (where all serious political strategy happens), I had a sudden flashback to the *post bus* from my Murphy's days: a cheerful red-and-yellow minibus that drove around the countryside offering stamps, parcels, and, if memory serves, a mild sense of adventure.

I wondered: **do post buses still exist?**
Google said yes.
The Post Office said maybe.
Damian Hinds said, "Let's give it a go."
(He's very agreeable when he hasn't had time to think).
After some lobbying, gentle, firm, and occasionally relentless, we got a trial mobile Post Office visit for Liss Forest.
Residents loved it.
They still do.
Nine years on, it's still visiting every week, a tiny victory on wheels.
The Post Office PR team thought it was a cracking story and persuaded BBC South Today to cover it in their evening news.
I spent hours doing interviews, walking importantly along

Forest Road, imagining I'd be the inspirational "before the weather" story.
The broadcast that evening?
Forty-five seconds.
I've seen longer trailers for dishwasher tablets.

The Temple Inn: Thirty-Two People, One Kitchen, and a Pub Saved
My second victory involved The Temple Inn, the heart of Liss Forest.
Then one day, Fullers announced they were closing it.
The community was horrified.
My inbox experienced the closest thing local government gets to a riot.
A group of residents asked if anything could be done.
EHDC's Communities Team told me that if we could prove genuine demand, we could get the pub listed as an **Asset of Community Value,** essentially a legal "hands off, you have to offer this to us first."
So, we organised a public meeting at the Evangelical Church.
It was *packed*.
Standing room only.
I haven't seen that many people in one room since free cake appeared at the West Liss Pavilion.
We gathered signatures and submitted them.
Two weeks later: success.
The Temple Inn was officially protected.

Now came the next challenge: forming the community committee.
We invited volunteers to Matt's house.
Thirty-two people showed up.
Matt's dining table had to be extended so many times I swear it ended somewhere near Guildford.
If the kitchen had been any smaller, we would've had to stack people vertically.

Matt and I retreated to the hallway to panic professionally, then returned with a plan:
- **Matt's team** - find a brewery/operator.
- **My team** - legal and compliance
- **Diana's team** - newsletters, website, general village morale

Matt's team excelled and identified three serious bidders.
We interviewed them like a very polite version of Dragons' Den.

One stood out: **Red Mist**, excellent reputation, solid finances, and a clear plan.
Their proposal:
Buy the pub outright, refurbish it beautifully, and build two small houses on part of the car park to help fund the work.

We checked with EHDC planning officers.
They nodded approvingly, a rare and treasured sight.
Red Mist submitted their bid to Fullers.
Weeks of silence.
Then: **ACCEPTED**.

The Temple Inn reopened, smartened up, refreshed, and full of life again.

It's changed hands since, but it remains exactly what a village pub should be, lively, local, and the kind of place where everyone knows your business before you do.

Two wins.
Two happy outcomes.
And proof that sometimes, all it takes is:
- an innovative idea,
- a lot of community spirit, and
- thirty-two people crammed into a kitchen saying, "I've brought biscuits."

The pavilion, the planks and the lesbian with the coat hanger

The new pavilion project was, without question, the most ambitious thing Liss Parish Council had attempted since someone in the 1980s said, "Let's donate these slightly wobbly agricultural buildings to the village, what's the worst that could happen?"

Quite a lot, as it turned out.

Some funding lay waiting in reserves, but nowhere near enough to build something modern, safe, and unlikely to collapse when someone sneezed too hard. Had we been allowed to borrow from the Public Works Loans Board when Paddy first drew up the plans, we'd have finished the project five years earlier and I'd have saved myself a great deal of grey hair.
But timing is a comedian, usually one that gets booed off the stage.

The Elderly Pavilion and the Vanishing Man
The old pavilion (and the adjacent 1st Liss Scouts hut) were relics from a time when "health and safety" meant putting your hands in your pockets and hoping for the best. Originally agricultural buildings, they had been gifted to the village already middle-aged. By the 2000s, they were held together mostly by memory, prayer, and an alarming quantity of hope.

There was wood.
There was glass.
There was corrugated something-or-other.
And, as we later discovered, **there was asbestos**.
A vintage selection, if you will.

Then came the day, a wet winter morning, when someone opened the main door, stepped inside… and vanished through the floor.
Gone. Just *gone*.

Thankfully, they weren't hurt. Under the boards was a sort of archaeological dig consisting of concrete piles, brick piers, and forty years of village odds and ends.

I remain unconvinced the building was ever *attached* to the piles.
I think it just sat on them the way we sit on sofas after Christmas lunch.

Plans, Pints, and a Problem of Money
Paddy, to his credit, had drawn up replacement plans years earlier, but that's where things had stalled, between the sketchpad and the land of "one day..."

As Chair of the Pavilion Committee, I gathered Vice-Chair Mike, Elwyn (who would later become a very dear friend), Paddy and a few other councillors. We reviewed every fundraising idea known to mankind:
- Buy-a-Brick? ✓
- Collection tins? ✓
- Publicity stands at village events? ✓

Useful.
Dependable.
About as financially impactful as a raffle for a lemon drizzle cake.
What we needed was *oomph*.
Or possibly "oomph!!!"

Comedy to the Rescue
I remembered how I used to spend evenings at Lakeside Country Club watching legends: Jim Davidson, Bob Monkhouse, Danny La Rue, Joe Pasquale, Michael McIntyre, Roy 'Chubby' Brown...

Over time I'd come to know one of the agents, Geoff, a man who lived somewhere between showbusiness and mild chaos.

"We're trying to raise funds for a new pavilion," I told him.
"How about a comedy night?" he said.
It was so obvious I felt silly for not having thought of it myself. Like discovering your glasses have been on your head the whole time.
The committee agreed and gave me a budget: **£500**.
In comedy terms, that buys you two up-and-comers, a headliner, and not so much as the *shadow* of a compère.
"That's fine," I said to Geoff.
"I'll MC it myself."
What could possibly go wrong?
(I know. I know.)

Geoff booked us Izzy and Craig, and as headliner, the wonderful Paul Kerensa, writer for *Miranda* and *Not Going Out*. A proper coup.

I did ask Geoff to warn the acts to keep things... let's say... BBC One rather than Channel 5 at 1am.

Opening Night: Two Jokes, One Prayer, and a Sudden Exit
The Village Hall looked magnificent.
Full house.
Buzzing atmosphere.
I put on my dinner suit, black tie and felt like a low-budget version of Bruce Forsyth.
I stepped onto the stage as compère, warmed up the crowd with two jokes, one true, one not, both reliable crowd-pleasers.
The first, absolutely true:
I recall visiting one of Liss's many retirement homes (we have more than anywhere else in Hampshire). Wearing my Chairman's chain, I sat beside a lady and asked:
"Do you know who I am?"
"No dear," she said kindly, "but if you go and sit on one of the chairs in the corridor, Matron will be along shortly, and she'll tell you."
The place erupted.
Best start I could have asked for.
The second joke, a little cheekier, also landed nicely.
Then Izzy took the stage.
Her first joke involved:
- a lesbian
- a dildo
- a bottle of lube
- and a wire coat hanger

I cannot overstate how quickly I considered pulling the fire alarm.
Through the hatch I saw most people laughing.
Some elderly ladies looked as though they'd just witnessed a séance.
And one gentleman, a potential wealthy donor, stood up, shook his head, and left the building like Elvis.
Thankfully, no one followed him.

Craig restored balance, then Paul blew the roof off.
Standing ovation, well earned.
When I returned to the stage and asked whether we should run more comedy nights, the hall shouted "YES!" so loudly it rattled the lighting rig.

Government to the Rescue (For Once)
Fundraisers continued, but we were still short.
Then, in a moment of legislative mercy, the Government announced parish councils could borrow from the Public Works Loans Board.

25-year loan. Fixed rate. 2%.

Practically money falling from heaven, if heaven did competitive interest rates.
The council agreed unanimously.
And that was it, the moment the new Liss Pavilion was truly born.

A triumph of teamwork, persistence, imagination, and one unforgettable night featuring comedy, community spirit, and a lesbian with a coat hanger.

What more could a village ask for?

Policing made practical

Within the East Hampshire Rail Partnership, we'd identified a recurring problem: a rotating cast of teenagers who treated our railway stations as if they were auditioning for *Jackass: The Hampshire Edition*.

They gathered at Liphook, Liss, or Petersfield stations, usually in packs, shouting abuse at passengers, vaping aggressively, drinking cheap cider, and inhaling nitrous oxide from little silver canisters supposedly meant for baristas. (If Costa ever runs out of whipped cream, now you know why.)

At Petersfield and Liss, they'd begun doing dangerous stunts, jumping down onto the track, then back up again. Not parkour. More like "stupid with extra steps."

Late at night, the behaviour escalated to urinating on platforms, swearing, punching ticket machines (which, frankly, I sometimes sympathised with), and generally intimidating anyone who wasn't wearing a hooded sweatshirt.

Fridays were the worst. The group was mostly male, but the girls were there too, the sort of girls who could probably set a bin on fire using nothing but a hair straightener and raw determination.

BTP reviewed hours of CCTV and were 90% sure who the ringleader was. As Chair of the Rail Partnership, they invited me to join them one Friday night to "see things first-hand."
I thought perhaps they wanted my strategic insight.
In reality, what they wanted was someone to hold the radio while they chased teenagers.
They issued me a high-vis jacket with OBSERVER on the back in letters so reflective I could have guided aircraft into Heathrow.

Patrol Begins (or: Two Policemen and the World's Slowest Civilian)
At 10 p.m. the BTP van rolled into Liss station. Officers Toby and Graham welcomed me in, both tall, fit, and clearly used to sprinting after fleeing youths.
I climbed into the back like a man boarding the last helicopter out of Saigon.

"We'll check Petersfield first," Toby said. "If they're not there, we'll try Liss, then Liphook. Mild weather, they'll be out somewhere."
Translation:
Tonight was going to be lively.
The control room in Southampton monitored CCTV and would alert us if trouble flared.
Petersfield: nothing.
Liss: nothing.
Even Liphook: empty.
I began wondering whether my presence was scaring them off, like a sort of anti-teenager talisman.
Then the radio crackled.
"There's a group on the London-bound platform at Liss. One just threw a bottle onto the track."
And we were off.
Toby hit the siren, swung the van around, and we headed down the A3 at a speed I associate only with ambulances and Domino's delivery scooters.
Just before reaching Liss station, the siren stopped. Then the blue lights.
"We want to catch them in the act," Toby said. "If they hear us coming, they'll leg it."
I nodded, trying to look authoritative, while clutching the seat like a man bracing for impact.

The Great Liss Station Sprint
We parked behind the station. Toby and Graham bolted up the ramp in full action-movie mode.
I followed them at the speed of a man who knows his knee joints have unionised and may go on strike at any moment.
The moment the teens saw the fluorescent yellow of justice approaching, they scattered like pigeons near a toddler with a breadstick.
Toby made a beeline for one boy, the suspected ringleader, who decided to play statue and hope camouflage-by-stupidity would work. It didn't.
Meanwhile, Graham shouted at another lad on the footbridge: "Fancy a night in the cells too?!"
The boy flashed his middle finger, then saw Graham advancing toward the stairs and vanished like a magician's assistant.
Toby ordered his suspect to empty his pockets.
Out tumbled approximately twenty nitrous oxide canisters, a plastic bag, and an expression that said, "I have made poor life choices."

"I'm over eighteen," he insisted. "These are all for personal use. I don't share. I don't sell."
The small roll of £10 notes in his other pocket hollered otherwise.
Toby, calm as a man reading the weather forecast, applied handcuffs and delivered the familiar script:
"You are under arrest…"
Into the van he went, banging and thumping like an angry washing machine.

The Unexpected Lesson
"What happens now?" I asked.
"Well," Toby said, "CPS won't take this. Not enough evidence. Normally we'd take him to Waterlooville, process him, interview him, release him with a caution…"
He paused.
"…but honestly? It won't teach him anything. I'd rather he had a bit of a shock."

What followed was gentle psychological warfare.
We drove down the A3.
Then around Horndean.
Then through a few random side roads.
Then back again.
The lad had no windows. No bearings. No idea where he was.
He kicked. He screamed. He hurled abuse.
Toby shouted back, "The more you kick, the slower I drive!"
It became a battle of wills.
Eventually the noise stopped.

When we arrived back in Liss, Toby called out, "Still awake, Joe?"
A small, sheepish "…yes" answered.
"Right. Here's the deal. Calm and sensible. No more stunts. No more canisters. Behave yourself. Or we do this again and THEN take you to custody. Understand?"
"Yes!"
Slightly louder.
Considerably humbler.
We released him.

He walked away, quiet as a church mouse after a sermon.

A Cup of Tea and a Thought
Back home, I made tea and thought about what I'd witnessed.
It was policing at its simplest:

- sensible
- measured
- human
- and completely devoid of the usual red tape

And best of all?
It worked.
Reports of anti-social behaviour at the stations stopped entirely after that night.
Not bad for a couple of officers, a van, a bag of canisters, and one extremely nervous OBSERVER with reflective lettering bright enough to be seen from space.
Well done, Toby & Graham - practical policing at its finest.

Decisions before dawn - leading through the Covid years

I'm not going to pretend otherwise: for me, as for most people, the Covid years were hard.

Hard personally.
Hard professionally.
Hard for my role as Chairman of EHDC.
Hard for my sanity.
Hard for my Amazon driver, who had to deliver more hand gel than any human being truly needs.

When Boris Johnson appeared on TV on the evening of 23 March 2020 and ordered the nation to stay at home, my first thought was identical to everyone else's:
"Right... and how exactly are we supposed to do *that*?"

Personal Fears and the Cult of Anti-Bac
For me, it wasn't just worrying, it was *properly* frightening. People younger and fitter than I were ending up in hospital, and my immune system was still behaving like a Victorian maiden who fainted at the sight of a strong breeze.
A cold could wipe me out for two weeks. Covid? I didn't even want to imagine.
So, I did what millions of people did:
- I bought enough masks to outfit a small amateur dramatics troupe.
- I switched to Tesco deliveries.
- I accumulated enough anti-bac wipes to *polish the entire village of Liss Forest*.

Did any of these products *definitely* kill Covid?
Nobody seemed entirely sure, including, I suspect, some of the manufacturers.
But they made me feel in control, and honestly, that was half the battle.

From 90% Full to 100% Empty
Then came the business shock.
My entire livelihood was built on being physically with clients three or four days a week. Workshops. Training days.

Interactive sessions. Whiteboards. Flip charts. You know, *people*.

Almost overnight, all of it disappeared.
Meetings were cancelled. Training postponed "until further notice" (a polite euphemism for "we have no idea when, if ever, life will restart"). Staff were furloughed. Everything stopped.
My diary went from a healthy 90% full to a heroic 100% empty in about 36 hours.
There was Government support for employees. Then support for the self-employed.
And then, for small limited company directors like me, there was absolutely nothing.
It was like an elaborate game of "Guess Who?" where everyone got rescued... except the people running tiny companies on their own.
Eventually the Bounce Back Loan appeared.
I applied, being honest, *too* honest, as it turned out.
The rules said I could claim up to three months of turnover. I sat down, looked carefully at the numbers, removed all the travel, hotel bills, and client-site lunches, and decided we only really needed **£8,000**.
The next day it appeared in our account.
Only later did I discover that many businesses of our size had quietly taken **£80,000**.
Morally, I still feel I did the right thing. But financially... well, let's just say my halo occasionally strangles me.

Reinventing the Business Overnight
If we were going to survive, we had to adapt. Rapidly.
We'd used PowWowNow before, expensive, temperamental, and with sound quality last seen on pirate radio in the 1970s.
Zoom, for me, was still something you did with a camera lens before taking a photo.
Then we tried it.

It wasn't flawless, but it worked.
We could deliver training.
We could meet clients.
We were *back in business*.
Covid taught me that the *perfect* business plan is a myth.
To anyone who still insists you must write one, take it to the bank, and frame it on the wall, I simply ask:
"Show me the person who had 'global pandemic shuts down all human contact' in their 2019 forecast."
Exactly.

Clubhouse: The Rise, The Fall, The £9.99 Gurus
Then came Clubhouse. The right app at the right moment.
I ended up running two weekly rooms:
- "GDPR: Ask Me Anything (But Preferably Not About Cookies)"
- "Rebuild the High Street"

Some sessions had over 100 people, including Theo Paphitis and senior politicians. It was like an unexpectedly lively conference in your pocket.

But when restrictions eased, Clubhouse emptied faster than a pub at last orders.

These days it's mostly people promising that, for just £9.99 a month, they can turn you into a millionaire.
I wish them happiness and keep my debit card firmly in another room.

Salvation Army on Zoom (a.k.a. The Choir of Chaos)
My friend Felix's wife Mary runs a Salvation Army group. When in-person services stopped, Felix filmed her giving short sermons. Lovely, but a bit... quiet.
Then I showed him Zoom.
They moved services online. Suddenly they had a congregation again, albeit one struggling with the audio equivalent of a car crash.

Group singing on Zoom is a special kind of chaos:
Everyone is slightly out of sync.
Everyone hears themselves perfectly.
Nobody hears anyone else properly.
The result?
Something resembling a choir rehearsing underwater.
But the togetherness mattered more than the tuning.

Councils Without Corridors
EHDC went from 250 staff in the office to around 245 working from home in under a fortnight.
A change we'd previously have said required a five-year plan, three feasibility studies, and possibly an exorcism.
Liss Parish Council went from *one* laptop to multiple, practically overnight.
To everyone's surprise, productivity didn't collapse. After a brief wobble, some teams actually became *more* productive.

EHDC used Microsoft Teams; Liss used Zoom.
I preferred Zoom. Teams always felt slightly like trying to drive a forklift with oven gloves on.

Democracy Goes Digital
Council meetings moved online.
Liss was manageable.
EHDC with 43 councillors? Less so.
We trained everyone to use the "raise hand" button. Some mastered it. Others raised their actual hands at the screen, which, as you can imagine, was less effective.
We set up a private WhatsApp group (myself, Richard, Julie, Gill, and David) to coordinate behind the scenes. It worked surprisingly well.
Voting, however, became a marathon.
Every decision needed a recorded vote.
Meaning:
- 44 councillors
- individually called.
- for every agenda item

I aged three years during every meeting.
Still, transparency increased. Engagement improved. And hybrid working has stayed.

Decisions Before Dawn
I was also a member of the Portsmouth NHS Clinical Commissioning Group. While normally just clinicians and a councillor from each local District/Borough/City council, for the duration of the Covid crisis, a police Superintendent was co-opted in too so that they were kept 'in the loop'.

We met **every day, 7 days a week, at 6:45am**.
It was... brutal.
Some decisions were desperately hard. Harder still without hindsight.
One meeting I'll never forget:
A hospital mortuary had run out of space.
We had to approve refrigerated shipping containers.
Decide where to place them.
And whether to tell the public.
We found a discreet location within the hospital grounds, screened off.
We decided not to publicise it.
The public mood was already on the floor.
That was the moment the scale of the crisis truly hit me.

When Old Battles Return
During the Covid years, my Non-Hodgkin's Lymphoma returned.
A small relapse, treatable, but unwelcome.
Did stress contribute?
Possibly.
Covid wasn't exactly a spa holiday.
But with treatment, I got through it.

What Covid Really Taught Me
Covid tested all of us:
- personally
- professionally
- emotionally
- and occasionally musically (see: Zoom choirs)

It revealed cracks in systems.
It revealed strengths in people.
It forced us to adapt in ways we didn't know we could.
If it taught me anything, it's this:

Resilience isn't about predicting the crisis.
It's about responding to it with imagination, speed, humour, and heart.

The night we became a Kingdom again

Of all the duties I carried out as Chairman of the Council, the one that touched me the most, and the one that felt heaviest on my shoulders, was guiding our community through the mourning period for Her Majesty Queen Elizabeth II.

If the jubilee celebrations had been moments of unfiltered joy, full of bunting, brass bands and people pretending Pimm's is a proper drink, this was something altogether different.

A strange, quiet mixture of sadness, disbelief, and reflection.

For almost all of us of my generation and younger, she had been the only monarch we had ever known. The constant in the background. The nation's screensaver. Like the family heirloom on the mantelpiece that's been there so long you don't even notice it, until suddenly, it's gone, and the room feels oddly unbalanced.
Prince Philip's passing had been deeply sad too. But this felt different.
This was the passing of an era.

We'd seen the news that the Queen was unwell, but none of us realised how serious it was. After all, she had been the living embodiment of "Keep Calm and Carry On" for seventy years.

Then, on 8th September 2022 at around 6:20pm, my phone buzzed. A message from the Lord-Lieutenant's office:
Sensitive - Embargoed until 18:30hrs
Her Majesty Queen Elizabeth II sadly passed away at Balmoral earlier today.
King Charles III has now assumed the monarchy.
God save the King.
The nation will be informed at 6:30pm. Further instructions to follow.

I gulped. The world seemed to slow.
I switched on BBC One. At 6:30pm, exactly to the second, the announcement came.
And like everyone else in the country that evening, I know exactly where I was, what I was doing, and the feeling in the pit of my stomach.

The Proclamation
Later that evening, my phone buzzed again. I had one eye on BBC News, one eye on Sky, and the sense that history was unfolding in real time.
Please check your email.
Attached is the text of the Royal Proclamation.
This must be read publicly on 10th September 2022 after 10:00 AM.
Please use the exact wording with no additions or omissions.
God save the King.

This wasn't something to take lightly.
There are moments in public life where ceremony actually *matters*, not the fussy kind done for tradition's sake, but the kind that roots us, binds us, reminds us that we're part of a bigger story.

This was one of those moments.
I contacted Sarah, our Parish Clerk, and several councillors, and we agreed:
the proclamation should be read beside the War Memorial, just before dusk.
Enough daylight to see each other's faces.
Enough dusk for the solemnity to settle in.

Clayre arranged a PA system, sparing the village the sight of me bellowing like a market trader, and Liss Band confirmed that enough musicians could attend to create the right atmosphere. Then I did something truly alien to my nature:
I practised.
For hours.
Word-perfect.
No improvising. No jokes. No "I'll just wing it" Keith-isms.
Just me, a script, and the heavy weight of history.

A Community Gathers
The evening came.
And the turnout was... extraordinary.
The pavements around the memorial green overflowed. People arrived from Liss, Petersfield, Greatham, Rake, some walking, some driving, but all drawn by the same quiet impulse to be present.

Families stood close, children trying to understand, grandparents remembering the coronation, and many just standing silently, hands in pockets, absorbing the moment.

I stepped up to the microphone.
I read the Proclamation.
Liss Band played the National Anthem.
And for the first time in my life, I led a community in singing:
"God Save Our Gracious King."

My brain had to wrestle my tongue into cooperation.
Queen wanted to escape every time.
Muscle memory is a stubborn thing.
But it was real.
It had changed.
History had turned a page.

And somehow, in our small corner of Hampshire, I'd been given the responsibility, and the honour, of helping mark the moment our nation said farewell to one reign and welcomed another.

A privilege I will never forget.

Bitten by the writing bug

One unexpected blessing to come out of Covid, tucked somewhere between the banana-bread craze and the national obsession with Joe Wicks, was my first published bestseller: *GDPR Made Simple*.
(Subtle plug, as requested: **the brand-new 2025 Edition is now available on Amazon**. Go on. Treat yourself.)

It may surprise absolutely no one that it was Michelle who finally pushed me to write it.

In those early, eerily quiet weeks of lockdown, when the world felt like it had collectively pressed "pause," we were sitting at home, still figuring out how to rebuild the business online, when Michelle looked at me and said:
"You know, for years you've been bleating on about the need for a simple, low-cost GDPR guide everyone can understand. You kept saying you were going to write it but never had the time. Well... you've got time now, haven't you?"

I had a fleeting, mildly suicidal thought like:
I knew from day one you were Miss Right; I just didn't realise your first name was Always.
But, miraculously, for once in my life, I swallowed it and instead said:
"Good point. I suppose I'd better start."

I remembered something my old business mentor, Shaa Wasmund, and her partner Matt Thomas, had told me years before:
"A book is the best business card you'll ever have."

They also insisted that writing a book could be joyful, not a chore, a claim I mentally filed alongside "absolutely no side effects" and "delivery guaranteed before 10am".

But Shaa and my more recent mentor, Brad Burton, had built whole portions of their careers on the back of their books, so I thought:
In for a penny, in for a pound, sat down, and started typing.
Covers, Quotes and KDP Confusion
When the manuscript was finally done, I wanted something eye-catching for the cover. Something that said:

"GDPR doesn't have to be boring... but also please take me seriously."

So, I rang Brad.

"Brad, I've written my first book. Can I put a quote from you on the front cover?"

"Yes, sure, mate. Give me a day or two."

And he did. Bless him. It was perfect, just the right mix of endorsement and mischief.

I decided to self-publish through Amazon KDP, the same platform this book will use. Some parts were easy. Some parts were... let's call them "character-building". But I muddled through, muttering only mild profanity.

A Launch with Prosecco and Panache

I also decided to host a launch event.

Naturally, I asked the local bookshop first.

Naturally, they declined.

(The joys of being an Amazon-published author. I think they'd rather host a séance.)

So, I thought laterally.

Signal, my business networking group, had just opened a prosecco bar and arts space at The Shed in Bordon. I asked if they'd open specially for a launch evening.

They agreed.

Everyone got a free glass of prosecco on me.

Anymore and they had to pay for it themselves.

(I love my readers, but not *that* much).

I sent out press releases. The Herald sent a journalist.

I felt it needed a bit of showbiz, so my VA suggested a balloon arch, and frankly, what screams "serious GDPR literature" more than an enormous balloon arch? She knew someone who could make one without bankrupting me.

The night went brilliantly.

My friend and fellow Signal member, Stu Morrison, he of the Liberace-meets-PE-kit suit collection, interviewed me on stage. We recorded it for The GDPR Weekly Show podcast (yes, that gets its own chapter).

By the end, I felt, dare I say it, like an *author*.

And then... The Writing Bug

Were Matt and Shaa right about the "writing bug"?

Well, considering you're now reading a *second* book from me... I think we know the answer.

In fact, I already have **four more** in the pipeline:
- A book about podcasting
- A book about the therapeutic magic of writing
- A book on business networking
- And my first novel - a crime thriller with the working title
  The Chain Gang Massacre
  (A title which, I admit, has caused certain members of the Chain Gang to give me nervous side-eye.)

My goal is to have them all published by the end of 2026.

So yes, Shaa, be proud.

I have been well and truly bitten by the writing bug.

And unlike Covid, it's one bug I plan to keep.

If only I'd known

In the first year or so after Enma passed away, I saw Michelle quite regularly. We supported each other as best we could, cups of tea, long chats, shared grief, and the sort of practical help that doesn't need words.

But as time went on, our lives naturally drifted in different directions.

I was busy with the business and parish council work.

She was navigating life with Carl and raising her young family.

After a couple of years, our contact had settled into the occasional text, usually something practical, like if she needed advice or if I needed a lift to the hospital, or a lift somewhere for business, plus the annual exchange of Christmas cards, birthday cards, and the obligatory chocolate eggs for the children at Easter. A gentle, quiet cadence.

And then, one afternoon in 2018, there was a knock at my door. I opened it to find Michelle standing there, slightly windswept, with a toddler clutching her leg, Lucy, just discovering the joys of walking, and a baby boy in her arms, Davy.

For a few seconds I had that momentary mental scramble you get when you bump into someone from school in Tesco and can't remember whether they're called Gary, Barry, Larry or Sarah.
Children? Hers? Carl's?
No. She and Carl had separated.
She was now living with someone new, T, at his place in Surrey. The children were instantly charming, full of curiosity, chatter, and the limitless energy I vaguely remembered having myself before the NHS file labelled *Medical History: Keith* began requiring its own shelf.

We sat and talked for ages, filling in the years like pages we'd skimmed. It felt warm. Natural. Easy.

After that, they popped round every few weeks.
A little family rhythm began forming again, soft, and familiar. I started buying the children small toys, nothing extravagant, mostly Poundland treasures: plastic dinosaurs, glittery

notebooks, things that make noise at a frequency only children appreciate, and adults endure.

Lucy and Davy loved them.
T came sometimes too.
He seemed polite, helpful, even kindly.

He did odd DIY jobs around the house for me, the sort of small-but-annoying tasks that lurk on a to-do list for six months until someone with a functioning knee sorts them out in ten minutes.

On the surface, it all looked positive.
Hopeful, even.
A new chapter opening quietly, page by page.

If only I'd known then what the next three or four years were going to hold.
Because that knock on the door...
was the beginning of the most turbulent chapter of my life.

Up a tree and out of reach

In the introduction to my family, I mentioned that my stepdaughter Michelle has five children, my grandchildren. And when I look at Michelle and two of her girls, Shona, and Lucy, I can see bits of Enma in all of them.

Mostly the ability to *command attention* with the confidence of someone who believes they were born under a spotlight.

Michelle is voluptuous, bright, funny, and absolutely aware she is all three. She's the sort of person who can walk into a room and have five people laughing before she's even taken her coat off. If charisma were currency, she'd be on The Sunday Times Rich List.

Shona inherited the same gift, with interest.
When she was small and Enma or I turned up, she'd say hello politely and then vanish upstairs. Five minutes later she would sweep back in wearing a princess dress, half a pot of Michelle's eyeshadow, and the facial expression of a child who knew she had achieved peak fabulousness.
We'd gush appropriately. She'd twirl. Peace would be restored. As she got older, the desire for attention stayed, she just upgraded the equipment.

One Christmas, I went to Michelle's house in Surrey. Lucy was at full toddler turbulence, Davy was just discovering walking, and the older three were upstairs.
Michelle called them down for Christmas dinner.
Hugh came first, tall, polite, very teenage.
Then Bethany, in a beautiful dress, fresh-faced and pretty as a snowflake on a postcard.
"Shona!" Michelle called again.
Eventually Shona appeared... wearing a black T-shirt.
Just a T-shirt.
A T-shirt that was *doing its best*, but gravity and adolescence were winning.
She crossed the room, spotted something on the floor, bent over from the waist, and removed all remaining mystery about what was, and was not, under the T-shirt.
She straightened up, beamed at me sweetly, and gave me a hug.
She *knew* exactly what she was doing, and she was *living for it*.

I retreated to the kitchen.

"Have you seen what Shona's wearing?" I asked Michelle.
"Yes," she sighed, "but if I say anything, she'll throw a strop and take the T-shirt off and sit there naked."
"She might as well," I muttered.
"Be nice," Michelle said. "It's Christmas."

After dinner, when she realised her outfit hadn't produced the level of chaos she'd hoped for, she vanished upstairs and reappeared in a bra top and jeans, grabbed her coat and declared:
"I'm going out. My friend's having a shit day".
And with that, she was gone, dramatic entrance, dramatic exit. Job done.

Lucy: The Adrenaline Junkie
Lucy, meanwhile, is cut from similar cloth, but with her own twist.
She loves the attention, but with fearless, autistic enthusiasm.
She doesn't *seek* drama.
She *creates* it naturally.

One day Michelle asked if I could have Lucy and Davy for a few hours. Lovely kids, lovely day. The garden had a couple of trees, one about thirty feet high.

When Michelle came to collect them, Davy ran in first.
"You okay, little man? Where's Lucy?" I said.
"She's up the tree," he said.
"What do you mean, up the tree?"
"Come and see!"
We stepped outside.
Lucy wasn't just "up the tree."
She was practically in orbit.

"Mummy! Grandad! I can see a long way from up here!"
"I expect you can," I said, trying to sound calming and not like someone silently calculating his home insurance excess. "Now... come back down."
"I can't!"
Great. Perfect. Exactly what my nerves needed.
Michelle tried in full Mum Voice.
Lucy remained unmoved.
There was no way I could climb after her, and no ladder on Earth would get me up there in my condition.
"There's only one thing for it," I said.
"We're calling the Fire Brigade."

I rang 999.

A fire engine arrived moments later, lights, helmets, the whole works. Lucy spotted it before we did.
"THE FIRE ENGINE'S HERE!" she yelled, delighted.
A firefighter in a white helmet took one look and fetched a long ladder. Remember, this was mid-Covid, masks, distancing, the lot.
He climbed up.
"Don't be scared, Lucy," he called. "I'm coming to get you."
"I'm not scared," she said. "But how do you know my name is Lucy?"
"Your grandad told me."
"Grandad!? Did you tell him my name is Lucy?"
"Yes," I said. "Now listen to the nice fireman."
He reached her and said, "Okay, Lucy. Just move one foot towards me and..."
"No."
"No?"
"No. Mummy says we must stay two metres away from strangers."
For a moment, the firefighter froze. You could almost see him thinking:
Of all the times for a child to obey a rule...

Michelle called, "It's okay, Lucy. He's got a mask, and you can trust him!"
"I'm not sure," she replied.
And then came the firefighter's stroke of genius.
"Lucy," he said, "if you come onto the ladder so I can get you down... you can sit in our fire engine. And you can press the button for the lights and the sirens."

Her eyes widened.
"Pinky promise?"
"Pinky promise."

"She's a right one," the firefighter at the bottom whispered to me.
"You don't know the half of it," I said.
Lucy edged onto the ladder, he lifted her, and down they came. Her feet hit the grass and immediately:
"Where is the fire engine? You promised!"

Davy piped up:
"Can I have a go too?"

No human could resist that face.

Both children ended up in the cab, lights flashing, sirens blaring, every setting they had.

If the neighbours hadn't noticed a fire engine outside before, they definitely had now.

"Grandad," Lucy said solemnly as she got out,
"I think I want to be a fireman."
"We'll see," I said.

The crew packed up and drove away.
Peace, and my blood pressure, slowly returned to normal.

"Tea?" Michelle asked.
"Definitely tea," I replied.

Staying on the line

This chapter probably needs a gentle warning: it talks about mental distress and suicide.

If that's something you'd rather not read, please feel completely free to skip ahead.

Life is heavy enough without picking up extra weight you don't need.

Michelle had been confiding in me for months that she thought T, her partner, and the father of Lucy and Davy, was having an affair.

He'd become cold.
Withdrawn.
Intimate only on his terms.

I tried to reassure Michelle as best I could. I told her T was probably just stressed, that work could easily explain his behaviour, that she could talk to me any time. And I meant it.

I told her, too, that if I ever sensed anything off in my conversations with T, I would tell her.

Then one Sunday evening, my phone rang.
"Hi Michelle," I said. "Everything okay?"
"No," she said. "T has confessed. I was right. He's been having an affair with some ugly bitch."
My heart sank.
"Oh, love... I'm so sorry."
There was a pause, a long one, and then, through sobs, she said:
"Daddy... you will look after the babies for me, won't you?"
I assumed she meant temporarily. A night. A weekend. Something practical.
"What do you mean?" I asked gently. "When?"
"Forever," she said. "I've taken tablets."
My stomach fell through the floor.
"How many tablets, Michelle?"
"All of them," she said. "Every tablet I could find. I'm feeling sleepy now."
No parent should ever hear those words.
No human being should ever have to.

"Michelle, listen to me," I said. "Do NOT go to sleep."
"Is T with you?" I asked.
"Yes," she said. "He's standing at the bedroom door, looking at me and listening."
"And the children?"
"They're standing with him. Daddy... he let them watch me take the tablets."

There are moments in life that sear themselves so deeply into your mind that they never fade.
That sentence is one of mine.
I'm not a violent man. Not by nature, not by inclination.
But in that moment, I could have taken T's head clean off his shoulders.

How could he stand there?
How could he *not* intervene?
How could he let his children, their children, watch something like that?

I will never understand it. Not fully. Not even partially.
But that was not the moment for questions or outrage.
That was the moment for action.

I dialled 999.
So, there I was, trying to keep my daughter awake on the landline while calling an ambulance on my mobile, something no doctor in the world would recommend for someone told to "reduce stress."

I told Michelle I'd stay with her on the phone until the paramedics arrived.
She talked. I talked.
I can't remember what about, only that every second mattered.
After what felt like hours but was probably minutes, she said:
"There's someone knocking at the door."
"That'll be the ambulance," I said.
"Lucy's gone to let them in."
In the background, I heard a man's voice. Calm, authoritative.
"Is that the paramedic?" I asked.
"Yes."
"Okay, Michelle. Do exactly what he asks. I'm going to hang up now so you can focus on him."

I paused.

"I love you. Everything is going to be okay. Just listen to the paramedic."

"Love you, Daddy," she said.

I ended the call.

And then I sat there, phone still in my hand, praying, really praying, that it wouldn't be the last time I ever heard her voice.

The long road back

Fortunately, mercifully, Michelle survived the overdose.

A day or two later, I received a call from Farnham Road Hospital in Guildford. She had been admitted for psychiatric support. Voluntarily, not under section, though they anticipated she would need several weeks of treatment.

My first question was about the children.
"They're with T," the nurse said gently.
It wasn't the reassurance she hoped it would be.
Given what had happened that Sunday evening, hearing that he was currently responsible for two traumatised children felt... challenging. But in that moment, there was nothing more I could do.

Children's Services inevitably became involved. The case was complicated by the simple fact that the children attended school in Hampshire but were now living, at least temporarily, in Surrey. Social workers visited Michelle in hospital, visited T at home, and visited me.
I filled in the gaps, the parts they didn't know, the parts no one else had witnessed.
It quickly became obvious to everyone that Michelle and T could not continue living together. A social housing property in Alton was found for her, and an informal plan formed: once Michelle was stable enough to return home, the children would go back into her care, with T having agreed access. Children's Services would monitor but not intervene unless anything deteriorated.

Six weeks passed.

Then came the phone call, breathless, shaking with excitement. "They're discharging me," Michelle said. "T is supposed to bring the kids to your house at five so I can pick them up without seeing him."

Carl, her ex, but thankfully still a good friend, had offered to collect her from the hospital and drive her home in her own car. They arrived at my house around 5:30 p.m.
Michelle practically flew through the door, hugged me, and immediately said:
"Where are the children?"

"They're not here yet," I said.
Her whole face changed.
"Call him. He's blocked my number."
I rang him.

He told me he'd taken the children back to his house, was feeding them, and would "bring them down later."
Michelle's response was instant and volcanic.
"We're going to get them."
Carl, sensibly, offered to drive. Michelle declined.
"No. You stay here. Dad's coming with me."

On the way, I asked, "What are you going to do if he refuses to open the door?"
"Call the police," she said. "I'm not letting him kidnap my children."

I didn't bother pointing out the legal nuance that they were his children too. Michelle was in full Enma Mode, and when she reached that level, even logic knew better than to interrupt.

About a mile from T's house, Michelle suddenly spotted his car coming towards us. She flashed her headlights. He saw us and accelerated. Michelle performed a three-point turn that would have impressed a stunt driver and we set off after him.

I reminded her, perhaps unnecessarily, not to drive too fast, considering he had the children in the back.

By the time we reached the A3 slip road, he had vanished.
I dialled 999.

A horrible part of me braced for what we might find around the next bend.

I gave the police his registration and vehicle description. They issued an alert and dispatched a patrol to check around my house.

Michelle and I drove home. Nothing.
I walked to the top of the hill in case he was watching. Still nothing.

By the time I got back, the police had called. They'd located his car. He told them he "felt intimidated" by me and would only come to my house if Michelle was outside on her own.

Why he felt intimidated, I'll never know. Guilt? Fear? Projection? He'd not spoken to me since the overdose. It made no sense.
But the priority wasn't understanding him. It was getting the children back safely.

So, we agreed.

Michelle went outside. The police confirmed she was alone. A few minutes later, T arrived. He handed over the children, who ran straight into Michelle's arms. He placed a couple of bags of clothes in her boot.
And then he was gone.

Carl offered to drive Michelle and the children home. I agreed without hesitation.

For the next few weeks, the arrangement was simple: T would have the children every other Saturday, with handovers done at my house to avoid direct contact between them.

It worked, until it didn't.
One Saturday he simply didn't arrive.
Lucy stood at the end of my driveway calling, "Daddy? Daddy? Where are you?"
It broke me.

We waited an hour. Nothing.
I called. No answer.
Michelle came to collect them. It was a horrible, hollow afternoon.

Meanwhile, Lucy's behaviour at school deteriorated sharply: escape attempts, disruption, emotional outbursts. Some of it was her autism. Some of it, unmistakably, was trauma.

Attempts were made to repair the arrangement, but eventually Children's Services made the decision everyone had been trying to avoid:
The children would need to go into foster care.
Michelle was devastated. T applied for sole custody, making everything harder.

We needed a solicitor, and because of the seriousness, a barrister too. Michelle wasn't working.

So, Bank of Dad had to open, as it has so many times in so many chapters.

The day before the hearing, Michelle made a brave, heartbreaking decision. She would not oppose the children entering foster care.
But we *would* fight T's custody claim.

Children's Services won. A bittersweet victory if ever there was one.

It was early November. The agreement was that the children could stay with Michelle until early January to keep Christmas stable, and then they would move to their foster family.

I still remember taking Lucy and Davy to a big firework display with Michelle. It was magical, the sort of evening childhood is supposed to contain in abundance.

They dropped me home afterwards. I hugged them all tightly.
I closed the door, sat down with my back against it, and howled.

How had life twisted itself into something so unfair?
How could this be happening to two children who deserved nothing but love and stability?
But tears, however cathartic, don't solve anything.
We focused on giving them a wonderful Christmas.
And we did.

Three years on, the children remain in foster care, and they are happy.
We are on the long, slow road toward reunification.
Will it be 2026? Probably not.
2027? Hopefully.

We see them regularly.
Handing them back still hurts but not like before.
It helps enormously knowing they are safe, cared for, and thriving.

They still love their Mummy.
They still love their Grandad.
And me?
I love them unconditionally.
Always.

Losing the seat, keeping the soul

Sometimes, as a local councillor, especially at District, Borough, County or Unitary level, it really doesn't matter how competent, diligent, or charming you are.

National politics rolls in like a tide, and however hard you paddle, you're still in it.

So, it proved in the 2023 local elections.

On the doorstep, I lost count of how many people said some variation of:
"Keith, we really appreciate everything you've done for the village. Honestly, you've been brilliant. But there is absolutely no way I can vote Conservative. The Government have simply cocked too many things up."

There are moments when you smile politely while your soul packs a suitcase and heads for the airport. This was one of them. Still, we campaigned hard. I visited as many homes in Liss and Liss Forest as my legs, and my rollator, permitted. Conservative colleagues came into the village for a couple of intensive canvassing sessions, which I appreciated greatly. If nothing else, it meant the residents realised it wasn't just me they were avoiding at the sound of a doorbell.
Looking back, there were two additional headwinds.
One was local and partly our own doing.
The other came out of nowhere like a custard pie.

The Two-Seat Problem
Liss is a two-member ward. My fellow councillor, Russell, had already told us he was standing down to focus on his Hampshire County Council work, entirely reasonable.
We found a local candidate willing to stand alongside me. Perfect.
Then, just as we were about to submit nomination papers and send everything to print, she withdrew.
We tried desperately to find another local candidate, but Liss is not exactly overflowing with Conservatives eager to leap into electoral combat. Eventually, we found a member in Froxfield willing to stand.

Legally: fine.
Politically: about as helpful as bringing a baguette to a sword fight.

Two obvious problems:
1. Nobody in Liss had the faintest idea who he was.
2. He was unwell and couldn't campaign.

With hindsight, that smug, sanctimonious word, it would probably have been wiser to run just one candidate: me.
But no. We ran two.
And we paid the price.

"Tory Dirty Tricks" and the Front Page That Launched a Thousand Swear Words

Then came the second problem, one entirely out of our control. One of our candidates in Horndean produced a leaflet criticising a Green councillor's attendance record. Perfectly fair comment, attendance is literally part of the job.

The local newspaper, the *Petersfield Post*, took a different view. On election day, *election day,* they ran a front-page headline: **"TORY DIRTY TRICKS"**
I stared at it in disbelief.
You couldn't make it up, and if you did, people would accuse you of exaggerating.
I wasn't furious about scrutiny, that's part of public life.
I was furious about the timing.
But the papers were printed, the headline was out, and the damage was done.

Reading Faces at the Polling Station

I spent most of polling day as a teller outside Liss polling station. Tellers don't campaign; we just record voter numbers. You're essentially a slightly decorative traffic cone wearing a rosette.
After doing this for several elections, I've learned to read faces. Some people emerge looking guilty, which usually means they voted for someone else.
Some throw a wink at another party's teller, which rather ruins the mystery.
Some look at you with the expression of a person hoping you won't take it personally.
Around 9:15 p.m., the flow dwindled.
East Hampshire wasn't counting votes until the next morning anyway, so I went home, put Sky News on, and watched

Conservative results collapse around the country like a poorly assembled gazebo in a gale.
I dared to hope I might squeak through. The big unknown was the postal vote. Historically, Conservatives did well there. We'd soon find out.

The Taro Centre Truth Bomb
The count started at 9 a.m.
But with the alphabet against me, "Alton" always hogs the initial action, there was no reason to arrive at dawn.
I walked into the Taro Centre around 11 a.m. and immediately saw Richard and Julie.

Their faces told the story before their voices did.
"**Fuck it, mate**," Richard said quietly.
"We're losing big time. I'm not even sure we'll have a majority by the end of today."

Alton confirmed it.
Apart from Holybourne, which Graham held only by the grace of God and a favourable breeze, we lost every Alton seat. Rural wards looked better, but even their majorities were down sharply.
Then came Liss.
Because every voter has two votes, counting takes longer.
As the piles formed, it was obvious Roger, the Liberal Democrat candidate, had secured one seat.
The second seat was incredibly close:
Me vs Ian, the Green Party candidate.
When the totals were announced, Ian had edged it.
Just like that, I was no longer a District Councillor.
Another chapter closed.

I congratulated Roger and Ian sincerely. Bitterness is pointless; the electorate had taken a free swing at the governing party, and we just happened to be standing in front of it.

That's democracy.
Sometimes you swing.
Sometimes you get walloped.
You dust yourself off and look toward 2027.

Kingmakers in Whitehill & Bordon
My drama was over. The council's wasn't.
The Whitehill & Bordon Community Party won every seat they contested. That gave them the balance of power.

The Conservatives remained the largest group but no longer had a majority.
They could try a minority administration, but that's basically governing with a constant nosebleed.
If the Whitehill & Bordon group aligned with the Conservatives, there'd be a healthy majority.
If they aligned with the Lib Dems, there'd still be a majority, slimmer, but workable.
That weekend my phone rang.
It was Andy, their leader.
He explained his dilemma and asked for my advice.
He very flatteringly referred to me as a local "wise sage," which I took to mean "the only ex-councillor who actually returns phone calls."
He asked:
"Should I go with the Conservatives? Or sign up with the Lib Dems?"
I told him I had to tread carefully. My bias was obvious.
But he didn't want bias, he wanted honesty.
So, I gave it.
"If I were you," I said, "I wouldn't sign a formal coalition with either side. I'd go for a confidence-and-supply agreement. You support the Conservatives on key votes so the council can function but keep independence on everything else."
My reasoning was simple:
If the majority party does something catastrophically unpopular, or ends up in a scandal, you get splattered with the same paintbrush, even if you personally did nothing wrong.
He thanked me and expressed genuine sympathy that I'd lost my seat.
I told him the truth: I wasn't thrilled, but I'm a democrat. You can't only like democracy when you're winning.
After our call, I updated Richard.
He was a little disappointed I hadn't pushed harder for a full coalition.
I explained: Andy asked for honesty. I gave it. Integrity outranks party tactics.
If you sacrifice your integrity just to cling onto influence, you may keep the seat...
but you lose something far more important.

Tip: Give honest advice, even when it's not in your short-term interest. Credibility outlasts any term of office.

A silver lining called Charlene

I wrote earlier about losing my EHDC councillor seat in the 2023 local elections. At the time, it felt like a personal blow, the end of something I had poured years of energy, evenings, weekends, shoe leather and caffeine into.

But as is often the case in life, every cloud really does have a silver lining.

Mine arrived wearing a Conservative rosette and an expression that suggested she would happily tackle a cabinet minister bare-handed if she thought they were wrong.

Her name was Charlene.
She'd just been elected as a brand-new councillor, determined, outspoken, funny, and fiercely protective of the people she cared about. During the long, slow, emotional purgatory that is waiting for an election count to finish, we got chatting.
And within minutes, we discovered something extraordinary.
Her son and I both have Marfan syndrome.
Until that moment, neither of us had ever met someone who *really* understood it from the inside. The rarity of Marfan's means most people never encounter it at all, let alone live with it or parent someone who does. People can care about you deeply, Michelle, my family, my friends, and they do. But they can't quite grasp that quiet, constant hum of fear.

That knowledge that at any moment, completely without warning, a major blood vessel could tear or rupture.

It's not drama. It's not imagination. It's not pessimism. It's simply the reality we live with.

And then suddenly, there was someone standing in front of me who *got it*. 100%. No explaining, no softening the edges, no "well I'm sure it'll be fine," just instant, mutual understanding.

From that day on, we became each other's unofficial Marfan helpline.

The one person each of us could ring when a new symptom flared up, or when a hospital letter arrived with wording that made our stomach drop. We talk frankly about things most people would find dark or worrying, and we laugh, because sometimes the only alternative is panic.

She checks on me.
I check on her.
We get it.

In losing my council seat, I thought I was walking away empty-handed.
But life has a funny way of rearranging your priorities.
2023 may have taken the title off my lapel...
but it gave me Charlene.
And on balance, I think I absolutely won that one.

General Election 2024

Rishi Sunak had much to learn about politics. One of the key lessons, and you'd think this would be obvious, is that if you're planning to call a snap General Election, it helps if your own party knows it's coming.
Sadly, nobody gave him that memo.
So, when he stepped out onto Downing Street on that grey, rain-lashed afternoon and announced a July election, he caught most of the country off guard... including several million Conservatives. He stood there, soaked to the skin, defiantly talking about stability whilst looking like a man who had taken a wrong turn on his way to a lifeboat.
The image of the Prime Minister, drenched, forlorn, blinking through sheets of rain, it will stay with me forever. He looked so much like a drowned rat that it was only surprising the tabloids didn't immediately nickname him *Roland*.

From the outset, we all knew the 2024 General Election was going to be brutal. The Conservatives were around twenty points behind in the polls. The national mood was sour. The public had sharpened its knives months earlier.

Victory? No.
Damage limitation? Yes.
That was the real game.

Still, here in East Hampshire, we were cautiously optimistic. Damian Hinds had built a reputation for solid constituency work and genuine community presence. If anyone could withstand the national storm, it was Damian.

The Pub With No Name... and No Free Evenings
A few days after the announcement, we held our first campaign meeting at The Pub with No Name in Priors Dean. It was an evening of hurried planning, strong coffee, nervous jokes, and several hundred "Right, who's doing what?" moments.
With canvassing and leafleting covered by the team, I took the job best suited to my mobility: logistics.
Specifically, organising public meetings for Damian across the constituency.
"How hard can it be?" I asked.
Famous. Last. Words.
What I assumed would be two days of emails turned into three full weeks of booking village halls, juggling availability,

wrangling last-minute cancellations, coordinating Damian's security requirements, and dealing with time changes that moved more often than Liz Truss's Chancellor.
At times, it felt less like political organising and more like herding caffeinated kittens.
And on top of that, I still had my formal role as Constituency Compliance Officer, making sure everything was within the rules, election spending, data handling, and all the thrilling paperwork the law requires. Not glamorous, but essential.

Of course, I did spend some time knocking on doors and delivering leaflets.

After the election I received a great testimonial from our Conservative Association President, Anthony. It read

I have always been a great admirer of the sterling way you battle through life with your infirmity delivering all those election leaflets . 99% of the population would not be up for that but you keep on pushing yourself for a worthwhile cause and that is incredibly commendable

Thank you Anthony, praise like that makes it all worthwhile.

Election Day: Rosettes, Rumours and Reality
Election Day dawned bright and early. I arrived at Liss Village Hall just before 7am for my shift as a Teller.
A quick myth-buster: giving your polling number to a Teller does *not* reveal how you voted. It simply stops your own party knocking on your door at 8:55pm asking if you've remembered to pop down. It's efficiency, not espionage.

I always think Tellers play a useful role. No campaigning, of course, but a warm smile and a "Good morning!" can genuinely sway a wobbling voter. Human contact matters in politics.
As always, my brother Roger travelled up from Portsmouth to join me. It made the day far more bearable, we swapped shifts, had proper conversations, and kept each other sane.
By 9pm, the last stragglers had passed through. I headed home briefly. Paul was due to pick me up at 9:15 to drive me to Damian's traditional election night supper.
At 9pm he called.
Minor accident. He was fine, thank goodness, but delayed.
"No rush," I told him. "We're not winning tonight anyway."

Exit Poll Shock
He arrived only a touch late and by 9:30 we were on our way. At Damian's, the mood was warm but tense. BBC One was already on, tea and wine in equal supply, and we even held a sweepstake on the final Conservative seat count. Predictions ranged from 80 to 150, which tells you everything about the expectations.
At 10pm the exit poll landed:
- **Labour:** 410
- **Conservative:** 131
- **Lib Dem:** 61
- **Reform:** 13

A curious cheer rippled round the room, not joy, but relief that it wasn't worse.
By the end, the Conservatives ended on **121 seats**.
Grim, but not apocalyptic.

The Count: Hope, Fear and Fluorescent Lighting
At 11:30pm, we headed to Petersfield Festival Hall. The Lib Dem team were buoyant, big smiles, big energy, big confidence. We did our best to match it, though inwardly most of us were preparing for the worst.
The count was close but never terrifyingly so.

As dawn crept in, the final numbers emerged:
Damian Hinds (Conservative) - *18,509*
Dominic Martin (Lib Dem) - *17,234*
Matthew Kellerman (Reform UK) - *6,476*
Lucy Sims (Labour) - *4,867*
Richard Knight (Green) - *2,404*
A narrow victory, a majority of just **2.5%**, down from **32.5%**. But a victory, nonetheless.

We were exhausted, relieved, slightly shell-shocked, and extremely grateful.

It wasn't triumph. It wasn't jubilation. It was survival.
But sometimes, after a long and bruising campaign, survival feels like victory enough.

Knocking, Smiling, and Sometimes Ducking

It's probably clear by now that campaigning has been a major part of my life for the past twenty years.

I've done the maths.
I have walked well over **500 miles** on the campaign trail.

If I'd had the foresight to make them sponsored walks, I could have funded a new wing at the QEII Hospital by now.

Health limits the mileage these days, but the lessons remain, vivid, funny, occasionally bruising, and always honest.
So, what has two decades of door-knocking taught me?

1. Smile. Be enthusiastic. Even if you're dying inside.
Let's be blunt: nobody *wants* a politician at their door.
We rank somewhere between "window salesman" and "Jehovah's Witnesses" on the list of visitors people pretend not to be home for. (Though even the Jehovah's Witnesses seem to have upgraded to mail-drops post-Covid).
But canvassing is really just marketing in sensible shoes.
If *you* don't sound enthusiastic about what you're offering, why should anyone else care?
Passion is contagious, but only if it's visible.

2. Beware the Liberal Democrat who smiles too widely
Some Lib Dem supporters absolutely **love** a doorstep debate. They know perfectly well they're never voting Conservative, but if they can keep me talking for thirty minutes, that's thirty minutes I'm not spending persuading someone who might swing.
Over time, you learn which doors to knock and which ones to bless from a respectful distance.

3. Data is your friend (and no, we still can't see how you vote)
Modern campaigning tools are remarkably sophisticated.
We know who *usually* votes and who doesn't.
We know if you registered for a postal vote.
But we **never** know *how* you vote.
That is, quite rightly, locked down tighter than Fort Knox.

In the old days, parties ignored non-voters: "If they didn't vote last time, they won't vote this time."
But then along came **Nigel Farage**.
Say what you like, and many do, but he has energised people who previously wouldn't have voted if you'd paid them. That is no small feat.
He also understands the media better than most MPs.
When Parliament is in recess, he holds weekly press conferences.
Why? Because Beth Rigby, Robert Peston and Chris Mason have nowhere else to be. With Westminster silent, they flock to him like moths to a UV lamp.
It still astonishes me that the major parties haven't learned from this.
If Reform can dominate the news with a microphone and a pint glass, surely the others can too?
But I digress.

4. Listen more than you speak
We have two ears and one mouth for a reason.
On the doorstep, and in business, people can instantly tell if you're listening or just reloading your next sentence.
Genuine support usually sounds thoughtful, curious, even hesitant.
People who fling open the door shouting, "Oh yes, absolutely voting for you!"
...are generally saying that to *everybody*.

Now for the fun bits: Campaign Trail Comedy

Aldershot: The Attack of the Stuffed Crocodile
I was helping with a by-election in Aldershot, strolling down a neat street with clipped hedges, when something suddenly *whacked me on the head*.
Then again.
I turned to see my campaign buddy doubled over, tears streaming.
Peering through the hedge, I found the culprit, a man wielding a three-foot stuffed crocodile, cheerfully bonking me with it.
"I take it you're not voting Conservative?" I said.
"Spot on," he grinned.
Fair enough.

Hill Brow: The Afternoon I Accidentally Gate-crashed a Garden Orgy
This one lives forever in my personal Hall of Fame.
It was a quiet Sunday. I walked up the gravel drive, heard voices in the back garden, and thought, "Ah, barbecue. Lovely family afternoon. I won't disturb them."
Then a woman called, "We're all through here! Come in!"
So, I did.
I opened the gate...
...and found around six people, all entirely naked.
In the middle, a woman astride a man turned her head, startled: "Oh! You're not who I thought you were!"
"No," I said brightly. "Just delivering a leaflet!"
I closed the gate and walked calmly back down the drive, holding in the sort of laughter that makes your ribs ache. I didn't dare look back.

A final request: Be kind.
If a campaign volunteer knocks on your door, of *any* party, please treat them kindly.
They're not paid.
They're not scheming.
They're not plotting a coup.
They're volunteers, giving up their time because they genuinely care about democracy.

Without them, our politics would be far poorer, far quieter, and far less entertaining.

Even on the days involving crocodiles and unexpected nudity.

Running on empty

I can't help but smile whenever I see people on social media complaining that some café or shop "won't accept cash anymore."
"Card only!" they moan, as if civilisation is on the brink.

I smile because it really wasn't that long ago that the *reverse* was true. Back then, lots of places wouldn't take a card at all, or if they did, they slapped on a "processing fee" that made you feel like you were applying for a mortgage.

And I have the perfect story to prove it.

The Scene: The Rising Sun, Clanfield

It was a perfectly ordinary evening. I'd been out at The Rising Sun in Clanfield with friends. I was driving, so on soft drinks only, a Coke, a lemonade, probably a packet of crisps if I was feeling daring.

In my wallet, I had:

- one ten-pound note

- an old Access card
  (Remember Access? The ancient ancestor of Mastercard, now spoken of only in museums and credit card helplines.)

I bought a round. Back then, £10 actually *meant* something. You could get a few drinks, a couple of snacks, and still have change to jangle impressively in your pocket. Simpler times.

The Problem: A Fuel Light With Attitude

I left around 10pm and walked to my car.
Then I remembered a small detail.

I was running low on petrol.

Well, that's fine, I thought. I'll just... top up somewhere. Except the somewhere would need to accept Access, and that narrowed it down considerably.

I turned the key.

The engine started.
The red fuel light came on.
It didn't blink politely, it *glared* at me, like a strict headmistress who knows you've forged your mum's signature.

I had just enough petrol to get to the top of the hill beyond HMS Mercury. If I made it there with enough speed, I could coast the whole way down through East Meon and on to Stroud Garage, one of the few places guaranteed to take my card.

A flawless plan...
in theory.

The Car: A Hero of Questionable Design

This was in my FSO days.
A car built, I assume, out of Soviet military leftovers.

- No power steering.
- No steering lock.
- A chassis that could withstand light artillery fire.

The steering lock was my trusted Krook Lok, a bright yellow metal device that probably cost more than the car.

But she ran. Mostly.

The Great Coast

I nursed the car up the hill, gently, lovingly, whispering encouragement like a trainer coaxing a boxer through round twelve.

At the summit, I knocked her out of gear, switched off the engine, and began gliding.

Fifty miles an hour. Perfect.

Silence, glorious, slightly eerie silence, as I rolled down through the dark countryside.

When I reached East Meon, I passed a group spilling out of the pub. The look on their faces as a totally silent car drifted past at 20mph...

They didn't know whether to run, wave, or summon the local exorcist.

I dipped the clutch, restarted the engine, and carried on the last stretch to Stroud Garage.

Victory (and Petrol)

I pulled in, triumphant.
They accepted Access.
Civilisation was saved.

I filled up, paid, and drove home feeling like I'd just completed a daring cross-country rally on a shoestring budget and sheer optimism.

A small win.
A tiny adventure.
And proof that sometimes, in life as in motoring, half the success comes from confidence…

…and the other half from luck.

An experience, if nothing else

I took my time to get over Ruth and was happy in my own life, but of course over time I missed the closeness, the spark, the sense of being chosen. I needed something in my life that felt *mine* again.

So, I decided to try online dating.

I'd never done it before. Years earlier I'd had a brief go at in-person speed dating, that's how I met Charlotte, but that had kind of fizzled out before it begun. Online dating felt like its modern descendant: throw out a line, see what bites, hope it's not a boot.

I set up a profile and began talking to a few women. But one stood out: Sandra.
We chatted for ages online, then swapped numbers. Before long we were messaging daily. It felt natural to meet. She lived on the far side of Basingstoke, not too far. We arranged that I'd pick her up on a Sunday lunchtime, go for a pub lunch, and see what happened.

When she opened the door, we both had the classic first-date micro-jolt. She said I looked taller than in my photos; I thought she looked a little different from hers, though in a positive way. Then she smiled and said, "Shall we go?" - and just like that, the awkwardness melted.

Lunch by the river turned into a long walk and hours of conversation. No fireworks, no violins, but warm, easy company. We agreed to meet again, and then again, and again.

After four or five weekends, Sandra invited me to dinner with one of her friends and her friend's new date. It turned into one of those cosy evenings with tasty food, too much wine, and a round of Trivial Pursuit that became, frankly, unreasonably competitive. Sandra offered me the spare room. It felt... natural. The next morning delivered an unintentionally comedic moment: I needed a wee. I opened the bathroom door and found her already in the bath. I froze. She didn't. "Don't worry," she said, "just get on with it," which led to the kind of awkward-shy-funny interaction you only get in early-stage whatever-this-is. We laughed it off and went downstairs for breakfast like two people who had survived a small, domestic farce.

The following weekend, things shifted. Sandra invited me over, just the two of us. We watched a film, she looked at me and said, "Shall we finish this in bed?" She said she wasn't ready to take things too far... and then nature did its usual thing. It felt right, mutual, unpressured.

After that, we settled into a pattern. Saturdays at Sandra's. A film. A night together. Sunday breakfast. Then back home. Enjoyable, easy, physical... but not especially emotional. We never argued, but we also never imagined a future together. It simply existed in the present tense.

The closest thing to a holiday came when her parents, Mary, and Felix, went away and we house-sat to look after the cats. It was a peaceful week: hot tub, quiet garden, nowhere to rush to. When they returned, Mary produced a meal fit for thirty people. I still remember her beaming and saying, "Ready for the main course?" while I felt like Dawn French facing her second Christmas dinner in *The Vicar of Dibley*.

I bonded with Felix especially. A kind man, thoughtful, easy company. We still speak every few weeks today.

But after a year, Sandra and I came to the same conclusion. The chemistry was lovely, but we shared nothing beyond that. No common interests, no shared ambitions, no spark that lifted things above the pleasantly physical. We ended things kindly, with no bitterness.

It was, and remains, exactly what I called it then:
An experience.
Nothing less. Nothing more.

And exactly the experience I needed at that moment in my life, something that reminded me I was still desirable, still fun, still *me*.

The railings saga

My mobility was getting worse, though, truth be told, I wasn't quite ready to admit it. According to me, I merely had "the occasional wobble." According to gravity, I had a tenancy agreement with the flowerbeds.

Dr Slaight, my neurologist, suggested extending the handrails from my front door all the way to the gate. Sensible, really. I'd had a few near misses at night, ending up among the begonias more than once. I always managed to stand up again, usually laughing and brushing off soil, but I knew that luck is not a long-term safety strategy.

So, I contacted the occupational therapist from my landlord, Abri.

She came out, took one glance at the garden path, and said, "Yes... yes we can definitely do something here." It was the tone of someone thinking, *how have you survived this long?*
She also agreed to have the crumbling bit of path resurfaced. Perfect.

A few weeks later, a cheerful workman arrived. "Here to do the railings and concrete," he announced. "Best avoid the path for the rest of the day while the concrete sets."

"Fine by me," I said, and left him to it.

For hours I heard drilling, scraping, the clang of metal, and the unmistakable sound of someone occasionally swearing at a stubborn lump of concrete. By mid-afternoon he knocked again. "All done," he said proudly. "Don't touch the railings until tomorrow. And you'll get an email with a satisfaction survey, if you could give me good marks, that'd be great."

I smiled. "No problem."

I glanced outside. Railings in place, path smooth... all looked in order. Job done, I thought.

A couple of hours later, my neighbour Chris got home. I saw him stop at the gate, frown, mutter something that was not a hymn, and then stomp up my path.

He knocked on the door.
"Hi Chris," I said. "Everything alright?"
"What numbskull put those railings in?" he demanded.
"A contractor from Abri," I replied. "He said they might be a bit wobbly until the cement sets."
"That's not the problem," said Chris.
"What is, then?"

He pointed. "Look at them! They've put railings all the way from your front door to the gate. How am I supposed to get the lawnmower onto your lawn to cut your grass?"

I looked at him. I looked at the railings. I started laughing.
"Well," I said, "it looks like I'm either never having my grass cut again, or you're going to have to throw the mower over."
He was not amused.

Sure enough, the next day the satisfaction survey email arrived. I filled it in dutifully:
"Excellent workmanship... however, I can no longer access my front garden."
Attached: two photos of the Great Rail Barrier of Liss.

The following morning, the occupational therapist herself appeared, slightly flustered.
"I'm so sorry, Mr Budden," she sighed. "They do this *all the time*. I'll arrange for them to come back and make an opening."
I thanked her.
Then waited.
And waited.

Eighteen months later, the railings remained proudly unbroken, functioning less as support rails and more as a state-of-the-art grass-preventing security system.

Until today.

This very morning, dear reader, a new occupational therapist, a man called Pat, knocked on the door. After introducing himself, he stepped onto the path, looked at the railings, and his eyebrows shot up so high they nearly left his forehead.
"I see they've still not fixed this," he said.
"No," I replied. "They haven't."
"Well, leave it with me."
I've heard those words before, and usually translated them as, "See you again in 2030."

But to my astonishment, this afternoon a van actually pulled up. Two contractors got out, tape measures in hand, marked where the new opening should be, and said, "We'll be back soon to sort it."

So, with slightly more optimism than usual, and only a faint suspicion that "soon" may be a philosophical term, fingers crossed, this time they actually will.

A night in casualty, the good, the bad and the ugly

It was late afternoon on the 9th of September 2025. I'd just stepped outside to put a rubbish bag in the bin when, halfway down the path, something hit me so hard across my left shoulder and upper chest that I genuinely wondered whether a sledgehammer had dropped out of the sky.

I staggered back inside, sat down, and tried to breathe through it, waiting for the pain to ease. It didn't. And then the unwelcome thought crept in: *Is this **another** heart attack?* I didn't want to take the chance.

I dialled 999.

Fifteen minutes later the ambulance arrived, two lady paramedics, calm, efficient and reassuring in that magical NHS way that makes you feel safer the moment they walk through the door. They ran the usual checks. "Your heart rhythm looks fine," they said, "but with that level of pain, we want to get you to QA."

No argument from me. I threw a few essentials into a bag, medication, phone charger, the "just in case" bits you learn to pack after enough hospital adventures, and off we went.

Every so often the siren wailed and reflected blue light danced across the windows. It's funny how you can be grateful and terrified at the same time.

At Queen Alexandra Hospital, the paramedics handed me over to A&E staff, transferred me to a trolley, and wished me well. I thanked them, sincerely. They'd been wonderful.

A junior doctor examined me and whisked me onto the "CT list," which turned out not to be so much a list as a geological era. "You're looking at about five, five and a half hours," he said. It was around 6pm. I did the maths. Midnight at best.
I finally got scanned at 3am.
The doctor apologised and explained that all the bays were full. "We'll set you up in the corridor," he said, positively chirpy about it. "Actually, it's probably better for you out there, staff are passing all the time, so if you need anything, just ask!"

I appreciated the optimism. Only the NHS could turn "We're leaving you in a corridor all night" into a customer-service benefit.

So, there I was. Corridor. Trolley. Blanket tucked around me like a sad human sausage roll.

Next to me was a bearded man whose left foot was facing southeast while his leg pointed due north. Even without a medical degree, you knew something was very wrong. Then I spotted the cuffs on his wrists, and across the corridor, two police officers babysitting him through the night.

They were there for nine hours.
Nine hours of officers who could've been out preventing crime, stuck instead in a corridor guarding a man whose ankle was auditioning for *The Exorcist*.

The NHS is full of moments like that, brilliant people trapped by a system that hasn't yet heard of common sense.

Eventually, my turn came. Scan done, I was wheeled back through a maze of tired faces and flickering lights, then seen by another doctor. "We're going to admit you," he said. "As soon as we find a bed."

That happened just after 6am.

A porter took me to a ward proudly described as "newly refurbished." And it *was* smart, fresh paint, shiny floors, bright lights. But the pièce de résistance was that every toilet on the ward was out of order.

Leaking. Badly.

Maintenance had locked them all and stuffed towels against the doors to stop water flowing into the corridor. To use the facilities, we had to shuffle to the unrefurbished ward down the hall.
I've been in hospitals enough to know that "water on the floor" and "patients with mobility issues" is not a combination that inspires confidence.
Late that morning, the consultant arrived. He explained that the scan showed nothing sinister; whatever had caused the pain had stabilised overnight. "You're safe to go home," he said. "But cardiology will need to see you again in a few weeks."

I felt relieved. Exhausted, but relieved.

So why title this chapter *The Good, the Bad, and the Ugly*?

The Good
The staff. Every nurse, doctor, paramedic, porter, radiographer, utterly brilliant. Under pressure. Undervalued. And still kind.

The Bad
The system. Those two police officers stuck in A&E all night summed it up. Not bad people, bad structure. An entire shift wasted because no one can coordinate basic processes.

The Ugly
The leaking toilets on a brand-new ward, and the complete lack of water coolers in A&E.

Instead, we had those old pump-top conference jugs, the kind you see in hotel meeting rooms filled with tepid water that tastes faintly of disappointment. There were about a hundred people waiting, and only four or five jugs, which constantly ran dry.

Nurses had to keep refilling them, wasting time they didn't have.
And that, really, is the NHS in a nutshell: breathtaking brilliance right alongside head-shaking absurdity.

That night, I saw both in perfect harmony.

Lest we forget - again

If all goes according to plan, this book should be appearing on shelves just after Remembrance Sunday.

Maybe it's because Dad and Grandad both served in the Army.
Maybe it's because Uncle Ben and Uncle Jim both did National Service.
Maybe it's simply because some traditions matter more the older you get.

Whatever the reason, Remembrance Sunday has always been woven into the rhythm of my year. Unless I've been really ill or physically out of the country, I've attended a Remembrance service every year for the past forty years. Liss, London, wherever life has taken me, there will always be a parade, a silence, and a wreath.
Yes, I go to honour those who gave their lives so we can have the life we enjoy today. But there's another reason, one rooted in something Dad said to me more than once.

Dad was shaped by what he saw in the 1930s: the rise of the far right in Germany under Hitler, and here at home, the British Union of Fascists under Oswald Mosley.
In 1936, he and his workmates travelled to Horndean and signed up for the Territorial Army. So, when war finally broke out, it was no surprise he was among the first to be called up.
Dad's message to me was simple, and it stuck:
"Always remember the evil that Hitler inspired, and that it could easily have happened here."

Whenever the National Front appeared on the news in the 1970s and 80s, Dad would shake his head and mutter, "There you go... people are forgetting already."

These days, when I watch the news and see hatred being stirred up again, often against immigrants or anyone deemed "different," I think of him. Occasionally I look up and mutter, "You must be turning in your grave, Dad."

The modern challenge
What is the answer to illegal immigration?
I'll be honest: I don't know.
But I do know that stirring up resentment, anger, and division isn't it.

The current craze of hanging St George's or Union flags from every lamppost is, for some, a show of patriotism. For others, it feels like selective symbolism, patriotism used as a divider, not a unifier.

True patriotism doesn't need to shout.
It doesn't need to claim territory.
It quietly stands for decency, respect, and remembrance.

Even stranger is the backlash. Council workers who take down flags as part of their ordinary duties are branded "woke lefties." But the moment anyone suggests that perhaps those putting them up may have a political motive rather than a patriotic one, they're shouted down.

It's as if everyone is determined to miss the irony.

What remembrance means to me
One of my greatest honours, as both a local councillor and as Chairman, is laying a wreath each year at the Liss war memorial.
To walk forward.
To bow my head.
To place the wreath.
To say a silent prayer of gratitude.

This year, 2025, was especially moving. The parade was led, as ever, by the brilliant Liss Band, but this year joined by an army officer on horseback. Then, as the Last Post echoed through the village, a Chinook from RAF Odiham passed overhead at the perfect moment. The timing was uncanny. The sound, the silence, the slow thrum of the blades, it brought a lump to my throat. A reminder that remembrance isn't just tradition; it's shared memory.

I sometimes see people complain when others don't observe the two-minute silence.
My view?
The very freedom *not* to observe it is precisely what so many laid down their lives to protect.
There's a saying:
"All it takes for evil to prosper is for good men to do nothing."

I'd extend it a little:

"All it takes for evil to prosper is not just for good men to do nothing, but for them to forget what evil looks like."

The Last Post at Ypres

On the subject of remembrance, one of the most memorable moments of my travels came on a trip to Belgium, when I finally had the chance to stop in Ypres and see the Menin Gate for myself.

I'd driven past the town countless times over the years, always meaning to visit "next time," but you know how life is, next time rarely arrives on schedule.

This day, though, it did. And by sheer luck rather than planning, I arrived just in time for the daily ceremony performed by the town's volunteer firemen.

Before that, I wandered through the Cloth Hall, a building that looks as though it's been standing serenely since the Middle Ages, yet the original was completely destroyed in the First World War and rebuilt brick by brick in the 1920s. The craftsmanship is astonishing. If you ever find yourself in that part of Belgium, both the Cloth Hall and the Menin Gate are worth every minute of your time.

The Menin Gate itself stopped me in my tracks.
I thought I'd seen impressive memorials before, but nothing prepared me for the scale of this one. More than **54,000 names** are carved into its stone, 54,000 young men whose bodies were never found, whose families never had a grave to visit. Standing there, reading some of those names, I felt two powerful emotions at once: pride for their courage, and a deep, almost physical sadness at the sheer waste and futility of war.

It's a lesson humanity still hasn't mastered. You only have to look at the ongoing war in Ukraine, or conflicts elsewhere in the world, to realise how quickly we forget. Maybe one day we'll learn. Maybe we never will.

At 8 p.m. sharp, the ceremony began, just as it has *every single day* since the 1920s, paused only during the Second World War when the occupying forces wouldn't permit it.
The road beneath the arch was closed. People gathered quietly, almost instinctively forming a circle of respect. Then the buglers stepped forward and played the Last Post.

There's something about that call that gets into your bones.
When it sounded, every sinew in my body seemed to tighten.
The hairs on my arms stood upright.
And yes, my eyes certainly weren't the only ones that found themselves a little damp.
Wreaths were laid.
A silence was held.
The Reveille sounded to close.

Simple. Dignified. Profoundly moving.

It was, without question, one of the most powerful experiences of my sixty-plus years on this planet, quiet, unhurried remembrance at its absolute best.

The Heathrow surprise

I'd known for a while that Enma had a sister, Mabi, still living in Spain. What I hadn't realised was that they hadn't seen each other in more than ten years. A decade. Michelle was in touch with her aunt now and then, a Christmas card here, a WhatsApp call there, but the sisters themselves hadn't been face-to-face in all that time.

It struck me how wonderful it would be to bring them back together. I could afford the flights. Mabi could stay with us for a week or two, share the bed with Enma, God knows they'd have plenty of catching up to do, and I'd happily take the sofa. I'd slept on worse things in my life, including a Lilo that slowly deflated over four consecutive nights.

The only hurdles were logistics and the slight issue that my Spanish vocabulary amounted to "hola," "adiós," and "dos cervezas, por favor." Fortunately, Michelle spoke Spanish far better than I did, and with the help of Google Translate we managed to orchestrate everything.

She was excited too, she'd get to see her aunt, and her children would meet their great-aunt for the first time. But she was sworn to secrecy. Enma must not know, under any circumstances, or the whole surprise would collapse.

By then, Enma had met my dear friend Jan and could see the bond we had. "You love him every bit as much as Roy and Roger," she once teased.
"Yes," I said. "Maybe even a bit more sometimes."
She gave that familiar mischievous laugh, the one that meant, *I know exactly what you're up to.*

So, the plan was simple: Enma thought Jan was flying back from Barcelona and that we were heading to Heathrow to pick him up for a night's stay. After that, I'd "drive him home to Milton Keynes," which worked beautifully because Enma's grasp of British geography was... let's say *creative*. In her mind, Milton Keynes was somewhere north of Hadrian's Wall.

When the day came, Enma wasn't feeling her best.

"You go, darling," she said. "I'll stay here and cook something nice for you both."

Absolutely not. I needed her at the airport.

"Please come with me," I insisted. "You know what Heathrow car parks are like, I'll never find a space without you guiding me."

"Oh, alright," she sighed. "But you owe me one. And you can buy the Indian or Chinese tonight. Whichever Jan wants."

"Deal," I said, trying to keep a straight face.

We parked in short-stay and headed to Arrivals. I got her into the wheelchair and pointed at the board. "Look, it's landed," I said, doing my absolute best impression of calm.

We waited. I'd only seen a few photos of Mabi from years ago, so I prayed she still resembled them and hadn't, say, dyed her hair purple.

Then the doors slid open... and there she was.

Enma's expression didn't just change, it *transformed*. Disbelief, recognition, joy, all in about half a second. Mabi dropped her bag and ran. Enma half-stood, half-bounced out of the wheelchair. They hugged. They kissed. They hugged again. It was one of those moments where your heart expands to three times its usual size and you pretend you've just got something in your eye.

"Mabi!" Enma gasped. "What are you doing here?"

"I've come to see you, of course!"

Enma blinked in confusion. "But... what a coincidence! We're here to collect..."
Then she stopped, turned slowly to me, and broke into the biggest beam I'd ever seen.
"You little bastard!" she said, her highest term of affection.

Back at our little bedsit, I made tea while the two sisters talked non-stop in Spanish. Honestly, I could have left the room for an hour, and I doubt either of them would have noticed. Their laughter filled the place, and I realised how long it had been since I'd heard Enma laugh that freely.

When it was bedtime, Enma told Mabi they'd share the bed and I'd take the sofa, as planned. Mabi came out of the bathroom in a long pink nightdress; Enma was already tucked in. I brushed my teeth, stripped down to my boxers, and kissed Enma goodnight.

"And me?" Mabi said with a wicked little grin.

I laughed, walked round the bed, and gave her a peck on the cheek. As I turned away, they whispered in Spanish and burst into giggles.

"What are you two up to?" I asked.

"Mabi said, 'Nice bum,'" Enma replied. "And I told her, 'I know. And that bum's all mine.'"

We all dissolved into laughter.

"Night-night," I said, turning off the light, still smiling as I made my way to the sofa.

And honestly? It was one of the happiest nights of my life.

From one phone on the wall to the world in your pocket

There's a whole generation of us who started life with one phone per family, and it was literally attached to the wall.

If you were on the phone, no one else could be. If you wanted any privacy, you stretched the curly cable as far as it would go into the hall and hoped no one was listening.

From there, we went to car phones the size of bricks, to early mobiles that needed their own rucksack, to the slim little smartphones we now carry around and occasionally, just occasionally, use to make an actual phone call.

We used to make a trip into town to buy a record if we wanted to hear a new song. If the shop didn't have it, we waited a week for them to order it.

Then came:

- Recording songs off the Top 40 onto cassette (complete with DJ talking over the intro).
- The first expensive CDs.
- MP3s you could only play on a computer.
- iPods that seemed like miracles.
- And now: streaming any track, any time, on a device smaller than the cassette we started on.

Computers used to live in big buildings with air conditioning and security passes.

Then:

- Our school had a special room with *the* computer. Singular.
- Then the first home computers that you could only use if you knew how to write programs.
- Then a beige box on your desk at work.
- Then laptops.

- And now? You carry a computer around in your pocket that has more power than the machines that sent people to the moon.

The internet was something we'd never even heard of.

Then suddenly we were:

- Plugging the computer into the phone line at home.
- Listening to that screeching dial-up tone.
- Waiting a minute for a single page to load.
- And having to disconnect so someone else could use the phone.

Now we walk around permanently connected to more information than the entire British Library, in a phone that also takes photos, films in HD, tracks our heart rate, counts our steps, and reminds us of when it's time to stand up.

Television? At one time we had three channels. That was your lot. If your programme was on at 8pm, you watched it at 8pm or you didn't see it.

Then came:

- The magic of the VCR, record now, watch later.
- Satellite dishes bolted to the side of the house so we could watch more channels... at the time they were broadcast.
- And now: watch anything, any time, on a TV, a tablet, a phone - on the sofa, in bed, on a train.

Films?

We went from:

- Having to go to the cinema,
- To hiring a video from Blockbuster or the local video shop,
- To streaming almost any film we like, whenever we like,

on whatever device we fancy.

Does all of this blow anyone else's mind as much as it does mine?

Because the technological changes I've seen in my lifetime are staggering. Things that were pure science fiction when we were children, communicators, video calls, computers you could talk to, now sit on our kitchen worktops and in our pockets, and we get annoyed if they take more than three seconds to respond.

I remember when **none** of this existed.

My children, and my grandchildren, will only ever remember a world where it **always has**.

And that, to me, is incredible.

It's a boy!
Adventures in the cardiac lab

For once, everything health-wise had been ticking along fairly nicely. No drama, no new diagnoses, just the usual daily dance with pills, appointments, and naps.

Then, over a couple of months, I noticed I was getting increasingly short of breath.

At first, it was just annoying. I assumed I was walking too fast, so I slowed down a bit. That helped for a while, then... didn't.

I'd built a weekly ritual I loved. Bags for life in the basket of my rollator, walk to Liss station, train to Petersfield, then down the hill to Marks & Spencer Food Hall, Poundland, WH Smith (or "TJ Jones" as it now insists on calling itself - surely a candidate for "Least Imaginative Rebrand of the 21st Century"), then Waitrose, then Lidl, then back to the station. Train to Liss, sit opposite the estate agents and wave at Lucy through the window, both of us waving like deranged cheerleaders who'd had too much Red Bull, then fish and chips, then home.

It was my end-of-week ritual. My "me" time. Predictable, quiet, and mine.

But over a few weeks, it changed. I was stopping increasingly often just to catch my breath. That three-hour loop quietly became a five-hour epic. By the time I got back to Liss, the estate agents had long since closed. Lucy was at home with her feet up and her dinner in front of her. No mad waving. No little shared moment.

Even I had to admit something wasn't right.

I rang my GP. Miraculously, I got a same-day appointment. (Take the small miracles where you can.)

She listened to my chest. Took blood. Sent me for a chest X-ray at Petersfield. Ordered an urgent referral to Cardiac Care. Booked an echocardiogram in Havant. If there was a cardiac test available, she ticked its box.

The initial suspicion was too much fluid retention. Solution: double my diuretics.

"Incontinent 50% of the time already and your big idea is tablets that make me wee more?" I thought. "Be still my beating heart."

Side note: adult nappies are genuinely brilliant. In eleven years, I've only had two proper leaks. The problem isn't the containment, it's the weight. As the day goes on and they quietly collect your "best work," they get heavier and heavier. Think: a two-litre bottle of milk taped into your underwear. It goes some way to explaining why some days my gait would make even John Wayne applaud politely.

Anyway, back to the heart.

The echocardiogram in Havant finally nailed it. My heart simply wasn't beating properly anymore. The valves weren't sealing reliably. One side of the heart was pacing regularly thanks to my pacemaker; the other side was doing its own thing entirely.

Imagine a couple on *Strictly Come Dancing*. The woman is gliding through a Viennese waltz; the man is enthusiastically doing the Charleston. That was my heart.

The proposed fix: replace my existing pacemaker with a newer model that would pace **all** the chambers in sync, so the heart didn't have to decide anything for itself. And while they were in there, they'd thread a long, thin tube with a camera and grabber up from my groin to my heart to assess the valve damage and decide if it was repairable or needed full replacement.

(I love that they call the procedure room "the lab." It looks for all the world like an operating theatre, but no - in cardiology, it's "the lab". I half expect to see bubbling green liquids and a spare Frankenstein on the trolley.)

At first, I was told it could be up to twelve months before they could do it. Deep joy.

Then the phone rang: there'd been a cancellation. Could I do next Tuesday? I'd need to be at the hospital by 7am. If all went well, I'd be home late afternoon or early evening. Bring an overnight bag "just in case," 50% chance of a two-three day stay. I said yes, obviously.

Diesel, a Flat Tyre, and Lord Lucan

Tuesday came. My neighbour, Chris, a self-employed carpenter/handyman, had offered to drive me, as long as I rang him at 5:45am to wake him. We'd leave at 6. It's about 40 minutes to the hospital, so that gave us a bit of wiggle room.

My alarm went off at 5. Shower, dressed, bags packed. I rang Chris. He answered. We were on.

"I need to stop in Petersfield to get some diesel," he said as we loaded my rollator and overnight bag into his van.

"I'll pay," I said. Seemed only fair given he was doing the favour.

Bang on 6am we set off. As we joined the old A3, Chris frowned. "Can you hear that rattle from the back?"

I listened. There was a noise. "Probably just my rollator clattering about," I said, optimistically.

We pulled into the petrol station. "How much diesel are you putting in?" I asked.

"Thirty quid will do," he replied.

I lifted my rollator out and walked into the shop to pay while he filled up. When I came back, he didn't look happy.

"Found the source of the rattle," he said, pointing to the rear wheel. The tyre was so flat the metal rim was almost kissing the tarmac.

"Have you got a spare?" I asked.

"Nope."

Oh, good.

"I know," said Chris, an optimist after my own heart. "I'll pump it up. Hopefully, it's just a slow puncture. If I drive steady, we should make it to Portsmouth, then I'll drop you off and head to Kwik Fit."

It was 6:15. The hospital was still 35 minutes away. I needed to be there by 7.

He inflated the tyre. It looked okay-ish. I peered at it like some amateur tyre engineer and declared, "Looks good. Let's go."

We made it. At the hospital, the tyre had sunk a bit but was still holding its shape.

"You'll make it to Kwik Fit," I said, like a budget Fairy Godmother approval service.

I thanked Chris for the lift. "Ring me if you need a lift home," he said. Another fellow councillor, Clive, had already offered, but backup plans are always welcome.

"If not, see you at home," he called, climbing back into his slightly wounded van.

Velcro Couture and a Treasure Hunt for Veins
Cardiac Care almost feels like a second home these days.

The receptionist checked me in in a pleasingly GDPR-compliant way. I was impressed.

"Take a seat," she said.

A few minutes later a male nurse appeared. "Mr Budden?"

He led me to a bed and pulled the curtains round. A small win: they've upgraded from those undignified back-tying gowns to Velcro pyjamas. Progress!

"I need to take some blood," he said.

Of course you do, I thought. Good luck.

After this many years of blood tests, my veins see a needle and vanish so efficiently even Lord Lucan would be impressed.

"And then I need to put a cannula into the back of your hand," he added.

Wonderful, not just hunting Lord Lucan, but Shergar too.

"Why not take the blood via the cannula?" I suggested, politely.

"I don't like doing it that way," he replied.

"All yours then," I thought.

He tried the left elbow first. Needle in, wiggle, wiggle, wiggle - like Indiana Jones hunting treasure.

"You're not in," I said.

"How can you tell?"

"Trust me," I said. "I know what it feels like when you are."

He admitted defeat, pulled the needle out. A blob of dark blood appeared as if the vein was poking its tongue out and saying, "Missed me!"

Gauze. Micropore tape. Round one to the veins.

He tried the other elbow. Same result. More gauze; more tape.

"Go for the hand," I thought. "Use the cannula."

Nope.

He felt along my forearm near the wrist. "I can feel one," he said, cheerfully. Needle in. Nothing. Wiggle. Nothing. Out again.

Another trickle of purple blood.

More gauze. More micropore.

"I'll use the cannula in your hand," he finally said.

"Hallelujah," I thought.

He actually managed to find a vein. Cannula in. He attached a vacuum vial, and lo and behold: blood.
He filled three vials with the glee of a small boy unwrapping his first Hornby train set.

"I'll leave you to get changed," he said. "And as we're going in via the groin as well, you'll need to take everything off underneath."

"Everything?"

"Everything."

"How long until the op?" I asked.

"About thirty minutes."

"You do know I'm incontinent both ways and wearing an adult nappy?" I asked.

He checked my notes. "So, you are. In that case, keep the nappy on and we'll remove it in theatre. Brought spares?"

"In the bag," I said. "They go everywhere with me."

It occurred to me that if he'd missed that, he'd possibly missed something else.

"You do know my pacemaker is on the right," I said. Most are on the left, but because my first one failed, they'd moved mine to the other side.

"Is it?" he asked.

"I think I'd know," I replied, pulling my T-shirt collar aside to show him the scar.

"Ah," he said. "In that case, I'd better go to the lab. They'll need to swap the equipment to the other side of the room, or the surgeon won't be able to reach your pacemaker and see the screens at the same time. Thanks for telling me. I'll leave you to get changed."

I stood there in my patchwork of gauze and tape, assembling the Velcro pyjamas. I caught sight of myself and thought I resembled a vampire's practice canvas from a Halloween episode of *Treasure Hunt*.

The pyjamas themselves weren't too bad. I'd seen worse.

The ward was mixed sex. On the opposite bed, a woman about my age was also in Velcro couture. Hers looked like the "Here's one I made earlier" version from Blue Peter. Mild pyjama envy crept in.

A woman in theatre scrubs arrived, a familiar face.

"Hello, Mr Budden," she said. "Good to see you again. I've left the team swapping the lab around, very glad we found out about that pacemaker location before you arrived in there. I'm assisting the surgeon today, so he's asked me to run through everything with you. Is that alright?"

"Of course," I said.

She explained the plan: local anaesthetic to the chest, heavy sedation, but not full anaesthesia because of my brain history. They'd replace the pacemaker, then go in via the groin to inspect the valves. Because of the heart issues and the Marfan's, there was a small but real chance they might need to "convert to open" if things went badly.

"I need you to sign consent that if anything goes wrong, we can open your chest," she said. "I want to reassure you, it's rare, and the surgeon and I have worked together many times. We've never had anyone bleed out on the table… yet."

I could have done without the dramatic pause before "yet."

"Now," she continued, "because you have incontinence, I need to check you don't have any sores 'down there'. We'll clean thoroughly before we start, but if there are sores, we may have to postpone. Is it okay if I take your bottoms off and check?"

"Well, that's a chat-up line I've not heard before," I said.

She laughed. "I like that one."

"Have it as a gift," I replied.

"Seriously though," she said, "because I'm going to examine you intimately, would you like a male chaperone?"
I couldn't resist. "A chaperone? Another person just to watch? If I'd known we could have spectators, I'd have sold tickets."

"You," she said, giggling, "are a very naughty man."

Inside, I was thinking: I'm actually a very scared one.

She removed my pyjama bottoms and nappy and examined everything with the focus of someone searching for the Holy Grail.

"All good," she said at last. "We can go ahead."

"Shall I put this nappy back on you?" she asked.

"Is it clean?" I heard myself say, immediately wondering why I hadn't just asked for a fresh one.

She looked inside it. "It's fine."

I breathed a quiet sigh of relief. She re-dressed me, binned the gloves, and said, "The porter will be here in a few minutes. The operation should only take a couple of hours, with luck, you'll be back for lunch."

Velcro Failure, Sandwich Chat, and the Lab
I decided I had time for a quick wee.

I stood up, grabbed my rollator, and pulled the curtains open.

Two steps towards the loo... and the Velcro on my pyjama trousers chose that moment to give up on life.

They dropped to my ankles.

The lady opposite valiantly tried to look away, then failed and burst out laughing.

A nurse came running. "You stand still," she said. "Let me help you with those."

"I was going to the loo," I replied. "They were going to have to come down anyway."
"In that case," she said, crouching down, "step out of them so you don't trip, and I'll help you put them back on afterwards. I saw the surgeon earlier, has anyone asked what you'd like for lunch?"

I started laughing.

"What's funny?" she asked.

"Well," I said, "you're crouched at my feet, eye-level with my groin, asking whether I'd prefer a ham or a cheese sandwich."

She burst out laughing. The woman opposite pretty much gave up any pretence of decorum and howled.

I waddled to the loo wearing just my green Velcro top and my nappy. At that point, even if I'd had any shyness left, it was gone.

When I came out, the nurse was waiting with my trousers and dressed me like a West End dresser prepping someone for a quick-change scene. They looked much better afterwards. My pyjama envy subsided.

The porter arrived. We trundled down to the lab.

I shifted from the trolley to the operating table. The anaesthetist placed a mask over my face.

"It's just sedative," she said. "If at any point you're uncomfortable, squeeze my hand and I'll increase it."

They draped green gauze so I couldn't see what they were doing.

The surgeon poked his head over.
"All okay?"
I nodded.

"Right," he said. "I'm just going to make the main incision over your old scar, so you don't get another one."

"Fine," I said. To be honest, by then he could have announced he was removing my leg, and I'd probably have said "Fine" to that too.
I don't remember much of the operation. I do recall, at one point, being acutely aware I needed a wee and hoping my bladder behaved itself while someone was wielding equipment remarkably close to my groin.

And then it was done.
"It's a Boy!" and a Scrapheap Heart
After lunch, the surgeon appeared at my bedside.

"I've got something to show you," he said. "But first, do you remember anything you said during the procedure?"

"I remember you saying you were making the incision, and needing a wee," I replied. "Other than that, not much."

He smiled. "Well, you didn't wee in theatre, which we appreciated. And you definitely kept us entertained."

"Oh dear," I said. "Go on..."

"I had some trouble getting your old pacemaker out," he said. "Your body was extremely attached to it, literally. I had to push and pull more than usual. When it finally came free, I held it up over the screen so you could see it. You looked up at it, looked at me, and proudly announced: 'It's a boy!'"

We both laughed.

"And later," he continued, "you launched into quite a passionate monologue about how, despite being a Conservative, you despaired of Boris Johnson's buffoonery. You were so animated I decided it was wisest to agree with you."

This did sound like me, to be fair.

He then produced two pacing charts.

"This," he said, pointing to a nice steady trace, "is your heart with the new pacemaker."

He showed me the second chart, my heart trying to pace itself. It looked less like a heart rhythm and more like a seismograph during an earthquake.
"We estimate that without a pacemaker, your heart only manages about twelve beats a minute," he said. "Put it this way: if it were a car, we'd be sending it to the scrapheap."

"Good job I've got a decent mechanic," I said.

He smiled. "We'll see you in clinic in a few weeks. For now, my colleague will keep an eye on you. Once we're happy, you can go home."

I tried ringing Clive, no signal where he was. So, I rang Sarah in the Parish Council office.

"Fancy a rescue mission?" I asked.

"Of course," she said. "Give me an hour."

And that was that.

Once again, I was going home.

Another unexpected chapter in this slightly ridiculous, very precious lifetime of moments.

A case of mistaken diagnosis

Just this week, I had a perfect example of what happens when communication falters, or when someone, somewhere in the NHS, puts two and two together and confidently arrives at five. About a week ago, a letter arrived inviting me to attend the Diabetes Clinic.

That was... surprising.

As you'll have gathered by now, my medical CV is already long enough to qualify as a novella, but diabetes has never been on it. My GP and hospital tests happen often enough that I'm practically on a loyalty card, and not once has anyone ever suggested diabetes.

I showed the letter to my GP. She scrolled through my notes, frowning.
"There's absolutely nothing here to indicate diabetes," she said. "But maybe someone spotted something during your last hospital stay, the pacemaker replacement. Best to go, just in case."

So off I went to clinic, a small knot of worry in my stomach. I didn't want another condition. My metaphorical medical mantelpiece is full enough.

Yes, I do have a sweet tooth. Yes, a Belgian bun occasionally "falls" into my shopping basket. And yes, I've been waking in the night more often for a wee, but at my age, that probably just means the plumbing is original.

I checked in and soon enough a nurse called me through. The diabetes specialist greeted me with a tentative smile.

"Mr Budden? Can you confirm your date of birth?"
I did. She glanced between two monitors and a stack of notes so thick it could be used as gym equipment.

"Well... I can't see *anything* here to suggest you have diabetes."

"That's a relief," I said.
"So, the obvious question becomes, why are you here?"

"Good question," I replied. "I got the letter, my GP was baffled, but she saw the referral came from a hospital doctor and thought maybe they knew something she didn't."

The specialist leaned back. "Right. Time to switch into Hercule Poirot mode."

She scrolled through screen after screen, murmuring under her breath, until suddenly -
"Ah-ha! I've cracked it."
"Go on," I said.
"You've been referred to Podiatry, correct?"
"Yes."
"And you've got peripheral neuropathy?"
"Yes-chemotherapy leftovers from twenty years ago."
"Thought so. Well, someone has seen 'foot issues + neuropathy + circulatory problems' and assumed diabetes. Quite common symptoms... but not in *your* case. I can confirm absolutely, you do not have diabetes. I'm sorry for the mix-up."

"That's excellent news," I said. "And please don't apologise. I'd rather come here and be told I *don't* have something than the other way around."

"We've still got ten minutes left," she said. "Anything else you want to tell me? I see in your notes that you've given up work and are writing an autobiography. How's it going?"
I filled her in on *A Lifetime of Moments*.
She smiled. "Will this appointment make it into the book?"
"It is now."
"Then I'll buy a copy when it's published. Right, coffee break before my next patient."

"Not too many sugars, I hope," I said.
She laughed. "You're funny!"
"That's good," I replied.
"What is?"
"When I came in, you were frowning. Now you're smiling. My work here is done."

I walked back down the corridor grinning like a fool.
"No diabetes," I thought.
"Time for a Belgian bun."

God, the universe and everything in between

My Dad wasn't one for long speeches or grand philosophies. But every so often, he'd share a thought so simple and so quietly profound that it lodged somewhere deep and never quite left me.

One of those thoughts has shaped how I view life to this day. He believed, and I believe, that the moment you're born, the moment you'll die is already fixed. The date, the hour, the second. Not the circumstances, just the timing.

Now, I know someone somewhere is already reaching for a spreadsheet, ready to plot a graph proving why that can't possibly be true. But bear with me.

If the beginning and the end are set, then the middle is ours. What we do with it, how we live, who we love, the mistakes we stumble into, the kindness we give away, what fears we face, where we wander, that's the part we get to shape. We can brighten the picture or darken it, frame it however we choose. But the length? That's beyond us.
And oddly, I find that comforting.

I've always described myself as Christian, Anglican these days. Over the years I've sat in Methodist pews, sung in Evangelical churches, and questioned my faith more times than I can count. I've seen religion bring out the best in people and, sadly, sometimes the worst.
But the older I get, the more I realise this: the things that unite the world's major faiths far outweigh the things that divide them. The Bible, the Torah, the Qur'an, different books, different prophets, different languages, yes, but the same core message: love one another, live with purpose, don't be a monster.

I don't believe any one faith has a monopoly on goodness. I'm not trying to convert anyone here. I'm just sharing the route I've taken through my own beliefs, potholes and all.

Yes, I believe in God. Yes, I believe in Jesus. But I also studied Natural Physics at university, and I believe in the Big Bang, in the expanding universe, in energy and matter and black holes and the laws of thermodynamics.

So, people sometimes ask, "How do you reconcile the two?"

For me, it's simple. Everything in physics begins with energy. And energy doesn't just pop into existence for a laugh. It can change form, light becomes heat becomes matter, but something had to start the process.

For me, that "something" was God. That first unimaginable burst of energy that became everything we see and know. I don't think science contradicts faith; I think it describes the mechanics of it.
And when people ask why Earth, of all places, is the one speck in the universe that seems to teem with life, I have two possible answers: either it's coincidence so vast it borders on miraculous, or something, or someone, set the conditions for it to happen. Either way, it's astonishing.

I don't think faith should switch off our questions. If God didn't want us searching, He wouldn't have given us the brainpower to do it.
Take Jesus. Was He real? Yes, absolutely. Did He perform miracles? I believe He did, though perhaps not always with quite as much theatrical flair as later written. The Bible wasn't a live blog, it was stories told and retold, preserved by people doing their best to honour what they'd heard. Stories have a way of growing, especially when passed down through awe.
And that's fine. Faith isn't weakened by honesty; it's strengthened by it.

Now for the belief that's earned me more raised eyebrows than anything else.
I don't believe only Christians go to heaven.
Imagine a young African woman living in a remote village. She's never heard of Jesus or the New Testament. She prays as her ancestors prayed, raises her children with tenderness, helps her neighbours, and lives a life full of kindness.
Are we seriously saying she doesn't get into heaven because no one happened to hand her a leaflet?
If that's the rule, then the God they're describing isn't the one I believe in.

When I was Chairman of EHDC, I met people of all faiths, but the Ahmadiyya Muslim community left a particular mark. Their motto, *Love for All, Hatred for None,* isn't just painted on banners. They live it. Their discipline during Ramadan astonished me.

I often joked that if most Christians were asked to fast, abstain, and pray five times a day for a month, they'd be under the pews by day two. Me included.

Would I convert to Islam? No. But do I respect it? Completely.

And then the big question: do I believe in heaven?
Honestly? I'm still not sure.
Medically, I've died three times. No pearly gates. No choir of angels. Just... white. A peaceful, silent whiteness. A calm I can't quite put into words. If that's heaven, then it's beautiful. If it's not, then it's still something I'm not afraid of.

But the rational side of me wonders. We're flesh and bone. We decay. The idea of billions of souls reuniting somewhere, do we keep our memories? Do we recognise our families? I struggle to imagine it, and I'm someone who can barely remember where I left my glasses.

Maybe heaven is somewhere. Maybe it's something. Maybe it's simply the peace we leave behind in the people who loved us. Maybe it's all of the above.
I don't know.

But here's what I *do* believe:
Life is short.
Love matters.
Kindness lasts.

And if we spend our days doing those things well, maybe, just maybe, we've already found our little piece of heaven right here.

Celebrities on aisle three, (and other Surreal moments of my life)

For someone who has spent most of his life being poked, prodded, scanned, wired up, observed, injected, and generally treated like a medical "try turning it off and on again" experiment, I seem to have accumulated a surprisingly glittering celebrity résumé.

Aside from once meeting wrestling commentator **Kent Walton** (whose voice alone could pin you to the sofa on a Saturday afternoon), I've somehow crossed paths with a whole assortment of famous faces. To any I've forgotten: apologies, blame age, not the encounter.

The first major surprise was **Michael McIntyre**.

At the inaugural A4U Awards (now the Performance Marketing Awards), I won a prize for my contributions to the affiliate marketing community. A young, sharply dressed, noticeably slimmer **Michael McIntyre** presented it. He was hilarious, fast as lightning, and already unmistakably *him*. Some of the jokes he told that night still show up in his modern routines like distant cousins.

My childhood brushes with fame were more observational. **Tommy Cooper**, for instance, was a regular visitor to Petersfield. Whenever he turned up at the Punch & Judy restaurant, the town buzzed like someone had spotted the Loch Ness Monster in a fez. I saw him through the window a few times but never went in to say, "Just like that."

Then came **Terry Wogan**.

He opened the Petersfield Comprehensive School fête, and for some reason I was chosen to present him with a gift. He bent down, smiled that warm, unmistakable **Terry Wogan** smile, and spoke to me as if I were the only person there. I adored him instantly, and rightly, he was exactly the lovely man everyone hoped he'd be.

Then came the moment I unexpectedly shared a train

compartment with **Sir Alec Guinness**.

I was travelling home from university on one of those old suburban trains with proper compartments, real doors, windows you had to lean out of, the works. There were just two of us inside: me, and an impeccably dressed older gentleman with a trilby, a three-piece suit, a macintosh folded beside him, and a fountain pen dancing across a broadsheet crossword.

I kept sneaking glances. He finally looked up, lifted a single eyebrow (the eyebrow of a man trained at RADA), and said:

"You're trying to work out who I am, aren't you, young man?"

I admitted I was.

"I feel I know you... do you live in Petersfield?"

"Close," he said. "Steep. And here's a clue: think *Star Wars*. Think *Obi-Wan Kenobi*."

And there it was.

Alec Guinness. Sitting opposite me. Not a Force ghost in sight.

We talked all the way to Liss. He was charming, funny, wonderfully normal. It's one of the only train journeys in my life where I was genuinely disappointed to reach my stop.

Which makes the next story even more ridiculous.

You'd think an avid motorsport fan like me would recognise **Lewis Hamilton** from several postcodes away. Turns out I can miss him from four feet.

I was at Silverstone for the British Touring Car Championship on a cold, windy day. A man with half his face hidden by a scarf stood next to me. We chatted about the rollator threatening to blow me down the hill, and he seemed *very* invested in the performance of one particular driver: **Nic Hamilton**.

Did I put two and two together?

No. I barely got as far as one and a half.

It wasn't until the cool-down lap, when he pulled his scarf down and cheered his brother, that the penny dropped.

"Well, it's been great to meet you, Lewis," I said.

"You too," he replied, giving me a friendly pat on the shoulder before vanishing into the crowd like Batman with a better skincare routine.

Not all my brushes with fame were surprises.

When I was Chairman of East Hampshire District Council, I helped open the new Alton Leisure Centre alongside **Colin Jackson** and **Mark Foster,** both lovely men, both consummate professionals, both very patient while I wielded the ceremonial scissors like someone defusing a bomb in an action film.

Then there was **Noel Edmonds**.

I visited his home in Devon before he moved to New Zealand, and I can confirm it is ridiculously hard to hold a serious adult conversation when there is a full-size Mr Blobby costume hanging on the wall and a "Gotcha" Oscar being used as a doorstop. Childhood nostalgia and absolute surrealism in equal measure.

But the one that truly floored me was **Bob Barrett,** Dr Sacha Levy from *Holby City*.

Michelle and I were at Treloar's for an event attended by HRH Sophie Wessex. I queued for tea, heard a familiar voice behind me, turned... and there he was.

Michelle still says it's the only time she's ever seen me *properly* starstruck. Not for royalty. Not for ministers. Not for titans of industry.

For a fictional doctor.

And she's absolutely right.

He was delightful, - warm, friendly, generous with his time. A proper diamond geezer.

And apparently trains are a magnet for celebrity encounters, because only a few weeks ago I was travelling first class to Manchester and found myself opposite **Fred Dinenage**, Southern TV legend, news presenter, and one of the hosts of the childhood classic *How?* The man who explained everything from how steam engines worked to why balloons pop. We spoke for the whole three-hour journey. Proof that sometimes first class isn't about the seats, it's about the company.

And finally, in the business world, I've met **Peter Jones, Theo Paphitis, Deborah Meaden**, and **Sir Alan Sugar**. No, before you ask, I've never been on *Dragons' Den* or *The Apprentice*. I've just been lucky. Incredibly lucky.

Each meeting left a little spark. A tiny moment in a lifetime of them.

And if you're wondering whether this entire chapter is just me shamelessly name-dropping...

...yes.

Yes, it absolutely is.

And I'm gloriously comfortable with that.

Final thoughts - Keep smiling

If you've made it this far through the book, then first of all, thank you.

Truly.

You've travelled with me through the nostalgia, the chaos, the medical dramas, the mischief, the heartbreaks, the victories, the loved ones gained, the loved ones lost, the laughter, and the occasional moment when I found myself naked, confused, or in a hospital gown, sometimes all three at once.

Hopefully, you'll also have noticed the thread running through it all: my cheerful, occasionally dark, often inappropriate, always stubborn sense of humour.

People who know me, friends, colleagues, doctors, nurses, paramedics, physiotherapists, occupational therapists, and anyone who's seen me fall into a flowerbed, often ask how I stay so upbeat.

"How do you stay cheerful with everything you've had going on?"
"Do you realise how much your attitude encourages other people?"
"Are you *sure* you're not secretly on something?"

But the truth is simple: I don't know how else to be.
This isn't an act. If it were, I'd have forgotten my lines years ago.

Do I have bad days? Of course. You've seen enough evidence in these pages. There are days when I wish to God I'd been dealt a different medical hand. Days when I wish certain people were still here to share a cup of tea, or a hug, or some laughter.

But those thoughts pass. You can't live in the "what ifs," or you miss the "what now's."

As I said back at the beginning of the book, life gives us a new hand every single day. Some good, some terrible, some baffling ("Why is my car full of balloons?") ... but it's still our hand. We don't choose the cards, only how we play them.

One thing I've learned, carved into me by time and experience:

A positive mindset won't guarantee a good outcome. But a negative mindset *will* guarantee a bad one.

And sometimes, I think I'm helped by a tiny bit of natural laziness. When I learned it takes fewer muscles to smile than to frown, that was it. Decision made. Why work harder than necessary?

As I've said before (and forgive me, I'm 60-something, repetition is practically a hobby): **smiling is the most contagious thing on Earth.** Not COVID. Not man-flu. Smiling.

Even reading the word "**smile**" makes you do it.

I'll bet a fair few of you just did.

So go on. Do it again. **Smile.**
It genuinely suits you.

And if anything in this book has made you smile, or laugh, or feel understood, or feel encouraged, then I'd like to ask you a small favour.

Nothing complicated. Nothing strenuous. No digging, lifting, fasting, or running marathons.

Just two tiny things:

**Please go onto Amazon and leave a review.
And then share the book on your social media.**

That's it.
Those two little actions mean the world to authors, especially new ones, and they help other people discover the book who might need it.

As for whether there will be a Volume Two?

If this sells well, and if I'm lucky enough to be given a few more years on this planet, then yes, absolutely. The first sixty years have been a rollercoaster... and I'm genuinely excited to see what the next ten might throw at me.

You'll find a few more pages of formal thankyous coming up. Feel free to skip them if you like, I won't be offended. (Well, I'll pretend I'm not.)

But please don't forget that Amazon review.

And those social media posts.

Thanking you in advance,
and thank you,
sincerely,
for walking through this lifetime of moments with me.

And one final thought to leave you with -

**People may be jealous of what you have, but no one is jealous of how you got it.
They want to enjoy the view but they don't want to do the climb.**

If you would like to continue to follow my story, and I hope you will, please go to

https://www.thinkofsomethingpublishing.co.uk/a-lifetime-of-moments

or simply scan the QR code below.

Those I must thank

No book writes itself, though this one has certainly tried its best to do it without me on some days.

A lifetime is built from moments, but moments are built from people.

These are the people who deserve thanks for appearing in mine, shaping them, saving me in them, or simply making the ride more joyful.

My Family

Mum and Dad - Without you, I wouldn't be here. Quite literally. Thank you for the values, the love, the laughter, and the quietly powerful lessons that still guide me today. I carry you with me always.

Roy and Roger - My brothers in every sense of the word: blood, bond, and absolute loyalty. You're two of the best men I've ever known, and I love you both deeply.

Michelle - My daughter. Fierce, brave, loving, and resilient in ways no one should ever have to be.
I am proud of you beyond words.

Lucy and Davy - My grandchildren. My joy. My hope. My reason for fighting on. You brighten every day simply by existing.

Friends Who Became Family

Jan - My brother from another mother and partner in so many misadventures. Your friendship has been one of the greatest gifts of my life.

Chris - The neighbour who keeps me upright, keeps me laughing, and keeps pointing out everything the contractors got wrong.

Rolf and Arjo - Dear friends and pillars of support, conversation, and occasional mischief. Thank you for your kindness and constancy.

Charlene - For the bond forged through shared challenges and shared strength. Your friendship has meant the world.

Andrea and Alan - Steadfast friends, warm, genuine, and always ready with good humour and good heart. Thank you for being part of my life.

Audere, Sonja and Laura - Loyal, generous, caring friends whose support has helped carry me through more than you know.
I am lucky to have you both.

Those Who Carried Me Through the Hardest Parts

Enma - For the years of love, laughter, and memories that shaped both me and Michelle. Thank you for everything.

Mabi - For crossing borders, brightening hearts, and bringing joy back into Enma's life, and for forgiving the Heathrow bum-incident.

Sandra - A needed chapter at just the right time. Kindness when I needed it most.

The NHS: the Good, the Brave, the Miracle-Workers

To every doctor, nurse, paramedic, physiotherapist, occupational therapist, radiographer, technician, surgeon, and specialist who has kept me alive long after logic suggested I should have expired like a budget battery.

A special thank you to **Dr Slaight** and **Dr Ann O'Callaghan**, and every GP brave enough to wade through my ever-expanding medical file.

Political Allies, Opponents, and Occasional Headaches

To my colleagues and sparring partners at **Liss Parish Council, EHDC,** and **the Conservative Party**, thank you for the debates, the camaraderie, the laughter, and the occasional headlines I could have done without.

To all volunteers, canvassers, leaflet-deliverers, tellers, rosette-wearers, and people who stood in the rain with me, thank you. Democracy runs because you do.

The Carers, Social Workers, and Guardians

To the incredible foster carers who have loved Lucy and Davy
when life became complicated.
To the social workers who fought the right battles.
To the solicitors and barristers
who did their utmost for the children.
You changed their lives, and mine.

And Finally... You

If you've read this book, thank you.
Thank you for stepping into my memories, walking through the laughter and chaos, the losses and triumphs, the absurdity and the tenderness.

If any part of it moved you, made you smile, or gave you a bit of motivation, please do me one tiny favour:

Leave a review on Amazon, and tell a few friends about the book.

(It keeps authors emotionally alive.
Medically, in my case, it may help too.)

Thank you, sincerely.
Keith.

Printed in Dunstable, United Kingdom